The Autobiography of Robert Rantoul

The Autobiography of Robert Rantoul
A Memoir Made at Beverly, November 1848

Robert Rantoul

Transcribed by Jeffrey Dauzat

Edited by Charles E. Wainwright

2018

Copyright © 2018 by Historic Beverly

All rights reserved. This book or any portion thereof may not be reproduced or used in any manner whatsoever without the express written permission of the copyright holder except for the use of brief quotations in a book review or scholarly journal.

First Printing: 2018

ISBN 978-1-891906-17-6

SC

Historic Beverly 117 Cabot Street Beverly, MA 01915

www.historicbeverly.net

The mission of Historic Beverly is to share Beverly history with everyone, through our 3 houses, 5 centuries and thousands of stories. We do that through collecting and preserving Beverly history, inspiring the community to engage with that history, and making history accessible to all.

Contents

Editor's Note xii

Preface xiii

Introduction 15

Author's Table of Contents 16

Memoir 20

    Genealogical tables of family connections [1] 21

    Correspondence with my English & Scotch relations [4½] 23

    Genealogy of the Preston family by Jedediah Herrick [24 ½.1] 40

    Early History, Last Letter of my Father, His Loss at Sea [32] 47

    First School, Susanna Babbige: Other Schools;
    Master Watson, Master Bentley, Master Southwick,
    Master Snelling, Master Long & Master Bancroft [43] 53

    Apprenticeship- Shipbuilding – Independence [50] 56

    Learning to Write [59] 58

    Master Lang [60] 59

    Schooling: Economy, Punctuality, Perseverance [63] 60

    Influence of my Father's Character on My Own [67] 61

    Luke Brooks [69] 62

    Corporeal Punishment in Schools [70] 63

    Salem School [71] 63

    Other Schools, Memory [72] 64

    Fishing Excursion [73] 64

    Ship building – *Grand Turk* [81] 67

    Eligius Fromentin – Senator in Congress [84] 68

    Run Over by Horses [85] 68

    Small Pox [85] 69

    Washington Hall [88] 70

    Apprenticeship Resumed [89] 70

    Obituary of Lucretia Osgood [92] 72

    Town Affairs [143] 94

    Proceedings of the town on my declining town offices [146½.5] 97

    Juryman [147] 99

Parish and Church Offices [155] 102

Sunday Schools – Hannah Hill and Joanna B. Prince [168] 107

Unitarian Association [179] 116

Rammohun Roy (of Calcutta, India) [183] 118

Remodeling the Meeting House [191] 122

Names of Parish Clerks [205] 128

Social Library [207] 129

School Committee – Schools [211] 132

William Burley's Legacy for Teaching Poor Children [219] 135

Private School Academy [221] 136

Cherry Hill Farm School [225] 138

South School District, New School House, Bibles [226] 139

Overseer of the Poor – Work House [231] 142

Application for Post Office [243] 149

The Long Embargo - Leveling the Common [244] 149

Justice of the Peace – Notary Public – Commissioner of Highways [247] 150

Asa W. Wildes [248] 152

Candidate for County Commissioner [249] 153

Candidate for Elector of President [254] 156

State Treasurer [254] 156

County Treasurer's Accounts, Settlement of [257] 156

Small Pox Vaccination – Henry Fornis, Mother & Sister [259] 157

Lectures on the History of Beverly,
the History of Essex County, and on a Variety of Subjects [261] 157

Trust deeds [266] 159

Thomas Barrett [268] 161

Beverly Marine Insurance Company [275] 162

Representative to the General Court – Senator [279] 163

Valuation Committee [288] 167

First Journey to Pittsfield; Albany, New York [289] 168

Essex County Convention of 1812 [291] 169

Hartford Convention [293] 170

James Monroe [295] 171

Party Spirit [296] 171

Columbian Sentinel – Benjamin Russel (Federalist Party paper) [297] 171

Impeachment of Judge James Prescott [299]	172
Town Treasurer - Mass Convention for Rewriting the Constitution 1820 [309]	175
Union Fire Society [313]	177
Fire Department [319]	179
Temperance Reform [328]	182
Health – Sickness Regimen [357]	195
Cholera - Health Committee 1832 [365]	198
Peace Society [376]	203
Capital Punishment [385]	206
Notice of Robert Stephen Rintoul, Editor of the London Examiner [404.1]	215
Robert Rantoul – Representative [405]	216
Institution for the Blind [405.1]	218
Essex Bridge [409]	220
Salem Turnpike & Chelsea Bridge [410]	220
Beverly Bank [415]	222
Joanna Quiner – Bust [417]	223
Beverly Charitable Society – Fisher Charitable Society [421]	224
General Lafayette: His Reception [423]	225
State Reform School [429]	227
Essex Agricultural Society [457]	241
Business in Probate Court – Guardian – Trustee [457]	241
Silas Stickney, Andrew Peabody & Others [457.1]	242
Installation of Dexter Clapp at Salem [465]	244
Celebration at Danvers, of the Incorporation of the Town [468]	245
Death of Son Robert [469]	246
Massachusetts 2nd Convention 1853 [477]	250
Index	253

Illustrations

All illustrations are from Historic Beverly unless otherwise indicated.

Author's Table of Contents	16-20
1808 booklet written by student William Rantoul Very	31
Signature of Robert Rantoul, Sr.	48
Robert S. Rantoul (1832-1922)	49
Robert Rantoul, Jr. (1805-1852)	49
Robert Rantoul (1778-1858)	49
Joanna Rantoul (1780-1848)	49
Samuel Endicott (1830-1891)	50
Robert R. Endicott (1833-1914)	50
Painting of the ship Grand Turk owned by Elias Hasket Derby, 1786	67
Robert Rantoul's Apothecary, corner of Washington and Cabot Street.	83
The home of the Beverly Union Sunday School, Front and Davis Streets, 1810	107
Christopher Toppan Thayer (1805-1880)	113
Abiel Abbot (1770-1828)	113
Joseph McKeen (1757-1807)	113
Joanna Batchelder Prince (1789-1859) co-founder, Beverly Union Sunday school	114
Hannah Hill (1784-1838), co-founder, Beverly Union Sunday school	114
Albert Thorndike (1800-1858) Superintendent of the First Parish Sunday school.	114
First Parish Meeting House, 1795. by Warren Prince.	122
Beverly Academy, Washington Street, 1833 by Charlotte Rantoul	136
Order of public services for the dedication of the Cove School, 1853	140
The Poor House, built in 1803, served as Beverly's Poor Farm until 1948	142
Obituary of Asa W. Wildes, December 7, 1857	153
Thomas Barrett, sexton of First Parish	161
Leather fire bucket, Beverly Union Fire Society, 1813	177
Petition from the Essex County Temperance Society	182

The Essex Bridge between Salem and Beverly, 1907	220
Bust of Robert Rantoul by Joanna Quiner	223
"Journey of Lafayette", poem by Daniel S. Whitney, 1825	225
"Lines", sung by children at the State Reform School, Westborough, 1848	233
Rantoul's invitation to meeting at the State Reform School November 23rd, 1848	234
Inauguration of William E. Starr, Superintendent of the Reform School Westboro	240
Newspaper article on the 1853 Convention	251

Editor's Note

Robert Rantoul wrote down everything, as anyone who studies Beverly history can attest. As First Parish Clerk and Church Deacon from 1808 to 1858, he was responsible for almost every official entry in Parish and Church registers. He maintained detailed records of his transactions as apothecary and trade merchant and penned extensive discourses on Beverly's history, parts of which ultimately served as the basis of E.M. Stone's "History of Beverly", and James R. Newhall's "Essex Memorial" of 1836.

Rantoul began his personal memoir shortly after the death of his wife, Joanna (Lovett) in November 1848, and made the final entries to record his attendance at the Massachusetts Constitutional Convention of 1853, shortly after the death of his son, Robert Rantoul, Jr. He added dated entries of clarification to the work right up to the time of his death, giving the manuscript more the feel of a journal than a memoir.

In editing Rantoul's manuscript, several conventions were employed to assist the reader in better appreciating Rantoul's manuscript:

- Manuscript page numbers: Rantoul meticulously numbered the pages of his manuscript, and often numbered pages he added with fractions. This, combined with additional unpaginated supporting material into the bound folio, make it difficult to precisely trace references between the printed volume and the manuscript. As a convention, Rantoul's manuscript page numbers are preserved wherever possible, including his fractional pages. Unnumbered pages are assigned the number of the last manuscript page, augmented with a decimal number, for example [14.1]. Manuscript page numbers are placed within brackets at the beginning of each manuscript page and are repeated in headings.

- Author's notes: Rantoul often wrote footnote-like entries in the margin or just below his text to explain or update information for the reader. These are retained in the form of footnotes. All underlines in the text are Rantoul's.

- Illegible and missing words: Like anyone writing a manuscript in pen, the quality of Rantoul's handwriting is inconsistent, and some of his words are simply illegible. These words appear as underlines, without footnote. In some instances, Rantoul left a number, word, or name out purposely, intending to come back later. He highlights these in the manuscript with an underline. They appear in the published volume as an underline, flagged with a footnote.

- Grammar, syntax, and word choice: Rantoul never proofread his manuscript, and he should, therefore, be forgiven for erring occasionally in grammar, syntax, or word choice. Word usage, to the extent it reflects the writing style of the early nineteenth century, was retained as much as possible. Otherwise, corrections were reluctantly and sparingly made to improve readability.

Charles E. Wainwright

Preface

"For about forty years there was no subject of much interest which came before the town, in which I did not take a decided course and use my earnest endeavors to carry through or to prevent according to my convictions of duty and of right."

Robert Rantoul

When you focus on local history and the people and events that connect to a particular place, there is a tendency to elevate the founding generation above those that succeeded them. Their courage and persistence were certainly admirable, and I take no credit from them, but it was also challenging to thrive and build community during the early years of this country. Robert Rantoul, who was born during the American Revolution and died only a few years before Fort Sumter, recounts his family history, major events, and his involvement with Beverly's civic realm in this autobiography, illuminating for us the many ways an individual can impact a community. Many tangible reminders of Rantoul's life and work remain, from a number of family homes to the street that bears his name. Rantoul "petitioned the county commissioners to lay out a new street parallel to Cabot street from Menasseh Trask's house on Cabot street, near to the entrance of Colon Street, southwesterly to the India Rubber factory near Ezra Batchelder's house," which was then named for him by the Selectmen in honor of his service to the town.

Our understanding of daily life, how ordinary people (like us) lived, often comes from this kind of source, the personal writings of an individual who reflects on his/her life and the people and events that were significant, either personally or to the community more broadly. It is critically important that we value and preserve these records of the past, so that we may all continue to learn from them.

This book would not have been possible with the support of the staff and volunteers of Historic Beverly. Very special thanks to Jeff Dauzat, who started the project by transcribing Rantoul's work, and to Charlie Wainwright, who edited the transcript, and added images and explanatory information based on his deep knowledge of the subject. We are very grateful to them.

Sue Goganian, Director
Historic Beverly

Introduction

The following biographical notes commenced in November 1848, a little more than a month after the decease of my wife, which event induced more thoughtfulness in regard to my own departure from life. They are intended for the gratification of the curiosity of my grandchildren, and with the hope of their deriving some benefit from their perusal. I shall probably bequeath them to one of my grandsons, whom I shall expect to pay particular attention to their presentation, in order that they may always be accessible by any of my descendants, under reasonable restrictions. Although these notes were begun, and mostly written in 1848, yet it will be perceived that they have been continued, from time to time, through several of the following years.

I have, in the latter part of my life, had a desire to investigate the characters and doings of my ancestors; and anticipating that some of my descendants may, in the course of their lives, have a similar desire, I suggest this a reason, that if these notes shall ever fall into the possession of one who has no such taste himself, that notwithstanding his own feelings in regard to their worth, that he will still carefully preserve them until the right one appears, who will appreciate their value.

These notes having been written on separate sheets and at various intervals will be found to contain some repetitions and some obscurity of dates which will require study to understand

Robert Rantoul

Contents of this volume

Genealogical tables of family connections .... 1 to 32
Early history, last letter of my father, his loss at sea, 33 to 42
First school, Susanna Bartlett, ... 42 to 48
Other schools, Master Watson, Master Bentley, Master ...
Master Snelling — Master Lang & Master ... — 45 & 50
Apprenticeship — Shipbuilding — Independence ...
Learning to write 59, Master Lang 60, Schooling 65
Economy, punctuality, perseverance .... 63 & 66
Influence of my father's character on my own 67
Luke Brooks 69, Corporal punishment in schools 70
Latin School 71, Other schools, memory 72
Fishing excursion 73, Election day 75 to 79
Ship building — Grand Turk 81, 82
Eliquett Fromenten, Soldier in Canada 84
Run away — lodes 85, Small Pox .... 85 & 87
Washington Hall 88 — Apprenticeship .... 89 to 95
Commencement of business 96 96
Martha Burke, Jenny Queen, Harry Barrick, Luther ...
Attendance on public worship ....
Courtship — marriage — housekeeping .... 114 to 115
Character of wife, her decease .... 116 to 117
Business .... 117 to 124
Washington Street .... 125 to 13...
Naming Streets 124 124
My military services .... 125 to 14...
Town affairs, Proceedings of the Town on my declining Town office as 146½ .... 143 to 14...
Juryman .... 147 to 15...
Parish & Church affairs .... 153 to 15...
Sunday Schools — ...

Contents of this Volume

	Pages
Genealogical tables of family connexions	1 to 30
Family history, last letter of my father, his loss at sea	33 to 42
First school, Susanna Rallege	43 to 44
Other schools, Master Watson, Master Bentley, Master [?], Master Snelling — Master Lang & Master Prannitt	45 to 50
Apprenticeship — Shipbuilding — Independence	50 to [?]
Learning to write 59, Master Lang 60 Schooling 62	
Economy, punctuality, perseverance	63 to 65
Influence of my father's character on my own	67
Luke Brooks 69 Corporeal punishment in Schools 70	
Latin School 71 Other Schools, memory 72	
Fishing excursion 73 Election day 75 to 79	
Ship building — Grand Turke	81, 82
Eliquel Fromentin Senator in Congress	[?]
Run over by — horses 86 Small Pox	85 to 87
Washington Hall 88 — Apprenticeship [?]	89 to 95
Commencement of business 96	96
Martha Burke, Jenny Owen, Henry Herrick, Larkin [?]	
Attendance on public worship	[?] to 100
Courtship — marriage — housekeeping	101 to 105
Character of wife, her decease	105 to 116
Business	117 to [?]
Washington Street	121 to 123
Naming Streets 124	124
My military services	125 to 140
Town officer	141 to 145
Proceedings of the Town on my declining Town Office 146½	147 to [?]
Juryman	[?]
Parish & Church affairs	
Sunday Schools	

Unitarian Association — 179 to
Rammohun Roy — 183 to
Remodelling the Meeting House — 191 to
Names of Parish Clerks
Social Library — 209
School Committee — Schools — 211 to
William Burley's legacy for teaching poor children — 219
Private School, Academy — 221 to
Cherry Hill Farm School — 225
South School District, New School House, The Bar
Overseer of the Poor — Work House
Post Office, application for,
The long Embargo — leveling the Common — 244
Justice of the Peace — Notary Public — Commissioner of Highways
Candidate for County Commissioner — 249
Candidate for Elector of President 254 State Freedom 254
County Treasurer's Accounts, settlement of
Small Pox & Vaccination — Henry Jones, mother Russel
Lectures on the History of Beverly — the History of
  Essex County and on a variety of subjects &c — 261
Hon'd Barrett 268 Trust Deeds 267
Beverly Marine Insurance Company — 275
Representative to the General Court — Senator — 279 to
First Journey to Pittsfield, Albany, New York — 289
Valuation Committee — 288
Essex County Convention of 1812 — 291
Hartford Convention 293–294 James Munroe 295
Party Spirit 296 Columbian Centinel, Benjamin Russell 297
        James Prescott

Congress House of Rep[?] 405
Town Treasurer 309
Mass[tts] Convention for revising the Constitution 1820 —
   "   "   "   "   "   "   1853
Union Fire Society
Fire Department
Temperance Reform
Health — sickness — regimen
Cholera — Health Committee 1832 —
Peace Society
Capital Punishment
Institution for the Blind
Essex Bridge 409 Salem Turnpike & Choate Bridge
Beverly Bank 415 Joanna Reiner — Probate — 417 418-419
Beverly Charitable Society — Fisher Charitable Society
General LaFayette — his reception
State Reform School
Essex Agricultural Society
Business in Probate Court — Guardian, Trustee — 456 & 457
Silas Stickney, Andrew Peabody, & others

Installation of Dexter Clapp at Salem   456 & 464
Celebration at Danvers, of the incorporation of the town
Death of son Robert   469
Massachusetts second Convention 1853   477
   Obituary notice of Mrs Lucretia Osgood   482
   "   "   "   Rev: William Rintoul — 489 485
Genealogy of the Preston family by Jedediah Herrick 24½
Correspondence & with my English & Scotch relations 40½
Dea W. Gilder   340
Notice of Robert Rantoul, Editor of the   485
London Examiner

19

Congress House of Rep. 305
Town Treasurer 309
Mass." Convention for revising the Constitution 1820 —
     "   "   "   "   1853
Union Fire Society
Fire Department
Temperance Reform
Health — sickness — regimen
Cholera — Health Committee 1832 —
Peace Society
Capital Punishment
Institution for the Blind
Essex Bridge 409 Salem Turnpike & Chelsea Bridge
Beverly Bank 415 Joanna Turner — Packet — 457, 415, 419
Beverly Charitable Society — Fisher Charitable Society
General La Fayette — his reception
State Reform School
Essex Agricultural Society
Business in Probate Court — Guardians, Trustee
Silas Stickney, Andrew Peabody & others

Installation of Dexter Clapp at Salem
Celebration at Danvers, of the incorporation of the town
Death of Rev. Robert
Massachusetts Second Convention 1853
Obituary notice of Mrs. Lucretia Osgood
    "   "   "   Rev. William Rintoul   489, 485
Genealogy of the Preston family by Jedediah Herrick
Correspondence & with my English & Scotch relatives
Dr. W. Hilder
Notice of Robert ____ in ____ of the
London Examiner

Memoir

Genealogical tables of family connections [1]

My Father, Robert Rintoul, Rentoul, Rantoul, (the first spelling of the name I consider to be correct and the others corruptions, although I and my descendants are under a kind of necessity from long use of writing it "Rantoul", my father usually in the later parts of his life, as appears, wrote it "Rentoul") was born at Middleton, in the Parish of Cleish in the county of Kinross, Fifeshire in the northern part of Scotland and in the same house where his father was born.

My cousin Sarah S Rintoul and two of her brothers, children of my father's brother William, were born in the same house, as she informs me in her letter of December 3rd, 1840. I have occasionally corresponded with my cousin Sarah, and with one of her brothers.

Kinross-Shire is a small inland county in the northern part of Scotland. The ancient shire of this name was divided about the year 1426, into the two counties of Fife and Kinross, and at the revolution Kinross, being thought too small a county as it then stood, was enlarged by the addition of Orwell, Cleish and Tullibole, which parishes before that time, were part of the county of Fife. But though these are now two distinct counties and are expertly represented in parliament, they are both comprehended in the Sheriff Dom of Fife. Kinross Shire is bounded on the east and south by Fife Shire, and on the north and west by Perth Shire. It extends, from east to west, from __[1] to Sycamore Bridge, eleven miles, and from Kelty Bridge nearly due north to Damhead, about nine miles and a half. Cleish is about twenty miles north of Edinburgh, has four considerable lakes, the largest is about a mile and a half in circumference, and the four cover about two hundred & fifty acres. Loch Leven a lake of the secondary class in Scotland is in the Shire of Kinross and has a surface of 3300 acres. For other particulars see Ree's Cyclopaedia article; Kinross Shire[2].

[2] For the etymology of my name I am indebted to my friend William Rintoul, of Toronto, Canada, who says in his letter to me dated July 11, 1831, "I have seen in a Heraldic dictionary that the crest of the Rintoul was an Elm tree, and I have fancied that, were it appropriate, I would add for a motto a part of the 14th verse of the 92nd psalm according to the Scottish Metrical version "aye be flourishing" (According to King James version "they shall be fat and flourishing.") I have sometimes amused myself with investigating the etymology of the name and the following derivation is probably as sound as others from which more important conclusions are attempted to be drawn, *Rhyn*, in the Celtic, denotes a mountain, cape or promontory. The same root I believe with Civ in the Irish, (pronounced something like Fool) denotes a den or cavern. So that Rintoul, may be the Den of the Hill. It happens that there is a place called Rintoul in the Braes of Kinross, but

---

[1] Rantoul erased this word in the manuscript.

[2] Rantoul's wrote in the margin, "for further information respecting my father's family see page 11."

I had not the curiosity, before leaving the old country, to visit it to see whether there were any caves about it from which the place, according to my theory, might get its name, which it had afterwards, I suppose, given to its possessor as there is or lately was, a Robert Rintoul of Rintoul.

Of the house in which my father, and his father, my grandfather was born, his brother, David Rintoul, writes under date of October 18th, 1774, at Elgin, north Britain, as follows:

"To Mr. Robert Rintoul at Jonah Archer sent at the Long Wharf in Salem near Boston in New England.

" Your sisters Jenny and Betty are at Mr. Gibbs, minister at Uphall, about 8 miles west from Edinburgh.

" your sister Jean is married to a wright at Edinburgh. She has two children.

[3] "Our brother William is at the sea. He has been twice at the East Indies. The first voyage he was with his Uncle and the Press being in London when he arrived, helped him on board another ship, but before he returned, his Uncle was dead, having died at the Cape of Good Hope in his return home, and William came home from China about five months ago.

" Sister Nelly is at Invernesh in service.

" I have been at Elgin these four years bygone, with my Uncle, who has given me education, & has put me home to be a wright. I am bound three years, which will expire in June next.

" Your uncle and aunts here:

" Your Uncle, Aunt & Cousins at Kelty - W Robert is a minister at Ireland & Charles is a baker at Aberdour (a small town of Fifeshire, in Scotland, on the Firth of Forth, about ten miles NW of Edinburgh) your Aunt & cousin at Edinburgh.

"As for our friends at Kirkcaldy, (a small town of Fife, on the north coast of the Firth of Forth, about three miles east of Kinghorn and near to Edinburg.) you know they would take no care of us when we were young, therefore, we have no concern with them. I am going to Edinburgh in June next, where I am to work with my brother-in-law, at Mr. Brodie's shop, a brother of Mrs. Rintoul's.

"A very exact account has been kept of what your father left behind him & how it has been expended, likewise the rent of the house & land, but the creditors have been so uneasy for the money our father borrowed, that they are threatening to force a sale of the house & land, which will consume a great part of the subject & besides, the great timber & roof of the house are failing, & will need a very expensive repair, for which reason all your friends here think that if you cannot bring or send home money to relieve it, by paying the debt, you should send home [4] a power to your Uncle to dispose of it, to the best advantage, and if there is any remainder, after all is paid, it should be divided among the children, as the law directs. The principle sums are owing to Mr. Adam in the Blair, & to our Uncle the Minister here.

"Our brother William was at China on board the *Duke of Kingstown*.

"Direct to the Rev. Mr. (David) Rintoul, Minister at Elgin, North Britain."

It seems that my father did not immediately attend to the request contained in the letter from his brother David, perhaps he was absent at sea, and a more pressing letter was written to him by his two sisters, Janet and Betty, dated Uphall, March 4th, 1775, wherein they urge him, who was the oldest son, to take measures for the settlement of his father's estate. They received a letter from my father on the same, 4th March 1775, and also acknowledge another letter which was written about three years before, but its date is not mentioned, and to which they sent an answer, but it appears not to have come to hand. By this it appears that my father came to this country as early as 1772. In their letter, they say:

"We are sorry to hear that you signify to us that you are thinking your will not come home to see us & all your friends.

"Your brother William went in a ship called the *Darling* to ye West Indies about Martinmas last. David is at Elgin with his Uncle. Jeanie, Janet, and Betty are at Uphall. Nelly is in a good family at Edinburgh."

My father's youngest sister outlived all her brothers and sisters and died unmarried December 13, 1835 in the 80th year of her age.

Correspondence with my English & Scotch relations [4½]

Copy of a letter from David Rintoul to his brother Robert Rantoul, from which extracts are made on pages 3 and 4:

"Dear Brother – I am happy to hear you are alive by a letter my Uncle received from Salem dated June 27th but there was no word of what year it was in, but all your friends were very glad you were alive. Your sisters Jenny and Betty are at Mr. Gibbs, Minister at Uphall west from Edin(burgh). They are both well. Your sister Jean is married to a wright at Edin(burgh). She has two children they are all well. Your brother William is at the sea. He has been twice at the West Indies & he is come from China about five months ago, he is also well. Sister Nelly is at Inverness in service & is very well. I have been at Elgin these four years by grace with my Uncle who has given me Education & has put me home to be a wright. I am bound three years which will be expired in Jun next. Your Uncle and Aunts here are very well. Your Uncle and Aunt at Kelty and your cousins are well. Mr. Robert is a minister in Ireland & Charles is a baker at Aberdour. Your Aunt and cousins at Edin(burgh) are also well. As for our friends at Kincaldy you know would take no care of us when we were young wherefore we have no concern with them.

"A very exact account has been kept of what your father left behind him and how it has been expended, likewise the rent of the house & land but the creditors are so uneasy for the money our father borrowed that they are threatening to force a sale of the house and land which will consume a great part of the subject & besides the great timber & roof of the house are failing & will need a very expensive repair, [4½.1] and for which reason all your friends here think if that you cannot bring or send home money to relieve it by paying the debt, you should send home a power to your uncle to dispose of it to the best advantage & if there is any remainder after all is payed it should be divided among the children as the law directs. The principal sums are owing to Wm. Adam in the Blain & to our uncle the Minister here. Be sure and send us a particular account of what you have been doing since you left this country, what you are doing and what you are desired to do & where we may direct a letter to you, you may try to find out our Brother William as he was at China on board the *Duke of Kingstown*, & we do not know but he may return again in it or some other ship, as it is uncertain where I may be write to my Uncle the Minister here who will communicate the contents to me & all concerned. Direct to the Rev Mr. Rintoul Minister at Elgin, North Britain. He & my two Aunts join in their best wishes with me to you. I am Dear Brother

Your Affc't humble servant

Elgin Oct. 18, 1774 David Rintoul.

The superscription is as follows; "Mr. Robert Rintoul at Jonah Archer, Gent. At the Long wharf in Salem near Boston in New England."

[4½.2] March 25, 1854, my grandson William Endicott Jun., left here for London and there made a visit to my cousins. He arrived home at his father's house on Thursday evening July 13th, 1854. He brought me letters from my three cousins Robert, William and Sarah and Mary. He also brought for me Butler's Folio Bible as a present to me from my cousins, with the following inscription "The family bible of the late Mr. Wm Rintoul of London, presented to his nephew Mr. Rob Rantoul of Beverly, in America, by his surviving children as a token of affection and esteem, and as a remembrance of the family." Cousin Mary sent a present to daughter Hannah and they presented Wm E(ndicott) Jun. with a gold pencil case. They received my grandson with great kindness and were much pleased and gratified with his two calls upon them and urged him to take up his abode with them while he remained in London. They appeared to be in comfortable circumstances, though not affluence. The letters received may be found with other letters received from Scotch and English relations. My cousins Robert W. and Mary kept house in a two-story tenement in a long building resembling Deacon Benj. Cleaves' house. Sarah with her husband boarded at a respectable house not far from the others. Her husband, George Laborin, looks like Peter Homans. Wm. Endicott Jun. says Rob't Wm is a printer. [4½.3] To these three letters I replied by a letter to my said cousins jointly under date of July 27, 1854. The draft of this letter, not an exact copy is on file. My grandson made cousin Mary a present of a pattern for a silk gown. This visit to them seems a renewal of our acquaintance and will serve as a connecting link with my descendants and I hope that they will duly appreciate the motive in sending the Bible to me which appears to be longer preserved in the family than if it remained with them- they, being without children and I, representing the oldest brother of their father. Whosoever's hands it may fall into I enjoin it upon them to preserve it with care and take all proper measures to secure its transmission to the succeeding generation. I am aware that the regard for family relics on antiquity is not universal, but I hope that enough of it will be found among my descendants to secure compliance with my directions for generations to come.

[4½.4] <u>Copy of a draft of my letter to my cousin.</u>

"To: Mr. W. Rintoul Beverly, July 27th, 1854

"Mrs. Sarah S. Laborin

"Miss Mary Rantoul

"My Dear Cousins,

"My grandson, William Endicott Jun. arrived at his father's house from the European tour on the 13th instant. He was the bearer of letters from each of you, and for which I make my best acknowledgements. He was also the bearer of an interesting and valuable present from you to me of a large folio Bible, being the family Bible of your late father and my uncle, interesting to me as a memorial of a brother of my deceased father, valuable and highly esteemed by me not only for its record contents, as a record of the revelation of the will of God to man upon his duty in this life and his destiny beyond this transient scheme, but as an evidence of your affectionate esteem and implicit confidence in this entrusting to my care an article having so many connections with your reminiscences of infancy, and of mature ages. I trust your confidence is not misplaced as I want to preserve this prospect with care during my short remaining period of life, and take the same measures for its transmission to other generations of my descendants that I shall in regard to other family memorials. I am pleased to learn from my grandson that he was so cordially received and heartily welcomed at the two visits he made to you, and that he was so well pleased and highly gratified with his reception. The habitual conformity of his only seeking manner to nature, to truth, to reality, and his freedom from all affect- [4½.5] tion must have made his visits agreeable to you. I am blessed in my children and grandchildren and hope that I shall be inspired with gratitude to the graces of all blessings therefor. The renewal of our acquaintance through the medium of my grandson is pleasant and agreeable to myself and to the several members of my family. I hope that you will continue to write to me whenever convenient. The remarks in regard to the existence of slavery in this country are in coincidence with my own opinions upon that subject. So far as moral power has influence, and so far as legal action is constitutional and just and right, I shall be found with those who are not only seeking but expecting in due course of time universal emancipation. My daughter Hannah will write you at this time and will supply my short comings. Give my respects to Mr. Laborin. Robt Rantoul."

August 2nd, 1857: I received a letter from Cousin Sarah by Wm. Endicott Jr. dated June 29th, 1857 from which I make the following extract and annex the certificate which she sent me:

"…with object of obtaining the information you wish I wrote to Southland to search the books in the Parish of Cleish, where I supposed it likely your father had been registered. But from the accompanying certificate which I received and which I forward to you it does not appear to be there. I think the Robt. Rintoul and C Miller in 1742 is our grandfather and grandmother because I know my father had an uncle of the name of Miller, which I suppose to have been his mother's brother, and the four names referenced of their children are the same as was in my father's family, I conclude it to be the name of my father and three younger children, but there were three older, your father and two sisters. The eldest Margaret and the other Elizabeth which I think must have been registered in another Parish. I am sorry it is not satisfactory, respecting your late parents. I only received it yesterday and thought it first came in time to forward it to you.

[4½.6] "Extracts from the Registrar of Marriages, Births, & Baptisms for the Parish of Cleish, county of Kinross.

"Robert Rintoul, younger son of Kelty in this Parish & Christian Miller, Parish of Kinglassie were married 24th Decem. 1742.

"Their son William born 29th Sept. 1754.

"Their daughter Helen --- 27th Nov. 1756.

"Their son David --- 13th Oct. 1759.

"Their son John --- 28th June 1762.

"Note there is an entry to the following effect viz: "Thomas Rintoul, son to Robert Rintoul & Margt Miller in Kelty, born 4th July, 1753" which I am of opinion are the same parties as the other, Margaret being written by mistake [4½.7] Christian. If so, & evidence to that effect can be given by Mr. Rintoul in London, or others, this error can be rectified.

"There is a very copious entry of the family of William Rintoul & Anna Browe at Kelty Bridge and, in all, eleven children extending from 1742 to 1765. There are entries of the name of Rintoul previous to these dates, but I cannot find the name of Robert as listed from the great interval between the marriages & the 1st birth entered viz. from 1742 to 1754. I am of opinion that the children if any born then may be registered in Beath, the adjoining Parish, the baptism more than the birth being the main end of registration.

"Cleish   Peter Cray, Twn. Clrk..

"16th June 1857

[4½.8] "From the time occupied & care employed in the search, the fee is 5/"

[4½.9] On the 6th day of June 1856, my daughter Hannah, received a letter dated May 19th, 1856, from Miss Mary Veitch, Park, Linlithgow in the county of Linlithgowshire, Scotland, and about sixteen miles from Edinburgh. She writes that her mother and myself are full cousins, if so, her grandmother was sister to my father. This letter is written in a hand that indicates a practiced writer, with a due regard to grammar and orthography, and the expression. This is a commencement of a correspondence which may be a means of continuing the connection between the families on both sides of the Atlantic Ocean. In Martin's Dictionary it is said "Linlithgow, a town of Scotland, large and well built, with a stately town house, and a noble palace of the Kings of Scotland. It is the shire town of the County."

January 1858: My daughter Hannah received another letter from Miss Veitch in reply to one which Hannah wrote to her. In this she mentions the death of W. Laborin, the husband of my cousin Sarah, he having lately died but does not mention the exact date of his death

February 15th, 1858: I received a letter from my cousin Sarah dated January 22nd, 1858 in which she says that her husband, Mr. Laborin died December 10th, 1857. She speaks well of his Christian character as exemplified from early life and that he died in faith of the one Atonement, that the scriptures reveal and that it is her "cheering hope that he has entered into rest."

[4½.10] April 21, 1857: I have received information from Matthew Stickney of Salem that he has in his possession a bill of one hogshead of molasses sold by Robert Rentoul to Capt. Derby of Salem, December 2, 1769. This will somewhat modify what is written on the next page. It would seem that he then wrote his name "Rintoul" but he afterwards wrote it "Rentoul".

[5] My Father was born in January 1753. He came to Boston in a public ship of war, as I suppose in 1772 or as soon as that. I find receipts among his papers for taxes for 1773, 1774 and 1775, and for 1776 & 1777, in which two last years he is styled Captain. He was Master of the Schooners *Caty* & *Hope*, owned by William Orne, Nathaniel Sparhawk & William Gray, and of the Brigs *Hopewell*, *Phoenix* & *Defense* owned by William Gray, Benjamin West, Theodore Lyman and others, from 1776 to 1782, in the West Indies and European trade and of the Ship *Iris* in 1782, belonging to William Gray.

When he left the ship of war, in Boston, he went to Salem, and boarded with Jonathan Archer, near the Long Wharf, as it was then called, but has since been named Union Wharf, and the street which leads from the Main street or Essex street to this wharf was then called Long Wharf lane, but now Union street, and I think that Jonathan Archer lived in this street. I remember him. He, being a very tall slim man, was called "Long Jonathan", to distinguish him from several others of the same name. My father, when he was married, hired rooms of another Jonathan Archer, at the westerly corner of Pleasant street and Essex street and lived there until March 25th, 1778. The first named Jonathan, taught seaman the art of navigation, as well as boarding them in his family.

In 1782 my father sailed from Salem, Master on the Ship *Iris*, December 28th, for Virginia where he arrived safe and wrote to my mother on the 10th, 16th & 28th of February 1783. The last letter was dated on the 28th at York river, ready for sea [6] but wind bound he sailed from thence on the 4th of March falling in company with two other vessels that arrived safe, but the Ship *Iris* was supposed to be lost in a gale of wind in the same month of March in which he sailed from Virginia and that all on board perished as they were never heard of more. The Ship was bound to France – Nantz[3].

Immediately after my father came to Salem, he found employment in Beverly, as a seaman, on board of a vessel commanded by Josiah Batchelder, who was afterwards surveyor of the Port of Beverly, under the United States government, and who, many years afterwards, when I was a tenant in his house, on my marriage, told me that he was an active seaman. One of the seaman who was with my father on his last voyage, and was lost with him, was Samuel Smith, the father of Samuel Smith, who has been my nearest neighbor almost as long as I have lived on Washington Street, he having built his house opposite to mine soon after I removed into mine which was in May 1805. Mr. Smith is about two years younger than myself. My father must have had energy, activity and intelligence combined with integrity to have got promotion, without the patronage of friends, so soon after coming to Salem an entire stranger. John Howard, who died in 1848, over ninety years of age informed me that he recollected my father well, that he could not

---

[3] Nantes: A French seaport on the Loire River.

perceive any resemblance between him and myself, but that he thought that he resembled my son Robert, being about his size and dark complexioned. I cannot myself recollect his appearance.

[7] In the latter part of the year 1776, his brother, William Rantoul, was captured by a privateer and carried prisoner to Newbury port, from which place, on the 9th of January 1777 he wrote to my father then in Salem. He informed that he had received a letter from him – that he has the liberty of the town, but had previously been in gaol for five weeks, and expected him to come soon to see him – I suppose that my father went to Newbury Port and procured the liberation of his brother and carried him to Salem, as I know from my Mother that he abided some time with her in Salem. He died in London, in his family, March 9th, 1823 in the 68th year of his age. He was born in October 1755 or as a latter account says Sept. 29th, 1754. He wrote several letters to my mother and to me, and when he was in China meeting with a Salem man, he sent my mother a present – the present consisted of a box of sugar candy and a piece of silk and comb by W. Greenwood, who brought also a letter dated "Ship *LaScelles*, second post, December 7th, 1789". Another letter was received from him, at St. Helens, Ship *Carnatie* April 10th, 1792 accompanied by W. Palmer, who called on my mother, with a present of one piece of Bengal Handkerchief, and a small box of Gun Powder Tea. These presents I afterwards, December 28th, 1819, reciprocated, by remitting him my draft on Samuel Williams, for a balance in his hands due to me, of about 19 pounds sterling. The receipt of which was acknowledged by his daughter Sarah Sinclair Rintoul, in her letter to me of August 15th, 1820.

William Rintoul, in the early part of his life, acquired so much property as to justify his quitting his seafaring [8] life, and to live on shore, but he interested his property in the hands of one, who became bankrupt, and paid him only one shilling and nine pence on the pound, which obliged him to resume his employment on the seas about 1799 or 1800, as in a letter from him dated August 14th, 1801, he says that he had returned from his first voyage to India. In this letter, he gives the ages of his children; Robert William born January 30, 1796, Sarah Sinclair born April 9, 1797, George born February 3, 1799 and Christian born 7th of October 1800. Another child, which we heard of afterwards, was born in September 1802.

After he left going to sea he had to labor for his living. This appears from his letter dated March 30th, 1817. William Rintoul of Toronto, when in London in 1840 visited the family and in a letter to me, after his return, says,

> "I had but a short interview with Mrs. Rintoul and her daughters, yet such as it was it was gratifying to me.
>
> "Your London friends, judging from the short interview I had with them, appears to be very excellent people. They are members of a Congregational Church, (the Orthodox only are known under that name in Britain), under the ministry of Doct. Reed, who some time ago, made one of a deputation to the Presbyterian & Congregational Churches in the States."

The widow of my uncle William Rintoul died in London on the 7th of August 1849 in the 82nd year of her age and his daughter Christian died on the 6th of September 1849 aged about 49. Of this I was informed by a letter from Sarah S Rintoul dated the 12th of September and received the 27th 1849.

[9] Just before my father sailed on his last voyage he made arrangements for building a dwelling house. The lot of land which my father bought of John Brown and Martha Brown of Boston, and Timothy Titch and Eunice Titch of Medford is on the main street now Essex street and at the westerly corner of Central street in Salem. The deed was acknowledged before Edmund Quincy at Boston, Dec. 5, 1782. The price was 850 pounds, equal to $2,833.33 for about twenty poles of land, say 50 ft. on Essex street and 120 ft. on Central Street[4].

This price shows a state of prosperity in Salem at the very conclusion of the revolutionary war. In a few years afterwards, there was a great decline, and after the adoption of the United States constitution, and the commencement of the war of the French revolution, another revival of prosperity. On the 3rd of November 1804 my sister Polly, my mother and myself, sold this same piece of land to William Shepard Gray and Benjamin Herbert Hathorne, for $8,500 being just three times the cost of it. Gray and Hathorne built a brick block of stores and houses covering the whole, or nearly so.

My father intended if he returned from his voyage, to have built a large dwelling house on this land, and in pursuance of this intention, he contracted, December 20th, 1782, with Eleazer Lindsey, for the rocks for a cellar 40 ft. square and 6 ½ ft. deep, with two tiers of front underpinning rocks and steps for two outward cellar doors, for 52 pounds and ½ paid in advance, and 3 pounds 18 pence given gratis, and paid in advance for <u>drink</u>. A part of these rocks was hauled on the land, and was sold by my mother, after it was believed that my father was lost.

[10] My father, when he was first married, hired rooms in the house of Jonathan Archer, at the westerly corner of Pleasant street on Essex street, and his first child was born there. He afterwards removed to Mrs. Elkins house, directly opposite to the East Meeting House, as it was then situated, but it was used for public worship for the last time, on Sunday the 28th day of December 1845. The society removing into their new house on Brown street on January 1, 1846 and the old house was taken down.

Here he occupied the easterly half of a double house, and there, I was born. After my father's death, my mother bought of her father, Andrew Preston, one half of his dwelling house for 140 pounds. The deed is dated April 15th, 1785. In this house, I lived with my mother, excepting while I was out as an apprentice until I removed to Beverly in 1796. At the time when she bought it the house stood end to the street, and somewhat back from the line of the same. It was removed and turned so as to have its longest side on the street. I remember it removed in 1785. While it was removing and fixing, my grandfather's family, and my mother's also, lived in the Silsbee house which is the next above. While living in that house, I recollect that my mother received from an adventure at sea, a crate of stoneware, of assorted articles, and among which there was only <u>one</u> mug or pitcher, and that of camel form, with a handle, containing about a pint. This pitcher was given to me and it has been preserved until this day, and is now in my possession, sound and unbroken.

---

[4] Rantoul wrote in the margin, "Deed recorded at Essex Registry Book 175, Leaf 100."

[11] The letters from the friends and relations of my father from which the forgoing extracts are made, are on file <u>with my papers</u>, and should be presented by my executor. July 23rd, 1850: I received a letter from my cousin Sarah Sinclair Rintoul, dated at London June 26th, 1850, wherein she informs that she has heard her father say that his parents both died within a few months of each other: That my father was a few years older than her father, who was born in October 1755; that their parents left seven children, three brothers and four sisters; that my father and two sisters were older than her father, the other three younger. They considered that a relative, who had been appointed to manage their affairs, did not act towards them with that justice and tenderness which orphans claim and in early life they were separated from each other, her father knowing nothing of his brothers than that they went to sea. The like employment he was put to. During the war between England and America, the vessel he was in being captured he became a prisoner in America at Newburyport & being out, one day, on parole, he entered a shop, when to [12] his surprise the shop keeper asked if his name was Rintoul, he said certainly it was, but how came he to know that. He replied that he so much resembled a neighbor of his that he thought they must be related. He soon obtained an interview and his brother Robert obtained a release from custody with liberty to continue in the state as long as he pleased. She says "I have often heard my father speak with pleasure of the very singular way he met with both brothers, not long before there were removed to another world, for as I before mentioned, it was unknown to him where they were but being on board a ship of war, for a few hours, he heard the name of David Rintoul, when upon inquiring he found it was his youngest brother, and it was the only time he saw him after their separation in childhood, for the next voyage he lost his life in an engagement with the enemy."

May 25th, 1852 I received from S. S. Rintoul a letter dated May 5th, 1852, wherein she acknowledges the receipt of son Robert's eulogy on Judge Levi Woodberry which I sent her. She and her sister get their living by dress making. She says that her sight and energy are somewhat impaired and that her sister is anxious and desponding. September 2nd, 1853 I received a letter dated August 17, 1853 from my cousin Mary Rintoul, aged 51, wherein she informs that her sister Sarah S Rintoul was married [13] on the 29th of July 1853 to Mr. George Sabourn, an elderly gentleman, a retired timber merchant, living at 9 Colet Place, Commercial Road East, and about half a mile from her former residence, N 3 Clarence Place, Stepney Green, London. He is represented to be in comfortable circumstances, a widower, without any family.

March 25, 1854: My grandson William Endicott Jun. sailed in a steamer from New York for Liverpool. I sent by him a letter to Sarah & Mary and a copy of son Robert's memoirs and writings, with an engraved copy of my likeness, to Sarah, and daughter Hannah sent to Mary a copy of A. P. Peabody's sermons and consolations.

My father was married in Salem to Mary Preston, daughter of Andrew Preston of Salem November 3rd, 1773[5]:

The first child by this marriage was Polly who was born on Sunday, October 26, 1777 at 3 o'clock in the morning and died September 29th, 1778.

---

[5] Rantoul added a notation in pencil, "or 1774 see Salem Register."

The second, Robert, born November 23, 1778 on Monday at one o'clock.

The third, William, born March 28, 1780 on Thursday at 6 o'clock a.m., and died, February 13th, 1783.

The fourth, Samuel, born July 10,1781 on Thursday at 9 o'clock evening and died at Bilbao in Spain, whither he went on account of being sick of consumption, April 22nd, 1802 at 7 o'clock PM.

The fifth, Polly, born July 22nd, 1783, Thursday 1 o'clock a.m. She was married to Andrew Peabody of Beverly, May 1808. He died December 19th, 1814 in the forty second year of his age, and she died at Portsmouth, in New Hampshire on Tuesday between nine and ten o'clock p.m., November 15, 1836.

[14] My mother, Mary Rantoul, married a second time, to Samuel Very, of Salem, September 26, 1793, and the only child by that marriage was a son, William Rantoul Very, but was always known by the name of William Rantoul only and died on board the Barque *Camel*- Holton J. Breed master, at sea, but his body was brought on shore and first buried at the quarantine ground at Salem neck, and afterwards removed to the burying point. He died July 7, 1816 at 5 o'clock AM.

1808 booklet written by Robert's half-brother, William Rantoul Very.

My mother, Mary Rantoul, died July 17th, 1816 at 20 minutes past 10 o'clock in the forenoon, aged 60 years and ten months, at my house, in Beverly, where she had resided some time but her body was buried at the old burying point on the westerly side in Salem, by the side of her son William who died 10 days before her. She was born Sept. 17, 1755. My sister Polly Peabody, removed to Portsmouth about a year before she died, her son, Andrew Preston Peabody, being settled there as the minister of the South Church. Andrew P Peabody married Catherine W Roberts, a daughter of Edmund Roberts, who died abroad as agent of the United States government at Macaw, June 1836. He, Andrew P. P., was born March 19,1811 and was married September 12th, 1836.

My sister's daughter, Mary Rantoul Peabody, married John P. Lyman, of Portsmouth, son of Isaac Lyman of York, Maine, October 23, 1843, who was born February 14, 1807. She was born September 23, 1813.

[15] I was born as before stated, November 23, 1778, in Salem and on the 18th of June in 1796, I commenced business as an apothecary in Beverly, and the first article which I sold was a half an ounce of spigelia, for six-and-a-quarter cents, but I did not begin to board in Beverly until the 31st and fully remove until the 22rnd of June. On the 4th of June 1801, I was married to Joanna Lovett, daughter of John & Elizabeth Lovett, who was born November 10th, 1780, and died September 23rd, 1848, a few minutes before twelve o'clock at night, of consumption, of a year's standing.

Our first child, Joanna Lovett Rantoul, was born January 13th, 1803, at 9 o'clock, Thursday morning and was baptized by Rev. Moses Dow Sunday February 27, 1803.

Our second child, Robert Rantoul, was born August 13th, 1805 Tuesday at ten o'clock in the evening and was baptized, by Rev. Abiel Abbot, on Sunday, the 25th August 1805. He died at Washington August 7th, 1852.

Our third child, Mary Elizabeth Rantoul, was born on Monday, August 14th, 1809, at 2 o'clock in the morning and was baptized by Rev. Abiel Abbot on Sunday the 20th of August 1809. She died August 14th, 1821, at 11 o'clock in the forenoon, of dropsy in the head.

Our fourth child, Samuel Rantoul, was born on Tuesday, March 23rd, 1813, at half past three o'clock in the morning, and was baptized, by Rev. Moses Dow, on Sunday the 4th of April 1813. He died on Friday, December 9th, 1831, at 9 ¾ o'clock in the evening of consumption, after a sickness of nine months. At his death, he was in his senior year at Harvard College.

[16] Our fifth child Charlotte Rantoul was born on Tuesday the 9th of January 1816 at two o'clock in the morning and was baptized by Rev. Abiel Abbot on Sunday January 28th, 1816. She died on Monday, December 2nd, 1839 at ten o'clock in the evening, of consumption.

Our sixth child, Elizabeth Augusta Lovett Rantoul, was born on Friday the 2nd of April 1819 at half past nine o'clock in the morning and was baptized by Rev. Doctor Holmes on Sunday the 11th of2 April 1819. She died on Tuesday May 23rd, 1837 at half past ten o'clock in the forenoon, of consumption, which commenced with Hemoptysis about two years before.

Our seventh child, Hannah Lovett Rantoul, was born on Sunday June 17, 1821, at six o'clock in the morning and was baptized by Rev. Andrew Bigelow on Sunday June 24, 1821.

Our eighth child, a female, was born on Wednesday June 16, 1824 at half past ten o'clock in the morning. She died unbaptized on Tuesday, June 22nd, 1824, at seven o'clock in the morning.

My son, Robert, died in the City of Washington, on Saturday night at about half past ten o'clock August 7th, 1852. He was at Washington as a representative in the Congress of the United States. His wife was with him at the time of his death, having left Beverly on hearing of his being dangerously sick, on Thursday evening and arriving in Washington on Saturday the 7th of August at about 6 o'clock in the morning. Although he was far gone and his mind wondering, he recognized his wife and desired that his eyes might be opened that he might once more see her. He would have been 47 years old on the 13th of August 1852.

[17] My great-great grandfather, John Williams, was born May 29th, 1664. He married Sarah Manning, who was born August 28th, 1667, on the 8th of December 1686. By this marriage there was,

Sarah Williams, born August 18, 1689.

Antriss Williams, born December 25th, 1700.

John Williams, born November 14th, 1702.

Henry Williams born, February 2nd, 1704.

Mary Williams, born May 8th, 1706.

George Williams born March 14th, 1700.

Ruth Williams, born August 25th, 1710.

My great grandmother, the above-named Mary Williams, was married to Joseph Lambert, and died at Salem, when she was about 90 years old. She died of the small pox in the autumn of 1773 and communicated this infection to others. She had a small dwelling house on the northerly side of the Common in Salem near where Milk street now is, and which was layed out over a part of the land where her house was. I used to visit with her often, when I was a boy. She said that she could remember when the common was overrun with whortleberry bushes, although the bushes were gone before my day, yet I can remember when there were six ponds of water in winter, each affording ample space for skaters, and a part of them had considerable water in them through the years. The children of my great grandfather and great grandmother Lambert were:

Joseph Lambert,

Sarah Lambert, married to __ [6] Underwood

Margaret Lambert, married to William White, and died November 16, 1803, aged 74 years.

[18] Priscilla Lambert, married to Daniel Ropes and died of Apoplexy, September 22, 1808 aged 69 years. She was born in 1739. Her husband, Daniel Ropes died October 1821 aged 83.

Elizabeth Lambert, married to __ [7] Phillips

Mary Lambert, my grandmother, born February 2nd, 1732, and died, November 17, 1810 in her 79th year. She was married to my grandfather Increase Preston or as he usually wrote it "Presson", though I think it should be "Preston" to conform to the original stock, which came from England February 4th, 1652. (See a letter from Jedediah Herrick for the genealogy of the Preston's dated Dec. 15, 1847, pages 24 & 5 of this book)

The following persons died of the small-pox, supposed to have received the infection from my great grandfather, Joseph Lambert. They were buried near the Pest House, a building on Salem neck, which was used for a small-pox hospital, before another was erected in the great pasture, near Castle Hill. This building stood where the Alms House now stands, and was standing within my recollection, viz,

Mary Lambert, wife of Joseph Lambert the son of the last-mentioned Joseph, died October 10, 1773, aged 45 years.

Hannah Townsend, wife of Moses Townsend, died October 14th, 1773, aged 37 years.

William Fairfield, Physician, died October 11th, 1773, aged 44 years.

---

[6] Rantoul left the first name blank.

[7] Rantoul left the first name blank. Elizabeth married Henry Philips on May 28, 1771 (Salem VRs).

Polly Ramsdell, wife of William Ramsdell, died November 5th, 1773, aged 27 years.

Samuel Barton, died November 9th, 1773, aged 36 years.

Hannah Cook, wife of Charles Cook, died December 27th, 1773 aged 23 years.

Hannah Stone, died January 8th, 1774, aged 51 years.

The disease must have been very virulent to have carried off such a number of persons in so short a time. The above was taken from their gravestones, November 1848.

[19] Inoculation was practiced in Boston as early as 1721.

My son Robert was married to Jane Elizabeth Woodberry, daughter of Peter and Debby Woodberry, August 3rd, 1831. She, Jane, was born October 10th, 1807, in Beverly.

Their first child, Robert Samuel Rantoul was born in Beverly, June 2nd, 1832, in my house at 4 o'clock in the afternoon[8].

Their second child, Charles William Rantoul was born in Beverly, April 24th, 1839 at 9 o'clock in the morning, in my house.

My daughter, Joanna Lovett, was married September 26th, 1824 to William Endicott, son of Robert and Mary Endicott. William Endicott was born March 11th, 1799.

Their first child, William Endicott, was born on Wednesday, January 4th, 1826, at one o'clock in the afternoon.

Their second child, Mary Elizabeth Endicott, was born on Monday, July 21st, 1828, at seven o'clock in the morning.

Their third child, Robert Rantoul Endicott, was born on Thursday, October 21st, 1830 at two o'clock in the morning. He died on the 19th of February 1833.

Their fourth child, Robert Rantoul Endicott, was born on Thursday, March 28th, 1838, at half past seven o'clock in the evening.

Their fifth child, Charles Endicott, was born on October 10th, 1835.

Their sixth child, Augusta Rantoul Endicott, was born November 13th, 1837. She died on Monday evening at about nine o'clock, February 5th, 1855 after a sickness from November 22nd; which she endured with great patience and resignation.

[20] Their seventh child, Henry Endicott, was born February 26th, 1840.

The six who were living at the time were baptized at their father's house, June 5, 1842, Sunday. By the Rev C. T. Thayer. I and my wife and other relations were present at the baptism.

The children of my nephew Andrew Preston Peabody are:

Andrew Preston Peabody, born August 7th, 1837, died April 13th, 1840.

Catherine Langdon Peabody, born October 14th, 1838, died January 24th, 1840.

---

[8] Rantoul added in pencil, "Latin School Boston, December 1st AD 1845.

Mary Rantoul Peabody, born December 14th, 1839.

Maria Ladd Peabody, born March 7th, 1841.

Robert Rantoul Peabody, born November 10th, 1844, died March 16th, 1846.

Ellen Langdon Peabody, born June 12th, 1846. Died August 13th, 1847.

Caroline Eustis Peabody, born June 8th, 1848.

Helen Peabody born September 20th, 1852.

The children of my niece Mary Rantoul Lyman named:

John Pickering Lyman, born February 8th, 1847.

Mary Rantoul Lyman, born December 18th, 1849.

Dora Lyman born September 18th, 1852.

[20 ½.1] My granddaughter, Augusta Rantoul Endicott, who died on Monday the fifth day of February 1855, at about nine o'clock in the evening, aged seventeen years two months and twenty-three days, was attacked with an acute pain in her side on Wednesday morning, November 22, 1854. This was followed with lung or pleurisy fever, which left her in a weak state with continual sickness at her stomach and vomiting. She endured her sickness, of about two and a half months, with much patience and met it's end with resignation to the divine will. She was kind and affectionate to all in their respective relations to her. She was distinguished for her literature and had been very studious and was well accomplished in the various branches of knowledge to which young ladies in this town usually attend. She was an amiable and lovely child and much esteemed by all who knew her. This is the second grandchild which I have lost.

[20½.2] Her funeral was attended at 2 ½ o'clock on February 7th, 1855. C. T. Thayer commenced the funeral services by reciting several appropriate and well selected passages of scripture. Then, Albert Thorndike and some sung a hymn accompanied with more on the piano, after which Mr. Thayer offered a prayer very well adapted to the mournful occasion. There were a sufficient number of carriages provided for all who chose to go to the grave.

In the autumn of 1855, her father caused a beautiful monument of marble to be erected at her grave. Beautiful for its neatness, for its simplicity and the inscription describes the same character. It consists of her name, Augusta Rantoul daughter of William and Joanna L Endicott, born November 13th, 1837. Died February 5th, 1855.

"The briefer life, the earlier immortality"

She was buried in the family lot in the town burying ground on Hale Street.

[20½.3] My eldest grandchild, Wm Endicott Jr, aged 31 years on the 4th of January last, was this thirty first day of March 1857, married to Mrs. Bonnie Thorndike Nourse, widow of John Freedom Nourse formerly of this town, but at the time of his death he was the principal teacher of a public school in Boston. She was at her marriage with W.E. about 32 ½ years of age, she has three children by her first husband, who are living. The wedding was at the Episcopal Church of the Messiah, Florence Street, Boston. By Rev. Mr. Randall, the minister of that church. I, with all of my children and grandchildren, and my son's widow Jane E. Rantoul and Harriett C. Neal to whom my grandson Robert S Rantoul is engaged, attended the wedding at the church at noon and afterwards we all repaired to Mrs. Nourse's house, No. 10, Indiana Place and there were entertained with cake and iced water. There was a room full of friends who retired at about 1 o'clock. Myself and all of my family above named (excepting Robert S.R. and Harriett C.N) came, and also her brother of New York and W Puffer, a border), came to dinner at about 4 o'clock. W(illiam) and his wife started for New York, there to take passage in the Steam Ship *Africa*, to sail April, for Liverpool. There were many more persons at the Church than at the House. They had received many handsome presents which were exhibited among which are a silver water pitcher of the value of $75 by C F Hovey and an elegant French Bible of the value of $50 by about 40 of the employees in the store of the firm of C F Hovey & Co, of which firm Wm E is a partner. I gave them half a dozen table spoons of the value of $21. There were many other articles of plate and some books, by many persons, manifesting the regard of a large circle of friends of the newly married couple. The numbers at the dinner table was 14. The day of the wedding was very pleasant, and everybody seemed to be pleased. We heard of their sailing from New York on Wednesday, April 1 under favorable auspices with about 111 passengers. The three children of Mrs. Endicott were put to board at Concord and went there about a week before the marriage. Her father lives at Worcester. Abel Rand, aged 73, did not attend the wedding. She is the daughter of Clarissa Thorndike and the granddaughter of Nicholas Thorndike of this town and a niece of Albert Thorndike.

They arrived at Liverpool in eleven days from New York and we received letters from them on Monday, May 4th, 1857. Their safe arrival was known on Friday of last week. The steamer *Africa*, in which they went having returned to New York. They arrived at Boston in the steamer *Eurofice* from Liverpool in the forenoon of the 31st of July 1859 and came to Beverly in the evening of that day, having left Liverpool on the 18th of July. Asa Rand was first settled as minister at Gorham in Maine in 1800. He lost his first wife while in Gorham and married Clara Thorndike of this town, and she dying he was again married and is now, 1857, living with his third wife.

[21] My great grandfather, Randall Preston, was born in Beverly April 3, 1702. He was the son of William and Priscilla Preston. His house was at Montserrat, near Hull's lane. He married to Susanna Stone, July 2nd, 1723. He was admitted a member of the first church, in Beverly, December 10, 1727 and died, March 27th, 1744, aged about 42 years. The children by his marriage were: [9]:

Susanna Preston, born July 2nd, 1723. Died July 16th, 1723.

William Preston born September 2nd, 1725 (settled at Gloucester).

Andrew Preston, my grandfather, born May 8, 1729. He learnt the tailors trade of Benjamin Cleaves and afterwards removed to Salem, and died there in February 1800, in his 71st year. He followed the sea through the active part of his life and at the time of his death was an inspector of the Customs.

---

[9] Randall and Susanna had two daughters named Susanna: The first was born July 2nd, 1723 and died July 16th, 1723. The second was born as Susannah in Beverly March 3rd, 1727 (Beverly VRs I, 268). She married Nicholas Biles on November 12th, 1751 (Beverly VRs II, 63).

Susan Preston, born May 16, 1731, died June 5th, 1731.

Benjamin Preston, born February 21, 1733/4.

Lucy Preston, born August 12, 1735

John Preston, born April 3, 1733. He lived near Mingoes Beach and his widow became the wife of Capt. Isaac Chapman.

My grandfather, the above-named Andrew Preston, was married in Salem to Mary Lambert, February 4th, 1752. By this marriage there were:

Mary Preston, my Mother, born September 17, 1755 and died, in Beverly, July 17, 1816, married November 3, 1773.

William Preston, born April 29, 1757, he married Hannah Neal who survived him many years and died May 10, 1849 aged 88 years.

Andrew Preston, born March 24, 1760, died June 8, 1771.

Susanna Preston, born September 3, 1761, died December 15th, 1834.

[22] Samuel Lambert Preston, born May 6th, 1763, died Nov. 6th, 1764.

Elizabeth Preston, born March 11, 1765, died April 6, 1766.

Samuel Lambert Preston, born February 17, 1767, died February 9th, 1788.

John Preston, born March 24, 1769, was lost in the ship *Iris*, with my father, supposed to be March 20th, 1783.

Elizabeth Preston, born April 12, 1771, married to Amos Lefavour, and died at Portland, where her children settled, May 1846.

Andrew Preston, born August 1775, died December 10, 1793.

Joseph Preston, born October 1, 1780, died August 27, 1840 at half past seven o'clock in the evening. He married Rebecca Peele, who still survives him. She was born about two years before her husband.

October 1850, Henry Larcom informs that my grandfather Preston's brother John Preston, lived near Mingo's Beach in Beverly. His widow married Capt. Isaac Chapman father of the present Homer Chapman who is now about 84 years of age. He, H Larcom, remembers the cellar of Randall Preston's house, near Hull lane. That William Woodberry, who married a Preston, lived in the house on Woodberry's point next, or next but one, to Curtis Woodberry's house, called the Garrison house, is now owned by John Prince's heirs that he, William W removed to Bridgetown, in Maine. Capt. Larcom is about 73 years old. The Garrison house was taken down many years ago and was reputed to be the first <u>framed</u> house erected in Beverly and was made secure against attacks from the Indians. I have seen some of the timber of the house which was used for fencing after the house was taken down.

[22 ½.1] My grandfather by my mother's side, Andrew Preston (he usually wrote his name Presson) was born in Beverly May 8th, 1729. At the usual age, he was put an apprentice to Benjamin Cleaves to learn the tailor's trade. At the expiration of his apprenticeship he went to Salem, and there became a seaman, and soon afterwards (Feb

4th, 1752), was married to Mary Lambert, daughter of Joseph Lambert of Salem. She was born February 2nd, 1732 and died November 17, 1810, in the 79th year of her age. My grandfather, from a common seaman, became the Master of a vessel and followed the sea in various capacities until, when advanced in years, he was appointed an Inspector of the Customs, in which office he died in February 1800, in the 71st year of his age. He became the owner of a dwelling house and fitted it for a Bake House, and in connection with his son William, who was born April 29, 1757, engaged in the baking business, which proved to be a losing business and involved him in embarrassment. He still held his dwelling house but was poor for the remainder of his life. His son William went to Castine at the entrance of Penobscot Bay and there carried on the baking business, his family remaining in Salem. He was never very thrifty. My mother loaned him money March 17, 1785, 252 pounds on a mortgage of land of his wife's on Chestnut Street in Salem after his decease her brother, Jonathan Neal, paid the original debt, with a part of the interest, and my mother gave up the residue of the interest. William had a large family, [22½.2] several of whom married and settled in Salem. Their decedents are still living there. My grandfather was noted for his persevering industry under many discouragements, misfortunes and afflictions, some of which in my boyhood and youth, knowing to. He was rather taciturn. I remember his teaching "scratch division" with a piece of charcoal on the hearth before the fire, but have entirely forgotten what knowledge I then acquired, and I do not now know what the rule is. My grandmother was more talkative, of a more active energetic spirit. She could do her turn at scolding her husband and her children whenever she thought it necessary. My grandfather for many years spent his evenings in Jacob Manning's shoe making shop, where there was a regular gathering of the old men of the neighborhood for conversation. Manning was called "Uncle Jake". He was a brother of Richard Manning Esq. and had three sisters. The five lived together to old age and no one of them married. Richard left a very large estate which was mostly inherited by the Hodges family in Salem. My grandmother Preston was a communicant of the East Church in Salem. [22½.3] My aunt Susanna Preston, in the latter part of her life spent several winters in my family and was kindly entertained and cared for by my wife and daughter. She died in Salem after some time of sickness in the house which I gave her for her life in 1834.

Sophia Rand, daughter of my aunt Elizabeth Lefavor, and widow of Rev. Samuel Rand, died in Portland, October 18th, 1854, aged 61 years. I visited her for the last time in October 1849 at her house in Portland, being at the Unitarian convention in that place. She used to visit at our house. Her husband was a free will Baptist Minister. He preached at Salem, but at Portland for some time before his death. He died at Portland and left a dwelling house at the west end of the city where his widow lived when I visited her. They had a daughter married to Mr. Small connected with one of the banks in Portland, as cashier and __.

[22½.4] William Preston, son of Andrew Preston, was born April 29, 1757, and married Hannah Neal daughter of David Neal. William Preston was a baker and had six children; viz William, David, Hannah, Polly, John who married __[10] Driver, was a baker and died in 1855, and left children. Jonathan who is a tinman, is married and has children.

---

[10] Rantoul left her first name blank. John Preston married Sally Driver on September 26, 1811 (Salem VRs.)

David Augustus Neal, son of Jonathan, born June 7, 1793 married July 26, 1818 to Harriet Charlotte Price, daughter of James and Mary Price of Boston. David Neal was officer of the Privateer *Diomede*, Capt. Crowninshield, in the war of 1812; was captured by the British and carried to Halifax, and thence to Dartmoor Prison, where he remained till the close of the war. On his passage from Halifax to England, he was badly wounded in an unsuccessful attempt made by him and a few others to capture the transport in which they were, and his wounds were dressed by Barry O'Meara, afterwards well known as the surgeon of Napoleon I at St. Helena after the peace. He was super cargo and master of several vessels, principally in the East India business, and subsequently was engaged in commerce in Salem in connection with his father and brothers. He retired from commercial business in 1846, having become President of the Eastern Railroad. Since that period, he has devoted his time mainly to railroad enterprises. He has had five children viz Theodore Frederick, born December 18, 1822, died in infancy; Theodore Augustus, born March 23, 1827, a merchant- he married May 30, 1849 Elizabeth Boardman Whitteridge daughter of Thomas Cook Witteridge and Susan Lovett Mead Whitteridge; Harriet Charlotte, born February 1, 1831, died March 17, 1837; Margaret Maria, born June 15, 1832; and Harriet Charlotte, born July 8, 1837. Theodore Augustus Neal has two children viz Elizabeth Martagini Whitteridge, born March 10, 1850, and Caroline Frothingham, born April 20, 1855. The foregoing was copied principally from the Neal Record, compiled by Theodore Augustus Neal and published under the date of November 5, 1856, of which he sent me a copy.

[23] John Lovett, my wife's father, was born Aug. 31, 1769 and died Feb 25th, 1792. It is said by Samuel Stickney who knew him, that he was tall and slim, with black hair and eyes and dark complexion. This information from Sam'l Stickney was obtained in January 1858.)

John Lovett, son of Josiah and Rebecca, married Elizabeth Herrick, daughter of Jonathan and Elizabeth Herrick December 3, 1767. By this marriage there were:

John Lovett born August 31, 1769, died October 14, 1805.

Jonathan Herrick Lovett, born February 24, 1772, died March 20th, 1844. He married his cousin Nancy Lovett, daughter of Joseph Lovett.

Elizabeth Lovett born March 7, 1774, died April 9, 1820. She married Rev. Rufus Anderson and survived him. He died at Wenham Feb. 7, 1814 aged 48 years.

Josiah Lovett born May 31, 1776, died February 1, 1794.

William Herrick Lovett born October 5, 1778, died September 10th, 1805. He married Abigail Dike who survived him many years but is now dead and had left two daughters.

Joanna Lovett born November 10th, 1780, died September 23rd, 1848. She was my wife.

Augustus Lovett born November 7, 1782, died September 3, 1833. He married Hannah Batchelder, daughter of Caleb Batchelder, who was the son of Josiah Batchelder Esq. She still survives and has three sons living viz. Augustus who married Miss. Bishop of Newbury Port. He is Secretary of the Hope Insurance Company in Boston. Fredrick, who is a ship master and Samuel Ingersol who married Miss Susan McDonald from Montreal in Canada. He is a Hardware merchant in Boston.

Charlotte Lovett born May 31, 1786 died Dec 25, 1787.

Edmonds Lovett born September 3, 1789. Died December 20, 1821. He was drowned on his passage from Antwerp to Batavia.

The first named John Lovett, my wife's father, died February 25, 1792 aged 48 years, 7 months and 13 days. His widow Elizabeth Lovett died October 31, 1825 aged about 81 years. She was born August 22, 1745.

[24] John Lovett and his wife Hannah who was the daughter of Josiah Batchelder Esq. both died in October 1805. John died October 14, 1805, and on October 22, 1805, Hannah died. They left four children viz. Elizabeth Augusta Lovett, John Lovett, Joanna Lovett and Hannah Batchelder Lovett. In March 1806 John and Joanna came to live in my family. John continued to live there for about six years and Joanna until she was married in April 1823. Thus, my wife not only had the care of bringing up her own children but also two of her brothers' children. The other two died young.

Edmonds Lovett married Judith Lamson, daughter of Francis Lamson, a hatter.

Hannah Batchelder Lovett daughter of John and Hannah died April 24th, 1816 aged ten years and six months.

Elizabeth Augusta Lovett died June 17, 1814 aged nineteen years and ten months.

Rufus Anderson, who married my wife's sister Elizabeth, was graduated at Dartmouth College 1791. Ordained at North Yarmouth October 22nd, 1794. Installed at Wenham July 10th, 1805. Died at Wenham February 1814. His first wife was a daughter of Hon. Isaac Parsons of New Gloucester in Maine by whom he had three or more children, but none by his second wife. He was born at Londonderry March 5th, 1768. The inscription on Elizabeth Anderson's grave stone is as follows:

"Enough for her that here her ashes rest, till God's own plaudit shall her worth attest"

Mrs. Anderson was always, from my first acquaintance with her, very kind and friendly towards me. She was distinguished from my wife, her sister, by her disposition to talk freely and unreservedly. Her mother was rather noted for her taciturnity as was my wife. Mrs. Anderson was always full of anxiety about the welfare and conduct of her relations, neighbors and friends and I might say of all the human race. Lamenting their errors and deploring their wants, sufferings and distresses.

Genealogy of the Preston family by Jedediah Herrick [24 ½.1]

"Hampden Maine, December 15, 1847

"Hon. R. Rantoul,

"Dear Sir,

"I have just received a letter from Mr. Alfred Presson of Gloucester, quoting largely from your letter to him, and from which I learn that your mother also was a Preston, and also probably a descendant of Samuel, Andover, 1670. From whence Samuel comes, I am yet in doubt, probably a son or grandson of Roger of Ipswich 1648-1666; but my purpose in addressing you at this time is to give you a concise sketch of the name Preston, generally, as far as I have been able to collate it from English & Scottish history, and such names of the early settlers in this country as have fallen in my way. It is my intention to pursue each enquiry to some definite result should my life & sufficient health be spared. But I am very feeble, seldom able to write at all, and with great pain when I do attempt it. All I can promise is to diligently pursue the collection of material, and to leave them in such form as may be available to any friend who will take them in hand.

"The European name is always Preston, both Scotch & English. It is of Scottish origin, territorially belonging to the family estate in Mid Lothian, Perth shire, Scotland. But in this, as in many other territorial names, it is impossible now to determine whether it was originated in the person or the estate. All we know in this Parish is that it was a Sir name before the Conquest[11].

[24½.2] "and are of the earliest on record. It was assumed as the Sir marque of the family at the time of King Malcome Cranmore early in the 11th century. The first of Knightly rank on record is Leolphus de* Preston, contemporary with William the Lyon 1165. His lineal descendant, Sir William Preston, was summoned to Batdinock[12] 1291 by Edward I of England, as one of the Scottish nobles required to decide upon the conflicting claims of Bruce and Balliol[13] to the Crown of Scotland.

"*de Preston. And here arises a not very unusual question as to the earlier origins of the race. I had taken it for granted that the prefix de indicated in all cases a Norman origin but W. Disraeli has thrown this to the winds. He says somewhere that many of the Anglo-Saxon gentry & nobility assumed this from regard to the prevailing fashion of the time, and thus an ancient landmark "few and far between" as they are, being so demolished and defaced as to afford us no longer any very certain guide. Whether our remote ancestors of this name were Celtic, or Anglo Saxon, or Danes. I am inclined to refer them to the early Anglo Saxons who populated the Southland districts of Scotland and held the country in common with the native Scots, with whom also they had become a mixed race of Scots, Saxons, & Danes & politically, at a later period, the Normans.

"The present head of this Kinse is Sir Robert Preston of Valleyfield, Perthshire, Scotland, 7th Baronet.

"At the battle of Neville's Cross 1346, John de Preston, another [24½.2] of Preston, Lord Dingwall was among the Scottish prisoners of distinction made by Queen Phillipas.

"At the battle of Otterburne, 1388, Henry Preston captured Ralph Percy of Northumberland, for whose ransom he received several luxurious manors. <u>Finissant</u>.

---

[11] Rantoul added a note in the left margin, "My g. grandfather Samuel, I believe, was gr. Son of the first Samuel, of Andover, came in 1707. His father died ante 1720 and his mother (who was Sarah Bridges) md. A Price of Ashford Conn. I first find my gr F. Samuel in Wilmington in 1740 where, about 1741 he md. Marcie Scales, dau. Of James & Sarah Scales who settled in Wilmington the same year. He being a Town clerk from 1707 to 1740 and it is quite possible that I may be."

[12] Badenoch is a traditional Scottish district located in the center of the Highlands.

[13] Robert the Bruce and John Balliol were clan leaders who had claims to the Scottish throne.

"Arms of the Preston family

> "Field: argent, 3 unicorn's heads, crossed, sable, within a bordeure azeure.
>
> "Crest: Ant of a Duceal coronet, or.on unicorns heads, sable,
>
> "Supporteurs. 2 lyons rampant guardants.
>
> "Motto: *Praesto ut praestem*[14].

"The English arms and motto are entirely different viz:

"Arms of Sir John Preston, Mayor of London 1332:

> "Field: Erminois, on a chief sable, 3 cressants or.
>
> "Crest: a Crescent or. Motto: *Pristinum spero lumen*[15].

"I can discover no material difference in the English arms. The colours and charges are uniformly the same. A difference only is found in the disposition of the Coronets.

"The English name is very numerous and seems to have set its mark upon many towns & places in several English Counties.

"A family at Boston, St. Lawrence County of Norfolk still retains its Knightly rank, of which the present representative is Sir Jacob Henry Preston, br. 1812, successor to Sir Thomas Preston, first Baronet.

"The name of Preston has been long & highly distinguished in British history, & especially in the army. A Captain Preston, you will remember, commanded the Company of English infantry when, by his orders, fired on the mob in King Street Boston, March 5, 1770, and if I do not misremember them with several others of this name among the British officers during our Revolutionary War. But there were no Tories and there are none now, altho there are some incorrigible __, by the way.

[[24½.4] "I had the pleasure of taking your son by the hand and thanking him, not so much for his loco politics as for his reliable service in in the effort to abolish capital punishment, and also in the great cause of public extended education.

"Sir Amicus Preston of London was among the grantees in K. James' 2nd charter of Virginia, 1609, and from the frequency of the name in Virginia, Maryland, Pennsylvania, and the Carolinas, I have supposed that persons of the name were among the early immigrants to New England. I have been only able to find Roger 1634, aged 21, settled in Ipswich, d. 1666, left a son Thomas and other descendants, who d. 1697. Son John.

"2. Daniel 1634 of whom I find nothing further.

"3. Edward 1634 settled in Dorchester age 13.

"4. William, with a family, settled in New Haven.

---

[14] "I undertake what I may perform."

[15] "Erstwhile light of hope."

"5. John d. in Boston 1663. Whether an immigrant or son of one of these does not appear.

"Samuel was of Andover 1671/2 when he and Susanna Gutterson md. D. 1738 aged 85 or 86. 2nd wife died same year, who was Mary Blodgett.

"Sons:

"Samuel b. 1672 from whence my g-grandfather Samuel of Wilmington 1740 was descended, I believe, as gr. Son.

"William b. January 11, 1674, who I suppose is your William of Beverly, I find him nowhere else.

"John b. May 1, 1685 settled in Windham Conn.

"Joseph b. January 26, 1687 m. ___ [16], settled in Windham Conn. d. 1737.

"Daughters

"Mary, Susannah, Elizabeth, Ruth, Lydia, Priscilla.

"I have a large number of families & names but am not yet able to track any unbroken line from the first immigrants. I hope ___ that some of my searches will find the clues.

"I am very desirous having [24½.5] taken this matter in hand, to trace out the lives directly from the original immigrants to the present time, so as that what I do, if I complete nothing, should be found valuable as a starting point for some future & more successful investigation. But I find this for little encouragement. The Prestons, like the Herricks, have been a migratory race seldom stopping longer than one or two generations in the same place, seldom more than two. Nor can the most perfect confidence be placed in the examinations of our __ affairs. I have always found myself well rewarded for the labor of gleaning after their harvest.

"I inclose a very rough draft of the armorial bearings of the Prestons, as far as I know. These arms are all transatlantic. I would very much like to ascertain whether the Prestons in this country have the same arms and, if different, in what particulars! If we ascertain a precise locality in England I apprehend we must find it by this, or by some accident yet unlooked upon.

"Most Respectfully, I am dear sir,

"Your greatly obliged humble servant

"Jedediah Herrick."

[25] "Genealogy of One Branch of the Lovett Family, Collected by J.P. Lovett February 1851

"3 brothers, John, James, & Joseph came to Beverly probably from England at or soon after its settlement in 1630. James moved to N. York, Joseph to N. Jersey,

---

[16] This name is illegible. Joseph married Rebecca Preston on December 21, 1709 (Andover VRs).

and John remained. John was at different periods, Surveyor of Highways, Constable, and Selectman. His descendants stand thus:

"1st John Lovett b. 1610 d. November 8th, 1686. His wife Mary d. June 1695 at 80.

"2nd John Lovett b. 1636 married Bethia --- d. Sept. 10, 1727

"3rd John Lovett b. abt. 1666 m. Mary Pride Mar. 5, 1695 d. bef. 1750.

"4th Josiah Lovett b. August 27, 1704 m. Rebecca Woodberry d. June 22nd, 1774.

"5th John Lovett b. July 1st, 1743 m. Eliz. Herrick 1767, d. Feb. 25, 1792 __

"6th John Lovett b. August 31st, 1769 m. Hannah Batchelder Feb. 17, 1794 d. Oct. 14, 1805. w.d. Oct 22.

"7th John Lovett b. July 1st, 1799 m. Mary Shaw January 3, 1826 (my father) died July 22, 1854.

"The Children of John (5th) & Elizabeth Lovett were:

"John m. Hannah Batchelder Feb. 17, 1794. Their child. Charlotte, b. Oct. 26, 1795, d..Oct.. 22, 1796. Eliz. Augusta b. Aug 26, 1797 d. June 17, 1817. John b. July 14, 1799 m. Mary Shaw Jan 3, 1826. Their children John Prince Nov. 4th 1830. Mary Sprague b. December 2, 1835 Eliz. Augusta b. Oct, 5, 1837. Frederick b. Sept. 11, 1844. Hannah born April 4, 1801 d. May 1803. Joanna Batchelder b. Feb 9, 1803 m. Albert Thorndike May 27, 1823 (their children living are Samuel, K, Lothrop b. Dec. 28, 1829, Wm. b. Apr 17, 1835 Albert b. __[17] Chas b. Nov. 8, 1843 Thos. Stevens b. Oct. 6, 1846) & Hannah Batchelder Oct 8th, 1805 d. Apr 2nd 1816.

"Jonathan Herrick married Nancy Lovett Oct. 6th, 1796. Their children who were married were Charlotte b. Apr 26, 1801 m. Henry Morgan chil. Charlotte b. who never enjoyed good health. 2d. Jonathan Herrick b. Dec. 30, 1805 m. Lydia Ray ch now living James Albert b. Apr 22, 1832, Horace Ray b. Mar 16, 1838 Henry Francis b. Mar. 2d, 1841 Wm Herrick b. Oct 26, 1808 m. Raney Foster ch Nancy Foster b. Nov. 8, 1833 Emily Francis b. Nov 18, 1836) 4th John C. Mar 29,1806 md. Charlotte Wallis ch. Geo. Augustus b. Mar. 26, 1839 d. Mar 4 1840. Raney May 18, 1813 (md. Amos Lefavour ch. Nancy Lovett b. Apr 22, 1857. 6th Chas. Thorndike b. Sept 11, 1817 m. Caroline Cressy no ch. D. md. 2nd. Ann Gage. 7th Mary Eliz. Dana b Sept. 4, 1802 m. G.W. Allen ch.

[26] "The Children of John & Eliz Lovett Cont'd

"Wm Herrick m. Abigail Dike their ch. 1st Abigail Dike (md. Wim. Foster their ch. Abby Stevens who md. Capt. Edward Meacom was b. Oct 29, 1822. Wm. Lovett b. Nov. 4, 1837) 2nd Eliz. Herrick m. Henry Heyde of Bath Maine ch. Henry b. Nov. 1831.

"Joanna m. Robert Rantoul their children now living are: Joanna Lovett b. January 13, 1803, m. Wm. Endicott their chil. Wm. B. Jan. 4, 1826. Robert Rantoul b.

---

[17] Rantoul left this date blank.

Mar 28th, 1833, Charles b. Oct. 10, 1835. Augusta Rantoul b. Nov. 13, 1837. Henry b. Feb. 25, 1840 2nd, Robert P. b August 13, 1805 md. Jane Woodberry three ch. Robt, Sam'l, Charles William Hannah Lovett June 17, 1821.

"Augustus m. Hannah Batchelder their children are:1st Augustus b. Dec. 30, 1813 (m. Mary Ann Bishop June 17, 1838 their ch. Now living Augustus Sidney b. Nov. 17, 1841 Henry Hall b. Sept 13, 1843 Sarah Ellen Everett b. Dec. 10, 1848). 2nd Frederick Wm. B. Feb. 4, 1816 md. Died Aug 3, 1854. 3rd Sam'l Ingersol b June 17, 1818 m. Susan MacDonald chil. Swan J. January 21, 1849.

"Edmonds m. Judith Lamson their chil. 1st Judith b. May 26, 1812 m. Hezekiah Lovett cheir chil. Sarah b. April 1832 Edmonds b. January 29, 1834 2nd Wm. Edmonds b. May 4, 1814 d. at sea June 5th, 1832. 3rd. John Francis b. June 19, 1817 m. Lucy Ann Fornis chil. 4th Eliz. Augusta b. June 21, 1819 m. Francis Montier children

"Josiah & Charlotte were not married. Elizabeth who m. Rob't Rufus Anderson left no children.

"Deaths arranged by year (6th gener.)

"John died October 14, 1805

"Jonathan Herrick died March 20, 1844

"Elizabeth died April 9th, 1820. Josiah died February 1794.

"Wm. Herrick died September 10th, 1805

"Joanna died September 23rd, 1848

"Augustus died September 3rd, 1833

"Charlotte died Dec. 25th, 1787

"Edmonds died at sea Dec. 10, 1821

[27] "John Lovett, son of John died July 21, 1854

"Frederick W. Lovett son of Augustus died Aug 3rd, 1854 on his passage from Philadelphia to Boston and which was brought on shore and buried in Beverly on Friday, the 4th August,1854."

[29] Robert Endicott, son of John and Elizabeth Endicott of Danvers was married to Mary Holt, daughter of Nathan and Sarah Holt of Danvers on the 1st day of November 1781. The time of the births of their children is as follows viz:

Mary Endicott, 29th of July 1782 at eleven o'clock P.M.

Robert Endicott, 5th of May 1785 at eleven o'clock A.M.

Nathan Holt Endicott, 31st of January 1788 at ten o'clock P.M.

Samuel Endicott 18th of July, 1793

A daughter 7th of June 1790.

William Endicott 11th of March 1799.

A daughter died June 10th, 1790, aged three days.

A daughter died September 10th, 1796 aged three days.

Mary Ellingwood wife of John Ellingwood died Jan. 6, 1813, aged thirty years.

Robert Endicott Jun. died August 27, 1813, aged 28 years.

Nathan Hale Endicott died July 2, 1816 aged 28 years.

John Ellingwood Jun. died November 7, 1816 aged 34 years.

Hannah Endicott wife of Samuel Endicott died March 14, 1825 aged 30 years.

Sarah F Endicott wife of Samuel Endicott died August 23, 1847 aged 38 years and 6 months.

Robert Endicott the first named died March 6, 1819 aged 62 years.

Mary Endicott wife of Robert died January 7, 1850 at 5 mins past 4 A.M. aged 88 years and 4 days.

[30] Births of Deacon John Beckford's children:

John Beckford was born August 2nd, 1725

Elizabeth was born December 17th, 1726.

Mary was born October 11, 1728.

Samuel was born August 23rd, 1730.

Benjamin was born June 4th, 1732.

Pinson was born July 14th, 1733.

Hannah was born October 1st, 1734.

Sarah was born February 11th, 1736.

Ebenezer was born April 9th, 1737.

Rebecca was born August 17th, 1738.

David was born October 5th, 1740.

Eunice was born December 10th, 1741.

Jonathan was born June 6th, 1743.

Births of the Herrick family & the deaths of some of them:

Jonathan Herrick born April 30, 1717.

Abigail Herrick born April 26, 1719, died June 1, 1719.

George Herrick, born March 11, 1721, died October 25th, 1726.

Abigail Herrick, born April 7th, 1723.

Andrew Herrick, born April 28th, 1725.

George Herrick, born January 4th, 1727, died August 9th, 1730.

David Herrick, born November 14, 1729.

Elizabeth Herrick was the wife of John Lovett and the mother of Joanna Rantoul, born August 22nd, 1745.

Elizabeth was the daughter of Jonathan and Elizabeth Herrick.

[31] Peter Holt was born in Andover Mass., June 12th, 1763. He was graduated at Harvard College in 1790. Josiah Quincy, who was afterwards President of the same college, was a chum and classmate and when Mr. Holt was aged visited him and made him a present of money. Mr. Holt was ordained minister of Epping, NH February 1793. He was married to Hannah, daughter of the Rev Nathan Holt of Danvers, Mass. April 23, 1793. She was a sister to Mrs. Mary Endicott, wife of Robert Endicott, whose family record is on the page but one before this. Mr. Holt preached in Epping for twenty-eight years and from thence removed to Exeter, NH where he lived six years and from thence removed to Peterborough, NH and was installed over the Presbyterian Church in 1827. He preached there eight and removed to Deering, NH where he preached until he was seventy-eight years of age when he retired from the ministry and removed to Greenfield, NH, where he died, March 25, 1867 at the age of eighty-seven years and nine months. Samuel Endicott of Beverly, son of Robert, married two of his daughters. Both of whom died before their father

Samuel Endicott was married to his third wife Martha Thorndike Giddings, widow of John E Giddings and daughter of William Leech, on Monday, June 7, 1852.

Hannah Holt, widow died in Beverly on July 25, 1857 at 9 ½ o'clock in the morning aged 88 years, 2 months and fourteen days.

[32] My Uncle Joseph Preston was married February 1, 1807 to Rebecca Peele who was born September 4th, 1778. Their children are:

Joseph born November 10, 1807. He died abroad.

Mary Lambert born July 25, 1812. She married Richard Noble.

William Rantoul Preston born October 28, 1814. He married Miss Marie Salter of Portsmouth.

Eliza Ann born November 10th, 1820. She married Nath. Henry Felt of Salem, tailor. He afterwards became Mormon and removed with his family to Salt Lake, Utah territory.

Margaret born August 31, 1822. She married Thomas Melzeard and removed to Norway Maine, from which place they removed in 1855, but returned there again.

My cousin John Preston of Salem, son of William P. died at Salem, August 14, 1855 aged 68 years. He was a baker, as was his father. No. 53 Summer Street, the house where his mother and his grandmother Neal lived within my remembrance.

Early History, Last Letter of my Father, His Loss at Sea [32]

The ship *Iris* in which my father sailed from Salem on his last voyage, December 28, 1782 bore a letter of marque and had a large crew. There were on the Ship *Iris* twenty persons, who being lost, left widows, nineteen of whom had a child after their husbands sailed from Salem. They lived in Beverly, Manchester, Salem and other places for some years afterwards, some of these Manchester women used to walk from Manchester to Salem to inquire of my Mother if there was any news of the missing ship *Iris*.

[33] My father left home on his last voyage on the 28th of December 1782, when I was about four years and a month old. I have no distinct recollection of his person. Having been thus early deprived of a father, who was supposed to be lost at sea on the 23rd of March 1783. I was almost wholly indebted to a kind and devoted mother for my rearing. My father for the short time he lived after I was born, was almost constantly absent at sea. From an examination of his letters, it appears that he must have had but little education in his youth. The last letter which my mother received from him is dated; York River, February 28th, 1783 and with corrections of the spelling and capitals is as follows viz:

"My Dear,

"These few lines come with my kind love to you hoping that they will find you and our dear children in good health as they leave me. I have been here ready for sea some time and wind bound and shall sail the first good wind. Your brother (John Preston) is well and in good health. I wrote to you to insure three hundred pounds on the ship *Iris* if the *Hind* was taken which I have had particular account that she is taken by the *Lion* man-of-war. You must act as you think best in regard of insurance. There is great talk of peace here, but I don't know what to think of it but hope that it is. Time goes away fast and the voyage much longer than expected but I hope to make a safe voyage. Remember me to mother, [34] brother and sister and all friends.

"I remain your ever mindful and loving husband,

 18

Probably the omission of "father" in connection with "mother" was that he knew that his father in law was at sea at the time. This was the last letter, but he did not sail until the 4th of March. Nothing was heard of him after that date. My mother did not give him up as lost for some time afterwards. I remember that information was received that there were some American seamen held in captivity at Algiers. This circumstance, though a year or two after he sailed from Virginia, revived the hope of my mother that he was still among the living and she made a journey to see a man who had arrived from Algiers to make inquiries of him. Other circumstances occurred from time to time to foster the belief in her mind that he was still living. She always remembered him with strong affection. The time of his being lost was connected with several severe domestic afflictions and trials. When my father left home he left three children, one of whom, named William, died suddenly of the Quincy, on the 13th of February 1783, and my mother had another

---

[18] Rantoul pasted here a signature of Robert Rantoul, his father. In the margin he wrote, "This signature was cut from another letter written at about the same time with foregoing."

Robert Rantoul (1778-1858).

Joanna Rantoul (1780-1848).

Robert Rantoul, Jr. (1805-1852).

Robert S. Rantoul (1832-1922),
Courtesy First Parish Church.

**Robert R. Endicott (1833-1914),
Courtesy First Parish Church.**

Samuel Endicott (1830-1891).

duty with great labor, perseverance and affection. She was little more [35] than eighteen years old when she married and lived with my father about nine years and was in the twenty eighth year of her age when he was lost. She had but little school education beyond reading and writing. At that time, females did not usually have the same advantages of acquiring common learning which were enjoyed by males and males had fewer, much fewer than at the present time.

My mother endeavored to impress upon my mind a regard for religious principles. I was instructed in the Westminster Shorter Catechism, in lessons from the Bible and was a constant attendant on the services in the Church on Sunday. She was especially anxious that I should have the best schooling which her limited means could procure in that part of the town where she lived. I was kept constantly at school, from four years of age until I was thirteen and a half years old. I was, in the main, obedient to my mother from a conscientious feeling of duty. I think that the great fault in the education of children at the present time is the want of parental reverence and respect. Unless obedience is secured in the earliest period of childhood it will be but rarely obtained afterwards. It should therefore be the first object of attention on the part of the mother to secure the obedience of her child. It should be done without harshness. It may be secured with the utmost kindness.

[36] During the years of childhood of myself and my brother and sister, my mother had a hard task. Although my father left some considerable property, yet it was so badly disposed of as to prevent, in a great measure, her realizing the proper income of it. The seven years following the peace with Great Britain were attended with great pecuniary

embarrassment in the seaport towns, of which the people of Salem had their full share. I remember the straits to which my mother was sometimes brought in regard to the support of her family. It was very difficult to obtain money from those from whom it was due, excepting William Gray, who kept on interest a part of the money which came to his hands, from my father being in his employ for several years, and from him it could be obtained always when due. I, being the oldest child, was more acquainted with my mother's difficulties than the others and was more participant in her cares and troubles than they. This early acquaintance with the cares and troubles of life gave a tinge to my character. I have always been careful, and oftentimes too much troubled about many things, for my own comfort or the comfort of those about me.

Cheerfulness, hopefulness should be cultivated by those who would enjoy life and it is particularly desirable that it should be attended to in childhood. I feel the want of these dispositions sufficiently in old age to lead me to recommend an attention to them in childhood, in youth and in mature life.

[37] The house in which I was born stands on Essex street (now 1848) directly opposite to where the East Meeting House stood. It belonged to the Elkins family and my father occupied the eastern half of the house, the western part of which was occupied by the widow Elkins. A son of hers, Henry Elkins, was a judge of the court of Sessions for Essex County and naval officer of the port of Salem. Among my first recollections and remembrances is the kindness of a negro woman, named Ancilla[19] who lived with Mrs. Elkins and who was so particularly attentive to me while an infant as to leave an impression which is not yet entirely obliterated, although almost seventy years have transpired since I could have been sensible of her caresses. To this circumstance of my infant years I have always attributed those kindly feelings towards the African race which I have invariably entertained and which are not diminished by old age. Rev. James Dimon, who baptized me in the East Meeting House was born Nov. 29, 1707 at Long Island, NY. He graduated at Harvard 1730. September 24th, 1783, William Bentley was ordained as colleague pastor with James Dimon, who was ordained pastor of the East Society, in May 1737. Mr. Bentley boarded with Mrs. Elkins, and the council at his ordination were entertained at her house. I remember that it was thought desirable to have me away from home on that occasion and I was sent down to my great uncle Joseph Lambert's house (corner of Becket street on Essex street) where I partook of the liberal entertainment which was at that time generally made on the day of the ordination of a minister. Wm Bentley was the first minister in Salem who publicly discarded the doctrine of the Trinity.

[38] Lord Cornwallis capitulated on the 17th October 1781, and his army was surrendered on the 19th. On the receipt of intelligence of this great event of the Revolutionary war at Salem, there were public demonstrations of joy, and although I had not then attained to three years of age, I remember that a Cannon was fired in Pleasant street near its entrance to Essex street and that I stood in a chair before a chamber window in my grandfather's house facing towards Pleasant street to see it fired. On the news of a peace being concluded between Great Britain and the United States in 1783 I remember that I was standing at the door of a little shop attached to the western end of Mrs. Elkins's house (but my mother lived in the eastern end) by the side of my mother, who was trafficking

---

[19] In the margin, Rantoul wrote, "this word means a "maid servant."

with a countryman on horseback for a quarter of meat, that, suddenly many persons came running down the street crying aloud Peace! Peace! And the first that reached the door of the East Meeting House, which was directly opposite to where I was standing, rushed in and began to ring the bell while others continued the cry of Peace! Peace! Thus, my mind was early impressed with national events, events which then excited more feeling and joy in the community than any similar events could have done at any time since that. Poverty and pecuniary distress followed the War of the Revolution in the country generally, and particularly in Salem and other seaports. Commercial businesses revived about 1788 or 1789 and Salem was visited with great prosperity, from the East India trade soon after this time.

[39] When I was a child it was not unusual to relate stories of ghosts to children, to entertain them or to frighten them. I had heard enough of such stories to lead me to a partial belief of the appearance of ghosts, representing the persons of departed human beings, as well as other animals. I will therefore relate a story, which I have never before divulged, of my own experience. Before 1785, my grandfather's house in Salem stood end towards the street and some thirty feet back from the street. The lower story was used for a bake house, for my uncle William Preston, who was a baker, and my grandfather's family resided in the second story. When visiting at my grandfather's I had, out of wantonness and sport, ill-treated and perhaps injured a stray cat which I found there. Not long afterwards, I was again at my grandfather's house, in the evening, sitting by the fireside facing the fire which was at the southerly end of the room, and I was sitting in front of the westerly side of the fireplace. While thus sitting, the cat, which I had maltreated, suddenly came and set herself down, very demurely, at my left hand. Her sudden appearance immediately brought to my mind the ill-usage she had experienced at my hand. My conscience reproached me. I then thought that I must have killed her, and that her ghost had come to rebuke me for my cruelty. I said nothing about it to anyone, but I layed it to heart [40] it worried me much. I repented of the evil which I had done to the poor cat and resolved to avoid all wanton injury to animals in future. As I grew older the belief in ghosts gradually wore out, but the moral influence of this occurrence remains to this day. This thing occurred about 65 years ago, and the particulars of it are still fresh in my memory. The absurdity and folly of relating stories of ghosts and other marvelous and preternatural events, to little children, is not the less to be depreciated because in this case it might have resulted beneficially to virtue. My mother at the time of her becoming a widow or thereabouts, had three aunts who were widows, Sarah Underwood, Margaret White and Elizabeth Phillips. Aunt Underwood had two sons who lived to manhood. Aunt White had no children and Aunt Phillips had a son and a daughter. These Aunts were the most frequent visitors at my mother's house and from them I received many impressions. They each had their peculiarities of temper, disposition and character. Aunt Underwood invariably gave a minute and entertaining description of the dinners and suppers which she had enjoyed and partaken of at the various places where she had visited in the intervals of her visits to mother. The impression made on my mind was that a large proportion of her comfort and enjoyment consisted in eating and drinking and I observed that she indulged [41] her appetite for food with greater freedom than most others whom we had an opportunity of witnessing at their meals. Aunt White was kind and affectionate and remarkable for her timidity. The sight of a mouse would almost throw her into convulsions. Aunt Phillips was a tailor and used to come to make the boys cloths. She was a

snuff taker and wore two large pockets, in one of which she carried her snuff box, handkerchief and other articles that would not suffer by their contiguity to these two, and in the other, she generally brought cake, gingerbread, apples, nuts or some other eatables, to distribute amongst the children, and this made her visits desirable and pleasant to us. Her going from house to house to work, made her the principal source of intelligence to the family. She was kind and pleasant to us, and we always anticipated her visits with much pleasure, we also were always glad to see Aunt White but had no particular liking for Aunt Underwood. My mother had other Aunts, but they were not frequent visitors, having families that required their attention at home. My grandmother Preston was sufficiently talkative, but not very much so. My mother's brothers and sisters were possessed of [42] humane and kindly feelings. It was under these domestic influences that I was raised and from them derived my own traits of character, modified by a vast variety of advantageous circumstances some of which I shall relate. A vast majority of our race owe their education more to the domestic influences arising from their intimate, daily association with brothers, sisters, uncles, aunts and other near relations and members of the household, than they do to the more direct modes of instruction which are thought so important in our day and the means of which are so vastly increased within the last half century. My associates, or rather those boys with whom I fell in with in the street, were many of them of vulgar manners, profane and indecent in their language, rough and course in their treatment of on another. Amongst these I had to learn to shun their vices and to profit by their good qualities. Self-discipline cannot be begun too soon, and boys should not be kept entirely away from other boys because of their imperfections, but they should be strictly guarded from contamination and thus gain moral strength by occasional association with those around them and with whom they must of necessity come in contact with when of mature age, and thus be gradually prepared to resist the temptations of such necessary contact.

First School, Susanna Babbige: Other Schools; Master Watson, Master Bentley, Master Southwick, Master Snelling, Master Long & Master Bancroft [43]

At about four years of age I was sent to school to Ma'am Babbige the great grandmother of Rev. Charles Babbige, who graduated at Harvard College in 1828 and is now a minister at Pepperell in this state. She kept a school for about fifty years and is said to have picked berries on Salem common. This good lady was very corpulent and advanced in age when I went to her school. She used to sit in an armed chair in front of a window on the easterly side of the house and near the easterly side of a great open fire place. The house is now standing though so much altered in its external appearance that the good Lady, were she to come, probably would not know it. The house is situated on the northerly side of Essex Street, a little below and opposite to the entrance of Union Street. She was so heavy that she could not easily perambulate her school room to apply her correcting hand to the urchins who were arranged on seats over the whole floor of the room. To remedy this, she kept by her side a cane pole, of sufficient length to reach the farthest boy in the school and when any one was seen by her, indulging himself in anything inconsistent with her notions of propriety, he was sure to be reminded of her displeasure by a good rap of the cane pole. Other modes of punishment used by her were to call the delinquent to her side and tie him to her chair with a piece of yarn or pin his clothes to hers. With the use of these means the school was well governed and I was taught to read, instructed in the West Minster Assembly's shorter Catechism, which was contained in the New England Primer. This small book so universally used in families and [44] primary schools at that day, was adorned with numerous cuts, if the hideous pictures there exhibited could be said to <u>adorn</u> it. Among these was John Rogers, the first Christian martyr in the reign of Queen Mary of England, burning at the stake at Smithfield in London surrounded by his wife with nine small children and one at the breast. But no one of the learned urchins of the school could settle the difficult question whether the poor woman had nine or ten children with her upon the melancholy occasion. There was, "In Adam's fall we sinned all", with a picture to represent this wide world calamity and to impress this dogma more strongly upon the infant mind. "Zacchaeus, he did climb a tree our Lord to see", "This book attend your life to mend" and several other wholesome and instructive sentences were arranged in a column, one under another, with a <u>picture,</u> an appropriate picture I was <u>going to say</u> (but cannot with regard to truth) placed in another column directly opposite, at the right hand of each sentence. My instruction in the scripture's consisted mainly in committing to memory a considerable portion of the second chapter of Luke's gospel, and however the practice of requiring young children to commit to memory select portions of scripture, at a time when they cannot be supposed to understand the import of what they thus learn, may have fallen into disrepute and [45] disuse. I am strongly impressed that it's influence on the heart and life is beneficial and useful in the formation of a religious character in subsequent years. I therefore think that pious mothers will do well to adhere to this practice of olden times.

At this Dame's school, although I acquired but little book learning, I was taught <u>obedience, reverence for age and for rank</u>. A daughter of hers, Miss Lydia, in another room, kept a higher school for young misses only. She was a more accomplished scholar, but needlework then was the prominent branch in such schools. The strongest and most durable impressions are made at the first school to which a young child is sent. Hence the importance of good principles, good temper and kindness, as well as decent literary attainments in the instructors of primary schools. My brother Samuel went to the same school after me and my sister Polly went to Miss Lydia after going through the course with the old Lady. In April 1785, when I was about seven years of age, I left Madam Babbige's school and went to Master Watson's school to learn to write and to attend to other branches of study. This school was kept at the westerly corner of Union Street on Essex Street, in a one story wooden building with a very sharp roof, which building remained there until preparation was making for the execution of the brick block which now stands fronting on Union and Essex Street. Here I became associated with larger boys and began to partake of the rough and tumble of life. In the athletic recreations which required [46] organization or leaders, the Crowninsheilds were generally put forward, they being the representation of the most distinguished family in the eastern section of the town, commonly called Wapping, which extending up as far and perhaps somewhat farther than the westerly side of the Common or to St. Peter's Street. The next division, and which was esteemed the most aristocratic was called St. James's and above this was Knocker's Hole. The Crowninsheild boys were Benjamin William Crowninsheild, who was afterwards Secretary of the Navy, acquired a great fortune and is now living in Boston and has a son, Francis Boardman Crowninsheild who is now Speaker of the Massachusetts House of Representatives. Another was Richard Crowninsheild (he died January 1851, age 76), who became a manufacturer and died a few years since. Another brother was Edward Crowninsheild who died young. At one time, there were several regular pitched battles between the Wapping boys, in line, on the Common and the Knocker's Hole boys, in another line, under their respective leaders. The battles were fought with stones and other missiles, neither side gaining the victory. The St. James's boys were considered as too effeminate to engage in such sports. Being young, I generally kept at a safe distance in the rear of the line. I went to Master Watson's School till Nov. 1785. At that time, the Town School in the East School House began, and Master Watson was appointed the instructor. This School House was the first <u>public</u> school house in the <u>eastern</u> section of the town. It stood on the southwestern corner of the Common, but a few years ago [47] it was removed farther east, on East Street and there altered and enlarged by the addition of a porch. It still displays its original form and its diminutiveness when compared with modern School Houses in Salem. Master Watson kept the town School but a short time, after which he resumed his private school and Rev. William Bentley, minister of the East Society, took charge of it temporarily. I continued at the town School with one or two short intervals until, in 1791, when John Southwick, who had been an assistant in the town School, under Master Lang, the principle instructor, set up a private school, and I was taken from the town School and sent to his school. Reading, Spelling, Writing and Arithmetic were all the branches attended to at the town School. The latter part of my attendance there, so many of the scholars as were desirous of attending to English Grammar were allowed to go to the Latin School, kept at the bottom of what is now Washington Street on the margin of the North river, two or three half days in a week. I was furnished with Perry's dictionary, containing his grammar and sent according to this arrangement to the Latin School kept by Thomas Bancroft, who was afterwards Clerk of the Courts for the County of Essex, and whose son, Thomas P. Bancroft now owns and lives on, in the summer season, the farm which has been in the hands of the first minister of Beverly, John Hale and of his descendants, from the time of his settlement here, to the present time, Thomas P Bancroft [48] being a descendent through his mother (he died in 1852). When General Washington, in 1789, visited Salem, to do honor to his reception the boys of all the town Schools, (there was then no provision for the instruction of girls at the expense of the town) were paraded on each side of Essex Street above Washington Street. I went with the Latin School which was led by John Pickering, son of Col. Timothy Pickering, he being the first scholar in the school. At that time and place I saw General Washington and again on the next day when he left the town[20]. The five years that I went to the town school I made but little progress in book learning. In Arithmetic, to which I happened to take a liking, I went ahead of most of the boys. I was furnished with Dilworth's School Master's Assistant and went through with nearly all the rules and studied out the curious miscellaneous questions at the end of the book. The town school at that time was very much below what it is now. Master Lang was a Silver-smith by trade and was taken from that employment to teach the school. He was a man of exemplary morals and dignified manners but had not the other requisite qualifications of a good teacher. He taught the school for most of the time that I attended it after Mr. Bentley's time. He had several efficient assistants among whom was Jonathan Snelling who was afterwards an instructor in the Boston public schools for many years.

---

[20] Rantoul inserted in the margin: "General Washington was lodged at Joshua Ward's house, west side of Washington Street near Rail Road station".

At the dedication of the new brick School House bounding on the Common in South Street and Essex Street, March 1, 1842 he was present and recognized me as one of his [49] scholars. He told me that although he had never spoken to me from the time of his leaving the Salem Town School till that time, yet he had always kept up the knowledge of my person, as he had frequent opportunities of seeing me in Boston when I was a member of the Legislature (He taught writing in the Boston Latin School at the time of his death while I was there RR.)

He was at that time about 74 years of age and was then a teacher in a Boston Public school, in which employment he had been ever since he left the Salem school. He looks hale and healthy, rather of short stature, pleasant and easy in conversation. He recollected Robert Stone, who attended the East School at the same time with me, and one or two others of his scholars at that time. The unexpected opportunity of conversation with me after so long a separation seemed to give him much pleasure. He died in 1848 aged about eighty years and held the office of teacher till his death.

I went to John Southwick's private school for about one year, and during that period I attended to many branches of school learning with assiduity. Southwick was a Quaker, but taught good manners, he was a very successful teacher for many years after I left his school. He afterwards became somewhat of a political partisan and was chosen a Representative of Salem in the General Court, one or more years, by the Democratic party, and I regret to add that at a more advanced age he became intemperate and sunk from his standing in society. In governing his school, he never struck any belonging to his first and second classes but if they were faulty he would when a leisure moment occurred in school time or after the school was dismissed, call the delinquent to him and by kind, persuasive [50] words and fondling would invariably soften his feelings, make him to see his failings in their true light and produce a resolution to amend. Upon the smaller scholars, he thought that he could not bestow the requisite time to produce the necessary result, he therefore occasionally visited them with the rod. He governed his school well. At his school, I attended some to Geometry, Trigonometry, Book-keeping, English, Grammar and the other studies usual.

Apprenticeship- Shipbuilding – Independence [50]

When I had entered upon the fourteenth year of my age I began to think that it was time for me to look about for some employment and I became uneasy at school and at the beginning of the summer of 1792, when I was about 13 ½ years old I left school and went no more excepting a few weeks in an interval between my other engagements, to study navigation. I also went one quarter to learn sacred music, in the evening before I left Southwick's school and with this instruction I went into the seats of the Choir of the East Society with the desire, but without the ability, to aid in the singing. I continued to sit with the Choir for some months, no one intimating that I was useless, or perhaps an injurious occupant of the place. Thus, it appears that my school education was imperfect and terminated early. In the spring of 1792, William Silsbee, who lived at one time in the house next above the one owned by my mother, and who was my playmate and school mate and but a few weeks younger than myself, procured a place as an apprentice with William Stearns, apothecary, father of Joseph E. Sprague the present Sheriff of Essex county, who has had his name altered from Stearns to Sprague.

[51] Learning that Doct. Stearns wanted another boy, I applied and was received I think about the first of June 1792. I boarded in the Doctors family, on the corner of Beckford and Essex Streets, and was kept very close at the shop the regular hours, from early in the morning till nine o'clock at night, excepting that on Wednesday evenings we were allowed to go to our homes after the lamps were lighted, to return so as to shut the shop when the bells rung at nine o'clock, and, on Sunday mornings we were allowed to leave at the ringing of the first bell for meeting, to prepare our dress and go to meeting in the forenoon and at the conclusion of the service to return to the shop and in the afternoon to leave at the ringing of the second bell, go to meeting and return to the shop at the end of that service. In the evening, we were allowed to leave after the lamps were lighted and to return when the bells rung at nine o'clock. This close, steady application to business laid the foundation of whatever industrious habits I have been possessed of through life. Doct. Stearns was punctilious in everything. Strictly economical, he suffered not the smallest thing to be wasted, adhered strictly to the principles of Justice and as for my services in the shop, I think the place was favorable for the acquisition of good habits of business. In the family, I was not happy. If any time was found to sit in the house, except while eating, our place was in the kitchen where there were three and sometimes four menial servants whose characters and habits of life were not agreeable. The children of the family were not well governed. From this circumstance and the associations with such servants, our residence in the family was unpleasant. [52] Silsbee and I generally agreed pretty well, though not without some occasional struggles for precedence. I was a few weeks older in years, but he came to the place a few weeks before I did, upon this last ground he claimed the precedence belonging to the oldest apprentice, this claim I was unwilling to yield to, thinking that from all the circumstances I was entitled to equality and whenever he endeavored to exercise what he considered his just prerogative I resisted. The spirit of independence and the habit of acting according to my own impressions was at that time, fully developed, as the results of my previous education, experience and observation. I think the same characteristics have continued to mark my course through my life thus far. By this no doubt I have fallen into many errors which might have been avoided by seeking and listening to the counsel of others, better informed and wiser than myself, but at the same time I think it is much better thus to suffer than to put in jeopardy one's independence, self-reliance, firmness of decision and energy of action. These should all be strictly adhered to and they may be without refusing the counsel of others, but my continual jealousy of the interference of others has led one to the extreme of caution. I hope that the exposure of my failings may prove beneficial to my posterity.

*One of the maid servants who lived with Doct. Stearns' family while I was there was Sarah or Sally Hale. She is now (1849) living in Beverly at the age of 83 years a widow partly dependent on charity and is named Anderson. She was a native of Salem.

[53] After all, self-reliance is the main spring of successful action. Without it one will be tame, wavering, indecisive, inefficient; he may not be vicious, but he is only negatively virtuous; he may avoid doing wrong, but he will be weak and slow in doing right. Better to stand <u>alone</u> even if it requires great effort, than to lean upon another. In the one case action will be a relief but in the other a burden. When one feels that he <u>alone</u> must think, resolve and act, he then may rely upon that inspiration from above, which under other circumstances he has no right to expect. "Yet I am not <u>alone</u> because the Father is with me" was the saying of him who was called to endure the greatest sufferings in

testimony of his fidelity to his mission of mercy and beneficence to our race. And thus, he was sustained under the greatest sufferings, with patience and resignation to the will of his heavenly father.

An indecisive character rarely attains to eminence in anything.

The habit of punctuality, order and diligence, the determination to concentrate the mind and action to one object at a time, to persevere under every discouragement and in short to be in earnest about every worthy object, great or small, are the sure means of success. Never affect depreciation of your calling or of any object which you think it right to attend to. If it is unworthy of [54] your attention, abandon it; if it is worthy, make it honorable to you by your fidelity and in discharging its claims. "Honor and shame from no condition rise, set well your part, there all the honor lies."

[55] An extract from the history of "David Copperfield" by Charles Dickens, August 22, 1850, which will illustrate what is written on the two preceding pages and add additional weight thereto:

"I have been very fortunate in worldly matters, many men have worked much harder, and not succeeded half so well, but I never could have done what I have done, without the habits of punctuality, order and diligence, without the determination to concentrate myself on one effect at a time, no matter how quickly its successor should come upon its heels, which has then formed. The man who reviews his own life, as I do mine, in going on here, from page to pare, had need to have been a good man, indeed, if he would be spared the sharp consciousness of many talents neglected, many opportunities wasted, many erratic and perverted feelings constantly at war within his breast, and defeating him. I do not hold one natural gift, I dare say, that I have not abused. My meaning simply is, that whatever I have devoted myself to, I have devoted myself to completely; that, in great aims and in small, I have always been thoroughly in earnest. I have never believed it possible that any natural or improved ability can claim immunity from the companionship of the steady, plain, hard-working qualities, and hope to gain its end. There is no such thing as such fulfillment on this earth. Some happy talent, some fortunate opportunity, may form the two sides of the ladder on which some men mount, but the rounds of the ladder must be made of stuff to stand wear and tear; and there is no substitute for thorough-going, ardent, and sincere earnestness. Never to put on hand to anything on which I could throw my whole self, and never to [56] affect depreciation of my work, whatever it was; I find, now to have been my golden rules."

Learning to Write [59]

As a caution against injudicious remarks, by influential persons in the presence of children, I have to remark that at the time when Rev. William Bentley was teaching the Town School, temporarily, and he, being on a visit at my mothers'; and, as is common with mothers, she inquired of him in respect to my progress in learning at school, he remarked upon my good progress in various branches but that I did not improve much in writing. Writing he said did not require talent or genius, it was a mere mechanical employment. This remark impressed itself upon my mind and influenced my conduct so as to induce me to pay but very little attention to improvement in writing for the remainder of the time that I went to the Town School, and not until I went to John Southwick's school did I overcome the impression, made upon my mind by this single remark of W. Bentley, leading me to think that the writing of a good hand was of but little importance. When I went to Mr. Southwick's school I began to try to improve my hand writing and when I left his school I wrote a tolerable hand. After leaving school I became careless about writing, and in consequence my handwriting deteriorated, and has remained but poor, till this time, though not without considerable diversity at various periods of my life as may be seen by my account books, record books etc. I am now strongly impressed with the opinion that the writing of a free, fair hand, is of very great importance, contributing largely to [60] comfort, happiness and usefulness and to success in very many industrial employments. I therefore hope that my example in writing will be guarded against and that the settled opinion of my old age will have its due weight in counteracting the influence of this example of my bad penmanship.

Master Lang [60]

Master Lang wrote a fair, but not an elegant hand. He ruled all the writing books used in school with a leaden plummet. The ruling of paper by a machine was not then practiced at all. He used a round ruler and was very expert, though with all his quickness it necessarily took much of his time. He also wrote copies for the boys on slips of paper, one of which was put into each book at the time of ruling on each page, a page being the extent of the writing of each boy at one time.

The school was large, sometimes as many as a hundred boys were present. Much of the time there was an assistant teacher, who was thought, by the boys, to have more learning than the principal. Opinions among boys which are unfavorable to the moral character, literary attainments, or practical efficiency of their teachers, are very injurious to the boys themselves, retarding their progress in good learning and impairing their reverence for virtue and goodness. The only school which I attended where daily prayer was offered by the instructor was the Latin School, kept by Thomas Bancroft, where I attended some two or three half days in a week to study English Grammar because it was not taught at Master Lang's school. [61] Devotional exercises where they can be seriously and feelingly performed are of good influence in a school, unless thus performed and followed by exemplary conduct on the part of the instructor they had better be omitted.

In 1789 while I attended M(aster) Bancroft's school General Washington visited Salem, and William Northey, who was a Quaker and chairman of the Selectmen, and wore a brownish wig, when the President was presented to him, he without moving his hat, took the President by his hand and said, "Friend Washington, we are glad to see thee, and in behalf of the inhabitants, bid thee a hearty welcome to Salem." I remember a son of Mr. Northey who went to Bancroft's school at the time when I did who did not conform strictly to the manners of the Quakers. A little more than one hundred and thirty years before that time the Quakers were persecuted and suffered many cruelties in Salem on account of their peculiarities, but then one of their number had the honor of leading in the reception of the first President of the United States. I was at the time but eleven years of age, but I can recall the pride that I felt in taking a part in the public proceedings of the day. There was a great degree of enthusiasm pervading all ages, classes and denominations of the people of Salem on the occurrence. It would be difficult to get up such a universal feeling of joy upon any occasion at the present time in Salem. [62] I enjoyed my humble part in the public proceedings of the occasion as much as I have on occasions of a similar character at a later period of life. On the next day after Washington's arrival, he rode on Horseback down the Main Street as far as Pleasant Street and there turned to go to Beverly to see the new cotton factory just put in operation. At the point of his turning the corner of Pleasant Street I had a full view of him. The cotton factory was in upper Beverly about two miles from Essex Bridge. The building was of brick. The spinning was with Jennies, which with a considerable number of spindles were moved by hand. This building was ultimately destroyed by fire and the bricks that remained were used in the construction of the first meeting house at Beverly Farms. This meeting house has since been taken down and a wooden one built in its place of a larger size and of more convenient arraignment and of a handsomer exterior. This cotton factory was the first that was <u>incorporated</u> in Massachusetts. It was a failure. Cotton cloth was afterwards for many years manufactured in the building by individuals or by partners. All the time it was incorporated, there was great difficulty in obtaining an act of incorporation. There was then great jealously of private corporation in the Legislature and among the people. Now hundreds are created every year, and many of the dangers anticipated have proved themselves to be visionary.

Schooling: Economy, Punctuality, Perseverance [63]

When I went to Ma'am Babbige's school my mother was particularly careful that my attendance should be regular and constant as far as practicable, and also punctual. She was sure to correct the offence of truancy and to prevent tardiness. I know not how much I am indebted to this early training for a habitual trait in my character of observing punctuality in all appointments and of keeping close to the particular object of pursuit, for the time at which it ought to be attended. Although I have often failed in these respects, yet I have experience enough of the great benefits resulting from an observance of the rules to induce me strongly to recommend them to my grandchildren. An established habit of the observance of punctuality will be found of incalculable advantage in every station in life. Equally important is the habit of doing, to completion, whatever is undertaken. Before beginning, consider well whether the object is deserving of the whole time and labor necessary to its accomplishment; weigh well its difficulties and estimate impartially your power and ability to overcome them and if you resolve to begin, then be sure to per- sever to the end. Avoid procrastination. Whatever belongs to the present time, that do immediately and without delay. With many persons, it is much easier to begin <u>many</u> things than it is to finish <u>one</u>. A habit of this sort is attended with innumerable vexations, disappointments and disorders. My first lessons in regard to business, when I went to Doct. Stearns's were favorable to the development of the principles of industry, punctuality, order and perseverance [64] and I have endeavored to act out these principles. Doct. Sterns was as remarkable for his strict economy as for anything else. He was very particular in instructing his apprentices not to <u>waste</u> anything. He never allowed wrapping paper to be torn, a practice which is very common in most shops, but required every sheet to be cut into halves, quarters, sixths, ninths, or some other number of parts so that none of it should be useless. The boys were to judge which of such parts were best adapted to wrap the article which they were selling and to use none larger than was necessary. So it was with the use of packing twine, it was to be passed around each end of the package and across its length and tied as near its end as a knot could be made and then cut without waste. For shot, flax seeds, mustard seed and other small round substances, that could not be wrapped up without an undue expenditure of paper, small paper bags were made, from time to time, with flower paste, and cut with the same precision as described above, so that no paper should be wasted. This systematic regard to economy was carried into every part of the business of the shop, so that economy with a strict regard to order, prevailed throughout. I have mentioned the course in regard to the use of wrapping paper as an exemplification of a rule which pervaded every part of the management in the shop. The habits that I formed there, continued with me in my subsequent service, with other employers, who were not particularly distinguished for their regard to economy or thrift.

[65] A very strict regard to order is very useful but still in the exercise of a sound, discriminating judgment an occasional departure from strict rules is right, proper and commendable. Let such departures however be infrequent and fully justified by the occasions, and not from frivolous considerations. There is no judgment to be entertained with greater caution than when exercised in regard to the dispensation with well-established rules of conduct. Generally, the temptation is all on one side, and reasons for yielding to the temptation will present themselves much more readily than those of an opposite tendency against this, the force and power of settled, confirmed habit is a great security system sometimes costs more than it is worth. It is important to observe rules, but it is hardly less important to be able to break them on a right occasion.

"A man who never breaks a rule is little better than a fool"

One who regulates his life by fixed principles of honor, honest, uprightness and religion will, whatever may the outer circumstances, have the unspeakable comfort and advantage of his own self approbation to sustain him amidst every adverse circumstance and will be enabled to resist away temptation which may beset him. Nehemiah, the governor of Jerusalem said when the men of property had done wrong by excessive usury in their transactions with their poorer brethren. "Then I consulted with myself"… "and I set a great assembly against them" Instead of consulting the noble and rulers. [66] This doctrine of self-consultation, is not so generally regarded as it ought to be. To relieve ourselves of responsibility we frequently go to others when it is very clear that we ought to rely upon ourselves.

Influence of my Father's Character on My Own [67]

That influence my father's character, manners and disposition might have had upon me during the few years of my childhood which passed before his death, most of which time he was absent from home, it is difficult to say. Of his success in getting employment and promotion is Salem, without friends or patronage is to be relied upon, he must have had elements of character which would have given him high rank among the mariners and merchants of Salem of that time, had he lived. In four years after he came to Salem he had attained to the command of a vessel and when he was but twenty-three years of age. He continued to be constantly employed as a Master of a vessel from 1776 to the time of his death in 1783. I think much of casual impressions on infant minds, and I am impressed with the belief that the few and short periods of association with my father must have given its due degree of shade to my character, though it was modified by other more frequent and longer continued associations. Of this early influence, I have no evidence besides a theory which I entertain and which I think is well founded. My mother, being quite young when she was married to my father, no doubt acquired from him some of the elements of her character from which mine derived some of its shades. [68] The Scotch are noted for their industry, economy, perseverance of enterprise as well as for their sobriety, temperance and thrift. They are universally instructed in the elements of common school learning and in the principles of religion. They are said to be parsimonious living in a somewhat high northern latitude the influence of climate upon character should be considered.

From the influence of education and the well-directed exertions of the clergy., the peasantry have long been distinguished for sobriety, industry and moral rectitude and in point of intelligence, are indubitably the first in the European world. Superstition still has its hold on the minds of many. The existence of witches, fairies and ghosts, is still part of the creed of the Scottish peasant, and the Highlander confidently believes in the power of second sight, or the capability of perceiving future events. The Scotch are said to resemble the New Englanders more than the English do.

The jealousy of foreign birth was not so much cultivated in Salem in 1773, '4, & '5 as it is now (1854). If it had had been, my father could not have had such rapid promotion in his calling. The intolerant and unjust feeling towards Roman Catholics and foreigners which now exist (1854) certainly cannot continue longer. It is too venomous, mean and un-Christian to stand.

Luke Brooks [69]

On the 22nd of November 1848 I met, in Boston, Luke Brooks of Salem. We recognized each other and after the usual salutations I asked him if he recollected our being at Master Lang's school together, he said that he did and that he had good reason to remember it from the assistance which I then gave him in getting his learning. He is 76 years of age, has a wife and three children, one son named Luke. He remembered Master Snelling, who died a few years since in the office of a teacher in Boston at the age of 78 or 79 as an assistant when he first came to school, but that John Southwick who succeeded Jon Snelling was the assistant for most of the time while he went to the school. Luke Brooks came to the school sometime after I had been there. He was about six years older than myself. He had made much less progress in school learning than I had for the want of opportunity to go to school. He came into the same seat where I was located and being of a kindly disposition, he conciliated my esteem and I used my best endeavors to help him along with his studies in which he was considerably behind me. It was highly gratifying to me, that after an interval of about sixty years, he still retained a grateful recollection of a service which I had rendered him without any expectation of reward at the time, but which now comes to me in old age in his gratitude. (Mary, widow of Luke, died in Salem, October 1853. aged 81.) The aid which I gave him was principally in arithmetic, my favorite study. I record this that it may encourage even young children to do good as they may have opportunity. (Luke Brooks died at Salem on Tuesday, May 14th, 1850 aged 77.)

Corporeal Punishment in Schools [70]

The infliction of corporeal punishment at Master Lang's school was a matter of daily occurrence and upon some particular occasions it was administered with a cruel severity which shocked the feelings of all those who were accustomed to a mild parental discipline while it very rarely prevented a recurrence of the same or equally heinous offences in the child who suffered the infliction. Truancy was the crime which was most severely punished, and the inefficiency of severity ought to have led to other means of cure, but the opinions of that day in regard to the utility of punishments were very different from what they are at the present time. The light of the present day had scarcely dawned upon the pedagogues of that time. A whip, commonly called a cow hide, was the usual instrument, and it was with the full strength of the master that it was sometimes applied. At that time, it was not an uncommon occurrence for men, and even <u>women</u> to be publicly whipped in Salem for stealing and other crimes. These flagellations were generally witnessed by a large number of boys. I am now of the opinion that both schools and families should be governed without the use of corporeal inflictions and that where they are not so governed it is the fault or the deficiency of talent in the parent or in the teacher or in both that prevents it. The best governed schools and the best governed families, so far as my observation has extended are managed without blows. Corporeal punishments are stricken from the laws of the state, saving in capital crimes.

Salem School [71]

My attendance at the Latin School to study English grammar brought me into acquaintance with boys from families of higher standing in Salem than those I had associated with at the East Town School. These boys were more refined in their manners and I formed acquaintances which continued more of less after I left school. While at the Latin School I was exercised somewhat in declamation and was furnished with the "Art of Speaking" for which I paid one dollar and bought it at the Gazette printing office. (Dollars were not as easily earned as they are now.) A book of some merit containing extracts from Shakespeare, Addison, Pope, and other standard authors. It strikes me that the selection was more judicious than some that are used at the present time. I read this book through and committed some of it to memory. It was a great defect in my education, that during the long time which I went to the East School, my memory was but very little cultivated. About all the exercises of memory there was the committing of the rules in arithmetic. In this branch it was a standing order that no sums could be done until the rule for them was learnt, and as I like to do the sums, I was willing to learn the rules so that I could work upon the sums. I remember when attending the Latin School that a dramatic piece was prepared from the "Art of Speaking", in which I had the very short part of the "nurse" in Dominic the Cortie. I was highly pleased to have any part assigned to me, but if it had been one of the longer parts, I do not know that I should have succeeded in committing it to memory. I think it desirable that children should have their [72] memory exercised when young and that continued attention should be paid to this subject through all their schooling.

Other Schools, Memory [72]

While I went to Mr. Southwick's school, a question in Permutation was published in the Salem Gazette requesting an answer. Mr. Southwick gave the question to me and I worked out the answer without any mistrust of the use he intended to make of my labor. In the next Gazette that came out, to my astonishment, it was commented that they had received an answer to their arithmetical question from <u>Master Robert Rantoul</u>, a pupil at Mr. Southwick's school. When the school boys saw the print, they hooted to me to my no small mortification. This was my first appearance in the newspaper which I suppose was to gratify the vanity of Master Southwick as to flatter me. Since that time, I have become less sensitive at the sight of my name in a newspaper whether for praise or for censure, having become accustomed to such notices, particularly the last. I have suffered much inconvenience and mortification as an extemporary speaker, from a defect of memory. I many times have omitted saying what I had premeditated, solely from this defect. Memory without a sound judgment, is in a great degree useless. I have known some who seemed to remember everything but to <u>know</u> nothing.

Fishing Excursion [73]

When I was about twelve years of age, in company with the other boys, two of whom were somewhat older, we procured a flat-bottomed boat, with two oars, called then most commonly a <u>Dory</u> and started early one morning on a fishing excursion, provided with bread and water for a day's consumption. With a favorable wind and tide, we rowed our skiff almost down to Baker's Island, enjoying the labor as much as the sailing, without any gloomy foreboding of what changes might come over our sunshiny prospect. We, on arriving at a suitable place for catching fish, threw over the hellock and went to fishing and were tolerably successful. The day passed along pleasantly until in the afternoon, there came up a sudden squall with heavy rain. We pulled up our hellock and took to our oars, against a strong wind and a heavy sea, thinking only how we should get home. I remember well how courageously I layed out my strength at the oar, not more so than my companions, all of us being impressed with the feeling that an extraordinary effort was required to enable us to reach our homes in season. After toiling for some time and making very slow progress, against the wind and sea, we held a consultation and it was concluded to make for the nearest shore. We turned the head of the boat from the wind and made for the Beverly shore, where we arrived before night. Having fastened our boat, we resolved to leave her with the fishing tackle [74] and walk home, a distance of some four or five miles. There was still a difficulty to overcome to get home, we must pass a toll bridge and none of us had any money to pay the tolls. In this dilemma, we opened a negotiation with the people we found near our landing place for the sale of the fish which we had taken in the course of the day and we were relieved from this ground of anxiety when we found one who compassionating our forlorn condition agreed to take all the fish and give us money enough to pay all the tolls for our passing over Essex Bridge to get to Salem. Having thus raised the funds for our journey, we immediately started for home and arriving in the evening, relieved our parents and friend from their great anxiety and fear that we had met with disaster in consequence of the Squall in the afternoon. The next morning, money was raised from the younger members of the company to pay the tolls of the two oldest boys who were commissioned to walk to the landing place and from there to row the boat up to the place of the owners. This was safely accomplished, and I acquired so much wisdom by the occurrences of this excursion as to prevent my ever engaging in another of the like kind. "bought wit is the best, if you do not pay too dear for it." I often went out in a boat a fishing but never before nor afterwards, with so young and inexperienced a crew, ventured so far from home. Although we were very much frightened, yet none of use lost our courage

[75] Wednesday, May 29th, 1850: This day brings to my mind the recollection of what has always been called Election Day being celebrated as the anniversary of the general election of State Officers from 1631 to 1831. Since the last date, by an alteration of the Constitution, its civil duties have been transferred to the first Wednesday in January, but its peculiar ancient recreations and amusements are not to be regulated by law. These are continued by the young. When I was quite a child of only three or four years, I was sent to my grandmothers to get from her garden the first blooming tulips and such other flowers as could be found. With these I was led about the streets to be caressed and admired by passing friends. As I grew older I was allowed to visit the places of amusement where the young usually assembled to enjoy their playfulness. These places were, for the children from the east end of the town of Salem, on the neck. At what was then called the old fort, now Fort Pickering, and what was then called the new fort and also sometimes at an old fortification called Juniper Fort. At these places there was cake, candy and other articles of refreshment for sale, of which the children were the purchasers and the consumers. Among the larger boys there were various games such as pitching coppers, throwing of props, running, jumping, wrestling etc. As I advanced in my boyish days I visited places at a greater distance from home and more particularly connected with other parts of the town. [76] These were on the Danvers road; Fry's tavern and the Bell tavern: In south Salem at Osgood's and Castle Hill and still further off, Putnam's tavern at Danvers plains. At these places, the amusements were more rough, rude and sometimes indecorous. There was more boisterousness. There was the Negro fiddler – dancing, by white boys with white girls, and by colored boys with colored girls. I never knew the whites to intermix with the colored in dancing, though the fiddler was a negro in almost all cases. Gambling with props, dice, cards and other implements was very much practiced. Drinking of egg-pop, beer, punch, flip, toddy and other intoxicating liquors and the eating of cake, pies and the more substantial articles of food was common among the young men and women who frequented these places. Horse racing was practiced at Danvers plains which was more of a resort for adult persons upon these occasions. Most of the amusements of the boys and girls were in the open air. The dancing was generally indoors, but not in private as the doors and windows were all open so that those without could see the dancing. On such occasions "Romp loving miss" "Is hauled about in gallantry robust". The manners of the times of my boy-hood are to be known now only from history. Coarse, vulgar dissipation is carried on now, if at all, more privately than at that time. I wish I could believe that it is only the beautiful flowers, the simple election cake, the innocent and humble drinks, the pleasant social interviews of the young that are continued to this day and that everything connected with the day which is vulgar, coarse or wicked has fallen into oblivion.

[77] Election Day was the usual time for changing from winter clothing to summer clothing, so that among other sources of enjoyment was the appearance in a new suit of clothes upon these occasions. The longest remembered pleasures of the day with me are

the new suit of clothes, the bunch of flowers, the election cake and the promenade. As I grew older these diminished in value or gave place to others better adapted to the changing taste, and progressive to those of youth. I never had any very strong desire for amusement or recreation. Election cake has preserved its celebrity from my first recollection to this day, a period of about sixty-eight years. Most indulgent mothers prepare it still, as they have done time out of mind. The election recreations of the times of my boyhood were usually continued for two days in succession and at some places there would be persons enough to congregate for four successive days and would only finish with the end of the week. At all the schools, there was a vacation of one or two days and at some of four days. Gaming and drinking to excess of the various intoxicating liquors were the vices which most frequently contaminated the young on these occasions. I think that there is an improvement in these respects since my first observations on the state of society. Election week continues to be observed in Boston by the anniversary meetings of most of the many religious, literary, moral, philanthropic, scientific and professional associations. Most of these anniversaries were established before the alteration [78] of the constitution changing the general election of State officers from the last Wednesday in May to the first Wednesday in January in that week although the principal reason for first establishing them at that time has ceased to operate for almost twenty years. The same thing has occurred in relation to the continuance of the Election holidays. They grew up with the government and although they were connected, for 200 years, with the general election of State Officers, yet they maintain their ground after they were separated from the occasion which gave rise to them. The winter season being unpropitious to their best enjoyment they will not forsake the season for flowers and genial warmth, for the ice and snows of our winters at the biding of the government of the State. On the very day placed at the head of this article, about 100 girls and boys are assembled at a fish house within a few rods of my dwelling, where they are, notwithstanding the unusual coldness of the weather, and rain and dampness of the day, amusing themselves with singing, dancing and eating and drinking. For music, they have two violins played by two young men of equal rank with themselves. They have been visited by parents and others, and I have visited them myself which will probably be my last observation of the conviviality of Election day. This visit and the anticipation of it has given rise to this article. Several of my grandchildren were there as participants and two of my children as spectators.

[79] The opportunities for recreation by the young are now much more frequent and diversified than when I was in my childhood. Perhaps the danger is now that they may become too frequent for the establishing of settled habits of industry, steady application and continued perseverance in the necessary labors of life. Those who have most influence in regard to such matters will bear this on their minds; There is always a tendency to extremes. In New England, as we change from the rigid puritanical manners and customs of the early settlers we are in great danger of going to the opposite extreme so that our young people may indulge in greater license of amusement and recreation than in those places where there has never been that degree of restraint which has been exercised here. Let all guard against extremes in everything. Sober, discreet, prudent persons should earnestly resist this tendency to excess in amusements and recreation.

[80] I witnessed the launching of the *Essex* Frigate and on Saturday, October 27, 1855 I witnessed the launch of the largest merchant ship ever built in Salem. She is between 8 and 900 tons. There was a large assemblage of spectators. I walked over but came home

in the cars. Enos Briggs was the eldest of the brothers engaged in building the *Grand Turk*. He established himself as a ship builder at south Salem, then called Stage Point and enjoyed a high reputation in his calling until his death. The Ship *Astrea* was built by E. Hasket Derby at the south shore in 1782. Enos Briggs was the builder and he and his brother removed to Salem to build the *Grand Turk* for Mr. Derby about ten years afterwards. The Ship *Astrea* arrived at Salem from Canton in June 1790 commanded by James Magee and paid 27,000 in duties to the government. I remember seeing this ship before their voyage and also the Light House about the same time which I think must have been about 1784. They were at Derby's Wharf and owned by Mr. Derby.

Ship building – *Grand Turk* [81]

In 1791, Elias Hasket Derby, who was then the principal merchant and the most wealthy inhabitant of Salem, undertook to build a large ship, called the *Grand Turk* of about 500 tons burthen and larger than had been before built in Salem. As builders, the two Briggs brothers were procured from the south shore of Massachusetts Bay, who afterwards removed their families to Salem and continued the business of ship building for some years. This ship was built at the head of the Derby Wharf next to Derby street and but little distance from the southerly terminations of my mother's garden. The novelty of the circumstance of the building of the largest ship and at a place which had not before been used for shipbuilding attracted the attention of many and particularly of the boys in the neighborhood.

Painting of the ship Grand Turk owned by Elias Hasket Derby, 1786.

I visited the spot daily and often many times in the day during the whole process of her building, so that there was hardly a timber of any considerable size but what I saw it in its perforation or in its place in the body of the ship. I thus acquired some general knowledge of ship building from the first stroke of the broad axe to the launching. So strong was my curiosity that my common course was to go to the ship yard before I went to school in the morning, again when the forenoon session of the school was ended and after school in the afternoon. When the time for launching came, which was May 28th, 1791, there was a great gathering (she measured 564 tons was 124 feet long and 32 fee breath of beam) [82] to witness it. She started on her ways but soon stopped and could not again be moved by all the force that could be brought to bear at that time so that she remained on the ways until some new arrangements being made at a subsequent time she was safely transferred to her appropriate element. While the *Grand Turk* was building, a smaller ship, mostly of pine, was built farther down the Derby wharf, and launched sideways into the water before the *Grand Turk* was ready for launching. She was 100 tons and named *Henry*. When vessels are launched in the usual manner a considerable number of persons are placed on board, but in the case of the *Henry*, the name of this pine ship, only a single person was permitted to be on board lest she should tip over before she was in the water and injure or drown those on board. I saw her launched and she went into the water beautifully and without the least incident. This was the only vessel which I ever saw launched sideways, but have seen many launched in the usual way, that is stern foremost. I think favorably of allowing children to view and examine mechanical operations in their various branches as opportunity presents. Generally, they have a strong curiosity which should be gratified and encouraged within reasonable limits. The frequent opportunities of gratifying this curiosity is one of the reasons why children who are raised in [83] large towns are generally more intelligent than those who are raised in the country. I think that I understood the manner in which ships are built better from observation of the building of the *Grand Turk*, when I was but twelve or thirteen years of age than I would have done by much study and instruction at a later period of life. All my knowledge of ship building came to me at that time and it was not without its use when for twenty years I served as a director of a Marine Insurance Company and for a considerable part of the same time as President.

I think it well to cultivate a taste for various mechanical employments in young boys. There are many situations in which such qualifications will prove to be highly useful and in all most every situation in life it contributes to one's comfort, independence and enjoyment of those about to be able to perform many small mechanical operations. I am also inclined to the opinion that it is well for boys to be taught many of those domestic employments which are usually preformed, in this country, by females; such as cooking, washing, mending clothes etc. There is a probability that they may occasionally be in situations where these qualifications will contribute much to the proper enjoyment of life. As an instance of this I will relate the following authentic story.

Eligius Fromentin – Senator in Congress [84]

When the whites were driven from St. Domingo, now called Haiti, by the colored population, they frequently were destitute of all property except such small matters as they could hastily secure and bring away. One of those sufferers was Eligius Fromentin, a Frenchman by birth and education. He was driven from the enjoyment of an independent fortune with nothing but his wardrobe and fourteen silver crowns equal to about fifteen and one-half dollars. With these things, he found himself in the City of New York, and he immediately set himself to contrive to live and to make himself respectable in his dress with them. By searching he found a French Barber who let him have a small room, connected with his shop, where he could lodge, cook and eat. He paid for the use of this room by making out the bills of the Barber. He procured cheap provisions by purchasing retuned ship stores at auction and by applying at the markets after the best had been disposed of. He did his own cooking, washing and ironing. He kept his clothes in such good repair as to enable him to appear well in public and for one whole year he thus preserved his independence and his connection with respectable society, and made his money serve to pay all his expenses for the same time. All this he was enabled to do by his having been in childhood instructed in the performance of domestic labor. In 1813, he was a Senator from the State of Louisiana in the Congress of the United States. He probably came to the United States about the year 1791.

Run Over by Horses [85]

An incident occurred while I went to Master Watson's school which I always esteemed as a providential preservation of my life. On Union street, just below the School house, Manning's Livery Stable was kept before my remembrance and was continued until the opening of the Eastern Rail Road between Salem and Boston. Horses were sometimes turned out without harness, for watering or for other purposes. On one occasion as I was running from the west side to the opposite side of Union street, two loose horses, following one another, came 'round the westerly corner of the street on the gallop. I had no time to retreat but in running from fright or some other cause, I fell prostrate upon the ground and both the horses went over me, as I supposed, without touching me at all. The fright might have led me to think that they went over me when in fact they might have only passed near my feet, but the occurrence made an impression upon my mind that has never been obliterated. I was at the time only about seven years of age. I have heard it remarked that horses are usually careful about hurting by treading with their feet, on human beings lying in their path.

Small Pox [85]

In October 1792 the small pox prevailing to a great extent in Boston and other places near to Salem, the town authorized the establishment of Hospital for inoculation with that disease in the environs of the town, and they were located in the Great Pasture and on the Neck. [86] I went to the Hospital in the Great Pasture with the first class that was admitted, numbering between two and three hundred persons. These were crammed into buildings which would have afforded decent room for only one third or at most one half of the number. I went into a room about eighteen feet square where, including a nurse, there were eighteen persons. At night when the sacks of straw for lodging were spread out, they covered the floor of the room; in the daytime they were piled up at the side of the room.

I was inoculated by Doct. Joseph Osgood of Salem and went through the disease in rather a mild form, though it was estimated that I might have a thousand pocks. One young man, who was inoculated, died in the same room where I was, and two others died of the whole class. Some had the disease with great violence and barely escaped with their lives. In the room where I was, Joseph Gardner a well-known Baker in Salem, but who supplied in a good measure the Beverly market with bread, had the disease very bad. His face was covered with pock so that he was entirely blind for some days. He recovered, but his face was very much pitted, which remained to be seen as long as he lived which was some 40 or 50 years afterwards.

There was a smaller Hospital at Castle Hill in the Great Pasture and one or more on the Neck. Some of my relations were on the Neck. After I got well I visited there and on one occasion, when returning, I was put into the smoke house with Rev. Wm. Bentley and he advised me to squat down near the fire to avoid most of the smoke while he stood up straight and received it freely. [87] The medical treatment in the Hospital was uniform in preparation for the disease. The first night the whole class were vomited. The next day a cathartic was administered of Glauber's salts[21] or Pill Cochia. The third day another and on the fifth another cathartic. When the symptoms of the disease began, if there was much fever, Nitri[22] was taken. On the days when the cathartics were taken, the diet consisted of

---

[21] Glaubers salts = Sodium sulfate decahydrate.

[22] Nitri = Saltpeter.

porridge, made by boiling Indian meal and water together a suitable time, sweetened with molasses. At other times we had bread, puddings and other vegetable food, but no animal food of any kind was allowed. After the symptoms appeared, the medical treatment was discriminating, according to the circumstances of each particular case. The system of generalization was not confined to medical treatment, but it extended to exercise, which was required to be in the open air and consisted in marching around, with or without the Drum, on a platform, laid around the sides of a parallelogram in front of the principal building, a certain number of times, morning and evening. When the febrile symptoms were considerable, it was practiced to get out of a warm bed and a warm room and to go into the cold air, with but very little clothing and with good effect. Those only who can remember the times of the small pox, can realize the vast amount of suffering, trouble and expense that has been saved by the introduction of vaccination. The small pox has ceased to be dreaded. My wife was inoculated with the small pox in Beverly and went to a house near Balles's Beach where several houses were used for Hospitals at about the same time I was in Salem. There was a general inoculation in Boston at the same time and in Marblehead.

Washington Hall [88]

While I was with Doct. Stearns there was a public dinner given in the Hall of the store, which was called Washington Hall, in commemoration of the French revolution. This was before the information was received in Salem of the beheading of Louis XVI and the enormities immediately preceding and which for a considerable time followed that event in France. The King was beheaded January 21st, 1793. This entertainment was about that time and was in coincidence with the general opinion in Salem at that time. The store on the corner of Washington street and Essex street was built in 1792 and Doct. Stearns removed into it in October 1792 and the Hall was finished after that time and probably this dinner was the first we made of it. Doc Stearns and his wife's father, Major Joseph Sprague, who were then among the leading men in Salem, were strong Democrats. Joseph Sprague, the brother-in-law of Doc Stearns was a Democrat throughout his life. Joseph E. Sprague, who was a son of Doct. Stearns and whose name was at first Joseph Sprague Stearns then altered by the General Court to Joseph Sprague, and again altered to Joseph E. Sprague, where it now stands was a Democrat until the expectancy of the presidential election of John Q. Adams, when he came out in his support, and from thence into the National Republican party, and there into the Whig party where he now remains. On the 9th of January 1843, just about a half a century after the above use of the Hall, I delivered there a lecture on capital punishment, not having been into the Hall for the half century.

Apprenticeship Resumed [89]

I remained with Doct. Stearns only about one year when I left in the following manner. We had received directions to lock the shop and go to the house to get our dinners at a certain hour, unless the Doctor was present to direct us otherwise. On a certain day, Silsbee and I went to the house at the appointed hour, when we arrived there we were informed that the Doct. had company to dine with him, and that our dinners would not be ready until a later hour than usual and that we might return to the shop and come again at that time. We left the house and after consultation we agreed to go to our mothers' houses and get our dinners which we did and returned to the shop as quickly as we well could. In the course of the afternoon the Doct. came to the shop somewhat angry and addressing both of use asked us why we hand not come to his house to get our dinners. Silsbee remained silent, but on his looking at me for an answer, with characteristic independence, I replied that I did not wish to wait so long for my dinner and therefore I went home and got it. He immediately said to me you may then go home again, and I took my hat and walked out of the shop and went home to my mother. Neither she nor I felt any disposition to seek a restoration for me to my place, although I have no doubt it might have been affected by a slight effort on the [90] part of either. The Doct. did not think it becoming in him to seek my return and so I lost a good place, as respected the acquisition of a knowledge of business from a very slight circumstance, which might after it occurred have been easily remedied if <u>pride</u> had not interposed her obstacle.

Silsbee remained but a short time after I was sent away but left without any disagreement to go to sea. He afterwards became a ship master and then a merchant. He married a daughter of Capt. Benjamin Hodges, and died of consumption some few years ago, about 1833. Rev. James Flint in his farewell discourse at the old East Meeting House December 28, 1845 says of him, "that he had been very kind and liberal towards him", and speaks in praise of his character, which I had no doubt was deserved. After we separated at Doct. Stearns we had little intercourse, and I knew but little of his character, but at the time of the separation he showed that he had more prudence and discretion than I had, and thereby retained his situation as long as he wanted it. I was not long without another place though a very inferior one, Samuel G. Mackey, who had served his time with Doct. Sterns and had set up a small shop in Beverly, next above Bell's building and on the same ground where Isaac W. Baker's shop now stands, the shop itself having been removed to Rial Side before [91] Isaac W. Baker's shop was built, was in want of a boy and he enquired of Doct. Stearns and obtaining a satisfactory account of my character from him (the only remark to my disadvantage was that "I did not like to dirty my hands",) he engaged me to attend his shop. Mr. Mackey was kind to me and treated me well, but the business was small and he, not being married, did not keep house, and I lived a part of the time in the shop and at other places without that domestic care which is so beneficial to young lads. I went to this place sometime in 1793 and remained about a year. The association which formed was, in part, of an unfavorable moral influence. I was exposed to temptations to which I had not before been in the way of. I parted with Mr. Mackey on good terms and I possessed his confidence to the end of his life. After I left him, he married Elizabeth, the daughter of Capt. Elias Smith who is still living in Beverly at about the age of 80 years and since the death of her husband to the present time, she has had recourse to me whenever she wanted assistance in relation to business. The occasion of my leaving Mr. Mackey was that he was about removing from Beverly to Hanover in New Hampshire, and my mother did not choose that I should go with him. He failed in trade and afterwards went to sea, became master of a vessel and acquired some property which he left to his widow. He was possessed of some good traits of character, with some very prominent bad ones. [92] While I lived with Mr. Mackey, I became acquainted with Ebenezer Smith, who was then an apprentice to Moses Adams, cabinet maker, who worked in a shop which stood between the house of Nathaniel Cox and the house of Samuel P. Lovett. This acquaintance was renewed when I removed to Beverly in 1796 and continued with a good degree of intimacy till his death, which occurred very suddenly by the Cholera, in the summer of 1848, at the age of 75 years, on Sunday August 6th. On Saturday morning, he was attending his business and on Sunday at 7 o'clock he was dead. He was kind, obliging, industrious, honest and faithful. While I was with Mr. Mackey, in the autumn, I was attacked with an inflammatory fever, went home to my mother and was sick for several weeks, and was attended by Doct. Edward Augustus Holyoke, who lived to his 101st year. On my recovery I lost my hair, which was of a brownish color, and from that time my hair gradually became white so that at an early age my hair was entirely white.

Obituary of Lucretia Osgood [92]

1849, May 7th, Monday: Mrs. Elizabeth Mackey, died at about 10 ¼ o'clock in the forenoon aged 80. She was born May 4th, 1769. She was the last of my master's wives. Doct. Stearn's widow died some years ago aged more than 80 as did Doct. Osgood's wife at an earlier age, say at about 61. Her name was Lucretia Ward and was a sister of Joshua Ward. She was an excellent wife and mother remarkable for her industry, her kindness to those in her family and to the poor that came to her knowledge. She presided over the Salem Female Charitable Society for several years.

[92½.1] The following obituary notice of her was published soon after her death, I do not know the author of it and copied from the newspaper September 7, 1854:

"Died

"In this town, (Salem) Mrs. Lucretia Osgood wife of Doct. Joseph Osgood, aged 61.

"The virtues and graces which beam forth with so mild and beauteous lustre in the female character, have a most powerful influence on society. This influence is often overlooked or known only in its consequences. It is noiseless, but lively and since in its operation, like the stream which, gliding silently along enriches and beautifies the adjacent grounds. Hence the death of a sensible and virtuous female must be severely felt within the sphere she illumined and warmed by her example, as the sod will lose its wont to endure when its fertilizing waters are dried up. Such was Mrs. Osgood. With mental powers naturally strong and inquisitive, enlightened and enriched by judicious reading and nebulous observation, her conversation was eminently instructive and entertaining, while the ease, gravity and dignity of her manners added their charm to render her the amiable, intelligent and truly refined lady. Her disposition was of the most social and communicative kind, and she had the happy facility, while she derived pleasure from the company and converse of others, to make them unusually pleased with her, and happy in themselves. In the circles of polished social life, many will long remember with what delight the resources of their memory her innocent pleasantry as well as her more serious remarks, [92½.2] enchained attention, so that her company was relinquished with regret, as it was welcomed with earnestness. In her heart, the tender charities and benevolent sympathies which adorn our nature had a favorable abode. Their influence was felt, if not always seen, in stanching the bleeding heart, and relieving the wants of hopeless indigence. As a private individual, and as Directress of the Female Charitable Society (a most laudable institution, which to say the least, she did as much as anyone to establish,) she had special opportunities for exhibiting that "chief grace below, and all in all above" a compassionate temper, and with what disinterest and active beneficence she engaged in the cause of the widows and orphan, their tears at her departure are the most eloquent answer. In the walks of domestic life she was a rare example of correct, hospitable and amiable deportments tenderly alive to the relations of wife and mother, she solicitously and faithfully performed the endeared and important duties attached to them, the well-being of her family was an indispensable bard of her own joy. But it was <u>religion</u> which tempered and purified the feelings and affections of her heart, which gave direction and animation to her life. In all her grief, and God had given her her share, it was <u>religion</u> which moderated their anguish, repressed the murmur of discontent and lighted up in the countenance the aspect of heart felt resignation. Piety, supported by faith kept her course unmoved amid the storm. On religious topics she conversed with the force and elegance of one [92½.3] well acquainted with and sincerely loving the, as educating the soul for a residence in Heaven. The Gospel with her was a rule of conduct, simple and well defined, to her view enough was clear for the guidance of a candid, docile mind, while she left elaborate speculations to those who esteeming faith as a tame, inactive principle, strive to explore, with human reason as a clue, the intricacies of God's word and government. The last hours of approaching dissolution were passed in tranquil contemplation and prayer, and solemn converse with her beloved family, and while lingering on the verge of the grave (when corporeal eye grows dim,) patient amid most trying pains and infirmities, she was blessed with an unclouded mental vision with an enlivening hope and humble reliance on the merits of the redeemer at whose feet she had long trod a loving disciple. Her bereaved family and friends have in her witnessed how a Christian should live, "how a Christian can die"". May they be comforted in the reflection, that "there is rest in Heaven".

[93] After leaving Mr. Mackey, I remained at home with my mother for some weeks, went to J Southwick's school and studied navigation, and entertained some thoughts of going to sea, if I did not soon obtain other employment. About that time Joseph Osgood Jr., son of Doct. Joseph Osgood, who had been keeping an apothecary's shop for some time had concluded to leave it and go to sea and his father agreed to take the shop and continue the business in his absence and to permit him to resume it on his return. Doct. Joseph Osgood being engaged in the practice of physic could not devote much of his time to a shop, it was therefore desirable for him to procure a boy who had some knowledge of medicine to attend the shop, under his supervision. He applied to me and I went into the shop. There again the business was small compared with that of Doct. Stearns. I was left alone with the care of the shop much of the time, but the association connected with the business of the shop was of a better cast than what I had fallen into while with Mr. Mackey. I resided in the Doctor's family and there I found satisfaction and enjoyment which thus far, I had been a stranger to, since I left my mother's house. His wife was a woman of superior mind. There were several children in the family some of them about my age. The children were well nurtured, and the family well governed. I was received upon a par with the children and treated, apparently, with the same kindness and attention [94] as if I had been one of them. I owe much to this family for their invariable kindness and I shall always feel grateful for the providential arrangement which brought me into it as a member. The time which I spent there had much influence in forming my character. It was the first family where there was attention paid to family religion within my knowledge.

Religion was not merely a profession, but it appeared to be an actuating principle guiding their daily lives. Doct. Osgood, his wife and all his children, save one, are dead. The one now living is the wife of Doct. Reuben Mussey of Cincinnati, who is at the head of his profession in the western country. The happiness I there enjoyed was not permitted to be of long continuance. In the spring of 1796 Joseph Osgood Jr. concluded to quit going to sea and to live at home, resuming the apothecary's shop, and as he intended to stay in the shop himself and to take in with him a brother several years younger than myself, he would not need my services. The profits of the shop, while I was connected with it, depended principally upon putting up the prescriptions of the Doct.'s and supplying his patients with such articles as one frequently wanted in sickness but do not usually enter into the prescriptions of the physician. The Doct. had at that time a good deal of business in his profession, and that brought a profitable business to the shop; but the trade was all in the small way. This son Joseph had married, or was about marrying, Polly Beckford, a daughter of Ebenezer Beckford, who was wealthy, but who would think it incumbent upon [95] his son in law to support his family by his own efforts and to wait patiently for the death of the father of his wife to realize any portion of the property which would in the usual course of events come to him from her father. Commencing housekeeping under these circumstances, he could not realize enough from a small apothecary's shop to support a family in the style of life which is to be expected by one having pretentions to wealth, but which could not then be realized. Under the presence of adverse circumstances, he died young, leaving several children, one of whom is now a practicing physician in Danvers, and has the name of his father and his father's father. While I was with Doct. Osgood I was attacked with the scarlet fever and throat distemper and went home to my mother's house until I recovered. The Doctor attended on me in my sickness without any charge for his services.

I ought not to forsake my testimony to the kindness and attention which I received from the only domestic servant in Doct. Osgood's family. She was somewhat advanced in years and in feeble health. Her faithfulness, fidelity, and amiable disposition, identified her with the family, all whose interests were her own. Rebecca Lutton, for that was her name, viewed me and treated me in the same manner as she did the members of the family. I can now recall to my mind her pleasant countenance and the recollection of her many kindnesses.

[96] After I left Doct. Osgood, Doct. Stearns having occasion for some temporary help in his shop, applied to me and I went and tarried as many days as he wanted me. I did not go into his family but boarded with my mother. He paid me to my satisfaction and did not appear to entertain any resentful feelings on account of the manner of our separation some two or three years before but treated me with respect and kindness. I mention this circumstance to show that although I had departed from these masters, none entertained any ill feelings toward me.

About the time of my leaving Doct. Osgood, Elisha Whitney son of Doct. Elisha Whitney, gave up keeping an apothecary's shop in Beverly not meeting with the success in business which was requisite to induce him to continue. He left, went to sea and afterwards became Master of a vessel and married Clarissa Lovett, daughter of Capt. Benjamin Lovett and a sister of Pyam Lovett. He died young and left no children. Doct. Osgood and some other friends advised me to avail myself of this opening and to set up a shop on my own account although I was then only seventeen years and seven months old and had served only four years apprenticeship including the intervals between my different services. I was nothing loathe to make the trial notwithstanding my youthfulness and inexperience.

[97] This I now view as an error in my life and I would not advise anyone to take the responsibility of business upon himself until he attains to the age of twenty-one years, unless there are special circumstances requiring it. My mother furnished me with some property, out of my father's estate, and I went to Beverly, hired a shop at $30 per year which then stood between the houses of Andrew Leech and Andrew Wallis on land which then was owned by my wife's sister Elizabeth and afterwards became my wife's. This shop was removed from thence some years ago. I went to Boston and purchased a small stock of medicines and other articles usually kept in such shops at that time[23].

On the 18th of June 1796, I opened my shop in Beverly and on the 21st went to board with the widow Martha Burke at three dollars per week and completed my removal to Beverly on the 22nd June. She was the daughter of Col Larkin Thorndike and the widow of Capt. John Burke, she was young and had two young children and by her industry and enterprise she contrived to support herself and them. Besides keeping boarders and working with her needle she kept a shop. I continued to board with her until I married on the 4th of June 1801 and near the same time she was married to Zebulon Ober, a son of Peter Ober. Her female domestic servant for most of the time while I boarded with her was Jenny Owens, who has expressed some pleasant remembrances of me very lately. She [98] is now the wife of William Claxton of Beverly. She was faithful and industrious and has maintained a good character up to this date. (Her husband died Dec 1848 aged 72.) While I was a minor, I found no difficulty in getting credit to any amount which I thought prudent. Honesty, industry, economy and punctuality in a young trader will always secure to him as much credit as is necessary for the prosecution of business within its reasonable bounds. I have always made it a rule from which I have but very seldom deviated up to this time, to observe a strict punctuality in my payments, and I think that a strict adherence to this rule in the main has secured to me all the advantages of credit which I have desired from the time when I commenced business, being then under eighteen years of age, to the present time when I am about seventy. I had credit in London as well when this country used to import medicines from Crawley and Elger.

The house in which I boarded with Mrs. Burke, for almost five years is situated on the corner of Briscoe and Hale streets and the next house easterly of the First Parish Meeting House. It was an old house and had been in the Thorndike family for two or more generations. It belonged to Col. Larkin Thorndike the father of Mrs. Burke and it came to him from his father John Thorndike, who kept a tavern in it, and who is found on the town and parish records under the designation of Landlord Thorndike. The house, of the old style, was in bad repair and would not at this time give gratification to boarders of the

---

[23] Rantoul wrote in the margin, "I bought some shop furniture and some other articles of Doct. Elisha Whitney which had been left by his son. The cases of drawers which I bought of Doct. Whitney were bought by him of Sam G Mackey and Mackey bought them of Doct. Nathan Read who kept an apothecary's shop in Salem and died at Belfast in Maine in January 1849 aged 89, see Salem Gazette of Jan. 30, 1849."

class which Mrs. Burke usually had, among which were the school masters Silas Stickney, Andrew Peabody, Henry True and Henry Herrick.

[99] Henry Herrick was a native of Beverly. He graduated at Harvard College in 1767. He was sociable and full of anecdote. His home was in the North Parish, but he got employment as a teacher of the public school in the south part of the town which rendered it necessary to board away from his family. I enjoyed his company much for a considerable portion of the time while he kept the school – But Alas! His besetting sin came over him before he had finished his engagement in the school. Under the influence of intoxicating drink, he became moody, melancholy, silent, reserved and instable so that he was obliged to leave his school before the termination of his engagement. He had, before he took the school, been occasionally insane, as was commonly reported, but at the time I boarded with him his partial insanity was manifestly the result of the use of intoxicating drinks. He excited the compassion of his fellow boarders, having, as he did, discovered such talents for entertaining conversation, they became attached to him and mourned over his fall. He left Mrs. Burke's house soon after he began to drink to excess and returned to his friends in the North Parish. This is one among many instances which have come under my own immediate notice and observation of the prostration of talents, intellect, usefulness, business and amiableness by the fell destroyer of character, comfort, happiness and even life itself. The danger of this issue is a sufficient ground for total abstinence from all intoxication liquors. He probably learned to drink strong drink in the conviviality of his college life.

[100] Henry True kept the private school in what was then called Dike's Lane. He did not acquire popularity and only kept through the time of his first engagement, which was short. He was thoughtful, demure and not very entertaining so that his leaving did not occasion much regret. He graduated at Dartmouth College in 1796. He is now and has been for many years a settled minister in Union, Lincoln county in Maine. My acquaintance with Mr. True terminated with his keeping the school, which I think was only for one quarter of a year. I have had no communication with him since but heard of him when I was at Brunswick last Autumn. Nathaniel Sterns a classmate of True's was teaching a school in Danvers at the same time and frequently visited him at Mrs. Burke's. I have seen Stone in Boston in 1851. There were some other boarders of whom I have not any distinct recollection. I kept up an acquaintance with Sterns while he remained in Danvers and spoke with him afterwards in Boston when I occasionally met him. I believe he still lives in Boston, at the North-end. He kept the Elliott School in Boston prior to 1826.

June 1851, Nathaniel Sterns died in Boston.

The newspapers give him a good character. He bequeathed from 4,000 to 6,000 dollars to the Massachusetts Colonization Society. From subsequent information I find that Henry True was separated from his parish in consequence of some difficulties, especially with one Samuel Hills, who was deaf and an unreasonable man and complained of want of edification. Oren Sikes the successor of Henry was settled in 1831 and dismissed in 1832.

[103] While the grammar school house was building in 1797, Mrs. Burke furnished dinners, only for Obadiah Groce of Salem, the contractor, and his workman. This building was ready for use early in 1798. While I boarded with Mrs. Burke her half-sister Betsey

Thorndike was married to Silas Stickney and I attended the wedding, the ceremony being performed by Rev. Joseph McKean, and her father Col. Larkin Thorndike who then lived in Ipswich, with a third or fourth wife, whom he married there, was present. He did not live long afterwards, for I remember that his corpse was brought from Ipswich to this town for burial and that I attended his funeral while I boarded with his daughter. The time that I boarded passed agreeably; there was a change of boarders from time to time and occasional visitors that afforded some variety. Mrs. Burke's brother, Doct. Larkin Thorndike, was there while he remained in Beverly. He had a college education, considerable talent, read much, skillful in his profession and social in conversation. The dark sides of his character it would be useless to expose. I enjoyed his conversation but escaped from any impressions from his infidelity. From my earliest childhood, I had been a constant attendant on public worship in the East Meeting House in Salem, and continued to attend there when I first removed to Beverly, but finding it to interfere with my business, I had a seat in Mrs. Burke's pew in the First Parish meeting house and commenced attending on the ministry of Joseph McKean, and have continued to attend with great constancy in the same house to this time.

[104] I think that a habit of constant attendance on public worship affords great security to youthful virtue although a young person may not become imbued strongly with religious principle by his attendance, yet I conceive he is in a measure protected against the insidious insinuations of the infidel, and of many of the allurements of sinful pleasure which beset the path of youth. I can truly say that it has been the habit of my life to attend public worship and I think that I have derived benefit from it and I commend it to the young that they early lay the foundation of this habit and that they never suffer themselves to be diverted from its claims by the indulgence of indolence, the allurements of pleasure or the calls of business. With six successive days of close application, followed with a day of rest from labor and worldly cares, as much may be accomplished by an industrious man s though he delved through the whole seven without intermission. This may not be true on an experiment for only a short time, but I am sure it will be "in the long run".

When I had become somewhat established in business like most other young men, I began to think about obtaining a wife. Although I had entertained thoughts in reference to some others, I never paid any particular attention to any one until I became acquainted with Joanna Lovett, a daughter of John & Elizabeth Lovett. Her father having died a few years before, she was then living with her mother. After short acquaintance, I made proposals of marriage to her, which with the assent [105] of her mother and friends, she assented to and on the fourth day of June 1801 we were joined in marriage by Rev. Joseph McKean at which time I was about 22 ½ years of age, and she was two years younger. I never regretted marrying at so early an age, and I recommend it to young men to marry as soon as they have a reasonable prospect of being able to provide for a family, and not to wait with the false notion that they should first get rich and then marry. If they make a judicious choice of one who "is a help meet" they will sooner attain their desire of wealth than if they remain single. I hired the westerly part of the dwelling house of Josiah Batchelder, at the corner of Front and Davis streets at $40 per year and in a few days after our marriage we set up housekeeping. We hired a girl to live with us at 58 cents per week and I had an apprentice, Francis Lamson, who boarded with us, so that our family for the first year consisted of four persons. For that year I kept an account of the expenses of my family, which amounted to about $400 and being satisfied that the expense was within my income, I discontinued my account and did not resume it again until some years afterwards. I now think it would have been useful to have continued it steadily to this time. It is attended with the very great benefit of enabling one to know for a certainty, whether he is living within his income, and if he finds it necessary to make any retrenchment in his expenditure, it will put it in his power to do it more judiciously by examining every item of expense [106] and lopping off those which can most conveniently be dispensed with and if on the other hand he thinks it proper to enlarge his expenditure, he may do it with greater safety and more satisfaction to himself and his family, from an accurate knowledge of his past expenses. I commend it to the young to commence life with it and to persevere in it to the end. I have practiced it for the larger part, but not for the whole of my married life. We continued to live in J Batchelder's house until his daughter Joanna Prince, having lost her husband in Maine, was desirous of living in her father's house so that in the spring of 1803 it became necessary for us to remove and at that time it was difficult to procure a suitable tenement and I hired and we removed into the old house where I had boarded for almost five years previous to our marriage, at the rate of $50 per year, about the middle of May 1803. Although our accommodations were inferior to what we had enjoyed for the first two years of our marriage, we contented ourselves in the place for two years until, in May 1805, we removed into my own house, on Washington Street, where I have lived to this time.

Rachel Osborne, who came to live with us when we married, continued to live with us until after our removal to Washington Street. When we removed there, there were no houses below Doct. Howe's brick house on the northeasterly side of the street, and none at all on the southwesterly side, from this circumstance we suffered inconvenience from snow in the street, being obliged to make our own paths to the Main Street, now called Cabot Street, and the travelled path when bare [107] of snow was in the state which it was found when the Street was layed out by the proprietors of the lands January, 1803 and accepted by the Town March 14, 1803. These inconveniences have been gradually diminishing so that now it is one of the handsomest and most convenient streets in the town, having on it a large Meeting House, an Academy and fourteen dwelling houses, besides other buildings. On each side, there is a good foot walk lined with trees and the carriage way is well made. There is a satisfaction in witnessing constant improvements about us, particularly if we are contributing our share, which more than counterbalances the inconveniences experienced by being the first settler in a town or even in a street. When in the spring of 1806 John & Joanna B. Lovett came to live with us, Hannah Boyles, who had previously lived with their mother, came to live with us and continued with us excepting a few short intervals for thirteen or fourteen years. Sometime after the marriage of Joanna B. Lovett in 1823 she went to live with her, where she continued some years until her death. So that for the first 20 years of our marriage, we were in a good measure exempted from that fruitful source of vexation, the frequent changes of help. Since that time, we have for the most part, dispensed with foreign aid in our domestic duties, my wife with assistance of her daughter's having been for most of the time able to do all our family work. Among the occasional helps was Nancy Nash who at several periods was with us more time than any other one beside the two aforenamed. She died some years ago, unmarried. Her faithfulness and honest simplicity was a strong ground of attachment to her by my family.

[108] It undoubtedly contributed very much to the comfort, happiness, good order and pecuniary prosperity of a family that the domestic labours should be performed by the female members of it, without recourse to strangers. The laborious calls are conducive to health and the physical education of daughters, as well as their knowledge of housewifery, so indispensable a qualification to prepare them for their expected situation in life, is very much promoted by their active participation in all the duties of the household.

For some 15 or 20 years, Phillis Cave was employed to do the washing of our family. She is now (1848) about 86 years of age and has washed for us until she was 84 or 85. She is of the African race. Her brother, Jupiter Bunn, lived with my wife's father. She, when she was a child, was sold, in Salem to a Mr. Cave of Middleton, who paid for her with iron. She remembers being carried in the bottom of the Chaise, hidden from view by the Boot, from Salem to Middleton, to Cave's farm, which is now the property of Judge Cummings. She came to this town at about the beginning of the Revolutionary War and had ever since maintained herself by her labor. The kindness of my wife and daughters to her has been the ground of her attachment to the family. She continued to wash for us after she had refused to work for others on account of her age. She never entertained a favorable opinion of the abolitionist, saying that if the slaves were freed they would not know how to live. She died January 20th 1852 aged about 90 years (See Beverly Citizen of January 24th - RR.)

[109] Of my beloved wife, who died of a lingering consumption on the 23rd of September, between eleven and twelve o'clock at night, 1848 – I will not now attempt to express my feelings. But will copy the notice of her death published in the Christian Register of October 7th 1848, which was supposed to be written by C.T. Thayer:

"Intelligence, gentleness, firmness, benevolence and piety, were happily and beautifully blended in her character. She was greatly respected and beloved, and justly regarded a model of fidelity in the various relations she sustained. Her departure is mourned, not only as a real bereavement to her friends, but a serious loss to the community in which her life was passed. Still it may and should be mourned as one to which Christian consolations apply with their most soothing and sustaining power. Such departures make heaven seem to be a reality and bring earth near to heaven."

In this I think all who knew her will concur. She gradually declined, when at about 9 o'clock in the evening of the 23rd of September, a sudden change took place, she became speechless and in about three hours she died in the same calm, tranquil, placid manner which was characteristic of her whole life. She was born on the 10th of November 1780 and aged sixty-seven years, ten months and thirteen days. We were married on the 4th of June 1801 and lived happily together for more than forty-seven years. Whatever abatements of the happiness of this long period were experienced, I must say, is firstly attributable to my own imperfections, [110] weakness and error, and in no degree to her. I heartily commend her example as most worthy of the imitation of her posterity. My son Robert, his wife Jane, my daughter Hannah, Mrs. Smith, wife of my neighbor Samuel Smith, and myself, were the only persons present at the time when she breathed her last. Her funeral was attended on Tuesday afternoon, September 27th. John P. Lyman & wife & Andrew P. Peabody, from Portsmouth, Hannah Lovett and two of her sons & daughter & S. Ingersol from Boston, Rebecca Preston & her daughter May, from Salem, together with the relatives of the family living in town, and a numerous body of our friends and acquaintance, attended the funeral. All my children, and all my grandchildren, save Henry Endicott, who was sick, attended the funeral. The sympathy and kindness manifested by a very numerous circle of friends and acquaintances during the whole of my wife's protracted illness, will, I hope, be long remembered with gratitude, not only by myself, but by my children and grandchildren. Scarcely a day passed for the last six months of her life, without some present of flowers, of which she was always most fond, fruits or some delicate article of food, which it was thought would be pleasant to her, being sent by one or more persons. For many weeks in succession Doct Augustus Torrey, sent twice in each week, beautiful bunches of flowers from his gardens, selected and arranged with good taste, he well knowing the love my wife had for flowers. From the first ripening of strawberries to [111] the end of the season for summer fruits, she had a regular supply of fruit, in great variety and of the choices quality, and from so many different persons, that I will not attempt to name them, as my imperfect recollections would lead to omissions which might be a subject of future regret. Every article of food of which it was supposed she would partake with satisfaction was sent to her. Young men sent her the birds which they shot and various contributions were from every class in society, from the poorest to the most affluent. Her appetite for food continued until the last day of her life. Through her life she had been particularly regardful of and indefatigable in her endeavors to relieve the sick and the suffering and now she had and employed some good measure of a return of her kindness to others, thus verifying the proverb, "Cast thy bread upon the waters and after many days shall thou find it"

Her piety, her devotion, her unremitted kindness, her prudence, her industry, her economy, her self-denial, her self-sacrifice, her habitual self-command, her cautious regard in conversation to avoid all evil speaking, are all strongly impressed on my mind, and cannot be too long remembered, by myself, my children and my grandchildren. By reflection upon her virtue our life, may all our hearts be made better, and whether we live many or few years may our last end come like hers, in peace with God and man.

[112] Five of our children preceded her to the grave. All of them, save the youngest who died suddenly received the most laborious, unremitting kindness and attention, from her hands, during their last sickness, which in each case was somewhat protracted. Three of them died of consumption and one of dropsy in the brain. They were lovely children, but their loss was borne by their mother with Christian patience and resignation. In the last sickness of her own mother, who died at the advanced age of 81 years, she left her own family that she might attend upon her dying parent. She was equally devoted to the care of my own mother, who died in my family in 1816. In addition to the care and nurture of her own children, she took into our family two of her brother John's children, soon after the decease of the parents, who both died of the malignant Dysentery which prevailed in Beverly in the summer and autumn of 1805. These children, John and Joanna B., she reared with the same care as her own, until they became settled in life. She was a kind mother to them as she was to her own children. To me she was a faithful counsellor, and I but seldom, if ever, had to regret that I followed her advice, but have to regret in some instances I did not listen to it more fully. As we advanced in years, her influence increased, and I became more sensible to the propriety of yielding to it.

"Blessings theirs": God Made her so,

And deeds of week-day holiness

Fell from her noiseless as the snow,

Nor hath she ever chanced to know

That aught were easier than to bless."

[113] John Lovett, who was reared in my family, died on the 22nd July 1854, at about one o'clock in the morning aged 55. Born July 1, 1799. At 12 o'clock on Thursday the 21, in the afternoon, I saw him for the last time. I attended to the execution of his Will, after which he took an affectionate leave, thanking me for all my kindness to him for which he appeared to be very grateful. He married Mary Shaw January 3, 1826. She survived him and has four children, two sons and two daughters. His oldest son John Prince Lovett was born Nov 24th, 1831. He is named Executor to the Will of his father. He proved the will on the first Tuesday in August 1854.

My wife's extraordinary industry and strict and preserving economy, enabled me to advance my pecuniary interests, under circumstances when had I been without her, I should have gone behind hand.

"The dead are like the stars by day,

Withdrawn from mortal eye;

But not extinct – they hold their way

In glory through the sky."

[117] When I began business in 1796 it was a time of great commercial prosperity in the United States, occasioned by the wars of the maritime powers of Europe while our country remained at peace and maintained her neutrality. Beverly partook of this general prosperity. There were several merchants who were engaged in foreign commerce and prosecuted the business with enterprise and with success. The cod fishery was carried on with greater activity, and with larger profits, than any time before. There was an increase of population and a rise in the value of land. This state of things continued for about ten years after I began & enabled me to prosecute my business with success and to add to the property with which I began. In 1806 there was a revolution and in Dec. 1807 the long embargo commenced, and prostrated foreign commerce and the fisheries. I think there never was before nor since such a favorable opportunity for ten successive years for a young trader to establish himself in business in Beverly. The embargo continued about a year and a quarter, at the end of which, in 1809, business again revived, and continued well until the commencement of the war with Great in Britain in 1812, excepting as it was checked by the removal of Israel Thorndike and other wealthy persons from this town to Boston. I devoted my whole attention to my business for some considerable time after I began. In the spring of 1798 I was under the necessity of removing from my shop and on the 19th of February 1798 I hired of Jeremiah & Ezra [118] Lovett a piece of land to build a shop on, at 9 dollars per year, situated where Washington Street comes into Cabot Street, and there built a shop, eighteen feet by thirty feet, and two stores in height, finishing the lower story only. It cost me about $400 and I removed July 9, 1798 to this new shop. Here I continued to carry on my business until June 29, 1801, when I bought of John Lovett of Wilton, New Hampshire, a lot of land with buildings thereon, situated on Washington & Cabot Streets, measuring 240 feet on Jeremiah & Ezra Lovett's land, whereon my shop then stood (and 144 feet including the way Howard Street) on Cabot Street, for

which I gave $2675, and only with a view of a shop lot in the central part of the town, and I afterwards sold parts of this messuage[24] to several person so that the land which remained cost me $711, on which I built the store 24 feet by 40 feet and two stories in height, which now stands at the northwesterly corner of Washington Street, and cost me about $900. It was at the time the largest for the retail business in Beverly. I moved into it in the summer or autumn of 1802, and on the 8th of November 1802, I removed my other shop from Jeremiah & Ezra Lovett's land at the head of Washington Street, to the land northerly of the above-mentioned store and let it for a mechanic's shop. Sometime afterwards I sold this shop with the land under and adjoining to John Appleton, who altered it into a dwelling house. He paid me a part of the purchase money and mortgaged the premises to me for security for the payment of the residue and he not [119] being able to pay the residue he released to me the equity of redemption and by that title I now hold it, having enlarged and improved if for the use of my daughter Joanna Endicott, who has lived there since her marriage to this time.

In 1804, and 1805, I built my dwelling house at the bottom of Washington Street, on land conveyed to me by Joseph Lovett, my wife's uncle, in exchange for land of my wife's conveyed to him and moved into it about the middle of May 1805, and have continued there until this time. Soon after it was built I let the northwesterly part to Thomas Woodberry for six months and afterwards for some years to Augustus Lovett at $40 dollars per year.

From 1796 to 1812 I traded largely (for me) with John Thorndyke of Concord NH. He finally settled with me in Sept. 1818 and paid me in full. I have 100 letters on file which I received from him. He died sometime in 1821. I used frequently to send adventures, and owned for a short time only, parts of schooners employed in the West India trade, with, upon the whole, but little profit. In as much as it diverted my attention from my shop and employed money which might have been used more advantageously in my shop, it was injurious as regarded my pecuniary interest. I therefore counsel my grandchildren that whatever business they undertake for permanency they should devote all their energies to its prosecution and not suffer their attention to be diverted into other channels, however flattering they may be. The desire of accumulation often overshoots its mark by endeavoring to hasten its accomplishment by a departure from the beaten path of [120] perseverance, industry and economy. I never was in any way of great or sudden acquisition, and the moderate competence to which I may venture to say I have attained at the age of three score years and ten, is the result, not so much of gaining as of <u>saving</u>. If my example is worth following, it is the last-mentioned cause that should command itself to special regard. I know not of any year of my life, after I commenced business, when my expenses were not less than my income. This has been accomplished not by refraining from what was necessary for the comfortable support, education and establishment of those who apprenticed to me, but by a most vigilant care to avoid unnecessary expenses in my established situation in life, and to refrain from all desire to imitate those whose income from business or whose accumulated property, or whose pride and vanity, or whose passion for show and slavery to fashion, let them to adopt a style of living

---

[24] Messuage: A dwelling house with outbuildings and land assigned to its use.

incompatible with my own view of duty and propriety for persons whose means were so limited as my own.

I continued to keep shop until, in 1824, I disposed of my stock to my son in law William Endicott, who commenced business, in my shop, on his own account on the 12th of April 1824. My shop business had gradually diminished so as to be very small when I gave it up. As my income from my shop lessened my income from other sources increased so that I continued to increase my property slowly. Since I left shop keeping my business has been various, but I have always found something to do even to this day.

Robert Rantoul's Apothecary, corner of Washington and Cabot Street.

[121] After I bought the estate at the corner of Washington and Cabot Streets, June 29, 1801, there was soon a movement among the proprietors of that and the adjoining lands in regard to the laying out of a street over their lands. In May 1802, an agreement was made to appoint a committee to lay out such a street. The memorandum of this agreement was as follows "The instrument shall be drawn authorizing the persons therein named to lay out a road over and near land of the subscribers for a high way. Said road to be fifty feet wide throughout from the main street to the bank of the river. The northern side to begin on the main street at seven feet from the southern bounds of Rob Rantoul's land and the southern side to begin on the main street near Isaac Appleton's shop. The road to run in such a course as will take nearest an equal part of the said road from the land of each of the proprietors of the land laying to the eastward of E & J Lovett's barn in proportion to their quantity of land and to make the road straight. There shall not be more than a piece of 25 feet wide and of the length of Doct. Whitney's taken from his lot of land in the whole. W Jackson shall have the land, if there be any, between his and road and it shall be the same respecting any other person who enters into this agreement."

The instrument was drawn to authorize Moses Brown, Thomas Davis and ---[25] to lay out a street in conformity with the above memorandum and also to apportion the damages to be paid. This instrument was executed by Jeremiah Lovett, Ezra Lovett, [122] Elisha Whitney, Joseph Lovett, Robert Rantoul, Amos Sawyer, Elizabeth Murray, and Ebenezer Jackson. The three last-named being persons to whom I had sold parts of the land which I bought in 1801. The committee laid out the street as follows and to be called "Washington Street". viz "beginning at the highway at a bound, 43 feet southwesterly from the northwesterly corner of Jeremiah or Ezra Lovett's land thence running south 44-30 'east, the distance of 29 poles and 3 links to the southeasterly side of Elisha Whitney's land cutting off on said Whitney's N.W. side 29 ½ fee and on the S.E. side of said Whitney's 24 feet and 8 inches. Thence running south 42' 30" east about 65 poles to high mark.

---

[25] Rantoul left this space blank.

The width of said way it cuts off on Ezra Lovett's land at said high water mark is 1 pole 10 links.

The N.E. side of said way begins at a stake at the highway standing 7 feet northeasterly from the south-westerly corner of Robert Rantoul's land thence running south 49'' 30' east distance of 7 poles 4 ½ links. Thence running south 42" 30' east to the high-water mark and said way takes off on the S.E. end of Jeremiah's son John's land 26 feet and at the N.E. end of said way on Joseph Lovett's land 1 pole & 16 links. The corner of land of Lovett's left by Jackson's lot contains about 1 pole and about 3 ½ poles more than the 50 feet in width it takes off of Lovett's land on the other side of said way. The damages to be paid as follows, viz E Whitney to pay Jeremiah Lovett 5 dollars & Ezra Lovett $33.50. Joseph Lovett to pay Ezra Lovett $70. R Rantoul to pay Ezra Lovett $60. A Sawyer to pay Ezra Lovett $25.50. Ebenezer Jackson to pay Ezra Lovett $46 and Eliz Murray to pay Ezra Lovett $24.

[123] The foregoing description was made with a plan by Jonathan Smith, May 14, 1802. This street was laid and accepted by the town March 14, 1803. I was very instrumental in procuring the location of this street and it has become settled under my observation. The reason why Ezra Lovett was awarded $259.00 out of $264.00 was that he owned part of the land fronting on the Main street measuring on the last-mentioned street about 43 feet the remaining 7 feet was take from my front land. Making the new street 50 feet wide on the Main street from whence it increased in width to the angle, 7 poles 4 ½ links distant 8.49 – 30" from the main street by the northeasterly line of the new street. So that at that angle the new street is considerably <u>more</u> than 50 feet wide and from thence gradually diminishes its width until it comes to the edge of the bank of the river so that the new street, is more than 50 feet wide in every part of it, excepting where it bounds on the Main Street and on the bank of the river. So, attention to this may prevent mistaken encroachments on the lines of the new street, under the wrong impression that it no more than 50 feet wide, while in fact, it is more in all its extent excepting at its two ends, and even the flat from the bank to low water mark. A plan of this street is with my collection of plans.

When I built my house on this street in 1804 & 5, it was thought by most people that I had committed an error in building so far from the main Street, but the taste of the people is now so much changed as to lead to the opinion that it is one of the most pleasant locations in the Town. It took some 30 or 40 years to bring about this change of opinion.

[124] At the annual Town Meeting in March 1838, Wyatt C. Boyden, John I. Baker and myself were appointed a committee to describe and to give names to certain of the streets. I proposed the name of "Cabot" for the principal or main Street in honor of John & Sebastian Cabot, who were considered as the discoverers of <u>North</u> America and "Colon" as the name for another street, in honor of Christopher Columbus or Colon the discoverer of the western continent – "Elliott" for the first town clerk, Andrew Elliott, "Conant" for Roger Conant, the first who had a house in Salem, but soon removed to this side of Bass River and died in Beverly in the 89th year of his age – "Dodge" because it had been long called "Dodge's Row". "Lothrop" for Capt. Thomas Lothrop who was killed in 1675 at Bloody-Brook. This last name I first proposed to the County Commissioners who inserted in their description of the location. Other names were suggested by the other members of the committee or grew out of particular circumstances connected with the streets or had

been previously used. Since this report other streets have been described and named by the Selectmen from time to time, as there was occasion, so that all that are much used are now named. The numbering of the buildings on the streets was begun in October 1855.

[125] My connection with the military deserves some notice inasmuch as it was so interesting to me for a time and then I entirely lost all regard and interest. When I first came to Beverly, I trained with the standing militia company, comprising the inhabitants from the meeting house to Manchester, and including Montserrat. There were then three companies in the town, and with the one company of Manchester composed the 3rd Regiment of the 1st Brigade of the 2nd division. The militia then consisted of every free, white, male citizen between the ages of 18 and 45 with a few exemptions. I once trained at a regimental muster under the command of major William Homans, the office of Colonel being then vacant by the recent resignation of Col. John Francis, Major Homans desired me to act as Adjutant on that occasion, that office having been also recently vacated by the resignation of Josiah Gould. I of course declined; my entire want of skill in horsemanship was an insuperable difficulty in the way, and my ignorance of military tactics would have rendered it equally improper to have undertaken it. After this, for one year, I was appointed, by the Selectmen of the town, without my request to be an Engine Man. Although not much gratified with this appointment, as I loved to train, I served at the Engine and was therefore exempted from military duty for a year.

In the autumn of 1800 there was a movement among the young men for the formation of a company of Light Infantry and I engaged in the movement. The persons who had previously expressed their desire in writing to [126] engage in the undertaking, met at the Town Hall (Briscoe Hall) on the 17th of October 1800. Doct. Josiah Batchelder, who is now living at Falmouth in Maine, was chosen moderator and they proceeded to select the officers for the intended company, and Jonathan H. Lovett, was chosen Captain, Robert Rantoul, Lieutenant, Benjamin Winn, Ensign, and William H. Lovett, Clerk. This meeting was adjourned to the 3rd of November following, when rules were adopted for organizing a Light Infantry company and for seeking for its Legal establishment, which could not then be done without a special act of the General Court. There were 38 persons subscribed at enlistment on the 3rd of November, and four more in the course of that month. These associates met once a week through the ensuing winter to learn the military exercise, and I engaged in it with enthusiasm. At the next session of the Legislature in November, J. H. Lovett, R. Rantoul & B. Winn, as a committee in behalf of the associates, petitioned for an act for the legal establishment of the company, but the session being a short one it was not finally acted on until the January session of 1801, when the act was passed authorizing Col. James Burnham to enlist a volunteer Light Infantry Company, and he on the 2nd day of June 1801, issued an order to me, (J.H. Lovett having gone to sea) to make the enlistment which I accordingly did, and procured 40 signers. Previously to the meeting for the choice of officers I made an address to the associates upon the subject of the election, a copy of which I have on file.

[127] List of Beverly Light Infantry April 1801

+Jonathan H. Lovett	+Enoch Goodwin
Robert Rantoul	William Webber Jun.
+Benjamin Winn	+Joseph S. Nelson

+Jonah Batchelder Jun.
died 1857

Nehemiah Smith, Jun. Aged 73 2/3
died Feb 15, 1857.

+Benjamin Lamson

+Ezra Mann

Joseph Littlehale

+Seth Rowe

Joseph Eaton

+John Hatch

+Gamaliel Hatch

+William Beckford

+William Dodge

+Ebenezer Wallis

Ebenezer Wallis 2nd
d. Dec 2, 1848, age 72

Bartholomew Wallis, Jun.

+William Herrick Lovett

+Peter Woodberry

+Samuel Baker

Isaac Appleton

+Nathaniel Treadwell

*Benjamin Pierce
(d Sept 10, 1850 age 75)

John Woodberry

+John Messervy

David Parsons

Samuel Stickney, Jun.

*John Fornis
died Oct 16, 1848.

+Edward Stone
died 1856.

Johnson Burbank

William Burbank

+Hammond Healey
died April 1802[26]

Simon Styles

+Israel Woodberry Roundy

Seaward Lee

Thomas Adams
(born August 1779)

+Joseph Gouldsberry

+Timothy Blake Gove

1801 June

John Wallis 2nd.

October Ebenezer Jackson

+Timothy Wyer

Daniel Adams, Jr.
(d. 1852 age 68)

Thomas Whittrage
(d. Jan 23, 1858 age 74)

Francis Lamson, Jun.

1802

Shaniliah Spaulding (died 1858)

+Caleb Wallis

+Dudley Abbot

---

[26] Hammond Healey died April 19, 1804 (Beverly VRs.)

John Wallis Ellingwood

Ebenezer Trask

Joseph Woodberry 5th

Samuel Morse Thissel

+Robert Baker, Jun.

[128]1805

John Porter Webber

1806

+Joseph Herrick

+Josiah Raymond (d. Sept 10, 1853)

Seth Dodge

1807 April

+Samuel Dodge

+Ebenezer Stickney

+Josiah Webber

1807 May

+Amos Stickney (died 1858 aged 72)

1807 June

John Allen

(he was Capt.) *Robert Tuck (died Jan 11, 1851 aged 66)

+Nathan Brown

James Brown

Israel Webber

July *Israel O. Stone

October Benjamin Cleaves

1808 September

Amos Durrant

+Robert G. Wood

+Daniel Symonds, Jun.

John Symmonds

Thomas Pickard

Henry Buck

+Thomas Carrico

John Dike, Jun.

William Lamson (1803 April)

John Chipman Baker

I was chosen Ensign June 15, 1801

Lieutenant Dec 24, 1801

Captain August 27, 1806

I was discharged by my own

request November 25, 1804.

Thus I served as an Officer

8 years 5 months & 10 days

Robert Rantoul,

Beverly, September 19, 1848

The foregoing is a copy

of a paper furnished

by John Proctor Webber

by his request.

December 11, 1848 Stephen

Homans informs me that he

trained with the Company

one-half day, it being the

last time that I command-

ed at a training.

Walter Brown

Robert Cary

+Ebenezer Bennet

Stephen Homans

Whole number 83 and Homans makes 84

Those marked + are known to be dead and probably many there are dead who had removed from town.

Sept 28, 1808, it was voted to admit Stephen Homans, but I do not know whether he joined the Company.

On the 15th of June 1801, [129] the meeting under the orders of Col. James Burnham was held for the choice of Company officers, and Jonathan H. Lovett was chosen Captain, Josiah Gould, Lieutenant; and Robert Rantoul, Ensign. Thus, Benjamin Winn was left out and I was put down from the Lieutenancy to a lower grade. This was all done with my consent and a principal object with those who engaged in effecting this change was, easily, to get rid of Benjamin Winn, who was a young butcher, a brother of Capt. Joseph Winn who at one time commanded the Salem Cadets. He had lived in this town but a short time and his character and qualifications for office did not seem to meet with general acceptance, and the choice of him in the first instance was thought to be inconsiderate. He soon withdrew from the Company, removed from the town and died young.

Josiah Gould would not accept the office to which he was elected. September 10th, 1801, the company met again for the choice of officers but Col. Burnham being prevented by sickness from attending, and not having appointed any officer to preside, the meeting was dissolved without proceeding to business. On the 24th of December 1801, a meeting was held, and I was chosen Lieutenant which, for most of the time, gave me the command of the company as J.H. Lovett was frequently absent at sea. The company was without an Ensign until May 17th, 1802, when Samuel Stickney was chosen, the votes being for 22 – Timothy Wyer 2 – John Hatch 1 Wm H. Lovett 1.

[130] S. Stickney accepted the office. He is still living and works at cabinet making at the age of 77. He was born in Boxford Nov 7, 1771. His mother was a native of Beverly.

On the 12th of May 1803, I was appointed a member of a Court Martial, to sit in Salem, for the trial of Capt. Daniel Usher of Danvers. This court consisted of thirteen members – Major William Prescott, the distinguished lawyer, who died in Boston at an advanced age, some two or three years ago, was President of the Court. John Prince, who was afterwards clerk of the Courts, and died Sept 22, 1848 aged 66, was Marshal and William Wetmore a lawyer in Salem, who died some years ago and whose widow married Judge Daniel S. White, was Judge Advocate. A guard composed of members of the Salem Cadets attended at the door of the Court House posting their sentinels according to military etiquette. The court was appointed to sit on the 1st day of June 1803, a Wednesday, and they continued to sit through that week, and for one or more days in the following week, and all this time, parade and expense was incurred to ascertain whether a poor, ignorant, militia Captain had been guilty of unmilitary and ungentlemanlike behavior, a question which might as well have been tried in a Justice's Court in half a day. He was found guilty and dismissed from office. This appointment however was of much advantage to me, inasmuch as it instructed me in many points, in relation to the conducting of public business, public spirit led me to improve all such opportunities for my advancement in knowledge.

[131] David Putnam, who is now President of Mercantile Bank in Salem was a signer of the complaint and John Page, who is now living in Danvers, was the first, there were four others. William H. Lovett, who had been clerk from the formation of the company, was discharged from that office by his own request on the 18th of May 1804 and I, as Lieutenant Commandant, appointed John Wallis Ellingwood to that office. He was then a silver smith but afterwards studied divinity and was settled as a minister at Bath in Maine, where he still resides. His first wife was a daughter of Deacon John Dike of this town and he has within a few months married a second from Portland.

April 14th, 1805: J.W. Ellingwood was, by his request, discharged from the office of clerk and Wm. H. Lovett was reappointed. June 10th, 1805 Jonathan H. Lovett was chosen Major of the Regt. And thus, the command of the Company devolved upon me entirely and on the 27th of August following I was chosen Captain. William H. Lovett, Sergeant & Clerk died September 10, 1805, and the Company attended his funeral, without arms and their usual dress, but with Crepe on the left arm above the elbow, in procession, two and two, before the corpse.

September 23rd, 1805: Timothy Wyer was chosen Lieutenant and on the 26th. William Webber Jr. was appointed Sergeant and Clerk in the room of Wm. H. Lovett deceased. October 8th, 1805, the company assembled at my house at 4 ½ clock in the morning, took breakfast there, and [132] then marched to Manchester to attend a Regimental muster. The Company was dismissed at Manchester. I rode home, and I never was more completely exhausted with fatigue than when I arrived.

July 4th, 1806: The company attended the celebration of Independence at Salem, making a part of the Escort of the procession to the South meeting house, where an address was delivered by Major Samuel Swett, who afterwards married a daughter of William Gray and now lives in Boston. After the address, the Company dined together on Washington Square.

April 23, 1807: Jonathan H. Lovett was chosen Lieut. Colonel and an attempt was made to elect a Major two being authorized by law. But after several trials no one having a majority, the meeting was adjourned to the 21st of May, when an election of a Major to supply the place of J.H. Lovett, promoted, was held. At this meeting Israel Foster and myself were chosen Major, but I declined accepting the office and Capt. Levi Dodge was chosen. Fortunately, my incapacity on horseback prevented my promotion in office. July 4, 1807 there was a public celebration & a standard was presented to the Company by Swan Whitney in behalf of the Ladies. A sermon was preached by Rev. Abiel Abbot and a public dinner was had on Watch House Hill, at which Col. Lovett presided. On the 28th of July 1807, A company was ordered to be detached from the 3rd Regiment to be held in readiness for service when called for by the United States Government. I, being oldest in commission of the Captains, [133] was appointed to the command of the Company which consisted of 1 Captain, 1 Lieutenant, 1 Ensign, 3 Sergeants, 1 Drummer, 1 Fifer and 40

Rank & File. August 20th, 1807: I inspected this detached company in Squads on the parade of the several companies in this town and in Manchester, assisted by Adjutant Allen Baker of the 3rd Regt.

October 14th, 1807: I attended with the Light Infantry at a Brigade Review at Danvers Plains, Marched up and home with the Company. It was a hard day's work.

July 4, 1808: There was a training and religious service at the Dane Street Meeting house at which I attended.

December 2, 1800: Another detachment was ordered for the service of the government when called for.

December 10, 1808: Gov. James Sullivan, aged 65, died and the officers of the Militia were requested to wear their uniforms and side arms for thirty days. This I complied with on four Sundays, omitting the Cap and wearing a surtout[27] over the uniform. On the 25th of July 1809, I attended a Court of Inquiry at Breed's Tavern in Salem, of which Mayor John Ledder was President. It was attended with little ceremony and was soon dispatched.

October 24th, 1809: The Company attended a Brigade Review which was the last time that it joined with the Beverly Light Infantry Company, and I resigned my commission soon afterwards and received a discharge November 25, 1809. [134] I served as a commissioned officer 8 years, 5 months, and ten days. Until near the conclusion of my service I was strongly impressed the importance to the country of supporting the Militia that they should be well armed, equipped and disciplined, and from a sense of duty I engaged with ardor in the formation and sustaining of this company of Light Infantry, the burden of which, in consequence of the absence or sickness of Jon H. Lovett, mostly devolved upon me. It required constant vigilance to keep it alive and it consumed much of my time to attend to its various requirements. It was of use to me in as much as it cultivated a public spirit, gave me some knowledge of the means and qualifications requisite for the management of bodies of men, created attachments by constant association which are not obliterated till this day. I occasionally see evidence of this feeling of regard and respect from those members of the company who are still living, comprising a considerable variety of characters. My long and active service in the militia, gave me a spirit of command, which is an element of power, and created responsibility. I have now entirely changed my opinion as regards the utility of a militia. I think that everything of the kind has a tendency to foster the spirit of war and therefore to promote and bring on war, and still if war should unfortunately occur, a militia affords no efficient means of prosecuting it, in the present state of society, with [135] that degree of vigor which is <u>supposed</u> to be necessary to obtain a peace. The division of labor is carried into the military line, in modern times, as fully as into any of the arts of civil life. Men must be hired and disciplined expressly for soldiers and officers must be educated for the same purpose, until the folly and wickedness of mankind shall be so far subdued as to terminate the brutal, savage mode of settling national disputes by wounding and killing one another. Being opposed to war, I disapprove of all that has a direct tendency to cherish the desire for it, or to promote the love of it. I think

---

[27] Surtout: A frock-like overcoat.

that all military displays should be discouraged and that a public opinion should be formed against them.

The Beverly Light Infantry, after I resigned the command, elected Timothy Wyer as Captain, and on his resignation, Robert Tuck was chosen; but the company dropped and died and was disbanded soon after I left it. Wyer was a house carpenter, of large stature and of fine personal appearance. In his youth, he contracted the habit of smoking and of drinking and finally ended his career in drunkenness and poverty. Robert Tuck is still living, with his children in Kentucky, where two of them are teaching schools.

My military career did not end with the leaving of the Light Infantry. After the commencement of the war with Great Britain in 1812, I was requested to take the command of a number of young men associated to meet once a week to improve themselves [136] in military exercises. I accepted their invitation on the 7th of August 1812 and commenced August 12th with 42 persons and continued until about the middle of the November following, when this association was dissolved.

On Thursday the 9th of June 1814, a barge, from a British Ship of War, pursued a schooner, belonging to Manchester, towards this harbor, she being unable to escape was run on shore at Mingoes Beach, where the British set fire to her and left her, when the inhabitants assembled and extinguished the fire. In consequence of this occurrence, a town meeting was held on the Saturday June 11th, and measures were taken to procure from the State, field pieces of Cannon, ammunition etc. for the defense of the town against the enemy.

A number of persons associated as Artillery-men, and on the 17th of June, at a meeting held for the purpose, Nicholas Thorndike, was chosen Captain, I was chosen first Lieutenant and Benjamin Brown second Lieutenant. Frequent meetings were held to exercise with the two brass six-pound cannon which the state furnished. The number of persons associated was 54. We turned out twice on alarms that the British were landing, which proved to be groundless, and we met frequently for exercise and practice, until February 13, 1815, when information was received in this town that a treaty of peace had been signed at Ghent, on the 24th of December 1814. In the afternoon, after the receipt of this news, the company [137] assembled and dragging the cannon on to the brow of Watch House Hill, near to Hale street, fired a salute of 18 guns, under my command, Capt. Thorndike being out of town. This was the last time that I wore a sword. This association soon afterwards was dissolved, and the cannon and apparatus were returned to the state arsenal. These two last undertakings after I had become legally exempt from military duty, grew out of circumstances connected with the war in which the country was then engaged. My reluctance to refuse to perform any public duty to which I might be called forbade my declining to comply with these invitations of my fellow citizens, upon such extraordinary occasions, although my taste for military parade had departed some years before.

I advise my grandsons to have nothing to do with the military, in any way whatever, for although I enjoyed my connection with it for some years, very much, yet in a retrospect of life it is not one of those circumstances which afford me satisfaction.

I think it would be well not to indulge young children in what is commonly called training that is in the imitation of the military parade and show of those who in riper years are organized into military companies. This indulgence fosters the sentiment that the military spirit should be encouraged and promoted which in my opinion it ought to be discouraged and if possible banished from the community. Let children be taught to love peace but not war.

[138] The spirit of the Militia was broken in Massachusetts when government began to pay them for their services. This was about 20 years since, the providing for the reimbursement of the Poll taxes of Militia men was by law passed March 19th, 1830. Since then a larger compensation has been voted which has been increased one or more times. It has now become a mercenary concern with some while others engage it on account of its affording the means and opportunity of conviviality or of dissipation and indulgence of gross vice. Formerly a spirit of patriotism obtained in a wholesome degree in the ranks and among the officers, which we now no longer can perceive to exist. The whole system is rotten and must be abandoned or means taken to put it on a new footing.

In Boston, I think that an armed police should be established which would supersede the necessity of having recourse to the military companies to dispense mobs or to protect property on sudden emergencies. The principle argument now in use for the keeping up the voluntary militia companies at so great an expense to the state and to the members of such companies is that their services may be necessary to suppress disorderly movements of the populace in large Cities. This can only be conceived to be necessary in Boston and Lowell, and in both these cities an armed police would supersede the keeping up of the volunteer militia at so great an expense and so much injury to the morals of the young.

[139] Much of my knowledge of military exercises and evolutions was acquired before I was 13 years of age by frequently attending and viewing the drilling of the Salem Cadets and the Salem Artillery, two volunteer companies formed soon after the termination of the Revolutionary war and also witnessing the less frequent trainings of the standing companies of the Salem Regiment an of the regimental trainings. Living at that time very near to the Common, where most of these exhibitions took place I was very rarely absent from any of them. The enthusiasm which at that time prevailed among the men actuate the breasts of the boys in favor of military display and exercises. So that when some six of seven years afterwards I was called to assist in drilling a newly formed company, the knowledge which I had acquired in boyhood and which had lain dormant for that period of time was revived and enabled me to perform my part in a superior manner to that of any other who was at that time connected with the movement. From this, my own experience, I infer that knowledge which is acquired at any period of life, particularly in childhood and youth, although long forgotten, may often be revived and made useful when circumstances shall make it needful to be known and used. Is not this an argument in favor of that theory which favors the doctrine of the continued existence of every thought and action of the human mind however they be forgotten and have seemed to have passed away.

[140] Robert Tuck who succeeded Timothy Wyer as Captain of the Light Infantry died at his son George Tuck's house in Petersburg Virginia, January 11, 1851 aged 66 years. In February 1851, I headed a petition of about 55 persons to the General Court praying for the repeal of all laws requiring or authorizing Militia drills. There were a few other petitions of a similar character presented about the same time, but not enough to indicate any very general prevalence of such views on the subject of trainings as were entertained by the Beverly petitions.

There was a hearing before a committee of the Legislature on the subject March 13th, 1851. Charles Brooks of Boston commenced the discussion and was followed by George C. Beckwith both of whom represented the petitions. An account of this hearing may be found in the "Advocate of Peace" for June 1851, page 73.

[141] October 12th, 1855: I received the following note:

"Hon. Robert Rantoul   Beverly, October 12th, 1855

"Dear Sir, the Beverly Light Infantry celebrates their 41st anniversary on Tuesday next, 16th inst. And invite your presence on that occasion. We should be pleased to meet you at Bell's Hall with other guests, at 12 o'clock noon, and escort thence to dinner. Enclosed please find a ticket, admitting you to dinner, and with three ladies, to the Town Hall in the evening.

"Respectfully yours

"John I. Baker for the Commonwealth."

After consultation with many of my family connections who all advised me to accept this invitation and notwithstanding the apparent inconsistency with my present views of military affairs, I have concluded after considering the various connected therewith to attend this meeting. There are now living in Beverly seventeen persons beside myself, who were members of the company while, or at some time while, I belonged to it. It will be pleasant and attended with many interesting recollections to meet with these my old companions in arms once more. The whole number of members who belonged to the company during any part of the period between April 1801 when the company was enlisted under orders from the Commander in chief to November 25th, 1809 when I resigned is 84. I had strong doubts of the propriety of accepting this invitation. There were difficulties on both sides of the question which I carefully considered before I came to a conclusion. October 16, 1855: I attended the meeting above mentioned with thirteen of my old associates in the old Beverly Light viz Samuel [142] Stickney who was Ensign for most of the time while I belonged to the company and is now 84 years of age, Edward Stone, Bartholomew Wallis, Ebenezer Trask, Thomas Adams, Samuel Morse Thissel, William Lamson, Francis Lamson, Thomas Whittridge, John Webber, Seth Dodge, Thomas Pickard and Robert Casey. About half of these are more than seventy years of age. We had a good dinner, Capt. Israel Wallis of the present Light Infantry presiding with modesty and with great propriety.

After dinner Charles Stephens made an enthusiastic speech, which indicated much feeling. I made some remarks which were listened to with respectful attention. In the evening, the Hall was well filled above and below principally with females. I attended with daughter Hannah. Ensign Stickney was there and some others of my old soldiers. There was music by the band, marching and dancing. Everything during the day and evening was conducted with much propriety and gave universal satisfaction. I left the evening meeting at about nine and Hannah at about ten o'clock. There were no intoxicating drinks to be had or to be heard of at any time in the day or evening, no gaming, no riotous verse or rowdyism, no quarreling; everything was peaceful and orderly.

Town Affairs [143]

As soon as I became entitled to vote in Town affairs, I began to attend the town meetings and interest myself in town and state affairs, taking an active part and at some periods of my life an influential part and I attended almost every town meeting for more than forty years. Of late I have not attended so constantly, partly from a defect of hearing from age, and partly from the declining influence which comes with age, to say nothing of other causes which are known although not mentioned.

For about forty years there was no subject of much interest which came before the town, in which I did not take a decided course and use my earnest endeavors to carry through or to prevent according to my convictions of duty and of right. The improvement of the existing public roads, and the location of new ones, was a special subject of my attention. The changes in the public roads have been very great since the commencement of the present century in almost all of which I engaged actively and heartily and as I believed influentially. I was for several years engaged in procuring in conjunction with others, the widening, straightening and new locating of the road from Grover's Hollow in Beverly to the meeting house and to Esty Tavern in Middleton. Most of this time however I was engaged in behalf of petitioners and in opposition to the town. This opposition came principally from the North Parish because it was apprehended that it would divert much of the country travel from that part of the town. Prosecuting this with great [144] ardor, I offended many persons whose feelings were as strongly enlisted against the measure as mine was for it, particularly Joseph Chipman, son of the minister John Chipman, who then was the richest man in that part of town, whose opposition to me upon all public occasions continued to the end of his life and even extended its effects to his family after his decease. Henry White, who then lived on the Cherry Hill Farm, was also much embittered but he was a passionate man and like most of that class his violent feelings subsided, and he yielded to the obliterating influence of time. There were others who entertained very strong feelings against me. I, being young, ardent, and sanguine, did not display in my public course that reverence and respect for the opinions of those who, compared with me, were aged and experienced men to which they were entitled. This is an error into which the young frequently fall and I caution my grandsons against this fault. Let them exercise the fullest independence of thought and of action with the greatest perseverance their own conviction of right and of duty but never to forget the reverence and respect which is due from the young to the old. In attending to the Rial Side Road from 1803 to 1811, I visited almost every town in the county my actual expenses being paid but I received no pay for my services. This road was finally located in 1811, four rods wide. I was also much engaged at several times and employed by the town to procure the improvement [145] of the road leading from the North Meeting House in Beverly, to the meeting house in Topsfield. These improvements which at first were advocated in the whole have been made by parts at several different times so at to afford a tolerable, direct road between the two points instead of the narrow, crooked, circuitous way, which previously existed. I was one of the representatives of the town at the widening and straightening of the road leading from the corner of Dodge & Cabot streets to Essex, in 1806; and also, on the widening and straightening of the road from the First Parish Meeting House to Manchester line. At a later time, I was one of the Town's Committee for opposing the alterations of the road leading from the First Parish meeting house to Essex. This alteration was strenuously urged by the Essex people, and opposed by Beverly because it was proposed to go over two high hills in Beverly & Wenham, the steepness of the ascent of both of which would deter teamsters from using the road with heavy loads, notwithstanding the saving in the distance. The road was however located over Rubly Hill and the anticipated result has taken place, for the heavy loads go generally by the Dodge's Row road. The hills are composed mostly of very hard stone and cannot be reduced much without great expense.

When the road was located from Cabot Street near the late Joseph Stephens's house to Cabot street near the Tavern House, October 23rd, 1826. I was one of the commissioners of Highways and assisted in locating it in that capacity only.

[146] I was actively engaged in procuring the location of Lothrop Street and in connection with it the widening of Water Street in many places. On many minor occasions, I was employed to attend to the interest of the town in reference to the alteration of roads.

The location of the piece of road from Stephen's house to the three-story tavern house, by the commissioners of Highways in October 1826, occasioned very much bitter feeling in many persons, notwithstanding its benefits to the public which will not now be denied by any.

Woodberry Page, who drove the Boston Stage continued to go around Nourse's Corner[28] by the old way, for many years. Jonathan Smith, who then kept the Post Office was much incensed. Thomas Davis, Edward Ford, Samuel Haskel, John Dike Jun. and others manifested their dissatisfaction. Abraham Edwards, as a petitioner to the commissioners, took the lead in getting the improvement and he deserves high commendation in carrying it through under great discouragements. July 28th, 1806, I was appointed in conjunction with Joseph Wood and Isaac Woodberry a committee to attend a viewing committee on the road from Fisher's corner in Beverly to Chebacco Meeting House in Ipswich then, by now Essex. This road was soon afterwards widened and straightened throughout.

[146½.1] October 1851, I have for several months preceding this date given much effort and active labor to aid the Selectmen, who by a vote of the town, petitioned the county commissioners to lay out a new street parallel to Cabot street from Menasseh Trask's house on Cabot street, near to the entrance of Colon Street, southwesterly to the India Rubber factory near Ezra Batchelder's house. This street is about a mile in length and is laid out four rods wide and nearly straight and I think will contribute much to the growth of the town in population and business and will give to the village a degree of symmetry, having thus three wide parallel streets of about a mile in length running through the length of the village. These will be crossed by numerous streets, though I am apprehensive they will generally be too narrow as most of the openings on Cabot street are now but narrow courts, that cannot be conveniently widened, but will be extended to the new street.

The widening of Bartlett Street from Michael Whitney's house to Lothrop Street has been prosecuted during the time and I have also given my attention to it. This, in the petition was connected with the laying out of way from Washington Street, through Lovett

---

[28] Nourse's corner is the intersection of Front and Davis Streets.

Street and from thence to Bartlett Street but this part of the petition failed, mainly in consequence of the opposition of Josiah L. Foster, of which I think he will hereafter repent.

[146½ .2] December 1851: The afore mentioned road from Ezra Batchelder's house was recorded by the county commissioners order. The damages allowed me is sixty dollars. Daniel Annable is allowed four hundred dollars, but in May 1852 he had a Sheriffs jury to assess his damages and they allowed him more than ten hundred dollars. I have staked out a street from Cabot Street, between Oliver Trask's and Stephens Baker's shops, over my land to the above-mentioned road and have named it Milton Street. From the westerly termination of Baker's land, it is fifty feet wide until it comes to said road. I have offered lots for sale on its north side.

November 1st, 1852: The new county road is now almost graded and finished for use and it now commends itself to many of those who were opposed to it at the beginning of the movement for it.

Col. Abraham Edwards and three others had a jury to assess their damages and in the aggregate the jury allowed them less than what county commissioners allowed them. The 27th November 1852, on Saturday, it was announced in the Beverly Citizen that in consequence of my services, the Selectman had named the new county road "Rantoul Street". I feel obliged to them for this compliment. It was noticed as follows in the Citizen: "Rantoul Street: Such in view of its intimate and long continued connection with the public affairs of this town, as well as for its eminent historical associations is the appropriate name which the Selectmen of Beverly have given unto the New County Road now building between the ancient ferry way and the old Hay Market." William Trask builds the 1st house on the street.

[146½.3] In April 1854, I sold to the Eastern Rail Road Company about five acres, being all of my land lying westerly of Rantoul Street and extending to the bounds of the Rail Road. In the course of the summer and autumn of 1854, that company have built a new and spacious Depot over the track of the road and adjoining to the land which they bought of me. The land they bought of me is now, November 4th, 1854, being reduced to a level with the rail road and to Rantoul Street. In consequence of this establishment of this Depot the county commissioners have been petitioned to locate a way from Cabot Street to Rantoul Street to the opening in front of the Depot. On this petition, the commissioners have received, and I attended and advocated the laying out of, a way from Samuel Dike's shop to Rantoul Street, although I did not sign the petition. The commissioners decided to locate the Way by Lawson Walker's house and stable. This Way is called "Rail Road Avenue".

The change of the Rail Road Station from Congress Street to Rantoul Street will be attended with important consequences in regard to the growth of the town in as much as its tendency will be to centralize business of almost every description, in which respect there has been heretofore great deficiency. Having the Depot on Congress Street at the very southern extremity of the town had a tendency to draw away a part of the business from the centre and thus creating a division and diversion where there was no need.

[146½.4] April 24th, 1855: Rail Road Avenue under the superintendence of the Selectman has been graded to the full width of 50 feet. It has required much laboring of hand rock and filling of earth and when entirely finished it will be a handsome street having a gradual decent from Cabot Street to Rantoul Street. It measures about 73 rods from Cabot Street to Rantoul Street. Milton Street measures about 68. This avenue has been Macadamized and has graveled sidewalks and will be the principal thoroughfare between Cabot and Rantoul Streets.

July 1855. I have graded Milton Street from Cabot Street to Rantoul Street. From Rantoul Street to the ledge of rocks it is made twenty feet wide and from thence to Cabot Street about twelve feet wide. The grading cost about $170. I have named the hill over which this street runs "Milton Hill". It has heretofore been called "Stephens's Hill", it having been for a long period owned by the Stephens family. In regard to the future disposal of this hill I intend to leave directions with my daughter Hannah.

Proceedings of the town on my declining town offices [146½.5]

February 14, 1854: I sent a note to the town clerk of which a copy is as follows viz:

"Beverly February 14,1854

"John I. Baker Esq. Town Clerk of Beverly

"Dear Sir,

"With the view of giving publicly thereto, I beg leave to inform, that, I shall not be a candidate for any Town office for the ensuing year.

"Very Respectfully, your ob't servant

"Robert Rantoul"

On the 13th of March 1854, the annual town meeting was held but I did not attend which I believe is only the second time that I have been absent from the annual Town Meeting since I was twenty-one years of age. At this meeting, my character and conduct were freely discussed, and the following votes were passed. "At a legal meeting of the qualified voters of the town of Beverly held on Monday and Tuesday, March 13 and 14, 1854 – Voted – that the town assume all the costs incurred by the Overseers of the Poor and the late Master of the Work House, in the prosecution against them and that the Town treasurer be directed to pay to each of the defendants in said suit the respective amounts incurred by them, and in expense in consequence thereof upon their several receipts.

Therefore, that the hearty thanks of the town be hereby given to Hon Robert Rantoul for his long, arduous, and faithful services as Overseer of the Poor, for a period of fifty years, and the inhabitants of the town most earnestly tender him their warmest wishes for his future health and happiness – voted - That the united thanks of the town be also given [146½.6] to Mr. Rantoul for his manifold other valuable services in behalf of this town and that the town clerk furnish to him a copy of the several votes under this article." Enclosing the foregoing votes I received from John I Baker town clerk the following letter.

"Beverly, March 15, 1854

"Hon. Robert Rantoul

"Dear Sir, your note of February 14th declining being a candidate for any town office was duly communicated to the annual March meeting and such of the enclosed votes as relate to yourself personally are responsive to their communication. To be the organ of communication of these responses is to perform a duty of peculiar pleasure, hover much that pleasure may be sobered by the realization that the occasion which calls it forth is the retiring from the counsels of the town of a venerable and faithful public servant. These votes were all <u>substantially</u> unanimous. The <u>two latter</u> especially so, evidently speaking the sincere and united voice of the town. And that they may afford to the recipient, but a proportionate degree of that consolation and gratification much as your most ardent friends could desire.

"Very respectfully – your Obed't Serv't

"John I. Baker"

This finishes my connection with Town affairs I began in 1799 and now finish in 1854. Being about 55 years. During this period, no individual has done so much in relation to town business as myself. I have attended nearly every town meeting that has been held during that time. And I do not recollect being from but two annual meetings and from a very few others during the fifty-five years prior to 1854.

[146½.7] March 10th, 1857: Notwithstanding my determination recorded on page 146½ 5 I was inclined to attend town meeting this day upon the subject of establishing a high school and being so advised by several friends I attended on that subject only. Rev C T Thayer and Doct. W C Boyden made lengthy speeches in favor of the measure. I followed them and commenced with stating that I had abstained from town meetings for discussions about four years. I came to the conclusion from considering my deafness and other infirmities of old age and the proceedings of the annual meeting of 1853 reflecting on me personally, but a special occasion now brought me out, nay, two reasons operated on me to induce me to speak, the first was to make my acknowledgement for the ample vote of thanks which I was informed was passed with a great degree of unanimity at the annual meeting in March 1854 and for which I now make my hearty thanks. I have attended up to 1854 almost every town meeting for 55 years from 1799.

The other reasons for attending this meeting and letting my voice be heard again after a silence of four years is the agitation of the question whether we shall have a high school as is required by law. This subject I esteem to be very important and have come to speak and vote in favor of the establishment of such a school I spoke at some length but by the result of the vote with very little effect as there was a large majority against the measure.

[146½.8] On Thursday October 8th, 1857, the town having been indicted at the court of common pleas for not establishing a high school, a town meeting being held. I attended and spoke in favor of establishing one. My grandsons Rob R Endicott and Rob S Rantoul were there. The last spoke in regard to the law of the case. A vote was passed by about 8 majority in favor of it and another vote was passed directing the school committee to establish it at the old school house in the West Farm district. With these votes, it is expected that the district attorney will generate the indictment. My grandson RSR appeared to have studied the case and spoke with modesty and propriety and was listened to with much attention.

Juryman [147]

In 1803, I was drawn and served as standing Grand-Juryman for the County of Essex. This was my first service as a juryman. The Jury was empowered at the Court of Common Pleas and General Sessions of the Peace, holden at Ipswich on the 10th of March 1803. There were 22 Jurymen. Deacon Jacob Saunderson of Salem was appointed foreman and I was chosen clerk. The jury at this time were sworn and charged but it was expected that they would make no presentment until the next term which was then held in Salem in June. The next in Newburyport in September and the two next terms at Ipswich in December 1803 & March 1804. By this arrangement the Jury attended the Court at five terms within the year for which they were appointed. I attended at each of the five terms and was probably chosen Clerk because I was the youngest, being then about 24½ years. This appointment led to a more particular acquaintance with the Jurymen as it was a part of my duty to keep the account of their attendance and travel, and of the general expenditures. A part of this expenditure was $10 for spirits. My acquaintance with these men, coming from every part of the County was beneficial to me in many instances afterwards in the course of my active life. Some individuals of the Jury from the acquaintance then formed were my particular friends afterwards. I believe they are all dead but one or two. I have lately heard from Jacob Gould, who has for about fifteen years lived in Rochester, NY but was then of [148] Boxford, who is now upwards of 80 years of age. All of them at the time of my service were several years older than myself and some of them were then old men. I was paid for fourteen days attendance at the five courts and for travel; $18.20. Abel Andrews of Ipswich was County Attorney in November 1805. I attended as a Juryman on the Jury of trials at the Supreme Judicial Court in Salem. I was paid for seventeen days attendance.

In September 1813, I attended as a traverse Juror at the Circuit Court of Common Pleas, holden at Newburyport by Judges Whetmore, Dana & Minot. I was chosen foreman of the Jury. John Peirpont, who is now a Unitarian Minister, was then a lawyer and argued a cause to the Jury of which I was foreman. I remember that we decided a cause against the opinion of the Court in matter of law. There had been a bona fide sale by a writing without a delivery of the article which was afterwards attached. The question arose between the person who held the bill of sale and the attaching creditors. The court held that the conveyance by bill of sale without delivery should be considered as fraudulent and therefore void and the attachment valid. The Jury were satisfied that the conveyance was fair and honest, and they found a verdict in favor of the party who held the bill of sale. This verdict was thought to be outrageous by lawyers and it was carried up to the Supreme Court and they decided that the giving a bill of sale of a moveable [149] article and retaining the possession was not in itself conclusive of its being fraudulent as against creditors although it might be considered as evidence of fraud, yet it might be controlled by showing the transaction to be honest and fair and the jury were the proper judges of this, so that our decision which was founded upon what we viewed to be justice, but not then considered as <u>sound law</u> was confirmed by the highest court and thus became law.

In 1805, at the Supreme Court sitting at Salem, the Jury to which I belonged, with Francis Lamson of this town as foreman for that particular case, Willard Peele of Salem being the stated foreman, tried an indictment against George Crowninshield and two or three others for a riot. The case was that Crowninshield, (who was father of Benj. W. C.

secretary of the Navy) owned land adjoining to land of one Ward. There was a dispute between Crowninshield & Ward relating to the boundary line between their lands. Ward put up a fence on what he considered the true line. Crowninshield having some ship carpenters in his employ when they had finished a job, say launching a boat, told them that he had another job for them and to take their axes and follow him which they did. He conducted them to the fence which they did. He conducted them to the fence which Ward had erected as the boundary of his land against Crowninshield and ordered them to cut down and demolish it, which they did forthwith, it being day time and Ward being [150] present and remonstrating against it. Crowninshield once the workman having been indicted by the grand jury for a riot, had been put on trial at a previous term of the Court, but the jury did not agree on a verdict. The trial at this term occupied several days and on Saturday, before the court adjourned for dinner, the case was submitted to our jury, we had permission from the Court to take moderate refreshment and being conducted to the tavern near Mechanic Hall, we soon had a good dinner and went to our room for deliberation, we soon found that there was no disagreement in regard to the facts in the case, all the important ones being admitted or proved. The Court had instructed us that the facts alleged constituted a riot in the law and if we believed them that we should find the defendants guilty. Not so with the jury, three of whom said that in their view the facts did not constitute a riot and they were therefore in favor of a verdict of not guilty, nine of them thought that in matter of law they would follow the advice of the Court and therefore were for finding the defendants guilty of a riot. Thus, differing in opinion, we continued to converse upon the subject but without any change of opinion until after sunset the Court having assembled directed the jury to be brought into Court and enquiring whether they could give us any further instructions in regard to the law, our foreman informed them that he did not know that they could and we were sent out again and I think that we were carried in and out a second time with the same result but of [151] this I am not now certain, finally, between 11 and 12 o'clock at night we were again carried into Court and Judge Theodore Sedgwick then presiding (his senior having left town) after some admonitions from him in regard to our disagreement and considering that the near approach of Sunday would prevent the setting of the Court again to receive our verdict, if we should agree, until Monday following and as we could give no encouragement that we should agree, he discharged us. In reference to this case it is remarked that at that time there was great political excitement, particularly in Salem. The family of the Crowninshields being at that time very influential not only in Salem but throughout the County of Essex and were the leaders of the Republican party. There was much exasperation and bitterness between the leading members of that and of the Federal party and it so happened that nine of the jurymen who tried this case were Federalist and three belonged to the opposing party and that the nine Federalists were in favor of finding a verdict of guilty and the three republicans were in favor of a verdict of acquittal. These circumstances occasioned much upon the jury and the imputation of improper motives. I can now very easily receive why individuals, not conversant with the principles of the common law, would in opposition to the opinions of learned judges, adopt the more popular motion of what constitutes a riot and strenuously adhere to the opinion that the cutting down of another's fence in the day time [152] without actual personal violence to any one, was not a riot. I hold to the right of the jury to judge of the laws well as the facts in criminal trials, paying all due respect to the advice of the Court in regard to the law. The case against Crowninshield and others was continued to the next term, but I think that it was not again brought to trial or if it was a verdict was not obtained in 1832, from October 15th to November 10th, I was foreman of the first Jury for the Circuit Court of the United States at Boston. I was paid for four travels 100 miles and for 19 days attendance $28.75 and my expenses were $19.67 by leaving $9.08 for my time. The Jury to which I belonged tried one important insurance case and a few other cases of small importance. Judges Story & Davis held the Court a few years after this and before I had attained to the age of exemption, 65 years, my name was left out of the jury box by the Selectmen, the popular movement about that time in Beverly being in favor of discarding the old and bringing forward the young for all public offices. The office of juryman began to be desired and coveted on account of the pay as well as the opportunity of acquiring knowledge. In the course of the time while I was eligible as a juror, I served twice or thrice on Coroner's juries of inquisition. The first was on the wife of Ishmael, called Sally Bowers who was found dead in the street. The second, of which I was foreman, was on the body of an infant found in the river but supposed to be born alive and immediately after its birth to have been drowned. The mother was never discovered. The fact of its having breathed was ascertained by the examination of its lungs by two physicians. Another case was that of Israel Pulcifer who was found dead in his workshop.

[153] I also served twice on Sherriff Juries to assess damages for the location of roads. The first was in Salem on a town way John Prince of Marblehead being the foreman. The second was in Wenham on a public road, August 3, 1836, and I was appointed foreman. We set late at night and finished the case in a day. Thus, I have served on nine juries.

There are some principles of the common law, which although this law is esteemed in this part of the country, as the quintessence of wisdom, which I think should be repudiated by Juries in criminal trials, and that commonsense should control common law. For instance, if a man should come into my yard intending to shoot and steal a goose which he knew to be my property and firing at the goose the ball perforating a fence killed a man who was concealed from view by the fence, this would, by the common law, constitute the crime of murder, although the same law defined murder to be the willful killing of a person with malice aforethought. Yet the malice is inferred because he is doing an unlawful act in shooting my goose. Now I think that men having commonsense would not convict a murder although the Court should thus define the laws to them. There are many other cases where I think common sense should control common law. The maxim that if one intends to do another felony, and undesignedly kills a man, this is murder should be received, if at all, with much allowance.

[154] In criminal cases, I do not think that the Jury are bound by the instructions of the Court in matter of law, any farther than such instructions produce conviction of their truthfulness upon their own minds. The advice of a learned, upright Judge should have its due weight but not a controlling power.

Jeffries, who was said to be learned in the law, was at one-time Chief Justice of the court of King's Bench, in England. Were Jurors bound to receive his arbitrary, cruel, tyrannical instructions as law? Other cases might be cited from the history of English Jurisprudence, as well as from our own, where it was the bounded duty of the Jury to give a verdict according to what they understood to be law, however much their opinions might differ from the Court.

Sir Robert Wright, appointed Chief Justice of the King's Bench by James II at a period subsequent to Jefferies, was said to be ignorant, poor, dissolute and <u>shameless</u>, yet Juries were found to take the law from his mouth.

In Judge Wilde's charge to the Jury on the trial of Abner Kneeland he says "In cases of doubt, the Jury would have the <u>power</u> but not the right to decide against the instructions of the Court, but I hold that they have the <u>right</u> as well as the <u>power</u> to decide every criminal case according to their own honest conviction of the law and the fact.

November 18th, 1850: I have just read in the Diary of President John Adams, that in 1771 he entertained the same opinion as I have expressed above in relation to the rights of Juries to Judge of the Law as well as the fact. -page 253- He was then about 35 years of age.

Parish and Church Offices [155]

My connection with the business of the First Parish and the first Church in Beverly has been as continuous as it has been with the business of the Town. I began to attend Parish meetings a soon as I was old enough to be entitled to vote. But I have no recollection of attending until April of 1801, at an adjournment of the meeting held on the 10th of March 1801.

Josiah Batchelder was moderator of this meeting and it was voted to add two hundred dollars to the salary of the Rev. Joseph McKean from May 1, 1801, thus making it 866 2/3 $. This vote met with some opposition and I voted with the minority. In March 9, 1802, this addition to Mr. McKean's salary was also voted and it was also voted to continue this additional grant for five years succeeding the current year, and Thomas David, Josiah Batchelder and Nathan Dane were chosen a committee to wait on him and communicate the votes in relation to his salary. June 14, 1802, Mr. McKean addressed a letter to the parish Committee, consisting of Joseph Wood, Richard Ober 2nd and John Low, informing that he had been elected President of Bowdoin College, at Brunswick, in Maine and that he was disposed to accept that office, and desiring the committee to call a parish meeting to act on his request for a dismission from ministerial relation to the Parish. A meeting was accordingly held on the 21st of June, for that purpose and after the necessary or usual preliminary measures it was voted that a dismission be granted to take effect on the 23rd of August following. There was mutual good feeling in regard to this reparation.

[156] After this reparation the Parish soon became agitated with the question of a division of the Parish and the settlement of a minister. With both these subjects I soon became zealously involved. On the 23rd of August 1802, Thomas Davis, Robert Endicott and John Dyson were appointed a committee to supply the Pulpit for three months, but before the expiration of this time a meeting was called to act on the petition of John Dike, Thomas Appleton, Daniel Herrick and others, requesting that they with such others as might join them might be set off and incorporated into a Religious Society. This meeting was held on the 25th of October, and Robert Endicott, Thomas Hovey and Francis Lamson were chosen to supply the Pulpit for three months from the 23rd of November, this meeting was adjourned to the 22nd of November. On the 29th of January 1803, a meeting was held on an order of notice from the General Court on the petition of Thomas Appleton and others praying to be incorporated into a separate Religious Society. The vote stood 83

yea's and 117 nay's, indicating a very general attendance of the voters. But afterwards a vote was passed, without a division, consenting to the incorporation, without the provision for a liberty of changing from one to other, after the expiration of six months. A large committee were chosen to draft a memorial to the Court upon the subject of "Open doors" as it was then popularly called and Thomas Stephens, John Dyson and myself were appointed a committee to present this memorial and attend to the interest of the parish at the Court.

[157] This was my first appointment to any office by the Parish. By virtue of this authority I attended to the subject of the incorporation of the Third Congregational Society at Boston. Being then strongly impressed with the opinion that the support of the public worship should be by a compulsory tax upon all the members of the community, I strenuously opposed the introduction of a principle into the relation between the new and old parishes which in my view would tend to the total abolishment of the then existing laws of the Commonwealth for the support of the public institutions of religion. That principle of the compulsory support has gradually yielded to the introduction of the principle of the voluntary support, and while this change has been going on in the public mind for the last half century, I have, however reluctantly for many years, at last come to the conclusion, that the voluntary support of religious institutions is the true ground upon which they ought to rest. That they should be totally disconnected with the government and left to be entirely sustained by the free will of the people. I maintained the conservative ground honestly and with much zeal, as long as it appeared to be of any use; my opinion was overwhelmed before it was changed. After having performed what I believed to be my duty not only to the Parish, but to the public, in relation to the division of the parish. I was on the 21st March 1803, chosen one of the standing committee for managing the prudential affairs of the parish in conjunction with Joseph Wood and Andrew Ober, and also one of the Committee for supplying the Pulpit in [158] conjunction with Thomas Davis and Andrew Ober, and I was continued on the Committee of supply until Abiel Abbot received a call to settle and on the Prudential Committee until March 15th 1814, when I declined a re-election, but on the 14th of March 1815, I was again chosen and have been re-elected annually until this time, so that I am now in the forty fifty year of my service in that office. After the decease of Joseph Wood, the Parish Clerk on the 21st January 1808 after nineteen years' service, I was on the 15th March 1808, chosen to the office of Parish Clerk and have been annually re-elected to that office until this time being now in the forty first year of my service as Parish Clerk.

On the 30th day of January and on December 7th, 1807, I was again appointed one of a committee to represent the Parish before the General Court in reference to the Third Congregational Society, and I again attended the General Court at Boston for that purpose and in the following spring I made a lengthy report upon the subject which is on the files of the parish.

After the decease of Abiel Abbot I was appointed one of the Committee for supplying the pulpit so that I have had an active concern in the settlement of two ministers, and from my experience, I advise that whenever a minister is settled with a good degree of unanimity and that he gives a reasonable degree of satisfaction every endeavor should be put forth to prolong the connection to the termination of the life of the minister. [159] The evils that accrue to a society during a vacancy in the ministry; the anxiety, the divisions, and even the bitterness of feeling that result from the many ineffectual attempts at a re-settlement of the ministry, and ultimately the secessions from a society which almost always follow from the settlement, even where there is an apparent unanimity in the public proceedings, should be a constant warning to all to avoid, as much as possible, all those matters which have a tendency to produce an alienation of feeling towards their minister and thereby hasten a separation. Both minister and people should habitually feel that the connection between them is to continue during his life and they should mutually forbear from every word or action that will create or foster any other feeling, particularly among the young. Evil speaking is generally the source of disunion and should be frowned upon by everyone who loves peace, harmony, social enjoyment and good order.

During Joseph McKean's ministry, there was a party who were dissatisfied with his preaching upon doctrinal grounds. They were sometimes called "New Lights", "Hopkinsians" but perhaps might have been more justly styled "Strict Calvinists". They preferred the preaching of Daniel Hopkins and Joshua Spaulding of Salem to that of J. McKean and some of the leaders of this party, occasionally went to Salem to enjoy what they considered as sounder preaching than that of the minister of the own Parish. They also set up a Sabbath evening religious meeting in the Parish, at the dwelling house of Mrs. Chapman, mother of [160] Capt. Isaac Chapman and grandmother of Abner Chapman who is now living and at the age of 80 years or more is still employed at Boston as an agent of the American Board of Foreign Missions. These meetings, being the only public resort on Sabbath evenings at that time, were usually conducted by laymen and were calculated to foster a feeling of dissatisfaction with the preaching of J. McKean, although there was little outward expression of such feelings. This course on the part of the Strict Calvinists, had prepared the way for a division of the Parish which was hastened by the dismissing of J. McKean and immediately after that event measures were set on foot for the formation of a new religious society. A Baptist Society had been previously organized and had built a meeting house about 1801. After J. McKean removed to Brunswick he was esteemed as belonging to the Orthodox part of the Congregational denomination and was spoken more kindly of by those here, who while he was with them spoke lightly of him as preacher. While he was here he was universally esteemed for social qualities and his excellent character. I attended on his ministry for about six years and as I hope with some religious improvement.

My wife and myself joined the Church Sept. 6th, 1801. Before Abiel Abbot was settled, the Third Congregational Society, now called the Dane Street Church, was organized and Joseph Emerson was ordained, and those who preferred the more decidedly Calvinistic doctrines joined the new Society and left the moderates as well as the liberals with A. Abbot. He probably had changed [161] his views in regard to several doctrines and particularly the doctrine of the Trinity from what they were at the time of his entering the ministry, but he had not become sufficiently grounded in his new views of doctrine to make them a ground of separation from what is now called orthodoxy, in his interchanges with neighboring ministers. He exchanged with Samuel Worcester of Salem, Rufus Anderson of Wenham, Joseph Dane of Ipswich, Samuel Dana of Marblehead and others of the same class.

He strove much to keep up this ministerial intercourse even after the orthodox had become much disinclined thereto. His prudence in the pulpit and in his intercourse with his people was of the same conciliating tenor, so that he preserved a good degree of harmony in his society, though there were from time to time seceding from his society of those who desired more explicitness of preaching in regard to doctrines. He refrained until near the end of his ministry from any public explicit denial of the doctrine of the of the Trinity, so that one distinguished member of his church, after his decease, declared to me that he was not a Unitarian and I could only prove my assertion by stating that I knew that he had joined the Unitarian association in Boston, had attended their meetings and had taken a part in their proceedings. In 1823 almost twenty years after his settlement, he was invited to join in Council at the settlement [162] of Ebenezer Poor, October 29th, 1823, in Salem & Beverly, commonly called the Upper Parish. Most of the members of the Council were orthodox. The members of the church and Parish were most strongly attached to A. Abbot and were desirous that he should have a prominent part in the exercises of the day, but some active persons of the Council interested themselves to prevent him from having any prominency in the ordination. This occasioned some discussion in the Council and some excitement among the members of the Parish, but it was finally compromised by A. Abbot being appointed to make the ordaining prayer.

I attended this ordination as a delegate from the church and my feelings were somewhat excited by this attempt to put down my minister. On my return, after an interview with Bernard Whitman, who was then studying divinity with A. Abbot, it was concluded that an account of the proceedings at this ordination should be submitted to the public through the newspapers. An account was accordingly drawn up for which I furnished most of the facts and B. Whitman did the rest. This was published in the Salem Gazette and drew out a reply, as it was supposed by David Oliphant, the minister of the Dane Street Church in this town. This led to the publishing of several articles written by B. Whitman, myself & others on one side and D. Oliphant, James Appleton of Marblehead & others on the other side. All these [163] articles may be found in the Salem Gazette from October 31st to December 30, 1823 inclusive, and in a pamphlet published, as was supposed, by James Appleton, in 1824. Even this public discussion did not induce A. Abbot to take very decisive and explicit ground in this own parish, in regard to the party lines which had been drawn in the Congregation Churches. I then thought, and I so told him, that it was time for him to make an explicit avowal of this opinions, but he replied that he knew the character of his parishioners better than anyone else, and that knowledge would be his guide.

During the whole period of A. Abbot's ministry, I took an active part in all the affairs of the Parish and of the church. On the 4th day of March 1812 Thomas Davis and myself were chosen Deacons of the church and gave notice of our acceptance of the office on the 29th of April 1812. Deacon Benjamin Cleaves died August 16th, 1808, at a great age of about 87 years and his place had not been supplied, and Deacon Robert Roundy had died January 5th, 1812, aged 89 years, so that the office was entirely vacant at the time of our election. Although we differed in our doctrinal views, yet we acted together in the office of Deacon with the utmost harmony and good fellowship until after the decease of Abiel Abbot, and the difficult task of settling another minister occurred. This led to a breach of friendship which had lasted for many years. He had always, from my first settling in the town, been a kind [164] patron and friend to me. It was this breach of friendship, as well as others, less distressing, that impressed my mind with the importance of the continuance of the ministerial office to the longest possible limits. Lacerated feelings very frequently if not always attend on a resettlement.

During the interval between the dismissing of J. McKean and the settlement of A. Abbot the following persons were hired to preach viz Joshua Bates, two Sabbaths, he was afterwards president of Middlebury College, was orthodox and was introduced here by J. McKean, he did not then give satisfaction to those who had before become dissatisfied with J. McKean. Samuel Vezia four Sabbaths, Pliny L. Dickinson, six Sabbaths, James Thompson twenty one Sabbaths, William Bigelow, three Sabbaths, Thomas Rich three Sabbaths, Elisha Clap four Sabbaths, Isaac Allen five Sabbaths, he was afterwards settled in Bolton and continued in the ministry there until his decease in old age. He never married, and he willed his property, which was some 20 thousand dollars, to the town of Bolton. John Brown, one Sabbath, Samuel Mead, one Sabbath & John Mellen, three Sabbaths. Abiel Abbot was paid for several Sabbaths before his salary commenced. The price was eight dollars per Sabbath and they were boarded at the expense of the Parish. I became acquainted with most of the persons who preached and with some of the acquaintances continue to this day. There were twelve different preachers employed in little more than a year, every one of whom, probably, made some friends but none of them [165] save James Thompson and Abbot seemed to make much impression. J Thompson got a majority in the Parish meeting in favor of his settlement, but the minority being so formidable, the vote was reconsidered, and it was voted to have him preach again, after hearing some others for a limited time, but before this time expired A. Abbot was procured and was afterwards settled with great unanimity, apparently, though there was really an unsubdued feeling in the minds of several giving the preference to J Thompson. He afterwards was settled at Barre and continues there till this time but has a colleague. James W. Thompson, minister of the Barton Square Church in Salem is his son.

I had the confidence of A. Abbot until a short time before the close of his ministry and I was frequently appointed as a delegate to councils upon various ecclesiastical subjects and was often appointed on committees of the Church when it generally devolved on me to draft their report, many of which are on file with the Church papers. My conservative views in regard to the permanence of membership in the Church were in coincidence with A Abbot's for several years, but I yielded my opinion in favor of the popular notion, which allowed changes at the will of each individual before _he_ had become convinced of the impracticality of the course which he and I had sustained. After the decease of A. Abbot June 27, 1828, the following persons were employed to preach viz Samuel Lothrop who created a strong party, perhaps a majority, in favor of his settlement, but the vote was not directly tried. He was first settled in Dover NH and afterwards in Brattle Street, Boston [166] Calvin E. Stowe, Benjamin Huntoon, Edmond L. Sewall, George W. Perkins, John Tessenden, James D. Green, David H. Barlow, Samuel H. Stearns, Jonathan Clement, Andrew Bigelow, David Austin, William H. Junis, George W. Burnap, Jonathan Tam, and Warren Burton preached. Christopher T received a call 76 to 38, December 28th, 1829. He accepted on the first day of January and was ordained on the 27th day of January 1830. During this interval the minds of the members of the Parish were much agitated. Several attempts were made to settle a minister. Benjamin Huntoon of Canton, procured a larger proposition of the votes than any other and received a call but his friends proposing 2000 dollars as a settlement which the Parish refused to grant, he declined accepting the call. I was not in favor of his settlement, but in a letter which I wrote for the use of his particular friends dated August 11, 1829, see letter book, I stated that "if the Parish shall see fit to call the Rev Mr. Huntoon and he shall accept and be settled as our minister I shall wave my objections to the manner in which he is ordained, and give him cordially and heartily all that support which my various relations to the church and parish justly claim of me". I also wrote a letter afterwards to Mr. Huntoon of a similar character to which he replied in October 1829. This letter is on file. It seemed finally to be settled that about one third of the Parish, with Deacon Thomas Davis at their head, wanted to settle an orthodox minister and about two thirds wanted to settle one of liberal principles, and with these I went. After C T Thayer settled, nearly one third of the parish seceded and went mostly to the Dane Street society.

[167] These repeated secessions have reduced the Parish within less than fifty years, from being among the largest in the state to one of ordinary numbers. Deacon Davis withdrew but was not dismissed from the church until January 29th, 1837 and he died July 17, 1840, aged 85 years. Joshua Lovett was chosen Deacon, September 30th, 1830 and died March 24th, 1842, aged 59 years. Albert Thorndike was chosen Deacon April 28th, 1842. During the 36 years I have been in office I have been very harmoniously associated with the three colleagues named, excepting the ever to be lamented occurrences which in 1828 & 1829 occasioned coldness and separation between Deacon Davis and myself. Such consequences attendant on a vacancy in the ministry should deter every lover of peace and harmony from every act of word that has a tendency to disturb existing happy relations between a minister and his people. Since the settlement of C T Thayer, the management of Church affairs, growing out of the views of the Liberal party, in regard to the rights of Churches in relation to the parish or society, has become comparatively unimportant. What little there has been done by the brethren has generally been with my approbation and I have been generally chosen as the delegate to represent the Church in councils, and thus far I have the happiness to believe that I have uniformly enjoyed the confidence of the minister. I have endeavored to crush in the bud every symptom of disaffection towards him and he has manifested great kindness and attention to me under all circumstances.

Sunday Schools – Hannah Hill and Joanna B. Prince [168]

In 1810, Hannah Hill and Joanna B Prince (now wife of Ebenezer Everett of Brunswick) established a Sunday school, with a view of benefiting the poor children in their immediate neighborhood. Their school was kept in a chamber in Mrs. Joanna Prince's house, at the corner of Davis and Front streets. My wife and myself visited their school, and July 18th, 1811 I procured a donation of six bibles and six testaments, from the Bible Society of Salem & it's vicinity, of which I was then one of the managers, and on sending the books to them I wrote a letter commending their efforts in the cause of religion (see letter book for 1811). This school, by Miss Hill and Miss Prince, was continued by them for several years, when

The Beverly Union Sunday School at Front and Davis Streets, Courtesy of First Parish Church.

it was removed to the First Parish meeting house, and other females took a part in its instruction. It was still without any systematic organization, and without any particular connection with the minister or parish, except what arose from its being kept in the meeting house. Some children belonging to other societies attended, before and after its removal to the meeting house. Abiel Abbot, at length began to think that it was proper for him to take some cognizance of the school. The Westminster shorter catechism had been considerably used in the instruction of the school and to do away the necessity of its continued use, A Abbot published a short catechism, called "The Parents' Assistant and Sunday School Book", about 1822 and he also, about the same time, commenced the organization of a Sunday school exclusively by appertaining to his society.

[169] In the spring of 1822, he first invited Isaac Flagg who was then teaching the Grammar school and who was the leader of the choir, to take the superintendence of the Sunday school, but he declined and he then applied to me and I accepted the appointment and commenced the school in the summer of 1822. I immediately organized the school with the aid of A Abbot, he inviting and inducing both teachers and children to attend, so that I had a very large school, say 214 scholars, divided into 40 classes and 44 teachers. I carried it through that season, with much effort, in as much as it was a new business to me and in the management of it I could derive but little aid from others. The school was discontinued in the autumn and was again assembled on the last Sabbath in May 1823, but there was much falling off in its numbers. The children were reduced to the number of 179 that is 114 females and 65 males. There were 38 classes and 41 teachers. The average attendance of the children was 110 of the 179. The school was again discontinued on the first Sabbath in October, and on the 8th of October 1823, I delivered a public address (this address is among my manuscripts) to the school in the vestry, in the afternoon which was well attended by parents and children and at the opening of the school in the spring of 1824, when near the close of the school for that season, A. Abbot left to make his voyage to the south to return no more. (1825) Bernard Whitman [170] and John S.C. Knowlton, delivered addresses at the close of two of the seasons and I think Doct. Wyatt C Boyden at the close of another (1826). At the close of 1827 there was no public address. In 1829 the desk being vacant there was no Sunday school, but it was reorganized under the superintendence of William Thorndike to whom I gave my assistance in 1830 and continued under the same head in 1831, 1832 and 1833 when William Thorndike declined attending and his brother Albert took his place, I still continued to give my aid and assistance and when he withdrew his services, C.T. Thayer took the superintendence while I continued to assist and to supply his place when absent. This arrangement has continued until this time, so that I have been more or less connected with the Sunday school until this time, being 26 years in the whole. In 1835, I prepared and read a series of scripture lessons to the school but was not encouraged to continue this course. Since the organization of the school in 1830, there have been some public addresses at the close of the lesson by William Thorndike, my son Robert and others. The teachers in a body have attended Sunday school celebrations in Salem and in the upper parish and in most cases I have joined with them. Upon the whole, I think that my connection with the Sunday school has been, though not without some abatement, pleasant and agreeable to myself and has been attended as it was sincerely meant to be, with some good fruits in others, and therefore I do not regret that I have given my time and attention to it to the extent which is stated.

**the close of my engagement in 1854, thirty – two years.

[171] From July 11, 1811 to May 11, 1822 I distributed 384 Bibles and 126 testaments, on account of the Bible Society of Salem and its vicinity, and during a part of that time I was a manager of that society and applied myself diligently to the business, particularly in regard to the supply of poor families in this town. I was also for a part of the time a trustee.

The names of the teachers in the Sunday school in 1822 are as follows viz:

Adeline Abbot*	Emily Abbot	Oliphert Tittle
Nancy Bridge	Elizabeth Leech	Thos. Wilson Flagg
Sarah D. Cox	Mrs. Hannah K. Fisk*	Robert Rantoul Jun.*
		(died May 15, 1850 aged 51)
Dorothy Whitney*	Lucy Glover	Andrew Wallis
Martha Leech	Sally Ober	Larkin F. Lee*
Nancy Giddings*	Abigail Dyson	Nath Batchelder 2nd*
Nancy Knowlton*	Eunice Haskel	Seaward Lee
Hannah Hill*	Hannah Little	Samuel P. Lovett
Hannah Whittridge	Nancy Brown*	John Groves*
Nancy Wallis	Nancy Gardner	Joshua Lovett*
Mary Worsley	Sally Haskel	William Endicott
Hannah Cole	Ann Whitmarsh	Eldridge Fisk*
Elizabeth Woodberry	Hannah Lovett*	Joseph Foster
Eliza Stickney*	Hannah Brimmer	Stephen Nourse*
Elizabeth Lovett*	Elizabeth Dempsey	John E. Baker

Those marked thus * are dead.

Albert Thorndike was Secretary

In the season of 1848, two of the above named attended to classes in the Sunday school, namely, Nancy Bridge and Martha Leech who is now the wife of John E. Giddings. (she afterwards was married to Samuel Endicott) [172] Mrs. Giddings only attended temporarily in a part of 1848 having retired from the school some years since. Nancy Bridge has been in the school, if not all the time, yet nearly all the time since 1822, when my connection with it began. Mrs. Susan Lovett has been a constant teacher for many years, but not from the beginning of the school. Several other females have continued their service through many years.

July 4, 1838, the children and teachers of the Sunday school assembled at 8 o'clock in the morning at the meeting house. Several appropriate hymns were sung by the juvenile singers and others, accompanied by the organ. Prayers were offered by Edwin M. Stone, and an address was made by C.T. Thayer. From the meeting house, the company went to the vestry, which was beautifully decorated with evergreens and flowers arranged in taste and there partook of refreshments, consisting of cake, cherries, apples, oranges and confectionary, with lemonade. The day was delightful and the whole was concluded by ten and a half o'clock and thus avoiding the heat of the noon day sun. At the same time, the orthodox societies in this part of town assembled their children in Briscoe Hall. My Sunday school lessons, eight in number, are in covers among my manuscripts.

Miss Nancy Bridge retired from the school in 1855.

In conjunction with Rev C.T. Thayer I was, in 1847, complimented by some of the ladies of the First Parish by being at their expense, made a life member of the Massachusetts Sunday School Society. This was gratifying to me and came unexpectedly and through the special efforts of Mrs. Martha Giddings. [173] I received a certificate of membership in the S.S.S. on the 23 of June 1847. On the 4th of July 1842, being Monday, there was a Sunday school celebration by all the schools in the town.

In the morning, the weather was pleasant but a little cloudy so that it was comfortable in the open air, the clouds mitigating the scorching rays of the sun. The bells rung at 5 o'clock in the morning, at noon and at sunset. At eight o'clock in the morning the children from all the Sunday schools in town assembled on the Public Square, near the Town Hall in the following numbers as near as could be ascertained viz; First Parish 207, Precinct of Salem & Beverly 72, First Baptist 257, Dane Street 225, Second Baptist (farms) 123. Orthodox Society in Upper Beverly (called the 4th congregational church) 60, Washington Street 138, Montserrat 44; total 1120.

Those numbers are inclusive of teachers who came with the pupils. Each school came to the square in regular procession and were assigned to their respective places. A hymn was read by Rev Thayer and sung by the children and others. Prayer was then offered by Mr. Thayer. Another hymn was sung, and an address was made by Robert Rantoul Jun. of about twenty minutes in its delivery. This was followed by the singing of another hymn and the services were concluded with a benediction. A procession was then formed of Children and their Teachers and it walked from the square, I, having been requested to take the lead, walked at its head. It proceeded down Cabot Street [174] To Union Street, through Union Street to Bartlett Street, up Bartlett Street to Cabot Street and up Cabot Street to the Town Hall. The procession in its length reached from William Lamson's corner down Cabot Street to Union Street through Union Street to Bartlett Street and up Bartlett Street to Samuel Endicott's house on Bartlett Street. The procession walked into the Town Hall, filing every part of the Hall, including the galleries. There a bountiful collection was provided with no drink but water, which was soon dispatched by so many hungry children and at about eleven o'clock the crowd dispersed to their homes. No unpleasant circumstance occurred to mar the beauty and harmony of the scene. Everybody seemed to be pleased and satisfied. The expense was paid by a subscription and the arrangements were by a committee appointed at a preliminary meeting, held in the First Parish Vestry, at which meeting I presided. This Union of all the Sunday schools was attempted on the 4th of July 1838, but failed in consequence of the objections of Nathaniel W. Williams, who was then minister of the First Baptist Society, to uniting with the Unitarians in religious exercises. This interference of Mr. Williams gave much dissatisfaction to many of the orthodox, which was freely expressed by them before the celebration of July 4, 1842. Mr. Williams had removed, and his place was supplied by Charles W. Flanders who threw no obstacles in the way.

[175] Wednesday August 16th, 1843 at 12 o'clock the teachers of the First Parish Sunday School assembled at my office with the view of attending the picnic got up by Edwin M. Stone and others for the Upper Parish Sunday school. The coach *Rambler* was drawn up before my office door and about twenty persons laden upon it, inside and out, including C.T. Thayer and myself. We rode to the Precinct Meeting House and after resting a short time proceeded to the vicinity of Wenham Pond, those who were provided with vehicles riding and others walking in procession. The ground chosen for the entertainment, was beautifully situated, the centre being covered with a fine growth of walnut trees and free from underbrush and the ground dry. The neighboring fields furnished ample space for walking. Berries were to be found in the pastures. Dodge's Hill, a little northwesterly of the grove, afforded a fine prospect of the surrounding country and a glimpse of the Ocean. Wenham, Hamilton, Ipswich, Topsfield, Danvers and Salem could be seen. On arriving at the grove, the company dispersed forming several groups. Swings were provided for those who preferred that sort of amusement. Music, instrumental and vocal enlivened the scene. After sufficient time had been given for amusement, the sound of the horn gave the signal for assembling around a table of sufficient length, including at each end a table at right angles with the principal one, to seat all the females and children, while the men standing behind the females [176] were conveniently situated to reach for themselves. A hymn was sung by the Choir, seated at the bottom of the table. A blessing was asked of C.T. Thayer, then each one helped himself or his neighbor to the refreshments spread over the tables. The tables were tastefully ornamented and there was an abundant supply of Ham, Beef, Cheese, Cake, Pears, Raisins, Pineapples, Cucumbers etc. etc. with clear spring water for drink. After all had partaken to their satisfaction, there was still much food remained untouched.

I was called on by E M Stone to speak and I gave some short account of the origin of Sunday schools in England and in this town, connecting my remarks with the recent custom of the alliance of these associations with our pleasures and our recreations as we then witnessed. C.T. Thayer spoke next, bestowing a compliment upon Mrs. Susan Lovett, who was present, and upon myself for our long-continued labors in the Sunday school. Next Andrew Bigelow, who had just arrived from Danvers, made some interesting remarks, another hymn was sung, and he pronounced a benediction after which, at about 5 o'clock the company separated. The weather was exceedingly pleasant, moderately warm with a gentle breeze. Everybody appeared to be pleased with the order, harmony, simplicity and taste displayed in all the arrangements and proceedings of the day. The coach *Rambler* was again loaded with some addition [177] to the numbers that it carried up, and proceeded slowly on its return to my office, where the company alighted and returned to their homes, well pleased with their afternoons entertainment.

July 19th, 1843: I went with the teachers of the First Parish Sunday school to a picnic in south Salem at E Hessy Derby's farm. The weather was beautiful, and everything went off well under the superintendence of Stephen Phillips. There were some three or four hundred persons present, including visitors from Beverly and Danvers. Refreshments were provided. My connection with the Sunday school having continued in various forms for the space of thirty-two years in March 1854 I gave notice to Mr. Thayer that I should discontinue my attendance after the close of this vacation and on the first Sunday of May (7th), 1854 I finished my connection with the school and Charles Davis was appointed to take my place. My connections with the Sunday school has afforded many opportunities of doing service to the young, which has given me much satisfaction. Old age warned of the time to withdraw. My deafness was particularly inconvenient.

[178] (Copy of the letter before mentioned written in 1811)

"Beverly July 18, 1811

"Miss Hannah Hill &

"Miss Joanna B. Prince

"Ladies. In behalf of the managers of the Bible Society of Salem & its vicinity, I present you six Bibles & six Testaments which they request you to accept for the use of your Sunday school, to be disposed of as you may think best. You will permit me to improve this opportunity to express the high opinion I entertain of your disinterested exertions to promote the Religious instruction of the rising generation. No method is better calculated to diffuse the diffuse the knowledge and practice of the Religion of the Redeemer than the early inculcation of its precepts on the tender minds of the young. We see the benign influence of Religious principles happily exemplified in devoting so much of your time & labor to this object. Esteeming, as no doubt you do the approbation of your religious friends and of your own minds and of your heavenly Fathers simple reward. That your labors may be blessed and crowned with abundant success, and that your example may excite an enlightened zeal for good works among all your Christian friends is my earnest prayer. I am very respectfully, Ladies,

"Your obed't Serv't

"Robert Rantoul"

While the Sunday school was kept by Misses Hill and Prince and others, and before its establishment as a Parish School, I gave the school, from time to time, many little books, particularly "Miss Barbauld's Hymns in Prose." This little book still maintains its standing amongst the great variety of children's books now used.

Rev. Joseph McKean (1757-1807), fifth Minister of First Parish Church 1773-1803, courtesy First Parish Church.

Rev. Abiel Abbot (1770-1828), sixth Minister of First Parish Church, 1803-1828, courtesy First Parish Church.

Rev. Christopher Toppan Thayer (1805-1880), seventh Minister of First Parish Church 1830-1858, courtesy First Parish Church.

Hannah Hill (1784-1838),
co-founder of the Beverly Union Sunday School.

Joanna Batchelder Prince (1789-1859) co-founder of
the Beverly Union Sunday School,
courtesy First Parish Church.

Albert Thorndike (1800-1858) Superintendent of the First
Parish Sunday school, courtesy First Parish Church.

On Wednesday, October 29th, 1856, I attended the Unitarian Sunday School Association of Massachusetts, at Salem, under the auspices of the four Unitarian Religious Societies of Salem. An invitation had been given to the Teachers and others of our Sunday school and there were a considerable number in attendance on Wednesday and on Thursday. The meeting on Wednesday commenced at 10 o'clock A.M. and at 10 o'clock P.M. adjourned to the Town Hall to partake of a bountiful and elegant collection provided by the four Salem societies. The tables covered the area of the Hall and the standing places around the sides of the Hall were filled with members of the Salem Societies while the tables were filled with their guests. Nathaniel Silsbee presided and with a short introductory speech welcomed the company to the entertainment. The Hall was beautifully decorated with evergreens, flowers and tapestry. Around the sides were portraits of the Ministers; Bentley, Bernard, Prince and others, also of the laity, Daniel A. White, Leverett Saltonstall, Timothy Pickering, Doct. Holyoke, Doct. Oliver, Deacon Saunderson and others; and busts of Nathaniel Bowditch and Joseph Tuckerman. The entertainment went off very pleasantly. The only beverages used were water, tea and coffee. The desert was of grapes, pears, apples and other fruits. Leaving the Town Hall at 2 o'clock and returning to the North Church it was found the children of the four Salem Schools there assembled. Addresses were made to them by several members of the convention after which they were marshaled in procession to march to the Town Hall to partake of the entertainment provided for <u>them</u>. In the forenoon as well as in the afternoon speeches were made in the Church by many persons. At five o'clock the conventions adjourned to nine o'clock on Thursday morning and notice was given that a conference and prayer meeting would be had at the Church commencing at eight o'clock and notice was also given that Rev. M Ellis, of Charlestown, would preach at the Barton Square Church at seven o'clock and after the services a levee would be held at the Town Hall. Daughter Hannah, Mary E Endicott and myself took tea, by invitation, at David S. Neal's house on Washington Street. In the evening, we attended the services in the Barton Street Church, which was filled so that many persons stood in the alley. The sermon was very good, containing many original remarks in relation to the history, character, general effect and present state of Sunday schools, as well many judicious suggestions in regard to their improvement. At about 8 ½ o'clock we repaired to the Town Hall which was thoroughly filled with company and at 9 ½ o'clock we left to ride home in the Omnibus with as many of our Beverly teachers as could find seats therein. On Thursday the 30th Hannah, Mary E. Endicott, Martha T. Endicott and some others went early to Salem to attend the conference in the North Church at 8 A.M. I went later so as to attend the Convention at 9 A.M. The Convention voted to adjourn at a quarter before one. There were many good speeches made by various persons and the church was well filled with hearers, many of whom, that came from a distance were lodged and entertained in Salem. We came home soon after one o'clock and dined at home. All were gratified with the proceedings and with the entertainment. Personally, I received many marks of civility and kindness for which I feel grateful. Such occasions, though not enjoyed with the zest of younger days, have a consoling and cheering effect on my spirits, and their influence is perceptible for a time afterwards. In my old age, I think more of the continuing effect of these occasions than I did in younger days when more objects of interest occupied my time and thoughts, and my feelings were more sensitive to enjoyment. About this time my health has been better than it had been in the summer months. I walked to Salem on that

day without much fatigue. C.T. Thayer and wife attended some of the meeting and he made some of the formations of thanks near the close of the conventions.

Thursday evening June 3, 1858, Charles Davis, son of the former Deacon Thomas Davis, deceased was chosen a third Deacon on account of the prolonged sickness of Deacon Albert Thorndike who is thought to be incurably afflicted with Dropsy. Mr. Charles Davis is about fifty years of age. At an early age, he was married to Helen M. Stephens, daughter of Thomas Stephens, on the 7th of September 1845, they were admitted to the Church. She died June 12th, 1846 aged 31 years since which he has remained unmarried. He has since, I left office, superintended the Sunday school as an adjunct to Christopher Thayer. At the meeting for the election there were nine votes given and all for him so that he is unanimously elected. I was not present at the meeting but here records my approbation of the result of the meeting.

Unitarian Association [179]

The Beverly Association Auxiliary to the American Unitarian Association, was commenced in 1830, soon after the settlement of C.T. Thayer as the minister of the First Parish. Most, but not all, of the members of this association have belonged to the First Parish. The annual payment to the principal society has usually been about fifty dollars. There has been an annual meeting for the choice of officers and for discussions for several years there were other meeting beside the annual meeting. I have been annually elected on of the standing committee and have generally made some remarks at the meetings. At the commencement William Thorndike was the principal reliance for speaking at the meetings. Edwin M. Stone has several times spoken with interest and effect. C.T. Thayer has always said more or less. There are some sixty or seventy of the tracts of the principal association distributed monthly among the members of this auxiliary. There was a degree of animation and feeling at the commencement which has gradually abated and declined. A <u>revival</u> is needed and according to the common course of things it will come before many years. It is more difficult to keep up and sustain such associations than it is to begin and establish them. The influence of novelty having died away, it requires the perseverance of the conservatives to keep them in existence. I have felt the importance of the conservative principle in reference to very many objects with which I have been connected and [180] which would have very prematurely seen their end had it not been for the operative of this principle with a very few of those who were concerned in such objects. The first meeting of the association was held on the 14th day of May 1830. Isaac Flagg, chairman. The officers were C.T. Thayer, President; Wm Endicott, Secretary; Charles Stephens, Treasurer; Robert Rantoul, William Thorndike and Samuel P. Lovett, standing committee constituting, with the other officers, the board of Directors. There were 120 subscribers about forty-five of whom are dead (May 1849.)

Quarterly meetings were held until May 1834 when the annual meeting was adjourned to May 1835, since which the meetings have been held annually. In May 1837, the number of members was 68. For several years past the annual meeting has been held on the first Sabbath in June. It was first held at that time in 1839. Others who have been elected to office are; Eldridge Fisk, Rev. Ebenezer Robinson, Josiah Lovett 2, Albert Thorndike, Joseph McLovett, John Patch, Stephens Baker and George W. Strickland. The annual meeting in 1849 was held on Sunday evening, May 20th on account of Frederick W. Holland, the general agent of the association, being in the vicinity and being desirous of addressing the meeting. Besides W Holland, C.T. Thayer and myself made some remarks. For several years past have collected many of the tracts received here and have returned them to the Agent for gratuitous distribution or have given [181] them, together with many other books and pamphlets to Edwin M. Stone, who for a time was a domestic missionary in the south part of the County of Essex and to John Bell, missionary for the City of Salem. Stephens Baker has been a liberal contributor of books and pamphlets as well as of the tracts of the association for the purpose of this distribution. About forty volumes were sent from the Sunday school library.

On Tuesday & Wednesday October 9th & 10th 1849 I attended a Unitarian convention at Portland in Maine and was lodged and entertained by John Murray. I was chosen first Vice President. I also attended a similar convention in Salem on Tuesday and Wednesday October 19th & 20th 1847 and was there appointed as Vice President.

It has been my practice for a long series of years to distribute among my acquaintances in every part of the United States my copies of the Christian Register, a weekly newspaper printed in Boston and to which I have been a subscriber for many years. I have also distributed many Unitarian tracts and publications in various places through the Post Office and otherwise.

On Tuesday, Wednesday & Thursday October 15th, 16th & 17th 1850 I attended a Unitarian convention at Springfield. There was a large attendance and the season was one of satisfaction and of improvement. My daughter, Hannah, granddaughter Mary Endicott & Mrs. Martha F. Giddings went with me.

[182] I have thus for many years given countenance to the Unitarian denomination. I attended some of the earlier meetings of the American Unitarian Association held in Boston and made myself a life member by the payment of the requisite sum. I am not very exclusive in my views in regard to religious sects. I think that there should be greater liberality and good fellowship among all the various sects, who profess to be followers of Christ. There always will, where there is freedom of thought, be a difference of opinion, but there need not be any alienation of affection. I think it to be one of the highest duties of Christians, at this time, to bring about a solitary change in the state of society in regard to the divisions that exist everywhere upon religious or sectarian grounds.

In October 1851, I attended the annual autumnal convention at Portsmouth. My daughter Hannah & myself were entertained at John P. Lyman's. The occasion was pleasant and edifying.

On Tuesday May 25th, 1852, I attended the annual meeting of the Unitarian Association in Boston and Hannah & myself partook of the collection. I came home in the evening, but Hannah lodged at Rev. Rufus Anderson's in Roxbury and on Wednesday attended several public meetings in Boston and came home in the evening.

Rammohun Roy (of Calcutta, India) [183]

April 16th, 1825: I received from Rammohun Roy[29] of Calcutta, Bangall the following letter by Capt. Israel Whitney, accompanied with one dozen pamphlets, mostly acknowledged publications of Rammohun Roy and which I afterwards had bound in one volume.

"Sir: you will be surprised at the presumption of one who is so perfect a stranger as myself in addressing you from a remote country, but I am sure that when you reflect on the motives which have led me to use this freedom you will excuse my intrusion. Having understood from Cap Whitney a friend of mine, that from the spirit of philanthropy you not only entertain sincere wishes for the welfare of your fellow citizens both here and hereafter, but also use every means calculated to direct them to the paths of pure Christianity which alone can lead man to peace and happiness, I am induced to do myself the honor of being known to a person so distinguished by his benevolence and religious zeal. After I had been tired of the gross absurdities of Hindu doctrines I directed my enquiries to the Christian faith, the name of Unitarian Christianity not then being known to me. But in proportion as I made myself acquainted with this system and its published defenses and illustrations, resolution increased to abandon it entirely, finding the Christian doctrines resembling those of Hindus in substance, though they are different from each other in minute interpretations. I, however, was so fortunate as to become intimately acquainted with a Scotch gentleman of great acquirements who kindly proposed to me to read the Bible with him and to examine whether it was more conformable to another system of Christianity [184] called Unitarianism and believed to have been the religion of primitive Christians. In following the advice of that best of all friends I have felt thoroughly convinced that the Christianity which the majority of Christians profess is a mixed system of the Romish and Christian religions and that pure Christianity has its support both from the revelation and from the human understanding, a circumstance which not only has happily deterred me from manifesting hostile feelings towards this religion but has rendered it incumbent upon me to exert myself in extending its influence by every possible means. I hope I shall at a future period lay before the public, a statement showing the close resemblance existing between the doctrines maintained by Hindus and the majority of Christians, and at present I entreat your acceptance of a few pamphlets which my friend has kindly offered to take charge of and beg to subscribe myself

"With respect and regard

"Your most Obedient Servant

"Rammohun Roy

"Calcutta

"December 28th, 1824

"(super scribed)

---

[29] Rammohun. Roy (1772-1833) is known as the "Father of India"

"To Honorable Robert Rantoul

"Beverly

"U.S.A

"*Beverly*

"Capt. Whitney[30]

(the ship by which the letter came was named "*Beverly*".)

[185] To this letter I sent the following answer, by Capt. Israel Whitney of the Ship *Beverly*:

"(Massachusetts) Beverly

"May 2nd, 1825

"Dear Sir,

"It is with great satisfaction that I acknowledge the receipt (by our mutual friend Capt. I. Whitney) of your letter of the 28th December last, and the pamphlets you were so good as to send me, for which be pleased to accept my most hearty thanks. I have found much gratification in reading your publications in defense of the Divine Unity and of pure Christianity. Whenever mankind can be brought to divest themselves of the prejudices of education and to examine impartially and thoroughly the nature of the Christian dispensation, its evidences as contained in the Jewish and Christian scriptures, its adaptation to the wants and character of man, the excellence of its precepts and the life of its founder their result will be (as in your own case) that they will not be content merely to receive it as precious to themselves, but will use every reasonable exertion to extend its influence among their fellow men. My native State, Massachusetts, was settled by the sect who, in England, were called Puritans. They were rigid and austere of manners and Calvinistic in their belief. They thought it their duty to protect and preserve what they called orthodoxy by such guards and restraints as seemed to them necessary to attain their object. But notwithstanding all restraints such has been progress and freedom of religious inquiry that Unitarian principles obtain more generally in Massachusetts than in any other part of the United States. But it is but of late, say within fifteen years, that these sentiments have been openly avowed. They long existed in the minds of many serious and intelligent persons, who from prudence, [186] Or defect of moral courage refrained from communicating them.

"Happily, the time has now arrived when an avowal, openly, of Unitarianism, in many parts of New England, does not lesson respect for character or influence in society. Prejudice gradually yields to rational inquiring and the changes of opinion in as rapid as is desirable, considering the danger to which we are all liable of running from one extreme to the opposite. The congregational clergy and other influential persons in the City of Boston have taken the lead in producing this change. The

---

[30] Rantoul notes "see also RR letter book "C" Aug. 1824 – June 1833".

Christian lives of these men has secured to their opinions that confidence which among the less informed is so necessary to give them a fair examination and comparison with the scriptures. To call such men Deists or Infidels is of no avail while the whole tenor of their conduct exemplifies the virtues that constitute the real disciple of Christ. Our college at Cambridge has contributed largely to the progress of liberal and enlightened opinions in theology. Your situation is singularly interesting, having to contend with and oppose the idolatry of your own countrymen as well as to combat with those who although they sincerely believe in the Christian religion hold it with many of those corruptions which have incorporated themselves with it since its first promulgation. Your path of duty is plain though arduous. Christianity, in its simplicity and original purity must and will recommend itself to enlightened minds among your countrymen and by their agency it will be gradually brought to the knowledge of their brethren. Christian missionaries have accomplished little in your country by their preaching though you give them much credit for the influence of their example.

[187] "You have given the reason of the failure. They preach incomprehensible mysteries to rational beings and expect them to be received, only, on an authority of which they have the most imperfect idea, if they have any at all. I am pleased with the prospect of the Unitarians at Calcutta being accommodated with a Chapel for worship. I suppose this will enlarge the sphere of Rev. Mr. Adam's usefulness to whom I beg you to present my best respects. Although we are strangers to each other, I am not without some knowledge of his history. He stands high in my estimation for the independence he has manifested in acting according to his visions of divine truth, under very trying circumstances. It will give me great pleasure to hear from you whenever your convenience will permit. Wishing you the greatest success in your endeavors to spread light and truth around you, I subscribe myself, Dear Sir, very respectfully

"Your Obed't Sev't Robert Rantoul

"Rammohun Roy Esq.

"Calcutta"

By the Ship *George*, Capt. Samuel Endicott, which sailed about 30th of June 1825 I sent Rammohun Roy about twenty pamphlets of different descriptions. This ended my correspondence with this extraordinary character. He afterwards went to England on a visit and there died Sept 27th, 1833. Wm. Adam, the Scotch gentleman, referred to in R Roy's letter afterwards came to the United States and has been employed as a preacher in several places and is now (1849) preaching at Chicago in Illinois.

[188] Rammohun Roy was born about 1780. He inherited a good estate. He began to study the English language about 1812.

[189] Tuesday October 18, 1853: I left home at about noon in company with C.T. Thayer to attend the autumnal Unitarian convention at Worcester. We arrived there at about 4 ½ o'clock and were directed to Mr. Trumbull's house Park Street where we were cordially received and very kindly and hospitably entertained. Mr. Trumbull is the cashier of the Citizens Bank, has a wife and ten children. There were said to be about 400 visitors at the convention. The weather was delightful and the services interesting. We returned

home on Friday in the forenoon. Mrs. Trumbull was indefatigable in her attentions to her guests, which numbered seven. She appeared to be an active, energetic woman and very kindly feeling. She was very kind in her attentions to my comfort.

Monday October 9th, 1854: In company with daughter Hannah and granddaughter Mary E. Endicott, I commenced a journey to Montreal to attend a Unitarian convention in that city. There were said to be about 300 visitors. About 138 of them were entertained by private families, the residue paid their expenses at the public houses. I was soon after my arrival attacked with disease which prevented my attending the meetings very much. We found the widow and three of the children of my friend, William Rintoul who, died about three years ago. They live at 18 E. Edward's Street. Mrs. Rintoul, her son William and her daughter called on me at Donegana Hotel. We were much pleased with them. They appeared to be kind [190] and amiable and intelligent. We, Hannah and I, left Montreal on Thursday morning at 6 o'clock and arrived home on Friday the 13th at about 3 ½ o'clock. Mary remained until the next day and came in company with A. P. Peabody & wife. Mary was attacked with Cholera Morbus after she arrived home and was seriously ill for a week. We had a pleasant journey upon the whole, my feeble health in abatement. Hannah was well throughout. It is the first time I have been without the limits of the United States. I visited the Cathedral which is a splendid building, and The Market House, built of stone and very spacious. In the Cathedral, there are many pulpits and confessionals. The pews below are numbered as high as 375. There are two tiers of galleries on the sides. The principal alleys running the length of the building are so wide as to admit of four rows of moveable seats. Going we lodged at Burlington arriving there at 12 o'clock on Monday night and leaving at 4 o'clock on Tuesday morning giving but little time for sleep. From thence we went on board a steamboat on Lake Champlain and in about four hours landed at Rouse's Point when we again took the rail road. Very many of the visitors were disagreeably affected by drinking the water of Montreal. I attribute my illness to this cause. Returning we lodged at Bellows Falls, arriving at about 4 o'clock in the afternoon of Thursday and leaving at 8 ½ o'clock on Friday in the morning, giving enough time to eat and to sleep.

[190.1] October 23rd, 1855: My daughter Hannah, my granddaughter Mary E. Endicott and myself went to Providence to attend the Unitarian Autumnal convention. We arrived there at about 6 ½ o'clock PM, went by direction of a Committee of arrangement to Mrs. Eunice Metcalf's No. 164th North Maine Street, where we were kindly and hospitably entertained. She is a widow, her family consisting of her son Frank, his wife and three daughters. We remained in Providence until the close of the convention on Thursday and arrived home on Thursday evening at about 8 o'clock. The services at the convention were interesting and the attendance large. Wednesday was rainy throughout, but Thursday was tolerably pleasant. From Beverly, there were beside those first mentioned, Mrs. Martha Endicott, Miss Hannah Adams, Mary Howe, Mary Weld, Paul Hildreth and his wife and Josiah B Prince. I attended at most of the meetings and at the social gathering, for which it was said that 1400 tickets were issued, and the persons present was about that number. Mrs. Metcalf's house is said to be on the site of Roger William's (the founder of Providence) house. My health was somewhat improved by this journey.

[190.2] On Monday May 25th, 1857 Hannah & I went to Boston to attend the anniversaries. We went to the house of Wm Endicott Jun. who with his wife is absent in

Europe but his Father, Mother, Sister and two Brothers, (Charles & Henry) have been keeping house there, No.10 Indiana Place, for several weeks past. On Monday evening I attended the meeting of the Peace Society at the Park Street Church. Address by Doct. Stebbins late president of Meadville College. On Tuesday, I attended the annual meeting of the Unitarian Association in the forenoon and the Collation in Faneuil Hall at five o'clock in the afternoon. In the morning between 8 & 9 o'clock of Tuesday, Wednesday, Thursday, Friday and Saturday, I attended the conference and prayer meetings in as many different Churches. Saturday afternoon we came home. This is the longest visit I have made in Boston since 1853. I attended many of the public meetings of various associations, filing up the time. My health was as good as usual, availing myself of the Horse Rail Road and Omnibus for ease of conveyance to different parts of the City. I was not much fatigued and came home somewhat improved. The morning meetings were all very well attended but principally by females. The speaking, prayers and singing were all impressive and devotional in their character, very much there appeared to be in the whole assembly at each meeting a profound seriousness and sincerity.

Remodeling the Meeting House [191]

First Parish Meeting House, 1795 by Warren Prince, courtesy First Parish Church.

In the first part of the year 1835, there was a movement in the First Parish in regard to the re-modeling or rebuilding their meeting house. At first, I did not favour this movement, thinking it was premature and knowing that it would alienate the minds of some members of the Parish and would be attended with a heavy pecuniary burden. However, as the thing progressed I came into the measure, not however without some fears of the consequences. In February 1835, a petition was circulated to request the Parish Committee to put an article into the warrant for calling the next Parish meeting "To see if the Parish will alter their house of worship, or take the present one down and build a new one on the same site etc." This petition was signed by William Leech and seventy-four or five others. The following analysis of the parishioners was made by a person who was favorable to the measure viz,

"the whole number of male persons on the tax list is 158. Of this number:

76 have signed the petition

36 are absent and not consulted

11 called on but declined signing but had no objection to the measure

32 were not called on

There are 39 females who are taxed in the Parish and who it is believed are very generally in favor of a new house."

It should be recollected that this statement was made by one whose feelings were engaged in the cause and that it did not show a majority in its favor. This state of things justified my views at the time.

[192] At the Parish meeting on the 10th of March 1835, there was a good degree of unanimity and a committee was appointed to report on the subject at an adjournment on the 7th of April following. This committee consisted of William Leech, Jacob Woodberry, Josiah Lovett 2nd, Edward Ford, Charles Stephens, Samuel Endicott and Robert Rantoul. Mark Knowlton was afterwards put in the place of Jacob Woodberry. The subject was fully considered by this committee and the unanimously agreed in favor of an alteration rather than to build a new house. By their request I drew up a lengthy report, which occupies eight pages in the Parish records, to which reference may be had for a full understanding of the circumstances of the case. This report was accepted by the Parish, without any dissentient voice. A building committee was appointed and the whole plan recommended was carried into effect. I from this time, gave my hearty support to the proceeding. A subscription paper was offered for individuals to take new Pews and only forty-four were subscribed for. The cost of the alteration was about $9,300 including $1,300 for the old Pews taken down, when it was estimated before it was begun at $6,000. The pews sold at auction for $11,444 and the surplus was applied for the purchase of an organ.

There were one or two seceding families in consequence of the alterations, but happily my fears appeared to be groundless in the main. I owned two whole Pews and two thirds of another Pew of those which were taken down and for which I received only a very moderate allowance, while I paid two hundred dollars for one of the new Pews so that my contribution to this object was not a small one.

[193] As I advance into the veil of years I find growing upon me a reluctance to join in impulsive movements. I find that society is much inclined to that mode of bringing about public objects, whether of a moral or material character. I have on several occasions held back, simply because I disapproved of encouraging the doing of things hastily and without a deliberate conviction, not only their propriety and fitness to be done., but also a full consideration and approbation of the means to be employed to bring them about, and a careful weighing of the consequences ether of success or of a failure. Acting under these impressions, which I feel to be right and true, I have lost in popularity what I have sacrificed to wisdom. Those in public movements of the young and sanguine should be restrained and controlled and kept within their proper limits by those farther advanced in years and who can take a more comprehensive view of the numerous bearings of a great public object. These may however be an excess of conservatism as well as to strong a desire for change, and he who resists all changes without reflection is no more to be commended than he who advocates changes, from no other motive than that they are changes. The rashness of youth, the impetuosity of the sanguine and head strong, the boldness of enterprise may all have their good uses as well as that they may more frequently plunge into irretrievable loss, suffering and ruin. My course in regard to the Town Hall was actuated by the same motives and was followed with somewhat similar results.

[194] The purchase of the organ and other expenses connected with the alteration of the Meeting House left the Parish some two or three hundred dollars in debt. This debt still remains although of some twelve or thirteen years duration. Painting the pews, painting the walls in fresco, shingling and repairing in consequence of damage by fire are the extraordinary expenses which have occurred since the alteration. The ordinary expenses are considerably increased in consequence of the purchase of the organ. And in regard to

the new Town hall the contingent expense of the town has been very much enhanced in consequence of its purchase. The general character of the voters who constitute the majority in our town meetings is very much changed from what it was some thirty or forty years ago. The introduction of shoemaking as a general employment has gradually changed the habits, manners and morals of the mass. From a fishing, seafaring and farming population, it is changed to a manufacturing population in the main. Many of the farmers, most of the fishermen and a large portion of the females work at shoe-making. A large number of females work at tailoring so that for domestic, household labor, foreigners are employed, and our own females are growing up without the practical knowledge of housewifery which formerly was their general characteristic. The young men of better education go to Boston to engage in the various branches of trade.

[195] The following is a copy of the report of the Committee on the remodeling of the First Parish Meeting House in 1835, which was unanimously accepted.

"The committee to whom was referred the fifth article in the warrant for calling the annual March meeting of the First Parish in Beverly in 1835, which article is as follows viz: 'to act on the petition of William Leech and others to see if the Parish will alter their house of worship, or take the present one down and build a new one on the same site, and act and do anything respecting the same, that they may deem expedient', have maturely considered the subject referred to them, and respectfully submit the following report. The principal reasons for dissatisfaction with the meeting house as it now is are that it is much larger than is necessary for the accommodation of the society with its present numbers; that its size in connection with the moderate number of persons who usually assemble in it, renders it burdensome to the speaker and sometimes prevents his being heard distinctly by a part of the audience, that in the winter season it is not comfortably warm, that the beneficial effects of religious instruction is diminished and impaired by the audience being scattered through so large a space, and from the circumstances before stated as well as from the want of compactness lessening the effect of the social principle, which is brought into action by assembling ourselves in large bodies. The foregoing may be considered as comprising one class of objections, which might be entirely removed or very much obviated by an alteration of the house attended with but a moderate [196] expense, that is by purchasing one or two rows of pews at each end of the house and putting up partitions from the floor to the wall so as to reduce the room to the desired size. But there is another class of objections which occasion extensive dissatisfaction and complaint and are equally deserving of attention and of remedy if practicable within reasonable limits. These objections are that the meeting house, being now about sixty five years of age, however well it was constructed, and adapted to the fashion of the time and to the convenience and comfortable accommodation of those who lived at that day, according to their notions of beauty and comfort, yet such have been the changes of opinion and of habit since that day, that it now must be considered as antiquated and obsolete both in the external appearance and its interior arrangement and as not according that reasonable and comfortable accommodation arising from adaptation to the feeling s and habits of those who use it, that is becoming, decent and proper in houses intended for public use.

"It must be conceded by all that both of these classes of objections are founded on facts. By remedying those of the first class only, we shall afford no relief in regard to the second, but in remedying the latter, we shall, of course, remove the first in the style of building Meeting Houses and other public edifices in this country, has so much changed within the last half century that it is no way surprising that the attention of the members of the First Parish should be drawn to this subject, at this time [197] especially, when they witness so many Houses of Public Worship which have been erected within a few years past in this and the neighboring towns, combining so much elegance in their external appearance with convenience and adaptation of their internal arrangement to the accommodation of both speaker and hearers. Changes in the form, embellishment and arrangement of buildings are continually taking place. It would be equally unavailing and hopeless to attempt to reason down the desire of change, it may be regulated but it cannot and ought not to be suppressed. Without it, improvement and reform would slacken their already too tardy place. In small towns, but little can be found in the outward appearance of private buildings that is ornamental and attractive, but something may be done to gratify the taste and please the eye of the beholder in the construction and outward appearance of <u>public</u> buildings. In New England villages, Churches and Meeting Houses are preeminent by the ornaments that attract the attention of the traveler. The general appearance of these buildings in regard to neatness and convenience as well as in respect to elegance and beauty, is considered as a sure indication of the prevailing disposition, habits and character of the inhabitants. In the march of improvement around us an effort must be made from time to time to preserve our relative standing. The history of the Town and Parish proves that in this respect the inhabitants have [198] not been wanting to their duty. As soon as there were sufficient number of settlers on this side of the river to justify the proceeding the first Meeting House was built, very near where the present one stands, in the year 1656, before either town or parish were organized. This soon was found too small to accommodate the growing society and was sold in 1682, in which year the second was built on the same spot where the present house stands, at an expense of 390 pounds sterling, equal to about 1645 dollars. This house with various repairs, alterations and improvements continued until the 89th year of its age, when in the year 1770 it was taken down and the present one erected in its place. In 1795, twenty-five years after it was built, it was found insufficient to accommodate the numerous worshippers who generally assembled within its walls. At that time, the Parish impressed with the importance of yielding to circumstances, caused the House to be enlarged by dividing it in the middle, removing the eastern half twenty feet from the western and finishing and filling up the space with twenty-seven new pews upon the floor and eight in the gallery. Since that period, what then constituted the First Parish has been and now is divided into four religious societies. The force of circumstances after the lapse of forty years calls upon us as loudly as it did upon them whose places we now occupy to accommodate ourselves [199] and our children and as we may reasonable hope our children's children, by a renovation of that which has thus far answered the purpose for which it was devised. In doing this generously and liberally we shall do homage to those principles which actuated our predecessors, who from the earliest settlement on this side Bass River, have up to our own time manifested a zeal for the common good, and have been ready and willing to bestow as much of their time and substance, as occasion required for the general use. We inherit their love of liberty both civil and religious. We have preserved their spirit of independence, we claim the same right of private judgment in matters of religion and shall we be behind them in public spirit, whenever occasion shall demand its free exercise?

"If then the time has arrived when a decided majority of the Parish are desirous of abandoning or of changing an antiquated, unfashionable and somewhat inconvenient house for one of modern structure, of fashionable appearance, combining comfort and convenience both to the Minister and hearers, and adding beauty and ornament to the town, let it be done without delay.

"The minority whose lingering regard for what is ancient, whose settled habits of life and whose staid opinions lead them to be contented with things as they are will cheerfully make the sacrifice which the occasion requires of them. They certainly will not throw any obstacles in the way of those whose liberal and [200] generous minds impel them to seek for the change only, because they are fully satisfied that the best interest of the Parish require it at their hands a unanimity of opinion may be wanting in regard to the expediency of the measure, but if it shall be determined to be expedient by the majority, a harmonious action and effort to accomplish the object will on this as on most other important occasions, characterize the inhabitants of the Parish. The subject is of great importance and should be carefully viewed in all its relations, seriously considered and proceeded upon with great caution and deliberation.

"For the purpose of obtaining information upon the subject referred to them, members of the committee have visited and examined several meeting houses in other towns that have been lately built or altered. The committee have also procured an architect, Mr. Richard Bond of Boston, who has had much experience in buildings of the kind, to examine the Meeting House in reference to an alteration of it. From his examination, together with their own view of the subject, they are of the opinion that the frame is sound, strong and well timbered, that the boarding is mostly in good order and that the northerly side of the roof is well and sufficiently shingled, and that the form of the body of the house is tolerably well accepted to a satisfactory alteration. They are therefore unanimously of the opinion that it is unnecessary [201] and inexpedient to take it down. With respect to a material alteration of the house, there are different opinions prevailing among the members of the Parish, in regard to the extent and degree of the alteration. While some would confine it to the inside principally and shingle one side of the roof, and repair the steeple, and paint the outside, leaving the windows and underpinning in their present form; others are in favor of such an alteration, both within and without, as shall be necessary to give it a modern fashionable appearance throughout. A majority of the committee are of the latter opinion, as the only mode which will give general and lasting satisfaction. Anything short of this would leave the subject open for further proceeding under much less advantage than to do all at this time that will probably be wanted or desired by the present generation. The additional expense probably would be paid by the greater price at which the pews would sell. Although this committee have for the convenience of the Parish, reported distinctly upon the separate portions of the work into which it may properly be divided, yet they are in favor of doing the whole. The expense of doing the whole is estimated at six thousand dollars, without including the indemnity to the present pew holders. They have procured a plan and draft of the various alterations which are proposed, which are skillfully and handsomely executed by Mr. Richard Bond, and herewith exhibited [202] to the Parish as a part of the report[31]. The committee are of opinion it is expedient, and recommend to the Parish to repair, alter and improve the outside of the Meeting House as follows viz:

"*First* - To take down the steeple and remove the porches and portico.

"*Second* - To raise up the house one and a half or two feet from the present underpinning stones, and to put under a new course of underpinning stones and to raise the earth around the house as high as the top of the present underpinning.

"*Third* - To new shingle the southern side of the roof

"*Fourth* – To put in five large windows on each side of the house, instead of the present windows, and three small windows in the western end

"*Fifth* – To finish the westerly end with proper embellishments and to have the entrance wholly at that end of the house and to erect a tower or cupola on that end of the roof and therein to hang the bell and place the clock and on the north and south sides to affix the dial plates.

"*Sixth* – To repair and paint the outside completely. The whole to be done in conformity with the plan accompanying this report.

"They are also of the opinion that it is expedient and recommend to the Parish to alter, repair and improve the inside of the Meeting House as follows viz:

"*First* – To make an entirely new arrangement of the pulpit, pews, galleries and seats and it is therefore expedient and necessary that all the pews should be taken up and that a reasonable indemnity should be allowed to the owners of the [203] pews, the amount of this indemnity to be ascertained by three disinterested appraisers appointed by the Parish and to be paid out of the Parish treasury as soon as may be after the sale of the new pews.

"*Second* – To make a porch at the western end by running a partition across at about fourteen feet from the end. This porch to contain two flights of stairs to the gallery.

"*Third* – To plaster the inside of the House furred out as far as the posts now project and arched overhead.

"*Fourth* – To build a new pulpit at the eastern end of the house of a fashionable form.

"*Fifth* – To build pews on two alleys running from the entrance at the west end to an alley crossing the east end in front of the pulpit, having a double row of pews between the two principal alleys, and a single row against the north and south

---

[31] This book of architectural plans is still in the First Parish Church archive.

sides and also a single row against the east end and reserving a convenient space for two stoves.

"*Sixth* – To finish and paint the inside of the house in a handsome manner, including a gallery at the west end sufficient to accommodate the choir and to contain some pews and some free seats and also to provide for warming the house. All to be done in conformity with the plan aforementioned excepting that the number and width of the pews may be varied if necessary.

[204] "The committee are also of the opinion and recommend to the parish to appoint a committee of five persons to make the foregoing alterations, improvements and repairs and to cause the whole house to be completely and handsomely finished at their discretion conformably to the foregoing directions and according to the plan as before stated.

"To authorize and request the parish treasurer to borrow from time to time such sums of money on account of the parish as may be necessary to defray the expense of the alterations, improvements and repairs not exceeding in the whole the sum of six thousand dollars and that the prudential committee of the parish draw orders in favor of the building committee or other persons as may be necessary to defray the expense and the treasurer to be authorized to pay said drafts out of the money which he shall borrow on account of the parish.

(signed) "Robt Rantoul

"Beverly April 7th, 1835 William Leech

"Saml Endicott

"Josiah Lovett 2nd

"Charles Stephens

"Mark Knowlton

"Edward Ford."

The foregoing report was drawn up by me, and I believe it gave very general satisfaction and was one of the means of promoting a unanimity of action so necessary in parish affairs.

Names of Parish Clerks [205]

The following is a list of the clerks of the First Parish from 1718 when the records were separated from those of the town to 1849 inclusive:

Robert Woodberry	4 years	John Ober	17 years
Robert Hale	5 years	John Cleaves	2 years
Israel Wood	13 years	Joseph Foster	1 year
James Lovett	2 years	Caleb Wallis	3 years
Joseph Wood	19 years	William Ober	3 years

Benjamin Lovett, Jun.	2 years	Benjamin Cleaves	2 years
John Lovett 4th	1 year	Moses Brown	1 year
Francis Smith	1 year	William Hazeltine	2 years
Joseph Rea	1 year	Larkin Thorndike	5 years
Livermore Whittrage	6 years	Robert Rantoul	42 years from 1808 to 1849 inclusive

The number of clerks is 20 for 132 years averaging 6 3/5 years to each. I have continued to be reelected until 1858.

For some three or four years after the incorporation of the Precinct of Salem & Beverly when a part of the town of Beverly was taken as a part of the Precinct, the Parish proceedings of the First Parish were recorded in the town book of records and this practice was continued until 1718 when the records of the Parish were begun in a separate book. Robert Woodberry was clerk of the town and of the parish. These offices were afterwards frequently held by the same person, though the records were kept in separate books.

[206] In November 1856, the gallery at the west end of the meeting house was altered by taking away the beam in front of the organ and extending the frescoing to the west end. The two half windows were enlarged at that end to double their size. The sitting bench was removed, and chairs substituted for the chairs and four pews, that is two at each end of the front of the gallery, fitted for sale.

These alterations are made under the superintendence of Seaward Lee, Warren Prince and Israel W. Wallis a committee chosen by the parish for the purpose, the standing parish committee having declined the service. In consequence of these alterations the usual meetings in the meeting house were suspended on Sunday the 23rd of November 1856 but were on that day held in the Vestry.

Social Library [207]

In 1802 I, in connection with others, got up a subscription for the establishment of a social library of 132 shares at six dollars each, that is five dollars a first and one dollar soon afterwards, making the sum 792 dollars. This sum was expended for the purchase of books under the direction of Nathan Dane, Joshua Fisher, Thomas Davis and Joseph McKean. Thomas Stephens was appointed clerk & treasurer which offices he held for some five or six years when he declined further service and I was chosen for twenty-nine years when I declined a re-election. Since which time I have had no concern in its management.

At this time, it is difficult to realize what was the utility of this establishment at its commencement, and for several years afterwards. Then, books were comparatively scarce and dear, now they are cheap and plenty. I rank this institution as among my most beneficial services for the public and as resulting from a conviction that I was performing a good service for myself and my fellow citizens. To encourage its establishment, Nathan

Dane & Israel Thorndike subscribed for twelve shares each, and several others subscribed liberally. For many years N. Dane was one of the trustees and took much of the management of it upon himself. The original number of shareholders was seventy-two. This number has since increased but without any increase of the aggregate number of shares. By a vote of the town the library was kept in the Town Hall and is still kept there, having been removed from the old to the new hall.

[208] I have from time to time given money, books and pamphlets to this Library. I think that this collection of books may be a nucleus around which a more generous and liberal supply may at some future time be gathered. It wants the particular attention of some enterprising individual who has a taste for reading himself and who feels strongly the desire of promoting reading among others to set about a revival of that interest which was felt by many at its first days. The room now appropriated to it in the new Town Hall is spacious and well finished and is used without expense, unless it be for fuel when it is opened which is on one evening in every week.

Some public spirited young man may appear who will have somewhat of the zeal and ardour which actuated several, nearly a half a century ago, in founding this Library and by devoting himself to the object may make it what it should be, in consequence of the growth of the town, an object of interest, of ornament and of general utility. Nothing is wanting but a generous effort.

In April 1851, a motion was made for improving the library but nothing effectual was ever done. In 1852 the library belonging to the First Church was removed to the social library room from the vestry. This was done in pursuance of a vote of the brethren of the church with the view of placing the books in a more accessible situation that they might be more generally read. The proprietors of the library to be allowed the use of them in conjunction with the members of the church.

[209] January 1853: I presented to the library forty-two volumes of United States documents which I had collected and purchased from 1834 to 1849.

At a town meeting held on the 13th of March 1854, the subject of establishing a town library was considered and referred to a large committee but at the adjournment of the meeting their report which was in favor was indefinitely postponed.

June 1854: I presented to the library three large octavo volumes bound in leather of the debates in the Massachusetts convention of 1853.

September 23rd: I presented to the library nine volumes of the Common School Journal from 1839 to 1847 inclusive.

March 1st, 1855: I presented to the library ten volumes of the Advocate of Peace.

March 12th, 1855: The Town voted to appropriate one hundred dollars towards establishing a Town library. At the adjournment of this meeting they voted a sum as large as should be procured by subscription but not exceeding five hundred dollars and trustees were chosen viz;

Richard Palmer Waters

William Endicott Jun.

Osgood Pierce

Charles W. Galloupe

Charles Haddock

These gentlemen have set about the business in earnest and I think their efforts will be attended with success.

[210] At the last annual meeting of the proprietors of the social library, on the first Monday in April 1855, it was voted that the trustees of the town library with regard to the union of the two libraries and if necessary to call a proprietor's meeting to act on their doings.

May 9th, 1855: I began the subscription for the town Library with one hundred dollars and Doct. Ingalls Kitteridge followed me with the same sum on the 10th of May. Afterwards William Larrabee, Charles W. Galloupe, William Endicott Jun., Augusta Ober, George W. Abbot, Edward Burley, Samuel Haskell of N.Y., F.B. Woodberry subscribed of smaller sums.

In July 1855, the proprietors of the social library voted to deposit the library with the town library.

In July 1855, the town voted to appropriate the room now used by the social library and the adjoining room now used by the sessions to the to the use of the town library.

The subscribers for fifty dollars each are Richard P. Waters, Charles G. Loring, Franklin Dexter, Franklin Haven.

The subscribers for twenty-five dollars each are W.C. Boyden, Wm Endicott, Andrew J. Leech, Phillip English, Charles Davis, John T. Baker, Austin D. Kilham, Daniel Hildreth, John Wilson, John I. Green, Wm. H Allen, Wm Decker, Richard Rickett, James Bryant, John Pickett, John P. Webber, William Porter, Edward Meacam, Joseph Wilson, Benj. Wallis Jr., Charles Haddock, Rob G. Bernett, Augustus N. Clarke, [210.1] Benj. Cole, Warren Filters, Charles S. Giddings, Samuel Porter, Wm. H. Lovett, Amos Lefavour, Isaac W. Becker, Rufus Putnam, C.T. Thayer, Josiah L. Foster, Jacob T. Woodberry, John P. Webber Jun.

March 3rd, 1856: I gave to the Town Library fifty-two bound volumes of Massachusetts Documents from 1812 to 1854. There is a volume of House documents for 1847 wanting to make the series complete for the later part of the time.

June 1858: I gave four additional volumes, unbound.

August 6th, 1856: The printed catalogue of the town library is received, the want of which has delayed the opening of the library to the public for some weeks.

Saturday September 20th, 1856: The town library was opened at 2 o'clock this afternoon for the first time for general use. I attended at that time with my daughter Hannah who then subscribed the regulations and took out the 2nd volume of memoirs of Sidney Smith. I subscribed the regulations on the 17th of September. The library contains over 3000 volumes, including about 700 volumes [210.2] which were formerly the social library and about 200 volumes now belonging to the First Church library. There was a goodly number of persons to take books at the opening and there were about 200 volumes taken out in the afternoon and evening. This propitious beginning induces the belief that it's utility will be great.

Saturday October 11th, 1856: Up to this date there have been about 800 volumes delivered from the library.

[210.3] The trustees of the town library having refused to receive the social library as a deposit, a meeting of the proprietors of the social library was held on Saturday evening, the 6th day of October 1855, when it was voted with one dissentient after a protracted discussion that the whole property of the social library (after the debts were paid) should be given to the Town library. I attended the first proprietors meeting of the social library in 1802 and I attended this meeting which will probably be the last, October 6th, 1855. I have attended about two thirds of the annual meetings of the proprietors. There is only one, beside myself of the original proprietors living in Beverly viz Livermore Whittridge. There are three others living in the other towns viz Nathaniel Goodwin in Plymouth, Abner Chapman in Malden and Josiah Batchelder in Falmouth, Maine. At the last meeting, there was a considerable amount of effort on the part of some to get a vote of the proprietors to sell the property and dissolve the corporation but notwithstanding the arguments of some leading individuals this was overruled by a large majority and the final vote to give was passed by yeas & nays, there being more than 40 voters represented by proxy. C.T. Thayer, Luke Morgan and myself were the principal advocates for giving and Edward Rowsland and Thomas Pickett for selling.

School Committee – Schools [211]

In the spring of the year 1816, I attended the School Committee in visiting most of the public schools in the town. I was not then a member of the committee but undertook this voluntary service with a view of acquiring a knowledge of the state of the schools and encouraging a disposition to visit them on the part of others by my example. Previously to 1816 I had taken an interest in the schools and had occasionally visited one or more of them with Abiel Abbot, chairman of the committee but I did not give any systematic attention to them until that year. October 31st, 1816: I addressed a letter to A. Abbot as follows:

"Dear Sir:

"In the course of the last spring I attended the school committee in visiting most of the public schools. My observation led to the opinion that some small reward to be bestowed at the visitation of the committee upon those scholars who had made the greatest proficiency in their studies and at the same time had maintained a reputation for good morals would have a tendency to excite a greater degree of emulation among the scholars and promote their improvement in knowledge and virtue. With this I take the liberty of offering to the committee a parcel of books, (ten or eleven copies of Mason on Self Knowledge) one for each school in order if they think proper to try the experiment they may be used for that purpose the approaching season. At the same time permit me to say that I shall be perfectly satisfied with the better judgment of the committee should they decide that it is inexpedient to accept the above measure."

The experiment was tried with these books in the spring of 1817, but the committee were of the [212] opinion that it was inexpedient to repeat the measure. I continued to visit the schools occasionally with the committee until I was in 1818 chosen a member. Since that time, I have considered it a special duty to visit the schools. I have been re-elected a member of the committee to this time, with the exception of some one or two years when I was left off. I have served about ---[32] years. I have never considered myself as entitled to take the lead on this committee as I have always been associated with one or more persons whose early education as well as their talents and acquirements qualified them for precedence. Most of the time A. Abbot and C.T. Thayer have been chosen chairmen, but not always without jealousy on the part of some other of the clerical members of the committee. I doubt however, whether there have been any clerical members since A. Abbot was appointed who would have bestowed so much time and labor as he and C.T. Thayer have done during the long course of years in which they have respectively served. A. Abbot served from 1804 to 1828 a period of twenty-four years during which time the schools rose from a great degree of depression to a very fair standing. C.T. Thayer has served in the same office with assiduity from 1834 to this time fourteen years but has been a member of the committee from 1830 to this time. In 1855, he declined a reelection. The intermediate years between the decease of A. Abbot and the year 1834, David Oliphant performed with fidelity the duties appertaining to the place of chairman until his [213] removal from the town. I have endeavored to aid and assist the respective chairmen in the performance of their arduous duties and have also endeavored to perform whatever service seemed to devolve upon me in a secondary capacity. My defect of hearing has inclined me to leave the committee, but other consideration shave induced me to remain although I am sensible of the diminution of my usefulness from the infirmities connected with age. During the period which is included in the foregoing history of school service, I have served as one of the prudential committee of the grammar school district for 1825, 1826 and 1827. In this office, I was principal and had much labor and care in commencing the district school in 1825 and its continuance afterwards Rufus Putman kept the school at its commencement and he has since become a very distinguished instructor in Salem where he is now in office as principal of the Bowditch (English High) School.

Mrs. Mary Weld and Miss. Sarah D. Cox kept the primary school. They are now not engaged in school keeping.

I have in the year previous to this time (March 1849) visited all the district schools within the town three times and several of them more including the spring examinations, all of which I have attended. I have made a greater effort the past year under the impression that I have arrived at that age when I should feel strongly impressed with the idea that my time is short and that I should do whatever belongs to me to do quickly.

[214] I thank that the common schools in this town have risen very considerably and that the last examinations justify the opinion that they are in a progressive state of improvement. The improvement in school houses as been very manifest. Within my recollection every school house has been either rebuilt or re-modeled. In the south district, there have been two new houses the present one is the arranged finished and furnished of

---

[32] Rantoul scratched thru his writing.

any in town. Briscoe Hall has been remodeled and is now well fitted for three schools of different grades.

July 1849, I have again visited all the public school in town. Some of them have very good female teachers and some indifferent ones. There are 14 public schools now in operation. That is one in each of 7 districts. 2 in the south district. In addition to these are the Beverly Academy kept by Teacher Lefavour and several schools kept by females for small children. J Lefavour has about 40 pupils and had a female assistant Miss Alice Penidges has a large school. Miss Mary F. Weld has a smaller number. Of the others I cannot speak, having no acquaintance with them. September 1849; I have visited 12 of the public schools a second time, since July 1849.

[215] December 20th, 1849: Yesterday, I completed my visitation of the public schools now keeping, saving a small school kept by a female in a private room in Bass river district, of about 20 small children. I have walked the whole distance to and from each school house. In returning form the Rial Side school I passed over the top of Brown's Hill, being the highest land in town. From this hill, there is an extensive view of the surrounding country as well as of the sea. This is probably the last time that I shall enjoy this view. I, returning from the Dodge's new school I passed over the top of Brimble Hill, which is the second in height in town. From this there is a fine view of Wenham Pond or Wenham Lake as it has been called since Ice has been largely cut and carried away from it, for use, to various parts of the American continent as well as to other parts of the world. It had been for sale in the City of London and has been presented to Queen Victoria. The surface of this pond measures about 320 acres. From this hill, there is an extensive view of the hills in Ipswich and Rowley and when there was a high steeple on the Ipswich Meeting House, near the Court House, it could be seen from this hill, but now I could not distinguish any object that would determine the exact location of the compact part of Ipswich. It is many years since I last before this, visited this hill.

[216] There is no public school now keeping in the South District, but there is a private school, kept by William E. Phillips, who last taught the public school there. The public schools are generally doing pretty well this winter. Some of them not so well as last winter and others better. The teachers are mostly from Dartmouth and Waterville Colleges. The Rial Side teacher is from Middleton, has been 10 weeks only at the Westfield Normal School & has not been at college.

The Dodge's Row teacher is a young man from Topsfield with moderate attainments but with great assiduity is successful. I made short addresses to all of the schools kept by male teachers. In some of them where I found there were some boys disinclined to attend to grammar and geography I stated my own school experience of more than sixty years ago when grammar and geography were not taught at all in the East town school in Salem where I then went to school. That the charge in common school learning had since then been gradually improving and that the idea entertained by some parents that as they when young did not attend to those studies therefore it was not necessary for their children to attend to them now is fallacious, in as much as their children are to come into life with a community better taught than when they the parents came into society and therefore their children should have the same advantages at school which others of the same rank now enjoy, so that they may stand upon an equality with their associates when they leave school.

[217] The long walks I have taken in visiting the schools this month (December 1849) have proved less fatiguing than at some other times, but I have been particular in choosing pleasant weather and dry hard ground for the time of my visits.

On the 20th December 1849 I visited the private school kept in the South District School house by Wm. E. Phillips, whole number 51, present 44. Order not so good as in some of the public schools. Writing books neat and some good writing. Some attend to drawing. The school did not appear so much better than the public school as I expected from the more select character of the scholars. I expected more exact order- closer application to study and more promptness in recitation.

December 27th, 1849: I visited the small school kept by Miss Wilson in the Bass River District which completes my annual visitation of the public schools. I walked to and from this school being about five miles in the whole.

March 8th, 1850: I have attended the examination of all the public schools now kept, excepting Miss Wilson but have rode to the distant schools with Rev C.T. Thayer. The whole number examined between the 22nd of February and the 8th of March inclusive is thirteen of which I have attended twelve.

July 1850: I have visited all the summer schools since their commencement for this season.

[218] March 7th, 1851: I have visited in the course of the last winter thirteen of the public schools one or more times each. I have attended the examination of sixteen of the public schools being the whole number and the largest number ever kept at one time in this town. The schools presented at this examination a better appearance than I have known them to do at any time heretofore. The attendance and attention of the Prudential committees without an exception was highly commendable. The presence of the parents and friends in every instance was ample. The order was good. The children clean and neat in their persons and apparel. The rooms were neat and clean and, in many instances, were dressed with evergreens and ornamented with artificial flowers. Singing is attended to in all the schools and in some there is a good degree of taste and skill manifested. The report of the School Committee was this year for the first time printed in the second number of the Beverly Citizen. The first newspaper published here.

June 4, 1851 I have this day completed my visits to the summer school for this year, fifteen in number. I rode to the farms and part of the distance in returning and went on the coach to Levi Dodge's corner to visit the Dodge's Row school (and walked all the rest)

In the course of the winter preceding the annual March meeting of 1854 I visited all the public schools in town excepting the Rial Side school to which I walked by & found that it was not in session and rode back. I soon afterwards gave notice that I should not be a candidate for re-election and at a meeting of the committee March 13th, 1854, voted me thanks on action of C.T. Thayer. This vote was printed in the Beverly Citizen of March 18, 1854.

William Burley's Legacy for Teaching Poor Children [219]

William Burley by his will gave to the towns of Ipswich and Beverly, fifty dollars per year to each for ten years to be applied for the instruction of poor children in reading and in the principles of the Christian religion. In 1822, December 22 William Burley died aged 72 years. In 1824, a committee was appointed of which I was the chairman to apply this legacy according to the directions of the donor. The plan adopted by the committee was to find out fifty poor children, from every part of the town, and induce their parents to send them to such a school for little children in their neighborhood as they chose. The committee agreeing to pay one dollar for one quarter's schooling for each child. School mistresses whose terms were higher than one dollar per quarter to favor this charity, invariably took such poor children as came to them for one quarter of the fixed price. The details of the administration of this fund devolved very much on me and this led me to visit all the female schools for the instruction of small children, where any of these poor children were sent. Before the end of the quarter I visited each school and paid the instructor for the quarter's schooling so that I had an opportunity of visiting and observing the state of most of the schools for young children kept within the town for ten consecutive years. These visits I almost invariably made on foot though it was necessary to go as far as the east farms and to the upper parish meeting house.

[220] The paper and vouchers relating to the management of this fund are wrapped in a separate bundle and are among my papers. These visitations continued for such a length of time, are among the means which have led to much improvement in this class of schools. The manner in which this money was employed led to no individual distinctions between the poor and others as would have been the case if separate and distinct schools had been established with this money. The town of Ipswich received at once the whole sum of five hundred dollars and with some other monies established a permanent fund, the income of which is to be applied to the same object in perpetuity.

My particular attention to the administration of this charity for the space of ten years is one among my public labors which gives me some satisfaction in the recollection in my old age. I recommend it to my grandchildren to avail themselves of opportunities of public usefulness in humble spheres. Many, who despise small things pass through life looking for opportunities to undertake great things, which not finding they suffer very much mortification and disappointment which would have been prevented by endeavoring to do the good which from time to time presented itself, heartily and truly however small it might seem in the eyes of the unreflecting. Let it be a maxim to do promptly and earnestly the duty that at the time presents itself not waiting for great occasions which rarely are found by those who seek them.

Private School Academy [221]

Beverly Academy, Washington Street, 1833 by Robert's daughter, Charlotte Rantoul.

In February 1833, a private school was projected by a number of persons, who associated for the purpose. They soon afterwards bought a lot of land on Washington street, containing about a quarter of an acre, and built a school house there on the land and building costing nearly one thousand dollars. The associates appointed a committee to manage the school of which I was the chairman. The school was organized and continued mostly under my supervision, until January 30, 1835, when it was incorporated into an academy and I being elected one of the trustees, and by them chosen chairman, it was still continued, principally, under my supervision, having the advice from time to time of my associates.

I thus continued to take the principal charge of this institution for eleven years form its first commencement, when an event occurred which terminated my connection with it in a different manner from what would have been agreeable to me or honorable to those who concocted it.

The immediate occasion of this disruption; although there were some anterior causes, was that the trustees in appointing a successor to Edward Appleton, gave the preference to John Nourse over James Woodberry Boyden as the instructor. To countervail this appointment, three of the proprietors, who were dissatisfied set about an intrigue, and finding that by purchasing some shares of proprietors, who were from [222] various motives, willing to sell, they could secure a majority against the trustees, they bought shares enough to give them the control. In June 1844, at the annual meeting, at which I did not attend, anticipating the result of the previous movements, I sent a letter addressed to the proprietors declining being a candidate for the office of trustee. Others of the obnoxious trustees declined or were superseded, and the Academy was put under a different set of trustees, including some of the former board, who as soon as practicable removed Mr. Nourse and appointed Mr. Boyden as instructor. After Mr. Boyden had kept until he was desirous of leaving to study law, Mr. Nourse was restored to the place and continued until he chose to go into one of the public schools in Boston. Issachar Lefavour was next appointed, and in 1848 the proprietors sold the land and building to him during the eleven years which I served as chairman of the committee of trustees, I performed much labor and endured much enmity, feeling the responsibility of the office which I held, and it would have been pleasant to me to have finished my connection more amicably.

The names of the three persons who were the principal conductors of this, to me, unpleasant transaction I shall not record. I have the satisfaction of reflecting that without pecuniary compensation, I performed eleven years' service (in my own estimation) with fidelity, integrity and uprightness.

[223]The instructors in this institution were Abiel Abbot of Wilton N.H., Charles G. Peabody of Farnsworth N.H., Edward Bradstreet of Newburyport and Thomas Barnard West of Salem; together with those before named. The females were Mary R. Peabody, Ann Wales Abbot, Mary E. Williams, Mary Thorndike Weld and some others.

This school was intended to furnish the means of a superior grade of education than could be found at that time in the public schools. Since its establishment there has been a progressive improvement in the public schools, particularly in the Grammar district where there are three grades of schools and the highest grade is almost equal to the Academy. From 1833 to this time I have had one or more of my children or grandchildren attending the Academy which increased my personal interest in its success. Since I ceased to be a trustee and until Mr. Lefavour purchased the estate and conducted the school upon his own account, I entirely disconnected myself from the school, but since Mr. Lefavour has become sole proprietor I have attended his examinations and addressed the scholars. The following is a copy of the letter which I sent to the proprietors:

To the proprietors of the Beverly Academy, Beverly, June 3rd, 1844.

Gentlemen – For a period of eleven consecutive years, since 1833, I have by your election been a member of the committee or trustees for the management of an institution, mainly intended for the education of our own children [224] but insubordination to this principal object, also for the education of the children of others, so far as compatible with its chief design and during the whole of that period, it has been the pleasure of the respective boards to allow me to stand at their head. This situation has been attended with some labor, great responsibility and much anxiety. All this was cheerfully borne while I had the satisfaction of believing that I was contributing to the attainment of the great object of the institution, and in some good degree answering the expectations of those who place me in this responsible situation. During the last year events have occurred which have changed the aspect of the scene, and which call upon me to change my relation to it. A combination of circumstances, which, although strongly impressed upon my mind, I refrain from detailing, induce me to request that you will no longer consider me as a candidate for any office within the institution. I regret that I could not have been permitted to close my services under auspices more agreeable to my feelings, but at this same time I have the consolation of believing that in thus withdrawing my name from consideration I shall diminish the number of objects respecting which a collision of opinion might exist among the proprietors, and may hasten the time when feelings and views which now prevail will no longer disturb that harmony which is so essential to the prosperity of an institution that has already accomplished much good and which it is hoped is still destined to accomplish much more. I am, very respectfully, Gentlemen,

Your Obedt Serv't

Rob Rantoul

The proprietors voted not to accept the report of the trustees for the year ending in June 1844. Therefore, it does not appear on their records, although it was prepared with labor and contained a full statement of the proceedings with led to the difference.

Cherry Hill Farm School [225]

In 1837, a school was commenced in the upper Parish on the Cherry Hill Farm, and incorporated as the New England Christian Academy. The school was conducted on the manual labor system and during its continuance averaged about 60 pupils. Its preceptor, for most of the time was Joseph Henry Siewers. The Academy remained in operation less than two years and was stopped from pecuniary circumstances. I was chosen one of the trustees but without any expectation that I should take an active part in its management. I however gave some money ($25, 26 volumes and pamphlets) and some books to the institution and I also visited the school several times attended the annual examination and made a short address to the pupils. This school was gotten up by members of what is called the "Christian denomination". The effort was laudable, though premature, and injudicious in as much as it attempted a great and good object with pecuniary means and patronage altogether insufficient. They contracted for the purchase of the Cherry Hill farm, built a school house, incurred expense in providing furniture and fixtures for boarding and employing the pupils, much of which was lost on the discontinuance of the establishment. Several suffered by this failure, among whom was Edwin M. Stone, the minister of the upper parish who had undertaken to board the pupils. Perhaps the failure was hastened by a sudden revulsion about that time in regard to the money market, which occasioned great embarrassment in business transactions.

South School District, New School House, Bibles [226]

In 1809, I took an active part in the establishment of an additional school district to be taken from the Grammar School district, this movement resulted in the formation of what is called the South District, being southerly of the entrance of Bartlett street from Cabot street. This district then built a brick school house which was then adequate to their wants, but in 1848 it was thought to be insufficient and a larger one with the improved furniture of the present day was erected on an eminence near the site of the first. This second house was publicly dedicated on the fifth day of October 1848, at which time I attended by invitation and made the introductory speech which was followed by most of the clerical members of the school committee, singing with instrumental music and prayers, made a part of the services. The room was comfortably filled with hearers.

In the winter and spring of 1839, by request of the school committee I delivered an address on the subject of public schools in the upper meeting house, the Farms meeting house, Briscoe Hall and the Cove school house. This address occupying more than an hour in its delivery, required much time in its preparation and probably aroused some degree of attention to the many facts which it contained.

[227] July 25th, 1851: I purchased ten octavo Bibles and had them lettered with the names of the several school districts and made a present of one copy to each district. I had frequently observed that the teachers had on their desks or tables a copy of the bible, of their own. Sometimes of a very diminutive size adopted to the pocket rather than for use in the devotional exercises of the school and I thought that one of a proper size should be furnished and kept for general use in each school which led me to adopt this course to supply the want.

December 19th, 1851: I have this day visited Dodge's Row and Bass River schools with completes my winter visitation of the schools, which I have accomplished on foot with the exception of a ride of about a mile on my way home from the farms, Bass River and Rial Side. I have been but very little fatigued not so much as last winter. Seventeen schools have been visited. They are all doing pretty well.

At the March town meeting in 1852, Mr. Thayer and myself were not chosen committee members but at the adjournment on the first Monday in April we were chosen to supply vacancies. Mr. Thayer had served on the committee since his settlement in 1830 and for most of the time as chairman and has done very much more of the labor of the committee than any other individual and certainly deserved better treatment than this to be dropped.

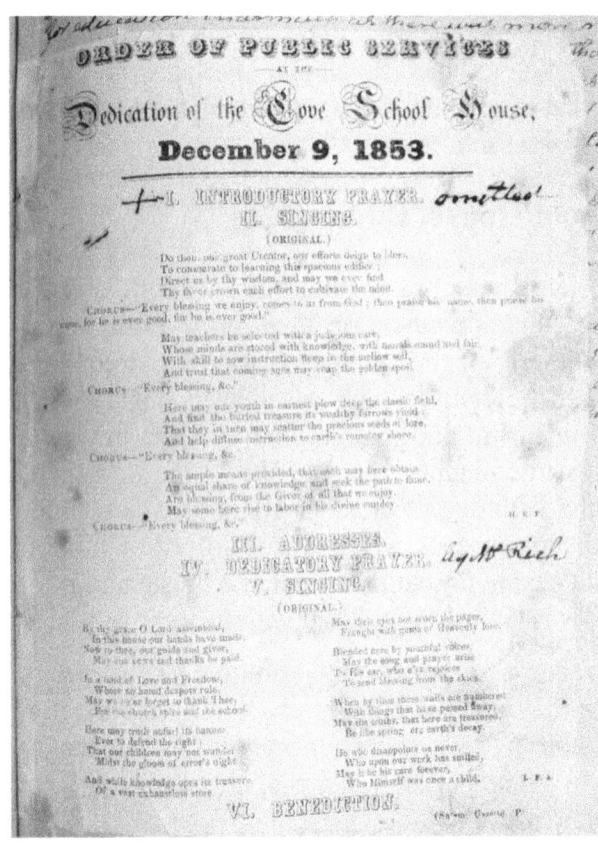

Order of public services
for the dedication of the Cove School, 1853.

[228] December 9th, 1853: In the afternoon of this day the new school house at the Cove on the easterly corner of Cross lane was dedicated. It has two commodious rooms in the lower story and one very spacious room in the second story. There are two flights of stairs and large entries above and below. It is handsomely finished within and without and furnished in accordance with the new style of accommodation. On this occasion, the upper story room was filled to overflowing. The larger number were females. The services commenced with singing by a select choir with some instruments. Then a hymn composed by a Lady of the district for the occasion was sung. Joseph Abbot, chairman of the school committee then addressed the meeting in some pertinent remarks in regard to ventilation, corporal punishment in school and other matters connected with schools. He requested me to follow him which I did with some historical reminiscences in relation to schools from the earliest settlement in New England to the present day. This I followed with remarks in regard to the duty of parents in connection with the public schools. Next Rufus Putnam spoke and then C.T. Thayer. Mr. Rich made a few remarks in relation to the study of the bible in schools and then prayed. Singing of a hymn composed by another Lady of the district followed and then a benediction was pronounced by C.T. Thayer. The tunes were composed in town so that in the branch of music it was all original. The day was very fine, and everything was conducted with great propriety and apparently to the general satisfaction of the inhabitants of the district.

[229] R Putnam advanced the idea that the introduction of Machinery in the arts had increased the demand for education in as much as there was more mind required in the use of machinery than without it so that a less proportion of manual labor is required to accomplish many times as much and increase in a greater proportion of mental power to the produce the increase results called for more education. This remark he strengthened by his own observation in the High School of Salem. When he first took charge of the school, parents found it difficult to procure suitable places for boys who had gone through the regular course of study but lately he found that there was such an increase of demand for well-educated boys that some were induced to leave school before they had completed their regular course of study.

[230] June 1852: I have this summer visited all the schools save for the Bass River district. I went to the school house of that district for the purpose but found it closed and

the school suspended by the sickness of the teacher, Mary Elizabeth Worsley. It is not intended to resume it this summer. Generally, the schools are doing well.

In the winter of 1852 & 1853, I visited all the schools. In the summer of 1853 I visited all the schools except Dodges Row. It being closed early I did not find a convenient time to visit it. I was in attendance on the Massachusetts Convention to revise the constitution from May to August which deprived me of the usual opportunities of visiting schools. In the winter of 1853 1854 I visited all the public schools save the one at Rial Side. The school house to which I walked but the school was not in session and I rode home. In March 1854, I attended the examinations in the Grammar District and in the South District only. In addressing the intermediate school in the Grammar District, I gave public notice that I should no longer be a candidate for re-election to the school committee and in consequence C.T. Thayer made a eulogistic speech and Rev. W. Coffin also in prayer commended me to God. I addressed the primary school in the South District on the 10th of March which finishes my public labors of about thirty-five years.

The proceedings of the School Committee upon my retiring from office was all that could be expected as complimentary to me. I had intended to withdraw from the committee some few years sooner, but circumstances occurred from time to time that seemed to me to render it inexpedient. I feel sensibly the importance of seasonable withdrawal from public offices of every description and hope I shall not delay in any case beyond the time of usefulness.

[230 ½] Copy of the vote of the School Committee

"Voted that the School Committee having heard with deep regret that the Hon. Robert Rantoul declines a reelection to the Board, cannot in justice to their own feelings allow the occasion to pass without some expression of their sentiments on his retirement from an office in which some of them have been so long associated with him, and all have found their association with him in its important duties so pleasant and valuable. They would, therefore, hereby express and leave on their records a cordial testimony of the persevering fidelity and warm and active interest with which for thirty-five years he has devoted himself to the schools and the cause of education generally among us, and, while they confidently trust that his entire sympathy and whose counsel will be continued to this great interest, they assure him that he will ever be attended with their sincerest and best wishes for his welfare.

"Joseph Abbot, Chairman

"March 13th, 1854"

Overseer of the Poor – Work House [231]

The Poor House built in 1803 served as Beverly's Poor Farm until 1948.

In the spring of 1804, I was chosen an Overseer of the Poor. This office had previously been exercised by the Selectmen, but a workhouse having been now erected, in to which the poor were removed in April 1804, it was thought best to separate these offices and Thomas Davis, John Dyson, Eleazer Wallis, Joseph Wood and myself were chosen.

I was much younger than the others and was appointed their clerk. I have served in the office of an overseer from that time to this being more than forty-four years. Some of these years my election has been opposed but in most it has taken place without any opposition. Within a dozen years past, a set of political partisans in their zeal to exclude all those who belonged to the Democratic party from all the town offices with reference to my political opinions, set on foot an intrigue to exclude me from this office, but upon communicating their views to others of their party they did not find that co-operation which they desired and therefore they let their scheme drop for that time. During the time I have been in this office I have been associated with Thomas Davis 7 years, John Dyson 3 years, Eleazer Wallis 2 years and Joseph Wood 1 year and Andrew Ober Senior 1 year, Samuel Ingersol 2 years, Nathaniel Goodwin 14 years, Isaac Rea 8 years, Thomas Stephens 10 years, Francis Lamson Junior 10 years, Israel Trask 3 years, Josiah Foster 3rd 6 years, Nathaniel Safford 1 year, Nathaniel Lamson 7 years, Samuel P. Lovett 3 years, Abraham Edwards 10 years, John Safford 26 years, Oliver Ober 3 years, William Thorndike 1 year, Henry Larcom 6 years, [232] Amos Shelden 8 years, James Dowling 8 years, Asa Woodberry 5 years, Stephens Baker 14 years, Ezra Dodge 7 years, Israel Trask 21 years, Andrew Ober (son of the first named Andrew Ober) 12 years. 27 persons beside myself whose average time of service is 6 17/100 years. Thirteen of them are dead. In each case where it will apply the current year, 1848, is included.

During the time of my service there have been three different masters of the house, viz; Charles Dennis who after 20 years' service resigned in 1824 and died in 1830 aged 63 years, Benjamin Lamson, who was appointed in 1824, and died of consumption in 1831, and Francis Lamson who was appointed in 1831 and is still in office. (resigned April 1853)

There has been a gradual improvement in the habits, manners and moral character of the subjects in the Work House. This is particularly noticeable in regard to travelling, transient paupers. Formerly they were more filthy, affected with vermin, coarse, uncleanly, brutal and profane than they have been of late years. In many of these respects similar changes have taken place in the constant residents in the house. It is but little known that the Work House is in the nature of an Inn for the travelling beggars and paupers, of whom there are many of foreign extraction, whose usual resort for a lodging and resting place is the Work House. I have acted in great harmony with the twenty-seven persons above mentioned with perhaps one or two exceptions. One of which I will describe as it will throw some light on the early days of the temperance reform. In 1804 the first board of overseers consisted of four persons who had had no experience [233] whatever in regard to the management of public paupers and of one, viz; Joseph Wood, who had long been one of the Selectman, and for a considerable portion of the time chairman and principle manager of the paupers of the town. The Selectmen acting as overseers of the poor previously to 1804. At the meeting of the Overseers of the Poor in 1804 to establish the rules of diet the question arose respecting the allowance of spirituous liquors to the subjects of the workhouse. Mr. Wood entertained the opinion which at that time was very prevalent that persons who labored hard ought to be furnished with spirituous drinks and he had always acted in conformity with this opinion in all his transactions. He was then about 65 years of age, had been connected with the public affairs of the town for about thirty-five years preceding. He spoke strongly and decidedly in favor of allowing spirits to those men who labored out of doors, who were inmates of the Work House. He was my senior by almost forty years. I entertained a contrary opinion in regard to the allowance of spirits to paupers and was in favor of their total abstinence from them. I was strenuous in urging my views upon the overseers and perhaps the ardent desire I entertained to have the rule adopted according to my views might have led me beyond the modest restraint which was becoming in a young man, in collision with one so much his senior and of so much experience. Whether I was blamable or not, he became angry and said some things directed personally to me which hurt my feelings very much

[234] but I had enough of the self-command not to retort or to express any resentment and bore the attack patiently. Enough of the overseers concurred with me in opinion and the rule of total abstinence was then established and has always been maintained as the rule until this time though I must add that the rule was not so inflexibly enforced by the first master of the house as it should have been, but I know not of any infringement of it for the last twenty-four years. At the end of the first year, Mr. Wood declined a reelection to the office of Overseer of the Poor. He died in January 1808. I was much connected with him in public business until the end of his life and always before and after the occurrence above related, he treated me with great civility and kindness. Although I regretted the occurrence, yet I have rejoiced that I was enabled to bear this attack without discovering any resentful feelings and I have reason to believe that he afterwards was more civil and kind to me than he would have been had the disagreement never occurred. In 1807 all the first chosen overseers having withdrawn, (although Thomas Davis came in again afterwards) I began to act as Chairman and with the acquiescence of my associates I have continued so to do until this time. I drafted the reports of the overseers to the town from 1804 to this time so that I have prepared forty-four annual reports, some of them lengthy and the others confined to the statics of the year.

[235] When I first entered upon the duties of an Overseer of the Poor, my mind was very much engrossed by the subject of the public provision for the poor. There are certain principles which I adopted very early which time has only served to strengthen my convictions of their justness. I have always been of the opinion that aid by the public in relief of the wants of the poor should be very sparingly administered in as much as it almost

invariably diminishes self-respect and self-dependence and impairs the energy, industry and economy of the recipients. This effect is not confined to the immediate subjects but is very often entailed upon their posterity for many generations. So that whenever application is made for relief by a person in middle age without any special misfortune it will most frequently be found on examination that one or more of the parents or grandparents of the persons have been chargeable to the town. This case of hereditary pauperism has been strikingly exemplified by a certain family in this town of whom I recollect that Joseph Wood said that always as long as he had had any concerns in the care of the town's poor there had been one or more of that family chargeable. He had been a Selectman before 1770 and my own observation confirms that same fact from 1804 to this very time, November 1848. There are now three very aged persons of that family in the workhouse. Vague tradition carries back the same [236] fact to an indefinite time before 1770. There is a town record of a Picket (the family referred to) being a pauper in 1721. Another principle of the correctness of which I am persuaded is that injudicious relief bestowed, encourages others who without this example would refrain from applying for aid from the public to seek for it. I have found it generally to be the case that new overseers have conceived it to be their duty to seek out and encourage persons whom they thought stood in need of relief to receive it from the town and I have also found that often a few years' experience in the office they have become convinced of the error of this course and have become cautious. In the dispensation of the private charity the kind and well-disposed may, nay should seek diligently for those who need and who will be comforted encouraged and strengthened in their moral principles by the hand of charity. But I think that it is not the duty of the overseers to seek for objects of relief. Pauperism is a great evil in society and it may be increased or diminished in any town by the judicious or injudicious course pursued by the Overseers of the Poor. I think that any perseverance in the course which I have mentioned has been influential in restraining the increase of pauperism in this town and that although there has occasionally been a manifestation of disapprobation and dissatisfaction among a portion of the inhabitants yet that upon a retrospective view of the whole course I think it well receiving the approbation of the judicious and considerate part of the community.

[237] For the first three years of my service as an overseer, Thomas Davis was the chairman and he being desirous of being excused from the labor of the correspondence which then was much greater than it is now, I was appointed clerk, with the intent that I should perform that service and do the other writing which for the first year was considerable. For my services as Clerk for the first year I had an allowance of eight dollars and I might have had, though I am not certain of it, for two or three following years, since which I have received no pay for any labor or service for one connected with the duties of an overseer, although I have bestowed much time and pains in the performance of these duties. I have long entertained an opinion that it is inexpedient that Overseers of the Poor should be paid for their services. Among the many subjects of the workhouse during my long service as an overseer, I have received the expressions of gratitude form several while others have manifested jealousy, resentment and displeasure but I have long ago made up my mind that the only sure and certain reward to be expected in this life must arise from the consciousness of having performed our duty in whatever station we are called to act, we should therefore look to ourselves for our reward and not to those whom we have endeavored to serve. If they are grateful, we should thankfully enjoy it but not repine if

they should prove to be insensible to our kindness knowing that we shall have our reward for the smallest act of kindness bestowed upon any of our brethren.

[238] I trust that my labors in the department of the poor have not been unavailing to the good order, pecuniary advantage and moral improvement of the town but this I submit to the judgment of the public. I comment to my grandsons my example in the discharge of the duties of this office earnestly exhorting them to shun my errors but to act up to the principle of self-devotion and disinteredness at which I have aimed, although I confess many shortcomings, and which should actuate them in whatever public station they may in the course of providence be called out to do.

Upon the subject of intemperance my views have somewhat changed. I fortunately never learned to drink spirits but used to drink cider and beer habitually for a number of years and wine occasionally until about fifteen years ago, in March 1833. I adopted the principle of total abstinence from all intoxicating drinks and to this I have adhered to this day. In the management of the poor I have endeavored to carry out my convictions in regard to this subject. Intemperance is the most fruitful source of pauperism. I have from a careful examination found that about one half the adults that have been subjects of our workhouse have been made so mainly by intemperance and to this half of the adults if we add the children aged and infirm persons, whom these adults would have maintained had they not been intemperate we may with safety call it three quarters of all the subjects for the forty-four or five years which have passed since the workhouse was established.

[239] From 1804 to 1821 the Overseers of the Poor followed a practice which had been established in Salem for many years before our workhouse was erected used to commit by an order under the hands of any two or more of them, common drunkards and other disorderly persons to the workhouse without trial or examination and during their pleasure about 1821, this practice declared to be in violation of the Bill of Rights, by the Supreme Judicial Court in a case that came before them from some town not now recollected, since which none have been committed to the workhouse for crimes without a trial and conviction before a justice of the peace or some court. These trials almost always have been had before me. One hundred and twelve persons accused of drunkenness since the year 1821 have been sent to the workhouse in this town. The number of commitments for drunkenness has diminished somewhat but cases still occur occasionally. But it is not alone those who are thus committed who are there in consequence of drunkenness. Many who come there from want of the means of living are in that predicament from intemperance. Some of the insane persons are there from the same cause, so it is with some of the lame, sick and infirm, their maladies having been brought upon them by their intemperance.

Although generally intemperate drinking of intoxicating liquors manifestly shortens life, yet there are very [240] noticeable exceptions, of these, one has first occurred in the workhouse here. A man had died at the advanced age of 69, who for fifty years has been an habitual drunkard. Donald McDonald, a Scotchman, who died while belonging to the Boston alms house at the age of 104 years was for a long period and up to the time of his death a confirmed drunkard.

From a careful examination, I can with confidence say that one half of the <u>adult</u> persons who have been subjects of the workhouse since its establishment in 1804 have been so from intemperance directly and that another one quarter part have been so from intemperance indirectly. To this last class belong children who have been there because of the intemperance of their parents disenabling them to support their children. Aged parents because of the intemperance of their children disenabling them to support their aged or infirm parents. Wives abandoned by their drunken husbands as well as others who would have been supported by relatives of remote degree had not such relatives been intemperate.

I can recollect the degenerating influence in several families in this town in three generations. The grandfather being a "moderate drinker" through the earlier and middle part of his life, as he became old and his vigor diminished he became a "hard drinker" and when old age was upon him "he was occasionally overcome by liquor" and went to his grave with a doubtful reputation for sobriety. The son went through the same course [241] but with great rapidity so that at the age of forty, none scrupled to call him a drunkard. The grandson becomes initiated in the custom of drinking at an earlier age than his father or his grandfather and passing hastily through the same stages becomes a confirmed drunkard at twenty or twenty-five years of age. I think there are many families in which this has occurred and which persons of my age by a short reflection may bring to their minds.

In 1804, I drafted a set of rules for the government of the Work House. In this work, I was much aided by the rules of the Salem Work House, I might have said governed by them. In 1838, March, I revised these rules with more independence than I allowed myself in 1804, when I paid great deference to the Salem rules which then, in a manner, had become obsolete. The revised rules I think may endure longer than those first adopted. The Salem rules were too antiquated and being, in 1804, without experience I did not venture far upon my own opinion and knowledge in making alterations.

March 1851 Andrew Ober was left off as an Overseer and Samuel Downing Gently Standley was chosen in his room. I served with Andrew Ober fifteen years. March 1853 Henry Lamson and S.D.G. Standley declined and Aaron Dodge, Israel Trask 5th and Frederick W. Choate were chosen in their stead, so that there were six Overseers of the Poor for the year 1853.

[242] January 10, 1853 Francis Lamson gave notice that he should resign the office of Master of the Work House at the expiration of his present year which will be in the first part of April next, when he will have completed twenty-two years' service. He has left a favorable character for humanity and kindness to the subjects under his care. His activity and energy are now somewhat impaired by the infirmities of age. He has served with fidelity and faithfulness __. His wife, who died ___ [33] 1834 was remarkable for her energy, prudence and discretion. Since her decease Mr. Lamson has been assisted by his two daughters one of whom was married to John I. Baker a few years since and from that time he has depended on the aid of his youngest daughter Judith.

At an adjourned Town Meeting on Monday the 4th day of April 1853 an excitement was gotten up which resulted in the censure of Mr. Lamson and the Overseers of the Poor. The town appointed a committee who contrived to get an indictment by the Grand Jury against Mr. Lamson and the Overseers of the Poor on which they were arraigned and pleading not guilty the Indictment was continued two terms and then *nol pros*[34] and

---

[33] Rantoul left the date blank. Martha Lamson died on February 16, 1834 (Beverly VRs.)

[34] Nolle Prosequi –" case dropped"

payment of costs. At the March meeting 1854 the town voted to reimburse the expense to the Overseers and to Mr. Lamson.

In April 1853 Ebenezer Roy having been previously appointed took charge of the house as the successor of Francis Lamson.

In March 1854, I declined being a candidate for re-election. I have thus served fifty years and have written fifty annual reports. I wrote the reports while Thomas Davis was chairman as well as while I was chairman. Here endeth my labors in this branch of duty.

(for notes of thanks see page 146 ½)

[242½] List of the Overseers of the Poor of the town of Beverly from the time the poor were supported in a Work House, April 1804 to March 13, 1854:

Robert Rantoul	for fifty years
xThomas Davis	for seven years
x John Dyson	for three years
x Joseph Wood	for one year
x Andrew Ober, Sr.	for two years
x Samuel Ingersol	for two years
x Nathaniel Goodwin	for fourteen years, died 1859 86 years
x Isaac Rae	for eight years
x Thomas Stephens	for ten years
Francis Lamson, Jr.	for ten years
Israel Trask	for three years
x Josiah Foster, 3rd	for six years
Nathaniel Safford	for one years
x Nathaniel Lamson	for seven years
Samuel P Lovett	for three years
Abraham Edwards	for ten years
John Safford	for thirty-two years
x Oliver Ober	for three years
x William Thorndike	for one years
Henry Larcom	for eleven years
x Amos Shelden	for eight years
x James Dowling	for eight years
x Asa Woodberry	for five years
Stephens Baker	for twenty years
Ezra Dodge	for seven years
Israel Trask	for one year
Andrew Ober Jun.	for fifteen years
Samuel D.G. Standley	for two years
Aaron Dodge	for one year (for the year 1853)

Israel Trask, 5th   for one year (for the year 1853)
Frederick W. Choate   for one year (for the year 1853)

Those marked with X are dead, being 14; living 17.

Thomas Davis was chairman at the first and for one or two years afterwards. Robert Rantoul was chairman from thence until 1854. Mr. Davis while he was chairman induced R Rantoul to write the annual reports, so that the whole, fifty in number, were written by R Rantoul. By recurrence to the records of the Overseers of the Poor it will be found that R Rantoul has attended almost all the monthly meetings for fifty years and that he has also in his turn made almost every weekly visit belonging to his place and has made as many extra visits as were necessary from time to time, has for the whole time carried on the correspondence necessarily connected with the office, Mr. Davis always declining this part of the duty of the chairman.

I had intended for several years past to retire from the board of Overseers of the Poor if I should live to complete a half century of service. If I contemplated this with too much self-complacency I have received a wholesome rebuke in the very great mortification I have suffered from being called into court to answer to an indictment for malfeasance in office. This is the only instance in the course of my life when I have been called on to answer for any offence before any judicial tribunal whatever. Perhaps I felt too much pride in the circumstance of fifty successive annual elections to office and this rebuke was permitted to humble my pride. I hope that even this marked adverse circumstance of my life may have a wholesome influence upon my character. I was worried about it for about a whole year, but now (March 1854) have received by the votes of the town, at a very full annual town meeting, and after a full discussion, all the amends which I could expect to my wounded feelings from that source. These votes will be found on page 146½. The conduct of certain individuals in regard to this matter may be attributed in some to good motives, earnestly or inconsiderately followed and in others to a malignancy of feeling which when and wherever known and fairly understood will be appreciated so as to throw blame from the Overseers of the Poor upon those who have been most active and bitter in their malignity. Time will give its true coloring to the whole proceeding.

Had it not been for this unhappy occurrence I probably should not have received from a very full town meeting such approval and commendation of my official character. The town has done everything to make amends for the distress and suffering which I have endured by the course pursued by their committee chosen last April.

The advice I give to my grandsons is not to hold on to any office too long. If I had left the office one year sooner I should have escaped suffering, but I should not have received such flattering testimonies of gratitude for my public labors. God be praised that I have been enabled to do so much in my day and generation, for the public.

March 17, 1855: This day two of the Overseers of the Poor of Topsfield (Mr. Gould and another) called on me for advice about a pauper case. Since I have left this office, as well as before, I have in consequence of its being generally known that I had been in the office very many years, been called upon occasionally by town officers and others for the like purpose. I have endeavored to comply with their wishes so far as my defective memory would permit.

Application for Post Office [243]

In September 1806, after the decease of Asa Leech, post master in this town, I made an effort to obtain that office which I believe is one of only two instances in which I have personally sought for office from the United States government or from the State government in both of which I had the mortification of being disappointed. This has rendered me very cautious in seeking office. I have made it a point to wait until my friends thought it proper to seek for me, or till the office sought me. This course has given me many offices of trust, of honor and of usefulness but very few of pecuniary emolument. The request for the Post office was signed by the most influential class of people in this town and was worded as follows viz; "We the subscribers request the appointment of Mr. Robert Rantoul as Post Master in this town. Mr. Rantoul's situation is the best in town to accommodate the inhabitants and he is a man of integrity, punctuality and fidelity and has a handsome property and his business requires his being constantly at the office." This paper was written and circulated by Thomas Stephens. This was sent to Gideon Granger, Post Master General, September 13, 1806. I also procured a letter of favorable commendation from Rev. William Bentley of Salem and also from Doct. Manasseh Cutler of Hamilton who was then, or a short time before had been a Representative in Congress from Essex North District. But it was all to no avail. I was a Federalist and Doct. Josiah Batchelder Jr. was a Democrat and he applied to Jacob Crowninshield, who was then the Representative [244] of Essex South District who wrote to the Post Master General and immediately procured the office for Josiah Batchelder Jr. It was disposed of with reference to party politics which method of disposing of public offices was not then in such general use as at present and was therefore less expected. This instance of disappointment to myself may be useful to my grandsons. I do not desire them always to avoid office seeking but to be very considerate and reflect much upon its probable consequences before they enter upon it. To do nothing in relation to it but what is perfectly fair and honorable; then if they fail of success they will have nothing to embitter the recollection of their failure in the subsequent years of their life and if they succeed the enjoyment of the office will be blessed with the satisfaction that nothing has been done to procure it but what will commend itself to the candid judgment of the public and of appointments, and above all to their own consciences.

The Long Embargo - Leveling the Common [244]

The long Embargo began December 22nd, 1807 and was raised March 15, 1809; thus, it continued 1 year, 2 months and 21 days. This prostrated the cod fishery and the navigating interest of the town. In blasting the rock on the Common, when it was leveled as is hereafter mentioned, some intermixture of green field-spar was discovered and at a subsequent period, handsome specimens were obtained there and in Ives's land adjoining the Common. This was done by Rev Cornelius and others from Salem in 1824.

[245] In May 1808, pending the long embargo, Jonathan H. Lovett who then commanded the third regiment of militia got up a subscription of money and labor for leveling the Common or Training-field, which was then uneven and encumbered with a large ledge of rocks. He obtained 148 subscribers mostly from one day to six days labor and some money. A town meeting was held, and it was voted that it might be leveled, and a

committee was chosen to superintend it of which I was one. J.H. Lovett engaged in it with his usual ardor and expended much of his time and the use of his team and some money in its accomplishment. His excitement was excessive and injurious to his health. He ordered the Regiment out for training on the fourth of July and previous to their dismission at noon, he gave notice that he would in the afternoon go to work on the Common to finish its leveling and invited the soldiers to join in the labor. This extraordinary movement did not take very well. I then commanded the Light Infantry and before I dismissed them for dinner I told them that such of them as chose to go to work on the Common in the afternoon would be excused from training but that I should attend for training for such as would join me. In the afternoon, almost all of the company appeared on parade for training and the time was occupied in the usual exercises. In the meantime, J. H. Lovett was thrown by his horse and in consequence was <u>bled</u> very freely, by the Surgeon of the Regiment, Josiah Batchelder Jun. and was much relieved from his previous excitement.

[246] Being carried home, the captains of the respective companies disposed of them as they thought proper. There was no work done on the Common on that day, but subsequently it was finished, and it was railed in at the expense of the town. The subscription paper for this object in on file with miscellaneous papers for 1808. The Town's committee were Moses Brown, Josiah Gould and myself. In leveling, many rocks were blasted a part of which were used in the building of the wall of the First Parish burying ground fronting on the Common and the remainder have been used for various purposes. Some years after the leveling the Common was surrounded with young Elm trees the expense of which was paid by subscription. The leveling of the Common grew out of the long embargo which threw many in this town out of their accustomed employment and left them at liberty to labor for a public object without interference with their private concerns. The getting up the scheme of doing it by voluntary contributions of labor was the plan of Jonathan H. Lovett and none but him would have carried it through in that form. He was always self-sacrificing in every public undertaking in which he engaged sometimes his ardor and his zeal outran his prudence, but he would generally listen to the counsel of particular friends to whom he was attached. The transactions of the 4th of July 1808 ended my desire of being connected with the military as it did my confidential intercourse with Col. Lovett upon military subjects upon which, till then, from 1800 I had been his adviser.

Justice of the Peace – Notary Public – Commissioner of Highways [247]

My first commission as a Justice of the Peace was by Governor James Sullivan and dated July 2nd, 1808. June 13th, 1815, I was appointed a Justice of the Peace and of the Quorum and this commission was renewed June 14th, 1822, June 1st, 1829, May 11th, 1836 and March 1st, 1843 and again in 1850. Immediately after my first appointment, I commenced business and have continued it to this time. The first entry on my record is dated August 9th, 1808 and is a case of assault and battery. From that time to this, which is more than forty years, I have attended to nearly all the criminal prosecution that have been indicted in Beverly. The number of these to December 1st, 1848 is 335. Synopses of all these may be found at the end of my second volume of records. I have attended to some civil actions and to more or less of all the other business usually transacted by country justices of the peace. My practice has been rather to discourage frequent prosecutions and to incline to the milder penalties of the law, when prosecutions are instituted. The course which I have thus pursued for forty years has, <u>in my own estimation</u> been favorable to the formation of habits of order and has conduced to the high reputation which the town has attained for its quietness and freedom from crime when compared with other towns in the county of Essex of about the same population. I would recommend to my grandchildren to be careful and solicitous to start right in every undertaking and having done so then be sure to persevere and not be drawn aside by any temporary unpopularity or by any improper influences.

In regard to the discouraging of prosecutions I have often, when persons have come to complain of an assault under the initiation of their feeling soon after occurrence, I have postponed action on the complaint until the next day when in many cases the complainant would relent and decline the prosecution which in a moment of passion he desired. There has been a very general feeling among the inhabitants of this town that it is expedient for them to refrain from commencing prosecutions against offenders unless under very peculiar circumstances. Hence, it is in some measure that so few offences and crimes are brought to public notice in this town. People not being familiar with legal proceedings are generally averse to engaging in the them. It is a characteristic which I have uniformly endeavored to cultivate and which I hope my successor in office will continue to promote.

June 18th, 1850: I was appointed a trial justice which confirmed to me exclusively what I had by general consent done almost exclusively for the last thirty-five years in relating to criminal prosecutions but only particularly in relation to civil suits. This appointment is under a law of May 3, 1850 and is to take effect from July 1st, 1850 and applies to both criminal prosecutions and civil actions. At the next General Court, the law authorizing the appointment of trial justices was repealed. The repeal takes effect June 23, 1851.

May 14th, 1858: I received from Gov. Nathaniel P. Banks a commission dated May 6th, 1855, whereby I was appointed a Justice of the Peace to try criminal cases in the County of Essex under a law passed at the last session of the General Court. On the 15th I wrote to the Governor that on account of the infirmities of old age I declined accepting the appointment. At the same time, I recommended the appointment of Charles Davis Esq. as the most suitable of any of the justices of the peace in town. I also wrote to the counselor for Essex Hon. George Cogswell and to the attorney General Stephen H. Phillips.

[248] Soon after the decease of Joseph Wood who was the notary public for many years, I was appointed to that office in 1808 and continued to hold it with the exception of one year, 1811, when John Burley was appointed until I regained it on receiving the appointment of a Special Justice of the Court of Sessions in 1822 which last office I held until in July 12th, 1826. I was appointed a commissioner of Highways which office I held for about two years, when the number was reduced from five to four and I was left off. During the time that I was a Commissioner of Highways I travelled into every town in the County of Essex in reference to the business of the Highways of which there was probably more done during those years than in the same period of time before or since, because the whole expense as well for damages as for making the road was paid from the county treasury which led many to seek for improvements who would have been deterred if the expense was to have been borne by the towns within which the roads were located. I

obtained considerable local knowledge which has at sometimes proved to be useful to myself or to others.

Asa W. Wildes [248]

I was associated with Asa W. Wildes of Newburyport who was the chairman and is still a county commissioner, Joseph Winn who died several years since at Salem aged ___ [35], William B. Breed of Lynn, who was the youngest of the board and apparently in the best health but he died soon after I was left out of the office & Stephen Barker of Andover who died March 14th 1849 aged 77 years. Asa W Wilds died at Newburyport on Friday Dec 4, 1857 aged 71 years & seven months.

[248.1] The following notice is from the Salem Register of December 7th, 1857

"Another veteran gone. The Hon Asa W. Wildes, so long and so well known to the people of the county of Essex as the veteran County Commissioner, died at his residence in Newburyport on Friday last, at the age of 71 years and 7 months. Mr. Wildes was a native of Topsfield where he still held an interest in a paternal farm to which he was much attached. He graduated at Dartmouth College in the class of 1809, with the late Hon Levi Woodberry, with whom, as long as the latter lived, Mr. W. was always on terms of friendly intimacy. At the earliest appointment of highway commissioners, some thirty years since, Mr. Wildes was elected to the Board, in which and in the more enlarged sphere of the office into that of County Commissioner, he continued, with the single exception of one term of three years, until about one year since, when failing to be re-elected to the office, he retired to his home, where he gradually went away to his final rest, but esteemed and beloved by those who know him best. Mr. Wildes has also been a member of the Executive Council for two or three years and but few men in the county have acted so often as referee, in matters of controversy as he was early engaged in teaching in different parts of Maine and Massachusetts including the grammar school in Newburyport and but few teachers have ever lived who have so long and so genuinely retained the good will and affections of their pupils. His wife, a sister of Hon. George Lunt, died about two years since we believe. He leaves eight children, including Rev. George D. Wildes of Boston, and the wife of Francis Chase, Esq. formerly of Salem.

In addition to the above my intimate acquaintance with him while I served with him as Commissioner of Highways of which board he was chairman and from my continued acquaintance with him afterwards to the last year of his life, that during this whole period he preserved his good humor always having some witty story to tell or some humorous jest which served to relieve the tedium of business and to infuse a degree of cheerfulness among those about him. During all this period, he was in straitened pecuniary circumstances and for several years previous to his death, his wife became insane, which afflictions, although they at times threw a gloom over his countenance, never extinguished his good humor.

[248.2] July 1st, 1858: This day my duties as a Justice of the Peace to try criminal cases terminates by law after a service of 50 years. I was reappointed under the new law

---

[35] Rantoul left his age blank. Joseph Winn died November 5th, 1839, aged 70 (Salem VRs.)

to try criminal cases, but I immediately declined accepting the office and James Hill was appointed in my place. During the fifty years of my service I have attended to 553 cases. 146 of which were for drunkenness during 35 years of the time from 1823 to 1858. And 137 for assault and battery for fifty years:

Whole number	553
Drunkenness	146
Assault & Battery	137
All other offences	270
Being an average of per year	11/

Before 1823 the Overseers of the Poor used to commit drunkards to the Work House by their own order and without judicial investigation. Before that time was only in a few cases and that mostly those whom the complainant and others were desirous of a commitment to the County House of Corrections, so that the prosecutions for drunkenness before me may be called for thirty-five years last past 146 or an average per year of 4.

Candidate for County Commissioner [249]

On the 26th of February 1838, I received the following letters:

Obituary of Asa W. Wildes, December 7, 1857.

"Dear Sir,

"It is the desire of several of my friends in this quarter (not of the same political faith as myself but of the antagonist school) to place your name before the County as a candidate for County Commissioner at the approaching canvass. And I am informed that they are ready to give you a hearty support. I am also informed by one of the number, that they now wait only to ascertain whether you would decline the nomination or the office if elected. The person referred to has desired to obtain the latter information thro' me, & as I have no personal acquaintance with you, I beg you to receive the facts above as an apology for this self-introduction and solicitation of your attention. An early reply is wished.

"Your Most Ob't S.

"George Osborne

"Robert Rantoul Sen. Esq   Danvers 26ᵗʰ Feb. 1838

"Beverly Mass"

This invitation I understood to be made with a principal reference to the Temperance Reform as it was supposed that the nomination then before the people comprised a majority who were in favor of licensing the sale by retail of spirituous liquors. With a special reference to this object I wrote an answer as follows:

"Doct. George Osborne   Beverly Feb 27ᵗʰ, 1838

"Dear Sir,

"I have the honor to acknowledge the receipt of your letter of yesterday [250] informing that it is the desire of several of your friends to place my name before the county as a candidate for County Commissioner, at the approaching canvass, and requesting to be informed whether I 'would decline the nomination, or the office if elected'. The partiality of your friends and your polite communication of the same, claim my best acknowledgements. In answer to your inquiries, I shall not think it proper to decline a nomination if made without any implied pledged on my part to any political or <u>other</u> party and made under such circumstances will place my name fairly and honorably before my fellow citizens of this County. At the same time, you will perceive that I ought to reserve to myself the privilege of judging of the circumstances under which a nomination may be made, and if not satisfactory, of withdrawing myself from the canvass. If I should suffer myself to be continued as a candidate until the time of the Election and it should so happen that a majority of votes should be cast for me, I should then consider it my duty to accept of the office. In thus frankly answering your inquiry I shall not be understood as soliciting the office or offering myself as a candidate here for.

"I am very respectfully, dear sir, Your Obed't Serv't

"Robert Rantoul"

I was, accordingly, put in nomination as a friend to the Temperance Reform, and by the Temperance Party. My opponents immediately assumed the [251] false pretense that it was a mere political maneuver to place a Democrat in a County office when that party were decidedly in the minority. The Whig partisan papers came out strongly against me and I failed of an election in consequent of the political bearing which it was given to the nomination. The temperance party in this town generally voted against me or omitted voting and towards them I felt some dissatisfaction which I then thought was justifiable and three years afterwards when another election was to take place, and Francis Lamson was appointed a delegate to a county convention to make the nomination of candidates I wrote to him as follows:

"Mr. Francis Lamson   Beverly February 15, 1841

"Dear Sir,

"Three years ago, I was nominated as a candidate for the office of County Commissioner, by a convention which was supposed, in making their selection of candidates for that office to have reference to opinions and habits which regarded the great Temperance Reform which has for many years past been going on in this country and in many other parts of the civilized world. In reference to the vote through the whole country, upon that occasion I have no remark to make other than, to return my thanks to my fellow citizens of the County for their suffrages. [252] bestowed upon me upon that occasion as well as upon various prior occasions, when I have had the honor of being a candidate for the voters of the county. Having thus express my thanks for the suffrages of the county, I cannot refrain from an expression of disappointment and regret at the course pursued by some of the leaders of the temperance reformers in this town, in with-holding their influence from the temperance list of candidates and in some notorious instances, bestowing their suffrages upon those whom they well know were of an opposite character. As there is good reason to conclude that the course pursued by those persons in this town in regard to the <u>whole</u> temperance list of candidates was dictated by considerations exclusively personal to myself, to prevent a like occurrence so prejudicial to an object, which for more than thirty years last past I have had so much at heart, and which has uniformly had my ardent, zealous support, I wish to withdraw myself from consideration as a candidate for the office of County Commissioner. To my friends in this town who upon that occasion bestowed their suffrages upon me, notwithstanding the defalcation of many of those who have the reputation of being strong temperance reformers, I tend my expressions of regard and esteem for their firm adhesion to principles, which I had the weakness to believe would on that occasion more generally have actuated the conduct of the temperance reformers in this town.

[253] "In thus declining the suffrages of my fellow citizens of the county of Essex, I trust I shall not be deemed wanting in a just respect to them. As it may be desirable to some of those who may attend the meeting to be held this evening for the choice of delegates to the Temperance Convention, to be holden at Ipswich on Wednesday next, to be apprised of my intentions, I have addressed this letter to you and request that it may be communicated in such manner as you may judge to be proper. I am with due respect

"Your Ob't Serv't Rob Rantoul"

Doct. George Osborne who wrote me in the first instance was a Democrat and, in his letter,, he informed me that my nomination was desired by some of the opposing political party and I could not therefore view it as having reference to general politics and wrote my consent to the proposed nomination under that impression. The conduct of some weak-minded partisans of the Democratic party gave some excuse for the course pursued by the opposite party but did not justify it at its commencement, as the conduct alluded to was subsequent to the attack upon me by my political opponents. This conduct added to the unpleasant feelings engendered by the whole transaction, but I cannot charge myself with any improper action in regard to it. I have often observed that justness of the saying "save me from my friends". This was probably the last time that I shall be a candidate for any County office.

Candidate for Elector of President [254]

In 1836, I was a candidate for Elector of President on the general ticket, Martin van Buren being the Democratic candidate for the office of President. The average aggregate vote of the state was:

Whigs	41,093
Democrats	33,228
	7,865

I received 33,416 votes. There were six Democrats who received a less number and seven who received a greater number. The highest on the Democratic list was Harvey Chapin who received 33,554 and on the Whig list General Thomas Longley who received 41,287 Leverett Saltonstall stood next to him and had 41,274.

State Treasurer [254]

In 1843, I was invited to be a candidate for the office of State Treasurer, but I positively declined the offer. John Mills was chosen State Treasurer that year but was superseded in 1844. My principal reason for declining this last office was my disinclination to ask the favor of rich men to become my bondsmen, as the amount of the bonds required is so large as to render it necessary to have men of larger property than any of my immediate connections or friends. The usual sum put into the bond is 100,000 dollars. Other reasons existed and particularly that an undue anxiety to discharge the duties of the office with propriety, might prey upon and impair my health. I have but very rarely declined any public situation of responsibility.

County Treasurer's Accounts, Settlement of [257]

In pursuance of a resolve of the General Court of February 25th, 1811, Ichabod Tucker, Parker Cleaveland and myself were appointed by the Court of Common Pleas, Commissioners to examine and audit the accounts of the Hon. Stephen Choate Esq., Treasurer of the County of Essex for such length of time as said Comm. should think proper so far as may relate to any monies received by him for the use of the Commonwealth. Under this commission I attended for three days at Ipswich to examine Mr. Choate's accounts. He was then very aged, but all his accounts were kept with perfect accuracy. He was County Treasurer for some twenty years and died at a great age with a high character of integrity and fidelity in many important trusts. I was gratified with this appointment though its labors were short and not very complicated.

I Tucker was the Clerk of the County in this county for many years. He lived to old age but out lived his mind. He died October 1846 aged 81 years. Doct. P. Cleaveland who was for a time the minister of the Tabernacle Society in Salem. He was one of the very small number who were members of the two Massachusetts convention for framing and for altering the Constitution in the years 1780 and 1820. He was very sociable and intelligent. I had other opportunities of intercourse with him at various times. He lived to old age and died much respected. While attending on this commission at Ipswich we boarded at Major Swasey's tavern, who was much esteemed for his social qualities.

Small Pox Vaccination – Henry Fornis, Mother & Sister [259]

The death of Henry Fornis, his mother and sister by the small pox, in the first part of 1812, occasioned some excitement and at a town meeting held subsequently I was appointed one of the Committee to ascertain the number of persons who had not had the small pox nor the kine pox[36] and to endeavor to induce them to be vaccinated. This duty was performed in the different sections of the town. In the section assigned to me there were 96. The measures pursued by the committee led to a very general vaccination. Since that time the subject has been left to the attention of individuals. There are always many poor persons who cannot easily abstract from their ordinary means the smallest fee for a purpose of which they do not discern the immediate necessity. It is on this account that public action is occasionally called for to converse the attention and sometimes to furnish the means of carrying out a general system of vaccination. The prevalence of small pox in Boston this year, 1850, has occasioned parents to cause their children to be inoculated with the kine pox, very extensively. At the time when Henry Fornis was attacked with the small pox at his mother's house I, by request of Doct. Abner Howe, visited him which was the last time that I saw any one with the disease, this was in January 1812.

Lectures on the History of Beverly, the History of Essex County, and on a Variety of Subjects [261]

In the spring of 1830, I commenced a series of lectures on the history of Beverly, which were read before the Lyceum. Each lecture occupying an hour in the delivery. They were delivered April 20th, 1830, November 30th, December 14th, and December 28th in the same year and March 22nd and 29th, April 26 and May 3rd in 1831. These eight lectures were followed by three describing the town, delivered November 15th, 1831, March 13th and March 29th, 1832. I next delivered four lectures on the history of the County of Essex. The services as Commissioner of Highways having given me some opportunity of acquiring some knowledge upon this subject.

These lectures containing a succinct history of each of the towns in the County of Essex to be delivered before the Lyceum in the winter of 1833 – 1834, but circumstances prevented their being read and 22 of these town histories were published in the newspapers, mostly in the Gloucester Democrat, but with some modifications and additions.

April 1, 1834: I read a lecture before the Lyceum upon the monied institutions of the County of Essex.

February 11, 1836 on modes of trial

December 8, 1836 on Economy

December 15, 1836 on Economy

January 24, 1839 on capital punishment. This lecture I also delivered in Salem, before the Washingtonian Lyceum, Jan 19, 1843, before the Manchester Lyceum, [262] March 7th, 1844 and in the Baptist meeting house, North Danvers, April 29th, 1844.

---

[36] Cow pox.

February 11, 1841: I read a lecture before the Beverly Lyceum on Agriculture.

May 12th, 1835: I delivered a lecture before the Union Temperance Society and on the 9th of December 1844 a temperance address to a large audience assembled in the new Town Hall. February 10, 1841 in the First Parish Meeting house, before the Daughters of Temperance, and November 25th, 1847 before the citizens in the Town Hall.

December 4th, 1843: I read a lecture on the life of Toussaint Louverture before the Washingtonian Lyceum at Washington Hall in Salem.

Thus from 1830 to this time, I have written more than thirty lectures, besides my address on the schools and my address at the opening of the new Town Hall, which have been mentioned elsewhere. All of these lectures I have delivered before public assemblies since 1830, excepting the four upon the history of the town in this county more of which were published in newspapers. In addition to my lecture on capital punishment, I published 10 articles in the Salem Gazette from March 22, 1831 to May 3, 1832. Twelve articles in the Experiment, a Lowell paper, published by Horatio Hastings Weld, from April 26, 1832 to July 12th, 1832. Fifteen articles in the Worcester Palladium from July to November 14th, 1838. Five articles in the Christian Register in 1838, from August to October. Some seventeen or more articles in the Gloucester Democrat in 1835 and 1836. Three articles in the Salem Advertiser April 1845. Some articles in the Prisoner's Friend and in diverse other newspapers which I cannot now recollect. All of these were upon the subject of capital punishment, which still remains unsettled[37].

[263] I very early had a propensity for writing scraps and articles for publication upon politics, public affairs, moral reforms & etc. I have sometimes indulged this propensity injudiciously and injuriously which is a source of regret, but I flatter myself that many of my hints and communications have upon the whole been beneficial and after an experience of more than fifty years, I cannot advise my grandchildren to abstain from the exercise of any talent for writing which they may possess, and which may be made a means of good to the community. I do however sincerely caution and advise them to be very considerate and careful and not to publish anything until after reflection they are well satisfied will do decidedly more good than hurt. I have written very many articles for newspapers some of which were crude and which a more mature mind and more serious reflection and regard for consequences would have suppressed. The heat of political excitement frequently leads to extravagant expressions and vituperative language in reference to opponents. I therefore advise not to withdraw from political action but to exercise great caution and use the utmost kindness and forbearance towards those who may differ from you in opinion and if they should pursue an opposite course towards you, to avoid all retaliation and not to weary in well doing. By perusing this course faithfully, should you attain to three score years and ten, it will not be a source of regret to you, that you have actively engaged in the [264] politics of your day. Nearly all my newspaper communications have been anonymous. There is something that is entitled to consideration which may be said on both sides of the question, whether a writer should put his name to what he lays before the public.

---

[37] Rantoul wrote in the margin, "The last of 17 numbers in the Gloucester Democrat was published Feb 19, 1836".

In 1835, I lent to James R. Newhall my lectures on the County of Essex, he being about compiling "The Essex memorial for 1836, embracing a register of the county". From my lectures, he derived many of his facts and in return he sent me a copy of this publication and a letter of thanks, January 4, 1836.

In 1842, I lent to Edwin M. Stone my lectures on Beverly and other papers, he being about to publish a History of Beverly. He presented me with a copy of his work and in its preface, made a suitable acknowledgement of the loan. I first suggested to him that if anyone would undertake to publish a history of Beverly he should have the free use of my manuscripts and I suppose this, among other circumstances led him to compile his history which has proved so acceptable to the inhabitants of the town, but still leaves room for a more full and complete history. In March 1849 I, at the request of Andrew P. Peabody wrote some biographical sketches of the Rev. Joseph McKean formerly minister of the first parish in this town, comprising about a dozen pages for the use of William B. Sprague of Albany to whom I sent the paper and received from him a handsome complimentary letter of an acknowledgement which is on file with my letters. W. Sprague proposes publishing the biography of the ministry of New England.

[265] November 6, 1813 and December 20, 1825: I wrote articles for the Salem Gazette upon the subject of the county prisons in Essex County and a House of Correction for the same county. These articles contain many suggestions which have since been carried into effect in the buildings which now exist. Whether they led to the improvements which have been made I cannot say but when it is known that the largest rivers are composed of single drops of rain, none should refrain from contributing their mite to benevolent objects because they cannot be assured of the degree of efficiency belonging to their efforts. Although the articles referred to are not exactly what I should write at this time, yet they were then somewhat ahead of public opinion in this county and were not carried out for several years afterwards. In September 1849, I rewrote for the Prisoner's Friend, three articles on Freedom, published in the Salem Advertiser in April 1846 and which were a revision of some articles on the same subject in the Worcester Palladium before the last-mentioned date. The Dictionary which I used prior to 1832, was the second edition of Benjamin Martin's, printed in London in 1754. This I inherited from my father and wish it may be preserved in my family. In 1832, I bought one of Johnson & Walker's by Worcester and in 1845 I bought Webster's in two volumes octavo for ten and a half dollars.

Trust deeds [266]

In January 1830, immediately after the ordination of C.T. Thayer, I wrote the following article for the Christian Register: "Rights of Parishes and Religious Societies." The third article of the bill of rights of this Commonwealth provides that Parishes and Religious Societies shall have the <u>exclusive</u> right of electing the public Teachers. Although it is now nearly half a century since the constitution containing this provision was adopted by the people, yet such has been the force of habit and prejudice in relation to ecclesiastical affairs that the most common course has been to have a concurrent vote of the church and parish or society in the election of a minister. Within a few years past public attention has been reluctantly drawn to this subject. The invention of <u>trust deeds</u> to secure this privilege of election (in express contradiction to the constitution) to the members of the church exclusive of any participation on the part of the members of the parish or society and the attempt made by a religious party to maintain and defend as a right, what has only been allotted to the church from courtesy has made at it the duty of Parishes and Societies to proceed upon the true principle which should govern in all elections of public officers in this country. In a republic, all power emanates from the people. How jealous are we of every appearance of interference in the free exercise of the elective franchise in regard to our civil officers? Should we not be equally jealous of the least attempts to usurp the right of electing the public teachers of piety, religion and morality? Are these officers of less importance than our civil officers or is the privilege [267] of choosing them of less value to the great body of the people? We were led to these remarks by the commendable course adopted by the First Parish in Beverly. We understand that their late proceedings in regard to the election and settlement of a minister were conducted wholly in the capacity of the parish. That at a parish meeting held for the purpose, they made choice of Mr. Thayer, of whose ordination we this day publish an account and that they notified him of his election and received his answer accepting of the office without submitting their doings to any other tribunal. They afterwards appointed a committee to ordain and induct him into office and this committee in behalf of the parish invited the aid and assistance of a suitable number of churches, who attended by their pastors and delegates and performed the usual ordaining services.

The reference to "trust deeds" was accessioned by the course pursued by the proprietors of a new church built in Hanover street, Boston for Doct. Lyman Beecher. This church was burnt down not many years afterwards and was not rebuilt. In the deed of the land on which this church stood, to certain trustees it was provided that no pew holders should have a right to give a vote in the election of a minister unless he was a member of the church in regular standing. The example of Hanover street church was followed by some others in Massachusetts, but it occasioned so much excitement that the practice was soon abandoned, and I know not whether it now exists anywhere.

[268] In July 1835, I wrote for the Gloucester Democrat two articles on the life and character of William Thorndike who died July 12th, 1835, in the 41st year of his age. One of these articles was the foundation of the article in Stone's history of Beverly on William Thorndike. The other article published in that paper was upon his political course and containing some party allusions was not noticed by Mr. Stone in compiling his notice of the deceased which was judicious in Mr. Stone.

Thomas Barrett [268]

In April 1846, I wrote the following notice of Thomas Barrett for the Salem Advertiser.

Thomas Barrett, Sexton of First Parish.

"Died in Beverly, on Sunday the 19th of April inst. Thomas Barrett, aged 87 years, Sexton of the First Parish in Beverly –

"History performs but half her office nor perhaps the most useful portion of it, if she commemorates only those who are the great lights of the world and preserves no line of men whose place is less ambitions, whose merits are more unpretending, but whose victories for that very reason are the more easily emulated and this may produce a more salutary influence. The subject of this notice, Thomas Barrett, was born in Newport Rhode Island the 21st of March 1759. At the usual age, he was bound as an apprentice to Shipley Townsend, a clock maker in Boston. Mr. Townsend was a religious man, kept his bible in his work shop, that he and his apprentices might consult it frequently. He was at the time of Mr. Barrett's residence in his family a member of the old South Church in Boston, but afterwards became a Sandemanian, and then a Universalist and was an officer of Rev Mr. Murray's [269] First Universalist Church in Boston. He published some small books for children and several essays upon theological subjects, which were collected and published in an Octave volume. During Mr. Barrett's residence in the family of Mr. Townsend his mind was imbued with a reverence for religion and his habits of order, diligence, fidelity and faithfulness were established, and the influence of this period in his life was exemplified in the various scenes and circumstances of his protracted existence. In June 1780, at the age of twenty-one years, he enlisted as a waiter in Captain Constance Freeman's company in Colonel Crane's regiment in the army of the revolution, and continued in the service about six months, which entitled him to a pension of twenty-five dollars, under the law of Congress of 1832. After his discharge from the army, he worked as a journeyman clock maker in Boston and afterward in Salem, and with Joseph Chipman, a son of the Rev. John Chipman, the first minister of the Precinct of Salem and Beverly. In 1784, he was married to Miss Lois Symonds of Salem, and in August of that year removed to Beverly and there set up his trade of Clock making. His first wife dying young, he subsequently married three others, the last of whom survives, to whom he was married on the 31st of December 1840. He was appointed to the office of Sexton of the First Parish in Beverly on the 4th of May 1797 and was annually reappointed till his decease, making [270] the whole term of his service nearly 49 years. In 1842, at his request, an assistant was appointed who performed most of the duties of the office of Sexton while the Parish continued Mr. Barrett in office and paid him the majority of his former salary. During the period of this active duty he buried two thousand, two hundred and fifty-nine persons. He faithfully and with the most exemplary care and fidelity performed every duty appertaining to his office. His punctuality was proverbial, those who knew him best and for the longest time have no recollection of his ever failing in punctuality or of his ever making any mistake in regard to the time of the performance of any of the duties of his office. His politeness and good manners were of the old school and procured the favorable notice of all those who met with him. In his domestic relations, he was kind and affectionate. He was in the full possession of his mental powers until within a short time of his departure and conversed cheerfully and feelingly of his expected dissolution, expressed his grateful sense of the kindness he had experience from his numerous friends, and his faith and hope in the gospel of his Lord and Savior, Jesus Christ."

I have written several other obituary notices for different newspapers. Thomas Barrett's first wife Lois Symonds of Salem, died September 1789, aged 29. His second wife Hannah Hamden of Salem died May 1818, 71 yrs. 4 mons. His third wife Lydia Smith of Beverly died April 26, 1840 aged 73 yrs. 8 mons.

[271] On the 22nd of March 1851 was issued the first number of a newspaper entitled the Beverly Citizen published by Andrew F. Wales and edited by Ira Washburn. It being the first newspaper published in Beverly. For this paper I wrote from a lecture which I wrote in 1841 and delivered in Salem in 1843, nine articles entitled the "Negro Chieftain" giving a history of Toussaint Louverture. The first of these articles was published April 5th and the last May 31st, 1851. I have also furnished several other articles for this paper upon a variety of subjects, such as I thought might be useful to my fellow townsmen.

This paper was entirely discontinued July 8th, 1854. Before its discontinuance and after the decease of Mr. Washburn, it passed through various phases of existence gradually declining in interest with the inhabitants. It proved to be a premature undertaking. Possibly Mr. Washburn, if he had lived and continued in the ministry here, might have kept it along. It was finally merged in the Bay State published in Lynn. We must wait for a longer growth in population and business before a newspaper can be well supported here. I have almost a complete file of the Citizens which is the only one which I know of.

Beverly Marine Insurance Company [275]

In the first part of the year 1804, I was actively engaged in getting up a subscription for a Marine Insurance Company and getting an act of incorporation therefore through the General Court. At the organization of the company I was chose a Director and continued by annual election until the expiration of the charger in 1829 and from 1817 to 1829 I was chosen President by the Directors. The income for the whole time was about equal to the lawful rate of interest and upon the dissolution of the corporation the remaining interest was vested in three trustees viz. Albert Thorndike, Charles Stephens & myself. Since our appointment we have recovered from the Spanish government an indemnity for a loss by capture of about 6,000 dollars of which as yet they have only paid the interest from time to time, which has been divided among the stockholders. Isaac Flagg, deceased, was the Secretary of the company from its commencement to its close, a period of twenty years. During its continuance it gave me daily occasion to devote some portion of time to its concerns and thus served to break the monotonous attendance on the shop. The first policy which I signed as President was on the 30th of August 1817. The first President was Moses Brown and the next Thomas Stephens whom I succeeded.

I was chosen President August 7th, 1817. The discontinuance of this Ins Company resulted from the opposition of a number of the stockholders to the renewal of its charter by the Legislature which was petitioned for by a vote of the company.

[276] An occurrence in relation to this insurance company broke up the friendship which had existed for many years, without any interruption, between Thomas Stephens and myself. He with others were the owners of the Barque *Washington*, an old vessel that had laid by during the War and had been fitted out for a voyage to Europe. She met with an injury and was condemned, having been insured to the amount of 5000 $, at the Beverly M. Ins. Office. The directors refused to pay the loss, upon the ground of her unseaworthiness. Thos. Stephens thereupon resigned the office of President and I was appointed in his room. The owners of the Barque, and the Directors, could not agree upon any terms of adjustment, and the owners commenced a suit against the Company. On the part of the Company, I was obliged by my office to attend to this suit. After a long time, it was tried, and a verdict in favor of the owners, on the question of seaworthiness but upon another ground of defense, a deviation, the court decided in favor of the M. I. Company. All these proceedings in the law served to confirm the alienation between T. Stephens and myself, and these feelings were never so far overcome as to restore the former cordiality of intercourse, though formal intercourse took place when it was necessary in the transaction of business. I regretted exceedingly, this alienation, but could not well shun the responsibility which seemed to devolve upon me.

[277] A second experiment in the business of insurance was begun by a company incorporated May 30th, 1852. It has not been successful to this time (1855.) Michael Whitney is the President. It is doubtful whether the commercial business of this town is sufficient to support an insurance company.

Representative to the General Court – Senator [279]

In 1809, I was chosen a Representative to the General Court with Thomas Davis & Abner Chapman & Thomas Stephens and Isaac Rea, all of whom are now dead excepting Abner Chapman[38] who now lives in Boston and is more than eighty years of age. At that time the town sent its full representation, but as the attendance of the members was paid for out of the town treasury, it was understood that the members should not attend constantly and I being the youngest of the delegation, it was expected that I should give place to my seniors, so that for the first years, that I belonged to the General Court, I attended only a portion of each session, lest the town should be unduly burthened in having so large a representation constantly in attendance. I was reelected from year to year until 1820, when I was elected a Senator for the County and was re-elected to the office of Senator for the years 1821 & 1822 and was a candidate for the next year but the election of senators going against the Federal party in this county, I lost my election but in the same year I was chosen the Representative and re-elected until 1827, when I lost my election but the following year, 1828, I was again chosen and was re-elected until 1833, inclusive. In 1834 and for five years following I was an unsuccessful candidate. During my time of service, when an alteration of the constitution went into operation, there were two elections in one

---

[38] In the margin Rantoul wrote:" Abner Chapman died October 1858 aged about 85 years."

year, so that from 1809 to 1833 inclusive I was elected as a member of the Legislature, twenty-four times, notwithstanding the omission in 1827.

[280] I did not fail of a choice in 1827 on account of party politics, but from various causes a disaffection had grown up towards me, among which causes the following were assigned viz:

1st That I had, in the preceding session, voted in favor of a free bridge from Charlestown to Boston, derogation of the vested rights of the proprietors of Charles River bridge, and indirectly of the vested rights of other corporations.

2nd That I held the office of Commissioner of Highways and ought not at the same time to enjoy the emoluments of the office of Representative to the General Courts.

3rd That in the office of commissioner of Highways I had not sufficiently regarded the rights of property in individuals, in aiding the laying out of a new piece of road from Cabot street to Water street in this town.

4th That a proper regard to rotation in office, required that I should retire after 18 successive elections.

There were many other good reasons for not voting for me, which did not take a tangible shape and therefore cannot be noted here.

In 1828, I was again elected notwithstanding this formidable array of opposition and continued to be reelected until the election for 1834 when I failed upon the ground of defection from the predominant political party. I then depended upon the Democratic party for support which has always been in the minority in this town, since I have resided here. I continued to [281] be their candidate until 1840 when I wrote the following letter which was read in a public meeting of the party at the Town Hall viz:

"Beverly September 22, 1840

"Capt. Josiah Lovett 2nd

"Dear Sir,

"The recent alteration of the constitution of this State, renders it necessary to reduce the number of the representatives to which this town has been entitled. This circumstance in connection with others, having drawn my attention to the relation in which I have stood to the electors in this town for the space of thirty-one years last past, I beg leave to address you as the Chairman of the town Democratic Committee upon the subject of withdrawing myself from the consideration of my fellow citizens as a candidate for office in the state Legislature. I was first elected as a Representative in 1809 a time of great political excitement. This election occurred in May following the raising of the long embargo, which was removed in March 1809. This measure of the National Government had operated with peculiar severity upon the business of this town and had produced a state of instability unexampled within the period of my recollection. Partaking strongly of the popular feeling as most young men do under similar circumstances, I was elected as an active partisan in connection with the Federal party. To that party I gave a hearty support not however without many fears that the influence of the leading men of the party tended to a consolidation of power in the

National Government and to the establishment of Aristocratic distinctions in society founded on [282] accumulated or hereditary wealth and family connections. I continued to be elected a Representative from 1809 to 1819 (inclusive) preserving my connection with the Federal party, considering their course in the main as preferable

"To that of their opponents, but still differing from the leading Federalists on several important points. In 1820, 1821 & 1822 I was elected by the Federal party as a Senator for the county of Essex, and was held up as a candidate for the same office in 1823 but the Federal party losing their ascendency in the county as well as in the State in that year of course I lost my election to the Senate but was in the same year elected by the town to the House of Representative of the town until 1827. In 1825 after the decease of Governor Eustis, who died in the first part of that year, an amalgamation of the two great political parties; Federal and Democratic was brought about through the instrumentality of the members of the Legislature then in session. I cooperated in the formation of this new party, in which some of the principles of Federalism were kept out of sight, and a union formed in favor of supporting the administration of President John Quincy Adams. At the formation of this party I objected (publicly) to what was falsely called the American system the leading principles of which I uniformly repudiated. With the National Republican party (as the new organization was called) I felt but little cordiality.

[283] "It soon became manifest that the protective system as it promised to be the foundation of the wealth of some of the more active partisans and to add greatly to the wealth of those who had already become such was the principle object of the party. Upon the protective system and the system of internal improvements by the nation government my earliest opinions have not changed, but upon another question, of great interest in the community I am equally free to say that the views which I now entertain are the opposite of what I held to formerly and that upon the constitutionality and expediency of a National Bank, I have changed my opinions. I once believed that a National Bank would afford great facilities to the government in collection and disbursing its revenues that it would be very beneficial to the trading portion of the community in equalizing exchanges, that it would be a great convenience to almost every class in the community in making remittances to every part of our extended country and that it would restrain and regulate the action of the State banks. The constitutional objections were obviated ty the apparent utility to the government in the arrangement of the financial concerns of the government. In most of these particulars the Bank has failed. But, admitting that all these benefits have been derived from its existence they certainly have been most dearly purchased. The dangerous power and influence of the Bank in controlling elections through a corrupt press by the use of its funds in loans or payment for services rendered its means of embarrassing the government in [284] any and every measure, in collusion with its interests, its means of influence in Congress though loans to its members or enormous fees, paid ostensibly for professional services but really to secure the votes and influence of the most gifted lawyers, holding seats in that body, its means of influence upon merchants and traders by granting or refusing loans of money, from political considerations, all combine to satisfy me that such an institution ought not to be tolerated in this free country. That our free institutions ought not to be put at hazard for any pecuniary advantages, any special accommodations, any convenience of arrangement, which

might be supposed to result there from. None of the real or supposed advantages would justify the hazarding of the supplanting of our free institutions by a monied power as despotic and cruel as any form of despotism to which poor humanity has ever been subjected. A National Bank is also dangerous to liberty when in harmony with the government and in conjunction with a corrupt administration may subvert every constitutional provision which might interfere with the aggrandizement of the one, or the usurpation of power by the other. There are two kinds of inequality, the one personal, that of talent and virtue the source of whatever is excellent and admirable in society, the other that of fortune <u>which must exist</u> because property alone can stimulate to labor, and labor, if it were not necessary to the existence would be indispensable to the happiness of man. But though property is necessary yet in its excess it is the great malady of civil society. The accumulation of that power, which is conferred by wealth, [285] in the hands of the few, is the perpetual source of oppression and neglect of the mass of mankind. The power of the wealthy is farther concentrated by their tendency to combination from which numbers dispersion, indigence and ignorance equally preclude the poor. This tendency to combination is promoted and facilitated by the creation of artificial corporate bodies by the government. In no country has the creation of private corporations increased with such rapid strides as in our own, and in none is there a louder call to awaken the jealousy and arouse the watchfulness of the friends of liberty and equality to the existing state, power and progress of such bodies and to guard the community against their deleterious influences.

"In 1826 the most exciting subject of consideration in the State Legislature was the granting of permission to erect a bridge, free of toll, over the Charles River between Boston and Charlestown. This question had ben agitated for several years previous to 1826 but without coming to a definite result and I had committed myself both in the Senate and in the House in favor of the right of the Legislature and also of its duty under certain circumstances to grant authority to construct such a bridge. In the winter session of the political year 1826 a bill was passed granting the free bridge by both branches, this bill was however vetoed by Governor Lincoln and returned to the House with his objections, March 10th, 1827, and again passed in the House by a vote of 99 to 45, being more than the constitutional majority of two thirds [286] and was then sent to the Senate and there again put upon it passage and the vote stood 16 in favor and 12 against it which not being two thirds it was lost. My vote was given in favor of this bill through all its stages. By this act I incurred the displeasure of some of the wealthiest men in Massachusetts, who were peculiarly sensitive at that time in regard to vested rights and the immunity of private corporations from Legislative interference without their consent. In 1827, I was again a candidate for Representative of the town and for the first time for (after) eighteen successive years, failed of obtaining a majority of the votes. Whether this result was occasioned by my votes upon the free bridge question or by any other acts of my public or private life, or by any omissions of duty on my part or whether it was simply that they preferred another (Thomas Stephens Jr) to me are questions which I had not then, neither have I now any right to ask.

"In 1828, (the free bridge question being settled) I was again a candidate and was chosen a Representative by a small majority and continued to be re-elected with more or less opposition until 1833. In 1833, resolutions were introduced into the House of Representative in favor of a continuance of the high tariff import duties. These resolutions I considered my duty to oppose. Previously to the elections for 1834 I avowed publicly my predilection in favor of the prominent measures [287] of President Jackson's administration and elected to join the Democratic party in support of his administration, since which, for six successive years, I have been indebted solely to the Democratic party for their support as an unsuccessful candidate for the office of Representative."

The particularity of the foregoing statement, without noticing the numerous other instances in which they have bestowed their free suffrages upon me for various important offices and trusts shows how much I am indebted to the partiality of my fellow townsmen and demands of me the expression of the grateful sense which I entertain of their continued favor. To the Democratic party in this town, I make my sincere acknowledgments for their cordial support for six successive years. Various circumstances now indicate the propriety of declining their suffrages at the ensuing elections of Representative. In doing this I hope it will not be for an instant thought that my zeal for the success of Democratic principles has in the least degree abated. I have faith in the people. I know that the cause and principles of Democracy must and will prevail. I see in the awakening attention to the subject of universal education, the increase of intelligence, the diffusion of information the progress of knowledge as well as in the vast and rapidly progressing improvement in the various arts, promotive of the health, the comfort and enjoyment of life, a sure evidence that the people of this happy and prosperous country never will relax their efforts until the true principles of liberty and equal rights and of security and protection of life and property are the essential characteristics of <u>all</u> our laws and institutions.

Valuation Committee [288]

During the time while I was a member of the General Court there was always more or less opposition upon the ground of party politics and sometimes from others who belonged to the same party with myself to my elections. I think that I might have been more conciliating without denigrating from my independence of which I thought so much as at sometimes to crowd out the thought of making difference of opinion as little obnoxious to opponents as possible consistent with firmness. Independence of thought and of action without a <u>due</u> regard to the opinions and feelings of other has at times, lessened my popularity.

In 1821 and in 1831, I was a member of the Valuation Committee which sat in the recess of the Legislature. The first time I attended, from November 7th, 1821 to January 8th, 1822 fifty-four days, and at the second time, from November 23rd, 1831 to January 3rd, 1832, forty days. The committee consisted in 1821 of 38 members and in 1831 of 41 members who were made up in the pay roll, there being some appointed that did not attend. Spending so much time with the gentlemen composing these two committees resulted in a particular acquaintance with many of them which has continued until this time. I was, for several years on the committee of accounts and this brought most of the members to a knowledge of me, as then, from almost every town in the state there was an account brought by its representative to be presented to the committee. This intercourse sometimes led to some collision but by a firm adherence to a strict interpretation of the laws although some temporary alienation [289] of feeling arose on the part of those whose views differed from my own, yet I think my course met with general approbation.

First Journey to Pittsfield; Albany, New York [289]

I was appointed in 1819 one of a committee with Daniel Noble and Wm W. Parrot to examine the Agricultural Bank at Pittsfield. I left home April 1819 and returned May 7, 1819. After I had finished the business I went for at Pittsfield I took the stage for Albany and remained there from Saturday until Tuesday forenoon, when I went on board a steamer to go down the Hudson river the City of New York. This was the first steamer that I had sailed in. We arrived at New York at about 7 o'clock in the morning and I took my small trunk in my hand and walked across the City from the north river to the east river and at the bottom of Fulton street I found a steamer which would leave in about 2 hours for New London, I engaged a passage and then walked about the City until near the time of departure went aboard and proceeding through Long Island Sound, stopped at New Haven at about nine o'clock in the evening to land and to take in passengers, from thence proceeded to New London arriving early in the morning of Thursday immediately took the stage for Boston and arrived at about 11 o'clock at night at William Smith's boarding house in Hanover street and the next day went home in the stage. Before this time, I had only been into New Hampshire as far as Concord in 1797, and to Exeter and Portsmouth in 1817 and to Portland about 1803, otherwise all my journeying had been within [290] thirty or forty miles from home, so that this my first journey to New York City gave me opportunity of seeing much which was new to me. I remember that when I awoke in the morning at William Smith's house, I found in my chamber what has been since called Doct. Wm E. Channing's Baltimore Sermon, delivered at the ordination of Jared Sparks. I was so much interested in it that I read it entirely through before I left my chamber for breakfast. This seemed to me to be the first open, decided, exposition of the ground upon with the Liberal Party then stood. I was at different times, while I was a member of the General court appointed on various committees for viewing turnpike roads, bridges, town lines, examining banks, treasurer's accounts, etc., etc. most of which services being attended to in the recess gave me opportunity of visiting many places which otherwise I should not have seen.

The persons who served with me as Representative besides: x Thomas Davis 11 years, Abner Chapman 7 years, x Thomas Stephens 2 years, and Isaac Rea 5 years, and x Nathaniel Goodwin 7 years, x Nicholas Thorndike 4 years, z Josiah Lovett 1 year, x Pyam Lovett 1 year, Oliver x Obear 4 years, William x Thorndike 1 year, Thomas Stephens Jun. 1 year, Henry Larcom 3 years, x Josiah Lovett 2nd 1 year, Amos x Shelden 2 years, Jesse Shelden 1 year, Charles Stephens 1 year, John Safford 1 year. In 1810, 1831 and 1832 I was the only representative from the town. In the Senate I served with from Essex County x Israel Bartlett, x Dudley L. Pickman, x Ebenezer Moseley, Robert Clark, x John Glen King, x Nathaniel Hooper, x Benjamin Osgood and Edward S. Rand[39].

---

[39] In previous lists, Rantoul used an "x" as an indicator of decease at time of writing

Essex County Convention of 1812 [291]

Immediately after the declaration of war against Great Britain in June 1812, a convention of the County of Essex was held at Ipswich composed principally of delegates chosen by the people, in legal town meetings called for the purpose but partly of delegates chosen by party voluntary meetings. Of this last description were the towns of Haverhill, Salisbury, Middleton & Lynn from which places delegates attended that were not chosen by towns in their corporate capacity. There were delegates from fifteen other towns in the County. The whole number of delegates was sixty-one. The town of Beverly was represented by x Moses Brown, x Joshua Fisher, x Hugh Hill, x Billy Porter, and myself who is the only one remaining of the delegation from this town. More than half of the whole number of delegates from the nineteen towns are dead. This convention met at Major Swasey's tavern in Ipswich, July 21st, 1812. Timothy Pickering, then of Wenham, was chosen President and Lonson Nash of Gloucester was chosen Secretary. The convention was of course composed exclusively of Federalists, who were opposed to war with Great Britain, the discussion, if so it ought to be called, was all one sided and it ended with voting an address styled a Declaration of the County of Essex. This address or declaration may be found in the fourth volume of Miscellaneous Pamphlets V 3. They also chose twenty delegates to represent this county in a convention of Delegates from the several counties in this Commonwealth, to be convened at Boston, in pursuance of their recommendation. [292] This declaration begins as follows:

"Our Country grievously oppressed by prohibitions of trade, under the name of embargo, and by other ruinous commercial restrictions which for many years have been wantonly imposed by the government of the United States; and its measure of iniquity being now filled up by a declaration of war against Great Britain, a war impolitic, unnecessary and unjust, and by which all our former sufferings will be aggravated, while our liberty and independence are put in jeopardy by the consequent connections with France whose government under every form stamped with despotism and perfidy is now in the bloodstained hands of a monster whose falsehood, injustice, cruelty ambition and tyranny have not in any period of the world been surpassed."

In this strain, the declaration proceeded at some considerable length.

I voted for this address, but I do not now approve of its spirit. The Federal party had then been wrought up to a high pitch of feeling against the dominant party. In this County they had suffered very much from 1806 to 1812 by embargo, non-intercourse, and other commercial restrictions and then by way. In 1806 when the principal trouble commenced by the rejections of a treaty which had been negotiated with Great Britain, commercial business was in the full tide of success and the check suddenly given to it was more heavily felt in contrast with the preceding years of the greatest prosperity. This violent opposition of the Federal party was kept up until the time of the Hartford Convention [293] with great virulence.

Hartford Convention [293]

October 5, 1814: the governor, with the advice of Council, convened the Legislature in an extra session which continued till the 20th of October. It was at this session that the far-famed Hartford Convention was resolved on. I voted for this measure which has since become so much a theme of reproach to those who acted in it I feel confident in saying that at that time, it was thought a prudent measure where by the feverish excitement which had become exceedingly violent might receive some abatement. That in selecting men whose years, character, connections and wealth, united with pre-eminent talents and whose patriotism was well known and highly appreciated in the community would have a tendency to prevent sedition, revolt and violent out breakings in opposition to the loss of the United States.

The result of their deliberations is before the public and I think that the coming age will pronounce it harmless. The uneasy feeling that has always been felt in the eastern section of the Union on account of the gradual departure of power and political influence from them and the increase of it in the west by its rapid growth in population and wealth will, when it is perceived to be hopeless of remedy, if remedy that should be called which can only be obtained by a narrowing of our limits cramping the resources of our common country retarding the increase of our population and restricting the progress of wealth, refinement, arts, science, learning and knowledge to a small section of the country because forsooth they happened [294] to be beforehand in all these. This is a local, narrow, illiberal feeling, which has had its day in New England, but it must vanish under the mighty power of a free press, the influence of steam power and of rail roads and of the numerous improvements of the means of intercourse by the post office and otherwise which present themselves at every day of the present time.

Of the twelve delegates to the Hartford Convention from Massachusetts, Samuel S. Wilde is the only one that I am certain is now alive. He is yet acting as a judge of the Supreme Court of the state, without complaint by the public of the diminution of his faculties for the transaction of business. I am in doubt whether Stephen Longfellow is still living. (He died August 3, 1849 at Portland aged 73) (Judge Wilde resigned his office October 1850) (died 1855).

Such at some periods has been the lack of political excitement in Beverly that in 1815 the whole number of votes given for the Representative to the General Court in 1815 was 23 as follows; Thomas Davis 23, Robert Rantoul 23, Nicholas Thorndike 23, which five persons were chosen and there was one more vote given which was for Ebenezer Everett. And again in 1818, the town voted to choose but one representative. Thomas Davis had 9 votes, Robert Rantoul 8, Nathaniel Goodwin 1. The whole number being 18, there was no choice. At a second trial Robert Rantoul had 11 votes and Thomas Davis 4 votes, whole number 15. This result was obtained through the influence of Thomas Davis who desired his friends to vote for me. There are other instances of the paucity of party spirit and extent of political excitement to be found on the Town Records.

James Monroe [295]

In 1817 James Monroe who had succeeded James Madison as President of the United States made the tour of the eastern states in the summer of that year. Israel Thorndike, who then resided principally in Boston, but made his house in Beverly his summer residence invited the President to stop at his house and breakfast. The principle inhabitants of Beverly and some from Salem and other towns in the vicinity were invited. Nathan Dane who had been acquainted with Mr. Monroe while in Congress, made a short address of welcome to him. I was introduced to him and breakfasted with him. After the outrageous violence of party spirit which had prevailed through the administrations of John Adams, Thomas Jefferson and James Maddison, this period was called the "Era of good feelings". The Federal party saw that it was in vain to prosecute their views of power in the violent manner in which they had at first struggled to maintain their preeminence and for sixteen years to regain it, now endeavored to conciliate their opponents. The principal merchants and other leading federalists in Boston and other large places in New England vied with each other in their polite and generous reception of the President upon this occasion. Symptoms of dissolution of the Federal party were apparent at this time and it was soon lost in the formation of the National Republican party by a practical amalgamation with the Democrats.

Party Spirit [296]

I think that party spirit has never been more bitter than it was from the commencement of John Adams' administration to the close of James Madison's a period of twenty years during which I steadfastly adhered to the Federal party. Israel Thorndike, a Federalist, was as violent a partisan pervious to the accession of Monroe as any to be found in this part of the country yet he was among the most forward in his attentions to Mr. Monroe in Boston and in this town. I do not recollect that he received any particular attention in Salem. The people here greeted him with cheers. On an occasion previous to this, in 1809 Mr. Thorndike opened his house for the public reception of Gov. Christopher Gore who made a tour from Boston to Maine, with much parade. I was introduced to Gov. Gore at Mr. Thorndike's house in my military dress in company with the other officers of the militia in their uniforms with their swords. There was firing of guns ringing of bells and huzzaing by the people. Gov. Gore lost his election the next year and probably the ostentation manifested on this town was one of the causes which led to his failure. It was something more than was thought becoming in a republican Governor of a state and was commented upon with great severity and sometimes ridiculed, exaggerated and misrepresented by the Democratic Newspapers. No other Governor within my recollection has made such an ostentatious display of grandeur. The leading Federalists promoted and cooperated.

Columbian Sentinel – Benjamin Russel (Federalist Party paper) [297]

The Columbian Sentinel, published and edited by Major Benjamin Russel was the leading paper of the Federal party. It ceased its opposition to the administration of the United States government on the accession of Mr. Monroe. It was with Benj. Russel that the phrase "Era of good feelings" originated and he acted according to its import. His paper which had been so vituperative and so exclusively opposed as never to utter a sentence in commendation of the Democratic administration before, now ceased to find fault and during the eight years of Monroe's administration the paper was free from all fault finding with that administration. Major Russel did not cease to be a Federalist until the last moments of the party. He then became a "National Republican" and then a "Whig". He died on the fourth of January 1845 in the 84th year of his age. I was a member of the Legislature with him for about 20 years. He commenced as a member in 1805, four years before I did. He was in both branches of the Legislature 27 years and 2 years in the Executive council.

He it was that in 1811 invented the word Gerrymander in 1811 when Mr. Gerry was governor, the Legislature made a new division of the districts for the election of Representative to Congress. An absurd and singular arrangement of the towns in the county of Essex, with Chelsea in the county of Suffolk was made to compose a district. Russel took a map of Essex and Chelsea and designated by a particular coloring the towns thus selected. He then hung the map on the wall of his editorial closet. One day, Gilbert Stuart, the celebrated painter looked at the map and said the towns which Russel had thus distinguished [298] formed a picture resembling some monstrous animal. He took a pencil and with a few touches, added what might be supposed to represent claws. "There" said Stuart, "that will do for a Salamander." Russel, who was busy with his pen looked up at the hideous figure and exclaimed "Salamander! Call it Gerrymander." The word became a proverb and for many years reproach to the Democratic Legislature of 1811. An engraving of the "Gerrymander" was made and hawked about the state, which had much effect in annoying if not in defeating the Democratic party. The new word did not find its way into <u>Webster's</u> dictionary in his life time, but I do not know how soon it may become a dictionary word.

Impeachment of Judge James Prescott [299]

In 1821, there was an extra session of the Legislature for the trial of the impeachment of James Prescott, Judge of Probate for the county of Middlesex for misconduct and maladministration in office.

This session commenced on Wednesday, April 18th, 1821 and ended on Friday, April 27th, 1821. Of the Senators William Gray, John M. Williams, Thomas Longley and George Mynick, were not present at the trial. The court of impeachment consisting of the Senate was organized and opened from day to day with much ceremony and formality. Samuel Hoar Jun., George Blake, Daniel Webster, and Samuel Hubbard appeared as counsel for Prescott.

There were 15 articles of impeachment. The following senators voted not guilty upon all the articles, viz Peter C. Brooks, John Wells, Jonathan Hunnewell, Samuel Eastman, Lewis Bigelow, and William Sullivan. The President of the Senate, John Phillips had but one opportunity or special call to vote and that was on the second article when it appeared that there were thirteen Senators voted that the respondent was guilty and twelve that he was not guilty when the President voted that he was not guilty, and this made a tie. It was generally understood that if there was a call for his vote, that he would give it in favor of acquittal on every charge. He seemed to have a strong sympathy for Prescott. They were classmates at college. Both their names beginning with the same letter brought them nearer in their recitations and there was a particular [300] friendship formed which had continued for a long time. I voted that he was guilty on the 1st, 2nd, 3rd, 4th, 5th, 7th, 11th, & 12th and not guilty on the other seven articles of charge. On 3rd article there were 16 voted that he was guilty and on the 12th article there were 19 voted he was guilty so that he was convicted on these two articles only. The result astonished me because it appeared so clear to my mind that the eight charges on which I voted that he was guilty proved beyond a reasonable doubt and if proved I did not presume how they could be otherwise considered than as misconduct and mal-administration in office. It is a striking instance of the different impression made upon men's minds by the same testimony. It was a time when there was no great excitement from party politics, but it had so lately been preceded by great excitement that the persons then in public life could hardly be considered as entirely divested of its influence. Prescott was a strong Federalist connected by friendship or otherwise with the principal men in Boston and no doubt had the sympathy of the conservatives and principal lawyers. All the Suffolk senators were for his acquittal upon all the charges. Two lawyers from the country voted to acquit on all and two more for condemning him on one article only. These were all Federalists. Of the Democrats two voted to condemn on 11 articles, two on 10 one on 9, one on 7, one on 6 and this comprised the whole number of Democrats. There were some of the articles although proved were not considered as containing a proper charge. There were several articles that were abandoned by the prosecution as not sustained by the evidence. On three of the articles there was a unanimous vote of acquittal [301] and on a fourth a unanimous vote for an acquittal save one. Upon the whole, I am inclined to the opinion that the method of proceeding by impeachment by one branch and the trial by another branch of the Legislature does not afford that protection against misconduct and mal administration in office which was expected by the framers of our Constitution or that of the United States. It is impracticable to exclude the undue influence of party prejudice upon the minds of those who are actively engaged in party politics at the time, as members of the Legislature and in times of great political excitement who can avoid, while they are members of the Legislature partaking of the feelings of the party?

My attendance on this trial increased my stock of knowledge in relation to many subjects particularly in regard to the constitution and duties of probate courts in which I have had occasion to transact much business from time to time to this day.

On Tuesday, April 17, 1821 a snow commenced about noon and continued through the night so that on Wednesday when the court commenced there was snow enough, though considerably drifted, for sleighing which continued for two or three days. The depth of the snow was estimated at from a foot to a foot and a half. The weather was cold pretty much through the session and vegetation very backward.

[302] The arrangement of the seats and tables in the Senate chamber were temporarily altered for the occasion so as to have all the Senators in two semicircular rows on the east side of the chamber and thus allowing the counsel and mangers on the part of the house of Rep on the west side of the chamber to face the courts. Jace C. Kuhn, messenger of the General Court was appointed Crier and made all the proclamations with dignity and propriety. Samuel F. McCleary was appointed clerk of the court and was sworn by the

President George Blake for the defense, spoke about six hours and Daniel Webster about the same length of time.

It was probably through the influence which resulted from this impeachment upon the public mind that from the 1st day of May 1824 all fees were abolished in the Probate Court and salaries were established for the judges and registers of Probate. In the House of Representatives, I took an active and I think an influential part in bringing about this change which in this county of Essex has given so much satisfaction. The fees demanded had become an occasion of great complaint and sometimes of altercation between the Register and persons doing business in the court. In January 1822, I received a letter from Nehemiah Knowlton of Gloucester making divers complaints to me as a Senator of the County a copy of my answer to which is on file with miscellaneous papers for 1822. I had some difference with the Register in regard to his fees on Joseph Stickney's estate in 1820.

[303] The fees of the Register on this estate remained unsettled until June 20, 1845 when I paid him $7.12 being the balance which I had retained in my hands of the said estate for more than twenty years during which time there remained between him and me some unpleasant feelings which were occasionally manifested. I advise my grandchildren to avoid all collision with public officers in the transaction of business so far as practicable. I suffered very much more pecuniary to say nothing of my feelings than the difference between the sum he demanded and what I thought he was entitled to.

An officer in his situation has very many opportunities of disobliging persons having business with him and when availing himself of such opportunities to gratify his resentful feelings may avoid doing or leaving undone anything that will afford a sufficient ground for public animediation upon his conduct so that the sufferer must bear in silence what he feels to be injurious without the satisfaction of complaining. The want of the pleasant, cheerful good will of a recording officer in any Court is attended with numerous disadvantages to a person having frequent occasion to transact business therein. I have suffered so much from this cause as to make me particularly desirous that my grandchildren should pursue a more conciliatory course with everyone in such situations with whom they may have occasion to transact business.

[304] Copy of a letter to Nehemiah Knowlton of Gloucester

"Beverly Jan 28th, 1822

"Dear Sir:

"Being at Boston last week I did not receive yours of the 17th until Saturday evening the 26th.

"I agree with you that <u>some</u> alteration has become necessary in the laws relating to the compensation of the Judge & Register of Probate for this County, but it is difficult to decide what alterations would give satisfaction to the public and at the same time present the respectability of the offices. The proper course for those who are dissatisfied is to petition the Legislature.

"Without petitions from the inhabitants it will be difficult to convince members of the Legislature from other parts of the State that the people of the County are dissatisfied and generally wish a change.

"It will always give me pleasure to receive information from any of my constituents upon any subject of Legislation in which they are more immediately interested."

[304.1] July 29th, 1857: the managers on the part of the House of Representatives of the impeachment of James Prescott were x John G. King, chairman. He died on Sunday July 26, 1857 at Salem. He was a son of James King and was born March 19, 1787 and was 70 years of age March 19, 1857. The other managers were Levi Lincoln, William Baglies, Warren Dutton and Samuel P. Fay, Samuel Hoar and Sherman Leland. In the course of the proceedings Horatio G. Newcomb and Francis C. Gray were substituted for Lincoln & Baglies.

The counsel employed by James Prescott were x William Prescott and George Blake x Daniel Webster x Samuel Hoar X Samuel Hubbard and x Augustus Peabody. Mr. King made the opening argument for the government. Those who I know to be dead at this time are marked x.

Mr. King was voted for the kindliness and generosity of this social feelings. He was a man of distinguished probity and eminent attainment and his death will cause a deep void in the community of which he was a useful member and an illustrious ornament.

[305] The largest number of members of the House of Representatives in the General Court was in 1812 when there were 747 chosen and it was calculated that there were 730 who attended on the first day of the session. The votes given were for speaker, Timothy Bigelow, the Federal candidate 420. John Holmes the Democratic candidate 290, gathering 3 = 716. For clerk Benjamin Polland, the Federal candidate 425, Charles Pinkney Sumner, the Democratic candidate 288 = 713

After the first day of the session when the strength of the two great parties was ascertained the attendance of members rapidly declined. It was then expected that the towns would have to pay for the attendance of their members, which the members mostly thought to be a good reason for shortening their stay in Boston.

1857 February – Charles P. Sumner above named was the father of Charles Sumner, Senator of the U.S. who has for some time past had the notoriety of being beaten with a cane by Preston S. Brooks of South Carolina while sitting in this seat in the Senate chambers at Washington. From this cowardly, brutal, murderous attack Mr. Sumner has not yet fully recovered and perhaps never will. Brooks has died, after a very short sickness, at Washington, the present winter.

Town Treasurer - Mass Convention for Rewriting the Constitution 1820 [309]

In 1817, I was chosen and served as Town Treasurer and was reelected to the office in 1818, but at the same time a reduction of the salary from what it had been previously was voted and in consequence I declined accepting the office for 1818. The reduction being made in a manner that displeased me. At a town meeting October 16, 1820, I was chosen a delegate to the convention for amending the Constitution of Massachusetts to meet on the third Wednesday in November 1820. There were four delegates chosen viz. Nathan Dane, Robert Rantoul, Nathaniel W. Williams and John Low. There were twelve persons voted for in all. The whole number of votes was sixty-four. Those chosen had from 52 to 55 votes each. Nathan Dane did not attend the Convention on account of deafness. The other three attended constantly. The principle effort of Williams and Low was to obtain an alteration of the third article of the Bill of Rights relating to the support of public worship and instruction.

Low was so heated with what he had experienced with relation to the division of the First Parish in this town that it seemed to engross his whole attention. Williams was as strongly impressed with what he called the oppression of the Baptists, of which denomination he was a minister but was active in his attention to all the points which were discussed. The convention sat from November 15th, 1820 to January 9th, 1821. At a town meeting in Beverly, previous to the one held on the 16th of October for choosing delegates on the question "Is it expedient that a convention be held?" the vote was 14 in favor of a convention and 18 against it. There were about 500 members elected to the convention they were not all present at any one time.

[310] This convention comprised a large amount of talent, probably more than was ever before assembled in Massachusetts. Every principle in the Constitution was fully discussed and that by the most able men. I spoke some five or six times, but my usual caution prevented my indulging myself in much speaking among so many whom I know to be my superiors in talent. There seemed to be a prevailing disposition to endeavor to <u>improve</u> as well as to <u>alter</u> the Constitution. There was a conservative party and a radical party, the first composed mostly of Federalists the other mostly of Democrats. There were several clergymen and others who would not choose to be ranked with any political party. Most of the towns that sent more than one, chose a portion from each party, so that though the Federal party had a large majority, yet there was a fair representation of the Democratic party. I generally but not always voted with the conservative party. The amendments so far as they were adopted made the Constitution more Democratic and such have been the amendments which have been adopted at different times since the convention and such will they continue to be here after Democracy is progressive but it is well that its progress is checked by a conservative party, they always exists of sufficient strength to prevent the evil that might result from the sudden changes which might be brought about without due deliberation by the fanaticism excessive ardor or improvident zeal of hasty reformers.

[311] My attendance on this Convention enlarged my acquaintance with the prominent men of Massachusetts and increased my knowledge of the principles of a free government. Daniel Webster and William Prescott, I think exercised a larger influence than any other two members. The first by his eloquence, the second by his policy combined with occasional speaking but not frequent. President John Adams was a member, but his great age and infirmities prevented his attendance after the 18th of December, when he had leave of absence. I dined with him at a party at Col. Israel Thorndike's. It was apparent that his mind was somewhat impaired by age, he then being 85. He died July 4, 1826 in his 91st year. He was born October 1735.

I was a member of the largest committee consisting of 29 respecting the Senate and House of Representatives of which William Prescott was chairman and I had in the sittings of that committee which were many, a good opportunity of witnessing his sagacity and adroit management, of which there was much need to bring them to a conclusion on a subject about which there was such a diversity of opinion. I went for the greatest reduction of number for the House that I supposed was attainable. I was of the opinion that 150 was a sufficient number to represent so compact and territorially small a state as Massachusetts, however numerous its population but so great a reduction did not then appear to be practicable. The time may come when a division of the state into as many districts as there are representative will be attainable, say 150, which I think to be the [312] true republican theory. The increase of cities which will continue to desire an aggregate representation chosen by the party being the strongest in the city without risking its weakening by a districting which might introduce one or more members from a minority party in reference to the whole is a growing obstacle to the introduction of this simple principle of representation. I would propose the same principle in regard to Senatorial representation. When the convention was held the principal obstacle to a system of districting was that a great number of towns would be deprived of a corporate representation by the smallness of their population. I think that before long this objection will be forsaken because of the undue power and influence resulting from the aggregation of the votes of Cities of which there soon will be some twelve or more comprising a third part of the whole population of the state, that will find it easier to combine its influence than the other two thirds distributed in three hundred corporations, each acting by itself. These 300 corporations will therefore prefer being represented in districts upon condition that the Cities shall also be divided into districts when entitled to more than one representative. I also think that the Senators should be chosen by single districts so that there should be the nearest practicable approach to a fair representation of the people in the Legislature.

Union Fire Society [313]

Copy of a Report to the Union Fire Society

Leather fire bucket,
Beverly Union Fire Society, 1813.

"The Treasurer of the Union Fire Society in Beverly having completed thirty years' service in that office and having recently been called on for a more full exposition of the pecuniary affairs of the Society than has been usually exhibited makes the following report viz: This Society was formed in 1804 and such has been its mutation that only two of its original members now remain. The late Thomas Davis Esq. was chosen as the first treasurer and continued in office until January 1811 when he, declining another re-election, the present incumbent was chosen and by successive annual re-elections has been continued in office to this time. On the 14th of February 1811, after a settlement with Treasurer Davis and with the clerk of the preceding year the funds of the society were found to amount to two hundred and seventy-four dollars which was then loaned on a Note to an individual. Since that time to January 1841 there has been received for assessments on the members twenty-eight dollars and twenty-five cents, there has also been received from the several clerks, by the treasurer for balances of fines and of sums of money received for admission of members, one hundred and seventy-five dollars and seventy-six cents. The receipts by the treasures from these sources for the period of thirty years amounting in the whole to the sum of two hundred and four dollars and one cent.

[314] "The expenditures of the Society are in part disbursed by the clerk and deducted from his receipts for fines and the admission of members the remainder of the expenses are paid by the treasury. There has been no assessment upon the members for any purpose whatever for about eighteen years last past. There has been paid by the treasurer for various objects which have been authorized by the Society and for the whole period referred to in this report, the sum of two hundred and thirty-eight dollars and twenty-five cents. Thus, the receipts into the treasurer form assessments, fines and fees for admission of members since February 14, 1811 has been less than the expenditures by thirty-four dollars and twenty-four cents. For the last three years nothing has been received from the clerk by the Treasurer whilst during that period the sum of five dollars per year amounting to fifteen dollars has been paid to Samuel Lovett, for storage of the sails and carriage, belonging to the Society in pursuance of an agreement made with him by their Committee.

"Thus, it appears that the increase of the Fund from two hundred and seventy-four dollars, it's amount on the 14th of February 1811, to the sum of one thousand two hundred & ninety-nine dollars and sixty-eight cents. Its amount at this time is exclusively to be assigned to the interest which has accrued on it from time to time and which has been regularly added to the principle. Of this fund, the members of the Society for the time being are the trustees and for the proposes for which it was created and for no other.

"The foundation of this fund was principally by assessments [315] on the members of the Society for the first seven years of its existence as will appear by the accounts of the first treasurer, its object will appear by the seventeenth article of the constitution to be 'for the express purpose of relieving such of the members as may unfortunately reduce in circumstances by fire' and by the nineteenth article this relief is also to be extended to the widows of deceased members. The usual annual account of the treasurer is annexed and makes a part of this report. At which is respectfully submitted.

"Rob Rantoul Treasurer

"Beverly January 11, 1841."

The occasion of making this detailed report was that at a meeting previous to the meeting in January 1841, the question had been raised about paying for an annual dinner out of the fund and a suggestion had been made in reference to the division of the fund among the members of the society. I resisted all such prospects. One ground of my argument was that the fund had grown from assessments and fines paid by the first members and they were then almost all dead and had many of them left widows who according to the articles of association in case of suffering loss by fire would be entitled to relief and that we could not without violating their rights, do anything that would prevent the society from satisfying such claims [316] on this occasion as well as a somewhat similar one prior to that, as a strenuous effort became necessary to secure an adherence to right principles on the part of the members generally, who were liable to be misled by the sophistry of one or two and by their own indolence and indifference.

[317] The Union Fire Society was formed in this town in 1804. I had nothing to do with originating it, but was one of its first members, and my long adherence to it deserves to be noted. It is now about forty-five years since its formation and I, only, of its first members remain. The whole number of persons who have belonged to it from its institution till this time is 108. Of this number, 51 are dead. Its present number of members is 42. I was Clerk for the first year and after the resignation of Thomas Davis who was the first treasurer, I was chosen to succeed him in 1811 and have been reelected annually to that office until this time, 1849, when 38 years are completed and I have entered on the 39th year. Although I have no claim to the originating of this association, yet I have special claim to its preservation. There has been more than one period in its history when, without special effort, it would have fallen to pieces. I have thought that its preservation was desirable and have therefore given at such times particular attention to the exigency. The fund has grown very much under my administration as treasurer and I have successfully resisted two attempts to dissipate it by convivial feasting. The fund of the society consists of 12 shares in the Beverly Bank and about 950$ in the Salem Savings Bank, amounting together to seventeen hundred dollars. When first I took the office of treasurer, Feb 14th, 1811 the fund was 274$.

[318] I am not very sanguine that it is of great importance that this institution should be continued indefinitely but if any one of my male descendants thinks that it had better be continued, he should join it and give his attention to its business with undiminishing constancy. Persevering therein against all obstacles and particularly against indifference which always affords ample field for the operations of any busy body, whether actuated by a spirit of putridity in reference to the division of the fund or by any other motive. There is frequently in a considerable number of associates, an individual who would take active means to dissolve the body with the expectation of receiving his distribution as a share of the fund and might succeed purely from the indifference of others unless opposed with equal activity by some generous, self-sacrificing opponent. My own experience in reference to this Union Fire Society for the space of forty-five years gives me confidence in recommending these remarks to careful consideration.

It is a good rule never to join any association until you are well satisfied that its establishment or its continuance will be useful and that you can bestow due care and attention to its interests. Having joined with proper motives, do not separate from it or neglect its interests because its novelty has disappeared but by your example encourage the perseverance of others who will be liable to fall away if left to depend upon their own resources.

Fire Department [319]

From the time of my commencing business in Beverly in 1796 until the introduction of those and other new machinery for the extinguishment of fires, it was my invariable practice, unless prevented by sickness, on an alarm of fire either in this town or in Salem, by night or by day, let the weather be what it might, with as much speed as practicable to take my fire buckets and proceed to the scene of devastation. It was then the prevalent opinion that it was an incumbent duty of all able-bodied persons so to do. This opinion had a favorable moral influence upon the mass of the community, promoting a generous desire to aid and assist one another by personal labors and sacrifices. The division of labor, an increase of refinement, the introduction of machinery and the general practice of insurance against fire has very much changed the state of opinion in regard to this subject. Whether the gain or the loss from this change predominates I do not feel ready to say. That there are great evils resulting from the almost universal practice of insuring against fire, I am well assured of. A diminution of carefulness, vigilance, watchfulness and activity in the laborious classes, the multiplication of fraudulent transactions in regard to insurance recklessness in reference to the loss or destruction of property, the lessening of sympathy for our fellow beings, the reserve and forbearance of personal labor in aid of others, grow out of this change aided by other changes in the social state consequent upon the increase of wealth.

[320] I know how ready the aged are to say that the former times were better than these. They are more sensitive to the evils of change while the young thinking little of these evils enjoy the inspiration of hope that change is improvement, when experience, sometimes at least, proves this hope to be fallacious.

The beginning of the shifting of the obligation upon every able-bodied person to repair to and aid in the extinguishing of fires, to certain persons appointed for that purpose was in June 18, 1825 when an act was passed authorizing the City of Boston to establish a fire department. Fire departments were soon after established in Salem and other principal places in the State and also prematurely in many smaller towns and villages, so that the change in the City which became necessary from the state of things in regard to its population was followed by a change in many other places when it has been injurious to the interests of the inhabitants but where they are fated to endure the evil, because they cannot restore the feelings and principles of action which have been thus inconsiderately sacrificed to the love of novelty, the desire of change.

[323] Before the formation of the Massachusetts Society for the Suppression of Intemperance in 1812 or 1813, I was much engaged about the existing practices and habits which prevailed universally in regard to the use of distilled spirits as a beverage. I had never learned to use them myself and I had become strongly impressed with the knowledge of the existing evils that resulted from their habitual use. The Massachusetts Society, although it existed in embryo before, was not fully organized until February 5, 1813, I joined at the first public meeting and my membership has continued to this time. I have during the same time been variously connected with other associations have the same object in view. I have attended many meetings upon the subject of temperance reform and in several different parts of this state. I have distributed in this town and elsewhere a large number of tracts. Beginning with Doct. Benjamin Bush's tract which, although very sound in the main, and sufficiently thorough at the time when published yet is not adapted to the present state of opinion, in as much as it proposes the cure of inebriety, when occasioned by spirituous, by resorting to the use of fermented liquors. Experience has since shown that this excuse is not to be relied on, that nothing but total abstinence from all intoxicating drinks can insure an entire change of the appetite. I distributed a considerable number of the first publication on the subject by the American Tract [324] Society, of which I was a life member from its first institution and in consequence of my paying twenty dollars I was supplied with a large number of their earlier publications for gratuitous distribution among which were some on the subject of temperance. I corresponded and co-operated with the Minister Abbot, who very soon after his installation proclaimed a series of

sermons upon this subject. I think that these sermons were delivered in 1803 and 1804. I remember that the <u>grumblers</u> of which class there are always more or less in every society began to say that they did not want to hear about <u>rum</u> all the time.

I have endeavored in various ways for nearly half a century to operate upon the opinions, practices and habits of society in regard to the use of intoxicating drinks. I have always refrained from the use of spirits as a beverage from a conviction of their inutility and a fear of the lamentable consequences of their use was so singular at the time that it was a subject of remark and frequently of unpleasant jeering, ridicule and sarcasms. In 1813 the public movement by association began and I formed in it heartily though this public movement was for a time involved in a cloud of odium and the power of ridicule was exerted to suppress it. My example in which I have been almost but not quite inflexible for about a half a century, (I might say seventy years) in regard to the drinking of spirits and altogether and entirely influenced [325] in regard to the use of any intoxicating liquors as a beverage, since March 1833 when I last drank some wine at a party given in Boston by Lieut. Gov. Samuel F. Armstrong the last year that I was a Representative to the General Court, my example I say has been confessed by several to have been the direct cause of their reformation from a habit of indulgence which if they had not then arrested would probably have proved their ruin and I am very confident that it has had and is still having a more extensive and effective influence in changing the habits of society than anything or all that I have written, spoken or said upon this great subject. I commend this to the particular attention of my grandchildren. There is no individual in society whose example for good or for evil is not more or less influential on the characters, habits, manners and morals of others. This example is in those of any class in society who are looked upon as more learned or wise, more intelligent or more virtuous operating with more power upon other classes in society than is generally appreciated. Therefore, in addition to all the other motives to a virtuous course, add this also; that everything that you say or do that is right, true and good will to a certain extent increase the virtue of others and that everything that you say or do that is wrong, false and wicked will to a certain extent, deteriorate the virtue of others. An example in regard to any particular change of the existing [326] habits of society which are thought to be wrong and to call for a change must not merely be commenced but must be persevered in, not merely for sixteen years, for fifty years or for seventy years but for the whole life or until the desired change should be brought about- Perseverance until the end.

In addition to my other efforts in this course, I have served as president of an association in this town called the Union Temperance Society which was organized at the time when there was a difference of opinion in regard to the propriety of <u>giving a pledge</u> to total abstinence. It was organized April 6th, 1835 and operated for a few years and then died out. I had commenced the <u>practice</u> of total abstinence more than two years before that time, but I did not think well then of insisting upon it in regard to fermented liquors, as a principle of association and requiring persons to give a pledge. I delivered an address to this society in the old Town Hall on the 12th of May 1835 in which I explained the principles which I then thought should be the ground of action by associations and be individuals to promote the progress of reform. This Society consisted of 52 members. The two articles in its constitution which distinguished it from some other societies are "3rd. The object of this society shall be to discountenance and suppress the use of spirituous liquors as a community and to promote habits of temperance." [327] "7th. Each member of this society shall make it a particular object to discountenance and prevent by his own example and influence the <u>intemperate</u> use of all intoxicating liquors." This society held a few annual meetings for the election of officers but was finally merged in the associations under the comprehensive pledge. The Beverly Total Abstinence Society was organized April 12th, 1838. I was chosen President in 1844 and have been continued to this time. I had previously signed the pledge of total abstinence which I had practiced since March 1833 but had entertained some scruple in regard to signing a pledge to do what I had resolved to do as long as I thought it best. Upon the whole, I think it was wise in me to yield to the current of opinion which was then strongly in favor of the adoption of a pledge. If I had continued to refuse my example might have encourage some to refuse to whom it might prove beneficial. Indeed, I think that in the attainment of any great object by combined action it is proper to concede our own individual opinions in regard to many of the details, to the prevalent opinion of others, when we do not think the positively wrong, otherwise it is in the power of every pertinacious or obstinate person to throw obstacles in the way which will seriously regard the main design. Latterly the "Sons of Temperance", and the "Daughters of Temperance" have taken to the lead in the Temperance reform, and I have endeavored to aid them by my occasional attendance and speaking at their meetings.

Temperance Reform [328]

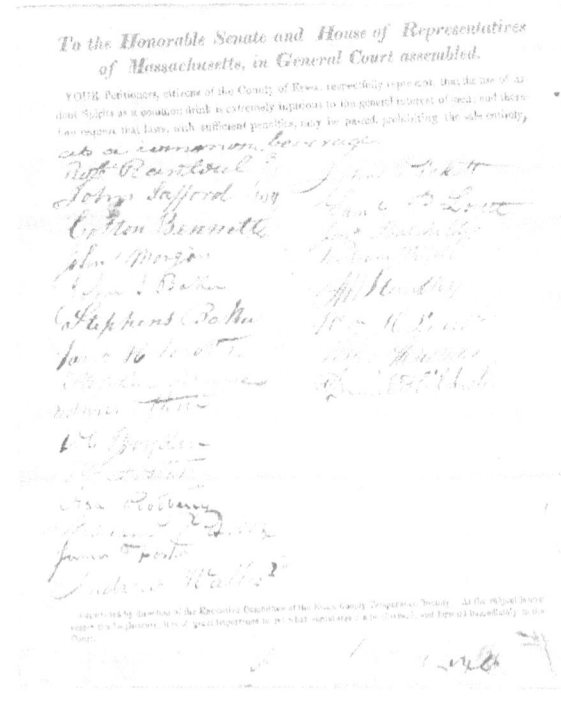

Petition to the Massachusetts Legislature from the Essex County Temperance Society.

January 29, 1835: I signed a petition to the general court praying for a law prohibiting the sale of spirituous liquors by retail. July 4th, 1833: I attended a public dinner at Gloucester and began to act in public upon my assumed resolution of total abstinence. Hosea Hildreth the minister and a temperance lecturer sat next to me at the table but before the toasts began to be drank he left the table band I <u>alone</u> filled my glass with water and refrained from wine entirely and it was a subject of remark, but I suffered no injury thereby. I did the same thing again July 4, 1835 at a public dinner in Beverly at which I presided and also at the ordination of Andrew P Peabody at Portsmouth in 1833. In the last-mentioned instance, I was supported by John Ball, now a domestic missionary at Salem and by him only. Other cases have occurred of a similar kind not requiring any special effort to meet them. September 15, 1837: I was appointed a vice president of the Essex County Temperance Society.

The pledge of the society which I am now president (Jan. 7, 1849) is; "We whose names are annexed agree to abstain, entirely, from the use as a beverage, of all intoxicating liquors that we will not be traffic, manufacture or in any other ways furnish them for such purpose and that we will use our influence to do away their use throughout the community"

By returning to my lecture before the Union Temperance Society, May 12, 1835 my lecture in the new Town Hall, December 9th, 1844, and my address to the Daughters of Temperance February 10th, 1847 and to gradual change of my opinions in regard to the necessity and importance of reform to the well-being of society I cannot say that my opinions have changed at all for the last half century.

[329] The first distillery in Beverly was erected before the Revolutionary war. It was on the wharf that is now Josiah Lovett 2nd's nearly opposite to Hildreth's Soap and Candle factory. Within the past year I have seen some of the brick foundation of the fire place. This Rum distillery at one time was said to belong to Joseph Lee, but I think it probably that there were other owners as well as him. He removed from this town to Boston and there died at a great age. The next distillery was Abel Laurence's and soon became Israel Dodge's (both of Salem) and was carried on by his son Caleb until the drowned himself in one of its cisterns. Being found with a kettle tied to his leg. Charles Dennis was employed as a foreman in this Distillery, he was afterwards master of the Work House and became intemperate. This Distillery was situated on Cabot street, bounding on the Court leading from Cabot street to the Work House. I think that Caleb Dodge died in the first part of the year 1798, that the business was continued for a short time by his brother Israel Dodge Jun., and was then abandoned and has not been resumed here since. I was the very first person who declined supplying <u>spirituous</u> liquors at funerals. This was in 1816. I was among the first, if not the very first, who refused to furnish spirituous liquors to persons who worked for me, by the day. It had been a universal custom in this town that when a mechanic or laborer was hired by the day, that he should be supplied with not less than half a pint of Rum, if he chose to drink so much, on each day that he was employed.

[330] Previously to those beginning to work, I gave them to understand that I should not provide any spirit so that they might take the circumstance into consideration in fixing the price of their work. This course was attended with much unpopularity for some time, but it soon became manifest to the more considerate that it was beneficial to both the employer and the employed and it has now become the general or, I might say, the universal custom in this town, for the employed to find his own drink. In the case of funerals, intoxicating liquors are now almost entirely dispensed with. In these two cases I claim much for my persevering example. Another case where I think my total abstinence from <u>spirituous liquors</u> has by example proved extensively useful was, while I was Commissioner of Highways and visited almost every town in the county under circumstances which customarily brought out the decanter at almost every resting place when viewing routes for roads petitioned for. I sometime exposed myself to ridicule when I refused to drink as others did but I persevered and now, my then singular practice, has become the prevailing custom. Although I derive much satisfaction from the reflection that by various bold and persevering methods I have contributed a large share to the promotion of the temperance reform, yet it is a subject of deep regret that I was once licensed as a retailer or Wines and Spirits and that I continued in the business for several years until I saw the evil of it and I then quit it, many years before I gave up shop keeping entirely. I think I left off selling spirits in 1813 or 1814 about ten years before I gave up my shop.

[331] July 4th, 1839: I attended the Great Temperance Dinner in Faneuil Hall Boston. Some 12 or 1500 persons were present. Edward Brooks presided. I offered and read a series of resolutions, which were prepared by my son Robert. These resolutions were published in the Salem Advertiser of July 6th, 1839 and about the same time in most of the temperance papers. February 12th and 13th 1840: I attended a temperance convention in Boston. About 1500 present. This was the most spirited Temperance Convention which I have attended. There was an effort to blend the temperance measures with party politics, which I opposed, and it did not then prevail.

My nephew Andrew P. Peabody, May 8th, 1842, Sunday evening delivered an elegant and thoroughly effective discourse on the subject of wines and wine drinking at the Marlborough Chapel in Boston, having delivered the same discourse in Portsmouth a few weeks before. This was the result of his determination to abandon the drinking of wine himself and to discourage the use of it by others. It had considerable effect in Portsmouth among the fashionable families who are much given to wine drinking. I note this as a demonstration in favor of the temperance reform by one of my family. I ought also to add that every member of my household has kept along with me in their habits of abstinence and that my son Robert has upon numerous occasions lectured and spoken upon the subject in many places in this and other states, to large bodies assembled for the purpose of hearing.

[332] At this time (Jan of 1849) and for a few months previously there has been a considerable degree of excitement upon the subject of Temperance, in this town. It has been mostly gotten up by the two associations called Sons of Temperance and Daughters of Temperance and has been attended with many meetings at Bell's Hall and one or two in the Town Hall. The clergymen of the town have agreed to lecture in the town hall on alternate Sunday evenings and in consequence of this arrangements C. Thayer delivered an interesting address on Sunday evening January 28th of about one hour, to a crowded audience there was singing of a superior grade and prayers by George Dole and benediction by Ira Washburn. My son Robert made an address at the town Hall a few weeks before which was very well received. I have attended most of these meetings and have spoken at some of them. Generally, there has been a good attendance and a more serious aspect has been given to these meetings than has been heretofore gained.

On Sunday evening February 1849 Charles W. Flanders minister of the First Baptist Society made the address in the Town Hall. Rev. Ira Washburn the prayer and ___ [40] Parks, formerly of Danvers the benediction. The singing was as before. C.W. Flanders' address was ingenious assuming a time about 450 years to come as the Millennium, he then described what the people of that period would say of the history of our own time in regard to the use of intoxicating drinks as it might come down to them in history. The Hall was filled, and the attention was profound.

[333] As a measure connected with the temperance reform in this town I will give some account of an occasion of considerable notoriety. On the 5th of January 1849 Jacob Lunt, Inspector of the Police came to me with an order from the Selectmen, directing him to institute a prosecution before me or some other Justice of the Peace against Daniel

---

[40] Rantoul left the first name blank. He was probably referring to Reverend. Harrison G. Park.

Pearson and Joseph W. Davis for selling spirituous liquor by retail, without a license on the 2nd of January 1849. I made out a complaint and issued a warrant thereon against Daniel Pearson for selling spirituous liquor to Eldridge Hildreth and also for selling to Benjamin Roundy and Similar complaints and warrants against Joseph W. Davis for selling to the same persons. Pearson was considered to be the keeper of the tavern called the Atlantic House and Davis as acting under him as Beer keeper. The four warrants were served on them by Constable Francis Lamson and they were brought to my office on Saturday, January 6th, 1849 at nine o'clock a.m. They were arraigned and pleaded not guilty. The produced a letter from Frederick W. Choate stating that he had been employed as their counsel and requesting that the trials might be postponed to Saturday next and I therefore adjourned the Court to Saturday the 13th January at 2 o'clock and recognized each of the respondents without any surety in the sum of $100 for their appearance at that time. Pearson suggested that he should like to have the trial in the Town Hall and the Selectmen caused the [334] Town Hall to be warmed and prepared for the purpose and on Saturday the 13th, at 2 o'clock I adjourned the court from my office to the Hall. There was a large number of persons in attendance so that the seats in the Hall were mostly filled and partly by females. My son Robert appeared for the government and Frederick W. Choate for the respondents. The trial of Joseph W. Davis was first commenced and on both complaints son Robert introduced the trial by a short speech justifying the Selectmen in causing the complaints to be made in these cases, setting froth the evils resulting from the sale of spirituous liquor contrary to the law. He then introduced the witnesses and the trial was continued, and the Court adjourned to Friday the 19th at 9 o'clock in the morning. On Friday, the Hall was again almost filled with spectators, male and female. The trial proceeded till 12 o'clock when it was adjourned until 2 o'clock and then resumed. Son Robert's closing argument was well spoken of by many persons. About sunset the trial of Davis was finished, and he was convicted for selling to Roundy. He was sentenced to pay a fine of twenty dollars and costs of prosecution, from which sentence he appealed to the court of Common Pleas and recognized in the sum of $100 to prosecute is appeal, with Andrew W. Standley and Alden Harris assembled. The Court was adjourned to 6 o'clock in the evening and the trail of Daniel Pearson for selling to Hildreth was then commenced and continued until 9 o'clock, [335] when the Court was adjourned to Saturday the 27th January at 9 o'clock AM. On Saturday January 27th, 1849 I attended at the town hall and immediately adjourned the Court to Saturday the 3rd of February at 1 o'clock in the afternoon by agreement of the counsel for both parties.

On Saturday, the 3rd of February the Court was held at the Town Hall at 1 o'clock P.M. There were considerable numbers of persons of both sexes in the Hall at the opening of the Court and which continued to increase until the recess at about 5 o'clock until six o'clock in the when the Hall was soon filled to the whole extent of its seats above and below. The order considering the large numbers of persons and many of whom were in an undue state of excitement both for and against the accused, was good. There was a slight attempt at applause when Choate finished his argument, but it was immediately repressed. More witnesses were examined on both sides and particularly with respect to the written lease from Annable to Pearson for 5 years from November 1847.

Annable's part of this indenture only had been produced and without being cancelled on a previous day and he then said that Pearson's part of this instrument had not been surrendered to him and had not to his knowledge been cancelled but now he brings

Pearson's part of the instrument with Pearson's release on the back of it to Annable, dated November 25, 1848, saying that since the Court on the 19th of January he had found it among his papers in his room but did not know how [336] it came there. The circumstances connected with this transaction induced his belief that the release on this part of the indenture, although it was dated on the 25th of November last, had in fact been written since the 19th of January last and that it had been done with the connivance of Annable, to help Pearson to prove that he was not the lessee of the Atlantic House on the 2nd of January last when the liquor was said to be sold there. On the part of the responded, Choate made a good argument, more carefully considered and freer of objectionable remarks than the one he made in defense of Davis on the 19th of January. He was followed by my son Robert for the government who fully exposed the tergiversation[41] of Annable in regard to the lease, justified the Selectmen for instituting the prosecution and impressed upon the assembly the great evils of intemperance and the great importance to the young in particular that the laws for the repression of the sale of intoxicating liquors should be faithfully executed. Although I was well satisfied that Davis did sell spirituous liquor in the bar room of the Atlantic House on the 2d of January yet there being no evidence of a direct sale by Pearson and as a Landlord not having fully completed the removal of his family back again into the house after having left it some two months before I did not consider the connection so far as proved, to exist between Davis and Pearson to be of that character which would justify me in considering Davis as the agent or servant of Pearson and thereby make Pearson answerable criminally for the violation of the laws by Davis, therefore acquitted Pearson and he was discharged.

[337] I have before mentioned that my family expenses for the first year after my marriage in 1801 were about $400 and by examining the items of expenditure I find about twelve dollars charged for wine, Brandy and Rum. Now, although my family expenses are much increased, yet it costs nothing for these items and it has not for several years past. Formerly I used to buy some three of four barrels of Cider in each year, but for several years past we have had none. Formerly we occasionally used beer in the family, but for several years past, I might say we have used no fermented liquors whatever. The opponents of reform say that nothing valuable has been accomplished but I say that the charge in regard to the use of liquors in families in middle life is an immense gain on the side of reform.

When I began housekeeping, the custom of treating visitors with intoxicating liquors of some sort, was all but universal; now those who do it in this town are among the exception to the general practice. At the former time, he who did not do it subjected himself to remark, to censure or to ridicule but at the latter period he who does it is considered as braving public opinion.

The first ordination which I attended as a delegate where there was no intoxicating liquor offered was at Lynn, October 11, 1843 when John Peirpont jun. was ordained. A cold collation was provided for the council and the Male & Female members of the society in the Town Hall. No other drink but water was furnished. Rev. John Peirce said that he

---

[41] Tergiversation: equivocation.

had lately for the first time attended a similar occasion in Boston where there was no intoxicating liquor offered.

[338] On Thursday February 15, 1849, I attended a Temperance Convention held in the Tremont Temple in Boston. Asahel Huntington of Salem was appointed President and Sam'l Hoar, Gersham B. Weston, Stephen C. Phillips, Moses Grant, myself and others were appointed Vice Presidents. The numbers assembled was large but did not fill the hall. There appeared to be a general enthusiastic feeling in favor of the cause. Much was said in approbation of the course which the clergy are pursuing and very little against them as has been the case at some meetings which I had attended. S.C. Phillips spoke for the Essex County delegation & S Hoar for Middlesex. John W. Hawkins said that there are more than 1100 places in Boston where intoxicating liquors are sold that three quarters of the persons carried into the Police court for drunkenness are foreigners that 300 of the places for selling strong drink are kept by foreigners. This large proportion of foreigners carried to the Police Court may in part be attributed to the circumstance that they are more generally friendless while the natives having friends more of them are carried home by the police and a smaller proportion carried to the courts, but still it may be true that drunkenness prevails in a greater degree among foreigners than among natives in Boston. I dined with Deacon Moses Grant at 7 Cambridge Street, as did A.Huntington. S Hoar & Barzillac Frost and left the Convention for home at 5 ½ pm. There was a large delegation from Beverly in attendance. They organized a new State Society with the view of uniting the power and influence of several of the existing [339] state organization in one body and thus increasing the efficiency of action beyond what could be attained to by many although acting in concert.

On Sunday evening February 25th, 1849, Rev. Joseph Abbot preached a sermon on Temperance at the Dane Street Church. Introductory prayers by ----[42], powerful singing and instrumental music. Text, Timothy 5-23, "Drink no longer water, but use a little wine for thy stomach sake and thine infirmities". Timothy was educated in temperance principles by his pious grandmother Lois and his faithful mother Eunice. He was a total abstinent, otherwise Paul would not have prescribed a <u>little,</u> as to a man in the habitual use of wine, a <u>little</u> would do no good. Paul did not prescribe for any on but Timothy and certain by not for any one at this day. If Paul was now here the present light of medical science might lead him to refrain from making a similar prescription for like complaints. The text cannot be pleaded in justification of ones prescribing for themselves and if recourse is had to a skillful physician he may know of some better remedy. The sermon was very well written and was conclusive against the use of wines and spirits, little or much in sickness or in health, under the sanction of the advice of Paul to Timothy – Benediction by C.T. Thayer. The weather being unpropitious the church was not crowded but was well filled.

[340] I have before mentioned the first ordination which I attended as a member of the ordaining council where there were no intoxicating drinks offered, this was on the 11th of October 1843, and to show <u>the great change</u> of custom I copy the following bill viz:

---

[42] Rantoul intentionally left the name blank.

"1785 May 11 & 12 Dr. The First Parish of Beverly to Lar. Thorndike to entertaining the council & delegates & other gentlemen at the ordination of Mr. Joseph McKean viz

CR

30 Bowles of Punch before the people went to meeting	3.0.0
80 people eating in the morning at 1/6	6.0.0
10 bottles of wine before they went to meeting a 3/	1.10.0
68 dinners at 3/	10.4.0
44 Bowles of punch while at dinner & after dinner at 2/	4.8.0
15 bottles of Wine at 3/	2.14.0
6 people drank tea at 1/6	0.9.0
40 horses	3.0.0
4 horses two days & nights	0.16.0
8 Bowles of Brandy	0.12.0
Cherry Rum	1.0.0
3 of the gentlemen's servants 2 meals each	
And drinks the day	0.12.0
	36.5.0

As it appears by the Bill of fare that Col. Larkin Thorndike is a

loser by the entertainment the committee agree to allow

$dlrs 2.0 (equal to 120.8.3)

36.5.0"

Of this bill, more than one third part was for strong drink which I suppose was not an unusual proportion of the expense upon such occasions. Ordinations were scenes of conviviality to the people generally who assembled from all the towns in the neighborhood. Fiddling, dancing and various other sports and amusement were usual on these occasions. For November 1772, the Bill of William Bartlett for entertaining the council of Joseph Willard's ordination was for 11 suppers, 7 breakfasts & suppers, and 6 dinners at ¼ each L 6.5.4.

This bill was a short time before the revolutionary war and the other a short time afterward.

[341] I first signed the Temperance Pledge at a public meeting in the Town Hall in Beverly on Monday evening March 4th, 1844. It was in the following form viz:

"We hereby pledge ourselves that we will not hereafter use any intoxicating liquors as a beverage and that we will not offer any such liquors to others as a drink."

I had conformed to this pledge in my practice for eleven years before, but I had doubts of the propriety of signing. At the meeting on the 4th of March 1844, there was enthusiasm in the course and an attempt made to procure many signers to the pledge, and to aid in the effort I gave public notice in the meeting which was a very large one, that I was about signing which announcement was received with some acclimation.

At that meeting Doct. Wyatt C. Boyden made a gavel speech against intoxicating liquors being kept in families for medicinal purposes and urged the impropriety as well as danger of having recourse to them for relief from trifling ailments.

January 8th, 1850 The Sons of Temperance, with their regalia had a meeting at the Town Hall and an address by Charles W. Stack. In his address, he took occasion to compliment by name some of the pioneers of the cause of temperance in this town, of twenty and thirty years standing. The hall was filled, and the meeting conducted with much decorum. Nothing ludicrous in the address as is sometimes the case in the performances of those of the same class with the orator.

[342] Rev. George Dole preached in the town Hall on Sunday evening April 1, 1849 on intemperance. The plan of his discourse was to show that intemperance is antagonistical to religion. The Hall was well filled and the audience attentive. On Thursday April 12th, 1849, being the fast day, there was a Washingtonian meeting in the Town Hall in the afternoon and evening. Rev. Mr. Warren of Windham in Maine prayed and spoke. Others spoke pertinently and ardently. I made some remarks at the evening meeting. I did not attend the afternoon meeting. W Thompson of Lynn presided. The Hall was full. There was much singing. The meeting went off well.

The arrival of Father Theobald Matthew at New York from Ireland in the summer of 1849 and his travels and labors in New York and in other places has given a new impulse to the Temperance reform in that city and in the city of Boston and in other places. His operations are mostly confined to the Catholics, most of whom in New England and New York are Irish by birth or by descent.

Rev. Caleb Stetson, formerly minister of Medford but now of Scituate is the only protestant minister that I have heard of as taking the pledge from Father Matthews. This was done by Mr. Stetson in Faneuil Hall, Boston.

[343] The distillery in Salem, which was the scene of the fiction of Deacon Giles's operations in the business of making and selling Rum, written by George B. Cheever was burnt in the night of December 18th, 1844 together with many other buildings. At the time of its destruction it was used as a planing factory. Cheever was prosecuted and convicted of a libel upon Deacon John Stone who then conducted the business of this distillery and died November 22nd, 1849 aged 68. Cheever was imprisoned in the Salem Goal in punishment of his offence. This prosecution probably doubled the number of the readers of the story of Deacon Giles.

June 1849: The arrival of the Rev. Theobald Matthew, an Irish Catholic, at New York gave some new impulse to the temperance reform in this country. He has been received with public honors in the City of New York. It is said that he has administered the total abstinence pledge to five millions of persons in Ireland and that the number who have relapsed is very small. He is about 54 years of age. He was received in Boston on Tuesday the 24th of July 1849 with a procession of all the temperance societies in Boston with others and addressed near the line of Roxbury, on the neck, by Doct. John C. Warren, the distinguished surgeon and physician of Boston.

Being conducted to the Adams house, he was there received by Governor Briggs in behalf of the Temperance organizations. In the afternoon, he was conducted to the common where there were other proceedings in compliment to him.

[344] On the 4th of July 1849, I attended a celebration of Independence at Gloucester. This celebration was commenced with the understanding that It should be carried on with reference to the Temperance Reform. The Sons of Temperance invited my son, Robert to deliver a public address upon the occasion to which he consented and made preparation there for but subsequently it was concluded that the election should be general uniting all the interests of the town and my son accordingly adapted his address to the new arrangement. There was a floral procession embracing all the children male and female, which was very pretty. There was the Sons of Temperance, The Cadets of Temperance, The Odd Fellows, The Free Masons, all these associations with their banners and badges. The officers of the town, Citizens and Military escort with a band of music making altogether a long procession which filled the first Universalist Meeting House.

The oration comprised a general view of the progress of reform through the civilized world going back far into the legends of history and tracing down to our own times and concluded with many sound views upon the four great subjects of present consideration viz; War, Slavery, Popular Education and Temperance, closing with the last subject. A collation was provided at the rope walk for 750 persons with no other drink than iced water of which there was a generous supply. The weather was pleasant and the whole entertainment passed off happily and thanks to the Temperance Reform, without the excess the disorder the intoxication which formerly always accompanied such public celebrations. The oration occupied one hour and a quarter in its delivery and it appeared to give general satisfactions and elicited much applause. The children partook of appropriate refreshment in the rope walk while the services in the church were performing.

[345] August 20th, 1849: I borrowed of Mrs. Emily Abbot three of the manuscript sermons of her late father Doct. Abiel Abbot late minister of the first Parish in this town, partly on the subject of intemperance. The first was preached here in 1804 where in he depicts the horrid feature of drunkenness with his usual plainness and fidelity but points to no particular modes of staying the evil other than what had been practiced by Christian ministers from the time of the Apostle Paul reasoning before Felix of righteousness, temperance and a judgement to come, down through eighteen centuries to our own times. It ended with an exhortation to cast off this work of darkness if any had indulged in it in any degree and for each to fix for himself the rigid boundary of temperance and not to indulge in the least degree beyond the innocent calls of nature. "you cannot calculate the consequence (of indulgence). We may say of it, as Solomon said of strife the very beginning of it is as one letteth out water – the breach once made upon temperance grows wider and wider till ruin is the final consequence. But again, I say cast off this work of darkness, this abuse of health, this ruin of mental faculties, this destruction of character and usefulness in time and prospects for eternity, for says the apostle – drunkards shall not inherit the kingdom of God." This sermon had been preached in Haverhill in 1799 & 1801 and was also preached here in 1804, 1811 & 1821.

[346] The second sermon was preached on the 9th of September 1813 the day of the national fast appointed by the President on account of the war with Great Britain. In this sermon, he describes intemperance as empathically our national ruin. He has recourse to the statistics which about that time were frequently published to show the immense consumption of ardent spirits in our country amounting to 33,000,000 of gallons annually and excluding slaves and children averaging seven and a half gallons to each individual. He dwells much upon state and other associations to check and diminish intemperance, to initiate reform by displacing the dangerous use of spirits by a salutary substitute. By this substitute it was understood to be meant Beer, Wine, Cider and other fermented liquors, to take the place of the habitual use as a beverage was little thought of at that time. Associations had then first commenced in Massachusetts and Connecticut and they were somewhat relied upon for diminished drunkenness by only a small portion of the community, and it required an effort of moral courage thus to encourage them from the pulpit. Doct. Abbot was among the first who engaged heartily in this mode of reform which then had its beginning but has since been carried to an immense extent producing societies under various names having the same object in view in [347] almost every town in the United States and throughout the civilized world.

The third sermon was preached on the day of the annual State fast April 1st, 1824. In this he is more bold in describing the character and condition of the drunkard and the evils that come on society by intemperance. He dwells on the uses of the law to diminish consumption and much of personal efforts and says less of associations and he adds that "Since so many are beguiled into intemperance by the daily habit of using ardent spirits, would it not be a dictate of sound discretion to substitute a safer refreshment for daily use and to resort, if at all, to the treacherous stimulate at wider intervals." This was as near an approach to the principle of total abstinence as the times would justify. In the stronger light of the present day we do not daily appreciate the labors of the process of this great reform. In 1814, 1813 & 1824 it required much more effort and courage to go as far in the pulpit as Doct. Abbot then went, than it would now to preach in favor of total abstinence from all intoxicating liquors

I generally co-operated with Doct. Abbot in his measures to promote reform but not always. He was desirous of forming a Temperance Society in his parish but Thomas Stephens, whose judgement was much relied upon thought it inexpedient and I concurred with him. [348] In regard to the occasional use of spirits as a beverage Doct. Abbot continued to use them in his family for some years after he was actively engaged in promoting a temperance reform. I do not now recollect when he first banished them from his house as a treat for occasional visitors, but it was subsequently to my doing of it. Wine, beer and cider were rarely denounced as dangerous in their habitual use until after his decease. He was ardent and assiduous in his endeavors to bring about a reform but had not discovered the necessity of total abstinence to the sure progress of reform. Had he lived a few years longer I think he would have acceded to the necessity of the measure and would have given his support to it. Many persons assiduously engaged in the reform of intemperance who could not be brought to the self-denying course of total abstinence from the drinking of intoxicating liquors themselves as a means of attaining that object. The principle difficulty was with the Wine drinkers. The Cider drinkers more easily adopted the self-denying ordinance. The moderate drinkers of spirituous liquors gave into the measure more readily than either of the other classes.

[349] September 14th, 1849: I went to Salem to visit procession on the entrance of Theobald Matthew into the city of Salem. He was received in Danvers, neat the Depot of the Essex Rail Road, on which road he came from Lawrence, by the Sons of Temperance and escorted by them, he rode through the principle streets of Salem attended by a band of musicians and a large number of Irishmen in an open barouche with six horses. As he passed his head being uncovered he bowed and kissed his hand as he passed through a crowd of people. He alighted at the City Hall and there I was introduced to him by Nathaniel Silsbee Jun., Mayor of Salem. I said to him that I welcomed him to our country and he gave me a hearty squeeze of the hand. After the introductions were gone through with he went to the Mayor's house, were he dined. He is modest in his demeanor, appears to be in good health and of a good constitution. About 59 years of age – of middling stature. The hall was pretty much cleared when he walked away with the Mayor. This man is remarkable for having administered the pledge of total abstinence in Europe and America to more than 5,000,000 of persons and for his unwearied labors in the great temperance reform. I returned to dinner at about 1 ½ o'clock PM. There were some of the Sons of Temperance with their regalia from the Beverly division in the procession, among them was Stephens Baker.

[350] I went to Salem again the afternoon, to see Father Matthew administer the teetotal pledge in the Town Hall. As many persons were collected at a time as could be, consisting of males and females, adults and children in front of his stand which was a little elevated. They were directed to kneel and to repeat the words of the pledge after him. When this was concluded he said to them collectively "God bless you", he then went to each individual and made the sign of the cross on each when the person rose from his knees and retired to another room to have his name recorded and take a medal. In addition to this he kissed the little children of whom there were many who kneeled before him caressing them. There were some women who kneeled with infants in their arms. This process was repeated from time to time as often as any could be found to kneel. In the intervals, he exhorted the people to temperance and to take the pledge from him. He frequently left his stand and passed familiarly among the crowd that filled the hall, to encourage the diffident or reluctant to come forward. It was supposed that about four hundred took the pledge. The Irish population of Salem is estimated at from two thousand to twenty-five hundred. He continued his labor until near sunset and then gave notice that it would be resumed at the Catholic church on the next day at nine o'clock in the morning.

[351] On Saturday Father Matthew resumed his labors in the Catholic church in Salem at an early hour in the morning and continued through the day with intervals for refreshment and left Salem at 6 o'clock P.M. for Quincy. The whole number who took the pledge in Salem is estimated at about 1200 including 50 from the Alms House. The enthusiasm of the Irish is great upon this occasion and I hope this visit by Father Matthew will be the means of rescuing many of them from their intemperance, in which they have in a larger proportion here than of our native population much indulged.

Father Matthew took the pledge of total abstinence himself on the 10th of April 1838. He took the lead of the Temperance Society of Cork and at the close of the year he had administered the pledge to 150,000. His next great effort was at Limerick, then at Dublin and at other principal places in Ireland until the number of pledged persons amounted to five millions. He also visited England and Scotland where he administered the pledge to half a million before he come to America. He died in Cork, Ireland December 9th, 1856, and his death was announced in Boston on the 22nd day of December.

[352] Sunday January 27th, 1850: Thomas B. Stone delivered an address in the Town Hall to a full house of more than an hour, without referring to notes and commanding close attention and making a deep impression. He ascribed the causes of intemperance of natural appetite to the desire and pleasure of excitement and to social influence. His presentation to education, embracing the moral and spiritual as well as the physical and intellectual. He dwelt feelingly on the sufferings of woman and on her power to prevent intemperance by making home agreeable as well as by other methods. I think this lecture of Mr. Stone's the most talented that has been delivered here.

On Wednesday September 10th, 1851, I attended a Temperance County Convention at Newburyport. The attendance was small. The Rev. Mr. Higginson appeared to be the leading man. There proceedings were not altogether satisfactory to me.

It should be noted that on Monday August 2nd, 1852, Samuel Dike is appointed agent and commences selling under the provisions of the new liquor law which went into operation on the 22nd of July 1852, for medicinal, mechanical and chemical purposes only. There is an opinion prevailing that intoxicating liquors are necessary for medication. It is said by some that three quarters of the whole number of families in this town are in the habitual use of such liquors <u>medicinally</u>. The agent being required to keep a record of the names of persons to whom he sells, this will enable us to settle the fact with greater certainty.

[353] Since Charles W. Slack lectured on the 8th of January 1850, there have been three lectures in the Town Hall by Ira Washburn, Thomas Stone and Augustus Woodberry of Concord N.H. and on Sunday evening February 24th, 1850, another by my grandson Robert Samuel Rantoul. At the last-mentioned lecture, the Hall was crowded, and many went away on account of the difficulty of obtaining admission within the hall. There were many standing in the entries above and below. There was good order and strict attention. This was his first appearance as a public lecturer in this town. He had previously lectured on another subject at Rockport and at Wrentham. I think he acquitted himself handsomely in the delivery of his address and that it was well written. The purport of it was on the importance of adhering to principle and not yielding to circumstances, of pursuing a settled purpose of life and of not being diverted therefrom by the locicitations of appetite, the thralldom of fashion or the bad example of others. If there was any fault to be found it was in the want of a more particular and forcible application of his subject to the temperance reform, but in regard to this point the modesty that became his youthfulness is a sufficient excuse for omitting a closer application. He was seventeen years old on the 2nd June 1849. The first public lecture which I delivered upon the subject of Temperance was on the 12th of May 1835. My son Robert and myself have delivered several since that time and now another generation has begun in my grandson who I hope will follow the example of perseverance set him by his grandfather.

[354] Sunday evening March 24th, 1850 Charles W. Willard, a student of Dartmouth College from Vermont, a teacher of the Bass River District school, delivered a Temperance lecture in the Town Hall to a large assembly. He discovered talents as a writer and speaker. His style was much ornamented. The general impression was favorable in regard to his performance. He spoke about an hour and was listened to with strict attention.

Tuesday June 11th, 1850: I attended the National Jubilee of the Sons of Temperance in Boston and rode in the procession in an open Barouche in company with a gentleman from Louisville in Kentucky and two other gentlemen and in the afternoon, heard some speeches on the common. The assemblage was large and proceedings exciting and interesting.

In the procession of adults in Salem on the 4th of July 1850, the Sons of Temperance and other Temperance associations had a place and there was a remarkable degree of order and freedom from intemperance among the immense assemblage of people on Salem Common. In the floral procession there were about 2000 children. At the public dinner on the Salem Common there was no intoxicating liquor used.

[355] 1850 May: -At a meeting of delegates of the Medical profession from all the states in the union at their public dinner where more than 400 were present, no intoxicating liquor was served. Doct. Reuben Mussey presided. He has long been a teetotaler.

It is also deserving of notice that the board of examiners of the West Point Military Academy at their annual visitation in 1849, passed a resolution requesting that intoxicating liquor might be excluded from their room while in session. This resolution was introduced by Horace Mann and unanimously adopted.

At the public dinner at Concord on the 19th of April 1850, the anniversary of the Lexington Fight of April 19th, 1775, there were no intoxicating liquors used and the same was the case at the Charlestown celebration of the Bunker Hill battle, on the 17th of June 1850. My son Robert delivered the oration at Concord and Edward Everett at Charlestown. Gov. George Briggs's example has a controlling influence at all the public entertainments to which he is invited and is expected to speak. He is an inflexible teetotaler and the Temperance reform owes very much to his example and his many addresses both public and more private in its favor.

July 1850: The commencement dinner at Harvard College was without intoxicating liquors

[356] Wednesday, September 4th, 1850: I attended the commencement of Bowdoin College Maine and dined with the government. There were no intoxicating liquors on the table, tea and water were the only drinks. I was absent from home six days and spent most of the time in Brunswick and Portsmouth and I did not see any intoxicating liquor, offered, sold or drank in anyplace during the whole time. At Brunswick, although there was a large collection of people, yet there was great stillness and good order, more than I have noticed at any other commencement unless it was at Harford at the commencement of the Episcopalian College there. This commencement did not much interest the mass of the community there, as it was considered a sectarian institution. A description of my journey may be found in my common place book of Sept 1850.

December 7th, 1850: Jacob Lunt, by direction of the Selectmen of Beverly, complained to me against Oliver F. Nelson, keeper of the Atlantic House and George Masury, a shop keeper at the corner of Union and Cabot streets, for selling intoxicating liquor. Nelson was tried and convicted on the distinct charges and was fined $20 with costs, on each. Masury was brought before me on the 7th but recognized to appear at the Town Hall on the 9th when he was tried and convicted on five distinct charges and was fined $20 with costs on each. Both of the respondents appealed to the court of common Pleas and recognized to proceed in their appeal. This is the second demonstration of the selectman for suppressing the sale of intoxicating liquors. This was followed on the 17th day of December 1850 by a well written address from the Sons of Temperance to the inhabitants of Beverly which was printed and extensively circulated in the town.

Health – Sickness Regimen [357]

I have enjoyed a good measure of health through my life thus far. I was at one time, for about a year, afflicted with complaints which seemed to indicate a disposition to the consumption. In the first place, I had the advice of Doct. Abner Howe who prescribed an alternative mercurial course and blistering but this did not remove the unfavorable symptoms, while it indicated a degree of debility which led to the disuse of much of the labor and exercise which I had habituated myself to in the open air. I then had recourse to Doct Joshua Fisher who without disapproving of what I had been previously done advised a course of tonics but still continued using the blistering and to pay strict attention to exercise in the open air. The medicine which he prescribed was the tincture of the sulphate of iron, three times a day, the use of a more generous diet than I had then of late accustomed myself to and for exercise he recommended hoeing. I immediately found relief in the course which he recommended and following it for about a year my health was restored. This was in 1810 or 1811. This was the only year of my life since my early boyhood when I omitted sea bathing in the summer season. Saving this one summer I have practiced sea bathing, more or less, in every year and of late years have been in the habit of washing every part of my person with cold water daily, for about half the year and occasionally with warm water for the residue of the year. I think that this course has been beneficial to [358] my health and I know that it has conduced to my comforts. I have, for about forty years past, been careful to intermingle exercise by walking or otherwise with sedentary employment and to pay particular attention to diet. As a general rule, I have eaten three times a day with an interval of about six hours between meals. I have generally eaten animal food in the morning and at noon with a large preponderance of vegetable food and at these meals have indulged my appetite somewhat freely, while my third meal has been light and sparing and the more sparing it has been the better have I slept. Taking this meal some three or four hours before going to bed, I have enjoyed sleep very much and I think that I have contributed to this by a habit of early rising. With respect to the quality of the different kinds of food in common use, I do not think it conducive to health or comfort to be very particular but when doubts are entertained of the adaptedness of particular types of food take a less quantity than usual and probably no inconvenience will result from their use. I have suffered occasionally from Dyspepsia and from Hypochondriasis. Although considered as distinct diseases, I think they mutually produce each other. For the first I have found bathing, a careful attention to diet, active exercise in the open air the best remedy. For the last, a diversion of the thoughts from that subject which by its entire engrossment seems to engender the disease, cheerfulness, active employment of body and mind, change of scene, diversity of employment are among the best remedies. [359] I have sometimes driven off a fit of it by walking several miles to visit a public school or by a visit to the workhouse or by some other public duty to which I have been called and which has engrossed my attention.

Ennui is not ranked among diseases, but I do not know but that it should be. It is undoubtedly a source of suffering and misery equally with disease. Moral measures and considerations are to be used. I have sometimes been afflicted with it but not very often.

With respect to external injuries I have suffered but very few. A habitual carefulness has probably saved me from many of those injuries which are usually termed accidents.

Riding in a chaise in Danvers, October 7th, 1828, in company with Joseph Winn and returning from Topsfield where we had been to view a road, he was driving, the top of the Chaise being thrown back, I was sitting with my hands wrapped under my cloak, when the horse stumbled, and I fell from the Chaise to the ground, dislocating my shoulder and spraining my ankle badly. This is what is usually called an accident, but had I been without a cloak, or had my hands been free, I should probably have saved myself from injury. Now ought this injury to be attributed to carelessness or to accident? It was a very serious injury. It required a great force to restore the bone to its proper place and a long time to cure the sprain. I was confined to my house for several days and then had to use a crutch for some time when I went out. I did not get entirely free from the effects of this sprain [360] for a whole year after it occurred. Time seemed to be the remedy. At first, by advice from Doct. Boyden I bathed my ankle with rum procured for that purpose as I had not kept anything of the kind in my house for some years previous. I was then satisfied that the use of it on my ankle did not promote a cure and I abandoned it and resorted to water, hot and cold, and also with common salt dissolved therein. I persevered in the use of these means, but I am doubtful whether any of these external appliances did any good. The natural state of the limb gradually returned. I repudiate the use of alcoholic liquors in such cases altogether. The use of cold water, hot water, & salt water may sometimes prove beneficial, but time is the great restorer. For some two or three years I was affected to a moderate degree with Rheumatism but have had no recurrence of it since my return from a journey to Cincinnati in September & October of 1846. I think that that journey produced some change in my constitution which has prevented the return of the disease. When this disease affected my knees, I used to apply warm water to them with decided benefit during the application and for a short time afterwards. Cold water did not produce the same alleviation.

In 1850 I was, after a cessation of four years, again affected somewhat with Rheumatism in my legs but in a much lighter degree than previously to 1846 and of short duration and it was not accompanied with a swelling of the joints of my knees as was the case four years earlier.

[361] The different short periods of sickness which have confined me to my house have been seasons attended with many circumstances of comfort and <u>enjoyment</u>. After recovering from the more violent symptoms of the small pox I remember the pleasurable feelings resulting from the expectation of the season of entire recovery and of emancipation from the necessary restraint from society to prevent the communication of the contagion of this formidable disease to others and this enjoyment of the season of partial seclusion after I left the Hospital and returned home, in subservience to the unreasonable fears and excess of caution which prevailed among the good people of Salem who had not had the disease. I was kept in a chamber with my brother Samuel, who had the disorder at the same time with myself, and our food was conveyed to us from the roof of the shed, through the chamber window. Soon we were allowed to walk abroad and to visit those of

our friends who had passed through and some who were still going through the disease at the Hospital on the Neck.

While I was with Samuel G. Mackey in the autumn of 1793, I was confined at home (at my mother's house in Salem) with a bad fever and I well recollect the vivid enjoyment of life during convalescence. My appetite for food was keen, my digestion good and I slept well. When I walked abroad the air seemed more pleasant and reviving than ever before. The gradual return of strength from day to day inspired the most pleasant feelings. The kindness of friends which had been manifested [362] during my sickness awakened feelings of gratitude. This period of convalescence was strongly impressed upon my remembrance for many years as one of the most pleasurable spots in my life.

My next confinement was with the Throat distemper about two years afterwards. This gave occasion for the special sympathy of my mother and other friends, but I have no very particular recollection of facts in relation to it. Doct. Joseph Osgood, with whom I had been living, attended me without any charge for his services. I have, since I have attained to manhood, several times been obliged to keep house for a day or two at a time. At all these times, I have been strongly impressed with feeling a sense of the kindness, sympathy and devoted attentions of my wife and my daughters. Away from the domestic fireside in the daily intercourse of business, between man and man, how little of these feelings are realized or enjoyed?

In October 1828, from a fall from a chaise, I was seriously injured and was confined to the house in consequence for some days. During this period, I examined the Church records from 1667 to 1825 and made notes of their contents to the extent of some sixteen pages which became of use to me when I afterwards wrote my lectures on the history of Beverly. At this time, I enjoyed my confinement, not being subject to pain. In addition to the indefatigable efforts of my wife and others to render my confinement pleasant and agreeable, I was particular impressed with the activity [363] and kindness of my little daughter Augusta, then about nine years of age and who was kept from school purposely to wait upon me. This she did so faithfully and kindly that I remember that, for some time, I styled her my "<u>little nurse</u>". How many kind friends called to see me and sympathize with me!

These seasons of suspension of active business and of retirement to one's family can only be enjoyed by those whose daily life is filled up with the calls of the multiplied claims upon his time and exertions under other circumstances. One who has very much leisure, I know from my own experience, since the diminution of my business, cannot so well enjoy the seasons of sickness. They are not however without their use's and pleasurable enjoyment, even in old age. A retrospect of my long life to this time (1850) gives full assurance of the merciful dispensation, of divine providence in sending occasional sickness as well as in the inestimable blessings of general health. "God tempers the winds to the shorn lamb," so in sickness, in civilized life, circumstances are so ordered that a bed of languishment, weakness and even of bodily pain and suffering is made to produce patience calmness, peace of mind, hope, content and acceptance in the ways of providence which dispositions of the mind and feelings make the time thus spent more replete with comfort, joy and happiness than is enjoyed in a like duration of time amidst the cares and turmoils of the world.

[364] March 1, 1852: Being on a visit to the East Farm School and riding in a sleigh with C.T. Thayer, Edward Pousland and my grandson Robert Rantoul – E. Pousland holding the reins, in turning the corner to go up to the School House the sleigh was upset and threw us all out with some injury to each excepting Mr. Thayer. I recalled a blow on my head and left shoulder. In consequence, I kept house two days and for some months afterwards the injury to my shoulder occasioned pain at intervals. My rheumatic pains when they occurred after this were in this shoulder mostly, which was not the case before.

On Saturday June 19th, 1852, I was walking on the side walk near John Lovett's house and first turning to cross the street to go to William Porter's reading room when I fell prostrate from the sidewalk into the street and sprained my right ankle severely. The effect of this sprain continued for many months and rheumatism seizing on my left knee deprived me of my accustomed exercise of walking to the extent to which I had previously enjoyed it.

In 1853, I am again able to walk as well as before the sprain and in December 1853, I walked to and from all the public schools in town with as much ease as for several of the preceding years.

In March 1854, I was afflicted with some disorder of my kidneys or bladder and on Sunday, March 19th I sent for Doct. Wyatt C. Boyden to visit me which is the only instance since 1828. This complaint has been gradually coming on for some years but without attracting particular attention as a disease. [364½] I have been confined to my house about three days by this complaint. I have to rejoice in the assiduous and kind attentions of my daughter Hannah, whose whole effort has been to make me comfortable. Since the decease of my beloved wife, she has devoted herself to my comfort. For which may God reward her. My daughter Joanna is very kind to me and does whatever she can for me consistently with her care of her large family. Hannah keeps my house and is with me all the time. Let not what is written seem to be in disparagement of the kindness of other friends and relatives of which I entertained grateful recollection. I have not been afflicted with Rheumatism since 1851. In 1855, I have had the piles considerably. I have been, for the course of the last fifty-five years of my life, repeatedly attacked with this complaint, but never as yet very severely.

Tuesday September 9th, 1856: I was attacked this morning with Cholera Morbus. Not very violently in its common symptoms but in one particular differed altogether from what I had ever experienced before that is, very great prostration. While the symptoms where moderate the weakness was alarming. I kept house about two days and in about eight or nine days was restored. This gave fresh opportunity for the assiduity of my daughter Hannah and for the kindness of many friends.

Cholera - Health Committee 1832 [365]

In the summer of 1832 there was great alarm in this town in consequence of the prevalence of Asiatic Cholera in various places in the United States and in our own vicinity and on the 4th of August 1832, a town meeting was held to consider what measures of prevention and remedy should be adopted. A committee was chose consisting of the five Selectmen and four others to be called The Health Committee. This committee consists of Edward Ford, James Dowling, Henry Larcom, Jesse Shelden, Ezra Ellingwood,

Nehemiah Roundy, Samuel Endicott, Charles Stephens & Robert Rantoul. The committee were authorized to take such measures as they thought necessary to prevent the disease and in reference to it, if it should prevail, among other measures the committee were instructed to publish and distribute a hand bill, containing directions in regard to the disease. The committee immediately met and elected me for their chairman and directed me to prepare an address to the in habitants of the Town, which was done and printed in two days afterwards. It was distributed to every family in the Town. This hand bill contained particular directions in regard to cleanliness, domestic and personal, food and general conduct. I have just now read this paper and I think that it most concisely explains what is necessary in regard to the preservation of health at all times as well as at the time of a prevalent or threatening epidemic. About that time there were [366] many publications of the kind which enabled me to compile one which I thought would be most beneficial in this town and in such a condensed form as would insure its being read in almost every family. I have preserved a copy and it is filed with miscellaneous papers for 1832. In addition to the circulation of this address the committee appointed persons in each of the school districts to visit every house in their respective districts and to examine all the premises and where ever they found any unwholesome matters to cause them to be removed or otherwise rendered in-noxious. These measures were the cause of a general clearing out of cellars and other neglected places which seemed to require it.

The alarm was not injurious but decidedly beneficial inasmuch as it led to many things being done which were permanently conducive to health comfort and sound morals and which would not have been done without some general cause of excitement. I feel a degree of satisfaction that the prudent influence, which at that time it was in my power to exercise was thus made to contribute to the substantial interests of my fellow townsmen. Two years later, political austerity would have impaired it not entirely destroyed that influence. The proceedings of this health committee were very harmonious, no case of Cholera occurred and as the excitement subsided the committee ceased to act.

[367] In 1849 the Cholera prevailed in different parts of the United States and with great mortality at Cincinnati, St. Louis, Nashville, New Orleans and some other places. The board of health in this town issued a notice in regard to the removal of filth and impurities from dwellings and other places and some additional attention has been given to the laws of cleanliness, diet, exposure to cold and damp etc. It has prevailed in Boston to some considerable extent, but a large proportion of its victims have been among the foreign population, which are principally Irish.

The disease prevailed at Bangor in Maine to an alarming extent. The disease found some few victims in many places in New England but in none excepting Bangor and Cabotville and Hadley on Connecticut river were the number of cases so great as to occasion many removals of the settled inhabitants. The deaths were generally from a third to half of the number who were seriously attacked. Doct. James Dowling Trask informed me that in a county house at White Plains New York, of which he was the physician, there were forty cases and twenty-five deaths. That there were very few cases out of the house in the neighborhood but that the Dysentery prevailed much and was severe. The deaths in Boston were 611 and more than two-thirds of them were foreigners. In Beverly, there was no very decided case of the disease but some cases of Cholera Morbus which proved mortal. The warm season upon the whole was [368] less sickly than usual with the exception of

Diarrhea which prevailed to a greater extent than is common and excited considerable apprehension from its being considered a premonitory symptom of the Cholera. I was attacked with it twice and had recourse to small doses of opium say 8 of 10 drops of Laudanum to check it, while in ordinary season I should not have had recourse to medicine at all under similar attacks. Generally, there was some peculiarity in the prevailing diseases of the bowels. They were often attended with febrile symptoms and much debility. The influence of the cause which produced the Cholera was manifested in the character of other diseases of a milder nature.

On Friday August 3, 1849, a fast was observed by <u>recommendation</u> of President Taylor, throughout the Union on account of the visitation of the Cholera in many parts of the states. Religious services were universally observed in consequence of this recommendation.

In the city of New York, the deaths by Cholera were more than 5,000 and about 3,000 by other diseases of the bowels. In the city of London there were 15,000 deaths by Cholera.

In <u>1832</u>, a State fast was appointed by the Gov. Levi Lincoln with the advice of the council to be observed on the 9th day of August, upon which occasion Christopher Tappan Thayer preached a sermon in the First Parish Meeting House in Beverly which was published by request and a copy is in the eleventh volume of my miscellaneous pamphlets.

[369] "Address of the Health Committee

"August 6th, 1832

"The Health Committee of Beverly in pursuance of a vote of the town address the inhabitants upon the subject of the desolating disease which now afflicts some parts of our country commonly called the Cholera. From a careful examination of the reports from every place where this disease has prevailed it appears that its first victims have been mostly among the intemperate, the filthy and the vicious. Those who habitually violate the laws of their nature by the excessive indulgence of those appetites and passions which were conferred upon man by his beneficent creator for his good and those who live in the habitual neglect of the laws of cleanliness inhaling air contaminated with the exhalations of decaying vegetable and animal substances and other deleterious effluvia are fitted and prepared to suffer from any peculiar atmospheric influence which produces epidemic disease while those of better habits resist its influence or suffer lightly from its effects. To obviate the general causes of disease is all that can safely be recommended as preventive of the introduction of the Cholera among us. Of the means of prevention, Cleanliness, domestic and personal is of the first importance. The Committee recommended that all filth and decaying animal or vegetable matters be removed from houses, yards, out buildings and other appurtenances. When such removal impracticable let all such substances be sprinkled frequently with [370] unslaked lime. Particular attention must be paid to cellars, that they be cleared of all vegetable remains and other foul substances, and that they be white washed with lime, dried and constantly aired. Lodging rooms beds and bedding should be well aired in the day time and every apartment in the dwelling house should be kept perfectly sweet and clean. In case the common means are insufficient, the recourse should be had to the Chloride of Lime, directions for the use of which may be obtained at the places where this article is kept for sale, always bearing in mind that the gas emitted by this substance is unfit for respiration. The free use of common lime in and about houses, barns and all other out buildings by frequent whitewashing is recommended. Personal cleanliness must be carefully attended to. All persons are in the daily practice of washing some parts of the body. If the face and hands require this daily attention why should the feet and legs which with many persons are equally exposed to the accumulation of dust, be neglected in this daily operation? In addition to the daily washing of those parts which are most exposed, the whole body should be washed once or twice a week during the warm season. To those male persons who are in robust health, the sea, the river and large ponds that are so easy of access, from every part of the town afford every desirable convenience for bathing. The chief precautions necessary to be observed are not to use the cold bath when the heat of the body is below the natural standard, nor when much raised above it, not to [371] remain in the water more than from five to eight minutes, and to be particularly careful to wipe every part of the body dry before dressing. But much the largest part of the population of the town cannot, for various and obvious reasons resort to these bathing places. To them it is recommended where the appropriate apparatus for warm bathing is wanting, to use a common washing tub with a pail-full of warm water, a large sponge or a cloth. The only precaution necessary is that great care should be used in wiping the person dry before putting on the clothing. In this process of washing, children should not be omitted. With these simple precautions, nearly all the advantages of expensive establishments for warm and cold bathing may be enjoyed by persons of every descriptions with very little or no expense.

"As few individuals as possible should live or be lodged in the same room. Crowded meetings especially in the evening and all exposure to the night air, to cold and wet and to the powerful heat of the sun and all unusual fatigue should as far as possible be avoided. The dress should be carefully regulated according to the temperature of the air. The feet should always be kept warm and dry. Woolen stockings and flannel worn near the skin, are useful for all persons but are particular necessary for persons in feeble health. When sleeping, avoid a current of air and keep the feet secure from cold and provide against sudden changes of the weather in the night by having an extra blanket over your feet.

[372] "In regard to food, more care is requisite in regard to the quantity than to the quality of our food. While there may be some who take too little, it is believed that there are many more who take too much. Both these extremes should be avoided. Tolerably healthy people should not eat without a good appetite and should finish their meal before their appetite is gone. In general, we may safely continue with moderation those habits of eating which have been found by uniform experience to suit our health and constitutions. Those articles of food which have been found hurtful should be strictly excluded. Those persons who take little exercise or are subject to indigestion, should guard their diet with greater precaution. The most wholesome articles of food are bread, eggs, fresh meat, fresh fish and rice. Thoroughly cooked potatoes and other vegetables in common use stand next.

"Pastry, hot bread, cade, preserves, pickles, spices, unripe fruit, cucumbers, and all uncooked vegetables as salads are unsafe at all times. Fruits that are fully ripened, when served as a part of the regular meals and in moderate quantities are generally wholesome but the practice of taking these fruits in the intervals of the regular meals, or in addition to the accustomed quantity of food should be abandoned. Total abstinence from the use of distilled spirituous liquors is absolutely necessary and [373] great moderation should be observed in the use of all other liquids. The best drinks are pure water, common tea and the common domestic herb teas. The use of medicines as preventives of the Cholera is said to be very dangerous. Should the Cholera appear amongst us every person who is attacked with a diarrhea or any other symptom of the disease should immediately send for a physician. In this stage of the disease a large proportion of the cases have been cured, therefore let no time be lost by night or day. Delay increases the danger exceedingly. Get your physician as soon as possible and follow implicitly his directions. Exercise that degree of moral courage which the occasion demands, avoiding fear and you will probably soon be restored to health. In all cases of severe sickness all those whose presence is not needed for the care and comfort of the sick, banish all fears and devote themselves to their service. In the fearless faithful and persevering performance of the duties of kindness and humanity towards our fellow creatures when suffering under sickness we may rationally expect to find security for ourselves. The influence of a national confidence in God, not merely as a preventive of alarming epidemic disease but of all the ills which flesh is heir to deserves the utmost consideration. [374] The removal of persons from their habitations in consequence of the occurrence of Cholera is thought to be inexpedient and unnecessary.

"The Committee assure their fellow citizens that they will devote themselves to these duties which circumstances may require of them, and they ask in return their co-operation and support in such measures as shall be found to be necessary for the common good.

"Rob Rantoul

"Nehemiah Roundy

"James Dowling

"Edward Ford

"Henry Larcom

"Jesse Shelden

"Samuel Endicott

"Ezra Ellingwood

"Charles Stephens

"Health Committee."

Of this address nine hundred copies were printed and one for each family sent to a committee in each of the ten school districts for distribution. After 17 years and a recurrence of the disease I see but little that I should alter in the address.

Peace Society [376]

In consequence of some writings of David L. Dodge in 1810 – 1812, a peace society was formed in the city of New York in August of 1815. Some months before Doct Noah Worcester's society in Boston and almost a year in advance of the London Peace Society. Dodge died in 1851 or 1852 aged 78 years.

[377] The war between the United States and Great Britain terminated in 1815, about which time the Massachusetts Peace Society was organized, say in December of 1815, under the particular care of Noah Worcester, its corresponding secretary. From its first establishment, I made it a point of attend its public meetings when I was in Boston, received and distributed its tracts and rendered such other aid in promoting its general object as I conveniently could but without trammeling myself with membership. For several years annual addresses were delivered in Boston on the evening of the 25th of December, many of them by distinguished scholars and orators. One of these addresses was by Josiah Quincy, late president of Harvard College, delivered on the 25th of December 1820 in the Stow Lyceum

I read this address of J Quincy's with the following introductory remarks:

"The Massachusetts Peach Society was formed in December 1815. Its founder and the most active and persevering promoter of its design was the remarkable Noah Worcester. The formation of this society it was hoped would have an extensive influence. Those who engaged in its formation were strongly impressed by considering the manifold crimes and tremendous calamities of public war and the melancholy insensibility which has been induced by education and habit, in regard to this most barbarous, destructive and unchristian custom. They were desirous that men should be brought to view war in a just light, to see clearly its baneful influence on the political, moral and religious condition of communities and its opposition to the design and spirit [378] of the gospel. They earnestly desired that men might be brought to feel that a spirit of conquest is among the most atrocious crimes, that the thirst for military glory is inhuman, delusive and ruinous and that the true dignity and happiness of people result from impartial justice towards all nations and the spirit and virtues of peace. They hoped that a change might be effected in public sentiment and a more happy state of society introduced. It is consistently the design and tendency of the gospel to subdue the lusts and passion from which wars and fightings come. And we are encouraged to hope that the time will come when the nations will learn war no more. A great majority of the people in every civilized country, when free from the delusions of party passions and prejudices no doubt have such an aversion to public hostilities, that they would rejoice if any plan could be devised which would both secure their rights and absolve them from the burdens and sufferings of war. It is clear that every popular custom must depend on public opinion and we know from history that many customs and usages which were formerly considered as honorable, useful and necessary have since been abolished as inhuman and barbarous and are now regarded with detestation and honor. One sect of Christians has, from its foundation, refused any participation in war, in any of its forms. A diversity of opinion exists among other sects in regard to the lawfulness of offensive or defensive wars and the duty of each individual in respect to engaging in warfare when thereto required by their government or voluntarily without such [379] requirement. It is not the intention of this society to enter into a consideration of any differences of opinion, but to act on such broad and liberal principles as to embrace all the friends of peace, although they may differ on this as well as on other interesting subjects. They wish to promote the cause of peace by methods which all Christians must approve, by exhibiting with all clearness and distinctness the pacific nature of the gospel and by turning the attention of the community of the nature, spirit, causes and effects of war. Great reforms are not wrought in a day. Evils which are the accumulated results of accumulated errors are not to be struck down at a blow by the nod of a magician. Free people may boast that all power is in their hands, but no effectual power can be in their hands until knowledge be in their minds. But how may knowledge be imparted to their minds? Such effective knowledge as shall render apparent to all the interest of all? IN promoting and diffusing knowledge of our subject. The means that have been used by this society have been the formation of societies in every part of this and in many parts of other countries to promote the same great object. The printing and general distribution of pamphlets and tracts calculated to draw the attention of readers and to enlighten their minds and to excite them to active exertions in inculcating and spreading around them sentiments which as far as they prevail will have the tendency to countenance that corrupting influence which is always at work to produce wars and bloodshed. One other method has been adopted, which is in harmony [380] with the prevailing taste of the day, I mean that of occasional public addresses to large assemblages of people convened to hear them. The effect of these means will first manifest itself in a more enlightened public sentiment and by the gradual illumination of the Christian world. A pacific spirit may be communicated to governments, to governments and in this way the occasions of war and the belief of it necessity will be constantly diminishing till it shall be regarded by all Christians with the same horror which we now look back on the exploded and barbarous customs of former ages. "

These remarks are a manifestation of my views in regard to the peace reform and in coincidence with their spirit I have continued to give my aid to the association. On Saturday, November 3rd, 1838, William Ladd, aged 61, President of the American Peace Society in which the Massachusetts Peace Society merged came to my house by my invitation and on Saturday evening he delivered an address upon a Congress of Nations in the Baptist Meeting House. On Sunday forenoon and afternoon, he preached on the subject of Peace in the First Baptist Meeting House, showing the inconsistency of the principles and practices of war with the gospel and on Sunday evening in the Washington Street Church in raising and answering objections which are made to the doctrines of Peace. He lodged at my house on Saturday and Sunday nights, dined at CT. Thayer's on Sunday and drank tea at Samuel S. Ober's on Sunday evening.

[381] Some particulars of his life which he related to me may be found in my Common Place book under date of November 3rd, 1838. I was elected a vice president of the society in May 1842. On the 8th of March 1843, I presided at a meeting for discussing the subject of peace in the Representatives Hall in Boston. William Ladd, the ardent and persevering advocate of the cause, was born May 20th, 1778 – died – April 9th, 1841. I made several pecuniary donations to the society at different times and in addition paid twenty dollars in 1841 to constitute my wife a life member, and afterwards forty dollars

to constitute my two daughters' life members. During the Mexican War, the secretary, Beckwith delivered an address in the Dane Street Church which from its bearing on party politics and his improper language in reference to the government of the United States displeased me. I was also displeased with the temper manifested in the periodical publications of the same period and emanating as supposed from the same source. This dissatisfaction will be temporary and now that Peace is restored it is hoped that a change will take place either in the <u>temper</u> of the <u>office,</u> of the Secretary and that I shall again feel <u>disposed,</u> cordially, to co-operate with the Secretary and other officers of the Society in promoting its great object. Another Noah Worcester or another William Ladd may arise to give an impulse to the society which is greatly needs at this time (January 1849). Perhaps it may be questionable whether the tome for the useful operation of Peace Societies has not already passed. Associations in the commencement of reforms may be useful and may cease to be so at subsequent periods.

[382] Elihu Barnett delivered a peace address in the town hall in this town, September 21, 1842. I presided at the meeting which was a large one. He did not confine himself to the subject of peace but dwelt considerably upon the slavery and temperance questions. He was generally acceptable. In December 1845, a petition was circulated in this town on the subject of a national tribunal for the settlement of national disputes. I placed my name at the head of this petition and forwarded it to Daniel P. King, member of congress from this district them at Washington with a letter of which the following is a copy –

"Beverly December 25th, 1845"

"Hon: Daniel P. King,

"Dear Sir: In behalf of the subscribers to the petition herewith sent, I respectfully request you to present the same and procure its reference to the appropriate committee of the House of Representatives in Congress. It is upon the subject of a National Tribunal for adjusting differences between sovereign states without recourse to critical force, to war. Whatever opinions may be held by myself and others respecting the practicability of any immediate efficient measures on the part of the government of the United States in relation to this most important subject, it is not the less important that the public mind would continue to be <u>agitated</u> in reference thereto. All great moral reforms have their 'day of small things', and such is the present aspect of the Peace reform. War is fraught with the greatest evils to humanity, moral and physical and every rational attempt to lessen the [383] frequency of its occurrence deserves the candid examination the cordial approbation, and the hearty cooperative of the Legislator, the politician and the philanthropist. The contempt and ridicule which have so frequently been bestowed upon the feeble efforts of the peace associations to stem the tide of public opinion which for ages and from the very earliest period of the history of mankind, has so strongly set in favor of settling difficulties between different independent states by recourse to arms, has in no wise discouraged the continuance of these efforts by those who have acted from the suggestions of an enlightened conscience. These efforts in our country date back some thirty or forty years and something has thereby been accomplished in the change of opinion in regard to war - its character – its morality – its necessity – the expediency of expending the recourse of a nation in preparation for its occurrence in time of peace – the utility of the militia and its discipline – the cost, usefulness and extension of a naval force, and a great variety of other matters intimately connected with the war spirit.

"Truly something has been accomplished but very much more remains to be done. Entertaining views in general co-incidence with the Peace societies, I have placed my name at the head of the petition of inhabitants of this town in favor of a Congress of Nations, but without in any degree compromising my right of private judgment, in regard to any ulterior measures which those engaged in the Peace cause may think proper to pursue.

[384] "I have taken the liberty to trouble you thus far that the imputation of the opinions of others with whom I may sometimes co-operate may not rest upon me and that I may not be made responsible for their measures without express assent. I beg leave to tender you my thanks for public documents which you have sent me and to request a continuance of the favor so far as my suite your convenience."

This letter, with the exception of the last sentence, was by D.P. King, published in the Christian Register of January 24th, 1846 but with my implied assent.

A great peace convention was held in Paris in France in the summer of 1849 at which there were many delegates from the United States. The Peace reform meets with countenance in all the Christian nations. Its progress has been slow, but here are sure indications that it is gaining ground in the opinions of very many wise and good men on the continents of the old and new world. In February 1851, I headed a petition with about fifty-four other signers praying for the abolition of Militia Drills by our State Legislature.

Capital Punishment [385]

In 1829 I, being then a member of the House of Representative, and Deacon Thomas Kendal, then a Representative from Boston, in January of that year offered a motion to the house respecting the abolition of capital punishment. This motion was referred to the judiciary committee of which committee Francis Baylies, of Taunton was chairman. This committee very soon reported against any alteration of the existing laws upon this subject. Deacon Kendal, made some remarks in opposition to the report when F. Baylies made an able speech in support of his report, but not confining himself to the subject of discussion, he in an ungentlemanly manner attacked Deacon Kendal personally, with his usual wit, ridicule and sarcasm but Deacon Kendal and the subject in which he appeared to feel a very deep interest found a ready defender equally able to say no more in Caleb Cushing then a Representative from Newburyport.

C. Cushing's speech was manly and philanthropic and had a forceful influence upon the House. The result was that the report of the judiciary committee was referred to a special committee who had under consideration the expediency of a revision of the Penal code, to which committee, C. Cushing and Theodore Sedgwick of Stockbridge, both of whom were known to be favorable to an alteration of the laws in regard to the subject under consideration, were added. At that time, I felt a desire to promote a change of the law. For many years before I was dissatisfied with the existing laws, but my mind had vacillated about the subject and had not come to a definite result.

[386] In March 1831, William Sullivan, Thomas Kendal, Oliver Holden, John B. Davis and myself were by the House of Representatives appointed a committee to consider the subject of capital punishment and to report at the next session of the General Court. I corresponded with William Sullivan and addressed the following letter to him which shew my views upon the subject at that time, this however is only the draft but not amended copy.

"Beverly June 28th, 1831"

"Hon: Wm. Sullivan

"Dear Sir, After you were authorized to prepare bills upon the subject of capital crimes I called at your office but missed of seeing you and being desirous of submitting to your consideration a few suggestions upon the topic, I beg you will excuse my troubling you with a letter. In the first place, I am of opinion that the punishment of death should be entirely abolished and secondly that there should be a gradation of punishment conformed to the moral sense of the community in regard to the more or less heinous character of crime as well as to the expediency of punishing with more or less severity according to political considerations growing out of the state of society and nature of our government. In regard to this last consideration we are in a degree relieved by the opinion I think of yourself and certainly of Edward Livingston, that it is unnecessary for any State of the Union to enact laws against Treason, so that a simple repeal of our statue against treason is all that seems to be necessary to be done in regard to that crime. The crime of murder in the view of almost [387] every person seems to call for the highest degree of punishment. Whether this crime should be divided into two degrees or not, I do not feel decided and there is the less necessity of it, when the punishment of death is abolished. What has been lately published upon the effect of solitary confinement, when protracted to any great length of time upon the body and the mind of the sufferer has led to the conclusion that it should be allowed for only a limited period of time and that somewhat at the discretion of the court, which might admit of a distinction in some measure according to the aggravation of the offence. I therefore am of opinion that murder should always be punished by confinement to hard labor for life with solitary confinement for a term not exceeding ___ months[43], to be applied at one time, or at certain intervals, say annually. Would it not also be expedient to consider the convict as civilly dead, the marriage contract to be dissolved and that all his rights in regard to property should cease and determine in the same way and manner as if naturally dead and that administration of his estate should follow and the whole be disposed of in the same way and manner as if naturally dead. The next offence that of personal violence to a female, to distinguish it from murder and to remove one temptation to its being followed by that crime, should be punished by a limited period of solitary confinement and confinement to hard labor. In the law made for the District of Columbia at the last session of Congress March 2, 1832 it is for the first offence punishable [388] by confinement to hard labor for a term not less than ten years nor more than thirty years, and for a second offence for life. By the same law Arson, for the first offence not less than one year nor more than ten years. For the second offence, not less than five nor more than twenty years.

---

[43] Rantoul intentionally left the number of months blank.

Burglary, for the first offence not less than three years nor more than seven years. For the second offence, not less than five years nor more than fifteen years. Robbery the same as burglary. I am aware that to follow this example in regard to these offences will also require a modification of the existing laws for punishing other crimes and I think this comes within your authority as incident to the principle subject. I rejoice that the whole subject is in your hands. As a professional man you will be able, readily, to discern the difficulties that really exist as well as the plausible objections that always arise against any considerable change in the criminal code. The principles of humanity which will be sure to guide you are a sure pledge that whatever can be done, will be done for the diminution of suffering while the principles of Christianity will control every feeling, so that whatever is done by you will be with reference to the whole character of man in society so that so that the greatest good may be attained by the best means considering our race in a probationary state for another of eternal duration. I again apologize for troubling you upon a subject which in every point of view is so much better understood by you than by myself."

[389] I received an answer from W. Sullivan of the date of June 30th, 1831 which is in my file of letters for that year.

January 18, 1831: I received a letter from James Seger, an Italian, accompanied with a volume on the subject of Capital punishment, wherein he refers to a resolution offered by me in the House which I do not otherwise recollect. I answered this letter on the 11th of January but did not preserve a copy. His letter is on file.

On the 10th of June 1831, an elaborate report prepared by Wm. Sullivan was made to the House of Representatives and ordered to be printed. This report was noticed in an article in the Christian Examiner for March 1832 and was ably reviewed in the same periodical by Andrew P. Peabody, July 1833. The first regular series of articles which I wrote for the Newspapers on this subject were published in the Salem Gazette in the summer of 1831. Since 1831, there have been several lengthy reports in favor as well as against the abolition of Capital punishment, and which have been printed by order of the Legislature. That of February 22tn 1836, written by my son Robert is the most thorough and comprehensive and was largely circulated throughout the United States. He also made lengthy reports in 1835 and 1837. Several editions of that of 1836 were published by the Legislature and one of a 1000 copies by a few individuals. The most full report against the abolition was by Charles Hudson in 1837, then a Senator from Worcester County but now a Rep. in Congress.

[390] My son Robert and my nephew Andrew P Peabody have done very much by their writings by their public addresses and by their conversation and discussions and by various other means to change the deep-rooted prejudices upon this subject. I recollect the first time when the subject was discussed in a debating society in this town and that when the vote was taken, William Thorndike and myself were all who voted that this mode of punishment ought to be abolished, while all the others being a considerable number voted on the other side of the question.

There have, from time to time to me but at a more recent period than debate, been petitions presented from this town to the General Court upon this subject. I have generally, if not universally placed my name at the head of these petitions and on several of the first here were but few signatures, but through the assiduity of Stephen Homans, the two last petitions have been more numerously signed. I have attended several public meetings upon this subject in Boston and in this town and have presided at some of them and have spoken at others. I have before mentioned some of the numerous articles which I have published in various newspapers and the lectures which I have delivered in Salem, Danvers, Manchester and Beverly.

Thus, it appears that I have been engaged in this reform for about twenty years. At the beginning, I found but few who would join me, there are now many more and the number is still increasing. [391] The laws have been so far altered as to abolish the punishment of death for Burglary and Robbery. Gov. Edward Everett recommended its abrogation in all cases except murder and Gov. Briggs has done the same, in two or more of his addresses to the Legislature. The makers of laws generally are behind the change of opinion which goes on in the community and it requires great watchfulness in them not to be too far behind, otherwise they jeopardize their power and influence.

January 1849, Gov. George N Briggs in his annual address to the General Court, says the subject of Penal laws has occupied very much of the public attention of late, in our own and in other countries.

"The number of capital offences has been greatly reduced and, in some governments, capital punishments have been abrogated. In our own Commonwealth, the number of crimes punishable by death is four. On former occasions, I have called the attention of the Legislature to this subject and recommended the propriety of abolishing the punishment of death, except in cases of willful murder. It seems to me that the reasons for such an alteration of our penal laws are every year gaining strength. I am satisfied that such a change in existing laws as will make only murder in the first degree punishable with death and subject the other crimes, now made capital to imprisonment for a long term of years or for life would meet with the public approbation, bad to the more certain punishment of crimes, and increase the safety of the community."

[392] I have corresponded with Charles Spear and John M. Spear and aided them somewhat with money to enable them to prosecute there designs in regard to this reform. Charles Spear has lectured twice in this town upon his subject and both of them have lectures much in different places upon the same topic.

The letter which I wrote to William Sullivan was after the committee of which he was chairman and after the committee of which he was chairman and I was a member, had made their report and in pursuance of that report he was authorized to draft bills for the House. The report may be found in my volume of Massachusetts documents for 1831 V 15 of the House documents. John B. Davis, I think, died about the time that the report was made, and his name does not appear on the report and was probably prevented by his sickness the names of the four others are appended to it. At the session of May 1831 W Sullivan was not a member and his report of June 1831 was referred to a committee of which I was chairman who reported that William Sullivan should prepare the bills and return them to the House at the next session and this was ordered by the House as will appear by House document No.3 page 49, 1832. I have witnessed only two executions. The first was an Indian in 1786 or 1787 named Isaac Coombs, for the murder of his wife. The other was Henry Blackbourne January 14th, 1796 for the murder of a man in a quarrel. Both were in Salem.

In March 1849, I placed my name at the head of a petition to the General Court for the abolition of this penalty. There were 82 signers, male and female, two of whom are ministers viz: C.T. Thayer and Ira Washburn. Mrs. Washburn headed the female list of signers. Stephen Homans was the active agent in procuring signers to this petition. [393] When I saw Isaac Coombs executed on Salem neck, I was but little more than eight years of age, it being in the latter part of 1786 or the first part of 1787[44]. I was carried there by the injudicious conduct of some of my relations. Michael Farley of Ipswich was then Sheriff. I remember his taking hold of the legs of the criminal and hanging his weight on them, so as to be sure of his death. The Sheriff was portly man and come on to the ground on horseback. The body of Coombs was in the following night after his execution disinterred by Doct Orne of Beverly with some associates and carried away for dissection. I remember the whole transaction was the common subject of conversation, with many disgusting details. At about that time, India Rubber was first brought into the town school where I attended and some of the larger boys who were so fortunate as to be possessed of a small piece, attracting the observation and exciting the curiosity of the smaller boys by its great elasticity, told them it was a part of the skin of the Indian who had been hanged. This story was believed by some. There were other topics of conversation among the boys of the East school growing out of the execution and the dissection which followed, some of them founded on facts and others on equally gross fiction. My conviction of the very immoral tendency of capital punishment commenced at that early age [394] of life has grown with my growth and strengthened with my years. I therefore think it wise in the Legislature were it any wise practicable that they have direct that executions shall be in private and thus in some small degree diminishing the bad influence upon the morals of the community. Notwithstanding the nominal privacy of executions, I know that a morbid curiosity still attracts multitudes and that to gratify this curiosity many ingenious devices are successfully practiced. There is no adequate remedy for these evils but the entire abrogation of the death penalty. The public processions formerly attendant on executions are got rid of by the new regulations.

Henry Blackbourne was a Chimney sweeper. He had a drunken quarrel with a man and in that quarrel stabbed him with a bayonet and killed him. Notwithstanding his legal conviction of murder, many at that time and at this present time, from an examination of the report of the trial were and are of the opinion that this conviction should have been manslaughter and not of murder. Coombs and Blackbourne were poor, friendless, intemperate, despised individuals and at the time of their execution there was none of that sympathy, comparatively, for those of their cast which now prevails amongst us. [395] Blackbourne on the day of his execution was carried from the Gaol to the Episcopal Church, where a sermon was preached by the Rev. Mr. Fisher the stated minister of the Church who was born in 1742 and died December 20, 1812. The sermon was accompanied with appropriate devotional exercises. The Church was filled, and I attended the services. At the gallows, there were several clergymen in attendance. When the drop was let down, the rope slipped or broke and Blackbourne fell to the ground, not dead, but somewhat paralyzed. He was set upon his feet and I remember seeing Rev. John Prince, assisting and was hoisted up to the gallows. I was about seventeen years of age. I then

---

[44] The warrant for executing Coombs was dated November 30, 1786.

lived with Doctor Joseph Osgood and was not in a situation to hear so much conversation about the matter as nine years before, when I was a pupil at the East Town School.

The next execution in Salem was in the summer of 1821 when Stephen M. Clark, a minor from Newburyport, was hanged for the crime of arson, which is the only execution for that offence within the county of Essex since 1780. This execution was on the Neck. I did not attend, but there were many spectators. John Francis Knapp was executed in Salem, on Tuesday September 28th, 1830 in the jail yard, and his brother Joseph Jenkins Knapp Jun., at the same place on Friday, December 31, 1830. Both of them for the murder of Joseph White who was killed by Richard Crowninshield Jun., the Knapps being accessories thereto. Crowninshield [396] hanged himself in the Salem Gaol before his trial. At the execution of the Knapps, there were supposed to be about 5,000 spectators, a portion of whom were females. Many of these spectators indulged in levity, profanity, intemperance and other low vices. How different are the sentiments which appear to occupy the minds of the spectators from that salutary terror which it is said to inspire in the breasts of the beholders and with that horror of crime which will restrain from its commission. I was not present at these two executions but learned some of the particulars from those who attended. Although they were executed within the Gaol yard, yet the fence was so low as to give an opportunity of all who chose to witness them from houses near and from stages erected for the purpose and other slight elevations.

There has been one other person executed within the county of Essex since 1780 viz; Pomp a Negro at Ipswich for the murder of a white man. He was hanged in the summer of 1795[45]. So that there have been six executions in the county of Essex since 1780. There was one, Bryan Shehan a few years before or about 1780[46], of which, when a child I often heard talk in our family but have no very distinct recollection of facts to record. I remember that the story used to excite sympathy for the criminal more that approbation of his punishment. Rev. James Diman, minister of the East Church in Salem preached a sermon on the occasion which was printed and is in possession of a relative of the wife of Wm. Lord, who is a descendant of James Dinmore. [397] Daniel H. Pearson was executed at East Cambridge on Friday July 26, 1850 for the murder of his wife and two of his children of about four years of age.

He confessed the crime before his death assigning no cause except that <u>he was led away</u> – by which it is generally understood that he became attached to a woman whom he wished to marry and to make way for this he killed his lawful wife against whom he had no just ground of complaint. He was thought to be truly penitent by Father Taylor of Boston, who visited him before and was present at his execution. The gallows was so placed in the prison yard that it could not be seen without the enclosure, still there was a large assemblage around the outside making indecent noises and shouts. There were about one hundred persons admitted within the prison yard. The effect of these executions is in my view deleterious to the morals of the community. I was one of the petitioners for a commutation of Doct John Webster's punishment from the death penalty to imprisonment for life, but I believe there was no considerable effort in the way of petition in favor of

---

[45] Pomp was hung in Aug 6, 1795 for the murder of Capt. Charles Furbush of Andover, killed in his bed Feb 11, 1795.

[46] Shehan was hanged Jan. 19, 1772.

reason. The only ground relied upon in his defence was imbecility of mind which was not sustained by the evidence. To brace up his nerves for the deed he had recourse to intoxicating drinks. Strong beer and gin are mentioned in his confession but for the stimulus of strong drinks conscience might not have been so blunted as not to have prevented the consummation of the dreadful deed.

[398] Friday August 30th, 1850: John White Webster aged 57 years, son of Redford Webster who died in 1833 aged 72 years was this day executed in the Gaol yard, Leverett street, Boston, at about 9 ½ o'clock in the forenoon for the murder of Doct. George Parkman of Boston. The murder was committed in the medical college in Boston. There were about 25 persons admitted within the prison yard to witness the awful scene. The roofs and windows of many of the surrounding houses and buildings were crowded with spectators. One man received a dollar of each person who he admitted into his house to observe the spectacle. Many of the spectators were females.

The wife and three daughters visited him yesterday from two to six and a half o'clock for the last time. George Putnam attended him and prayed with him in his cell in the morning, a short time before he was led out for execution. On Thursday, there was a crowd of people in Leverett Street to witness the last visit of Mrs. Webster and her daughters to her husband. They were on account of the crowd admitted at and came out of a private door. Some were so vile and barbarous as to hoot after the carriage in which they left the Gaol.

There were 125 Constables and Police officers on duty during the execution and 50 of them within the prison and 75 without. There was no disturbance of a riotous character but there was some noise without while the warrant was read, which was decidedly disorderly and indecent. Webster appeared to be in good health. His countenance was pleasant. Mr. Putnam conversed with Webster after he was on the platform shook hands with him and parted with him affectionately.

[399] Doct. Parkman was murdered on the 23rd of November 1849 and Doct. Webster was arrested on suspicion about a week afterwards and the public mind has been agitated with the subject continually until this last act in the tragedy. I hope that this event will draw the attention of any enlightened minds to the laws of this state as well as all the other states in the Union (except Michigan) upon the subject of the death penalty. Michigan about a year ago abolished the punishment of death. Massachusetts, from time to time, has diminished the number of capital crimes and it is hoped that the time is not far distant where it will be abolished entirely. The execution of Webster will operate upon the sympathetic feelings of a class in community who have not heretofore felt as they ought to have done in reference to this subject. Executions have almost always fallen upon the low, ignorant, debased, friendless members of society for whom the upper class have but little sympathy, but in the case of Webster it comes home to the refined, educated and fashionable class.

Some of the occupants of the houses on Lowell street from the rear windows of which a full view of the gallows could be had, kept their doors and blinds closed. The crowd was very great and from those who had no possibility of seeing the gallows, loud noises and expressions disgraceful in the extreme to those who attended them, continually fell upon the ears of those who were compelled from duty, to witness the execution. [400] This execution will and has already occasioned the discussion of the subject of the death penalty in newspapers that have heretofore been silent upon it. In the Atlas on the 31st August 1850 there is a well written article upon this subject taken from the London Times, an article which editors of the Boston Atlas would not have republished a year ago. I think that a new order of talent will be drawn forth and that the subject will be considered in a different aspect form what it has been of late years. The conservative class in society have felt as if they ought to oppose all innovation in regard to it because a change is urged principally by that body of persons who are styled reformers and who in pursuit of some of their measures of reform are fanatical, disorganizing and radical and that in conceding to them any particular reform which they have agitated will weaken the resistance which the conservatives think should be constantly sustained against these reformers, lest they should break down and destroy the fabric of society. I think that a prudent, discreet amendment of whatever is decidedly wrong in the constitution of society is the true ground of security against violent convulsions or great revolutions.

I was particularly acquainted with Doct. Webster's father Redford Webster, who was an Overseer of the Poor for about thirty years and a Representative of Boston in the General Court for several years while I was a member. I always entertained a good opinion of him. He was a Representative from 1824 to his death, not constantly. He was in the Mass. convention of 1820 and always esteemed a very worthy man.

[401] Deacon Thomas Kendal who made the first motion in the house of Representatives on the subject of capital punishment while I was a member of the house died in Brookline near Boston on the fifteenth day of November 1850 aged 80 years. In the active part of his life he was a tailor in Boston, where he acquired property which enabled him to retire from business and to spend the latter part of his life out of the city. He was a Deacon of the Baptist Society in Charles Street, Boston of which society Doct. Sharp was the Minister. He was a Representative of Boston for several years and a Representative from Brookline in 1843; 1844 to 1845. He spoke occasionally in the house, having the appearance of self-complacency. His talents and acquirements by reading were moderate. He was conscientiously desirous of doing what he could for the good of his fellow man.

In 1851 a report was made in the House of Representatives for the abolition of capital punishment in all cases but in May 1851 the report was refused acceptance by a vote of about 172 to 97. It afforded some encouragement that there were so considerable a number of our Representatives in favor of abolishing it. The report is a valuable document and deserves a reading by those interested in the subject.

May 20th, 1852 the Legislature passed an act providing for the punishment of Treason, Arson and Rape by imprisonment with labor for life, thus abolishing capital punishment in all cases except murder and when a conviction [402] of the crime of murder is had, the convict is not to be executed until a year has expired after his conviction, thus giving time for discovery of error in the proceeding, for the subsiding of vindictive feelings on the part of the people, for repentance on the part of the convict and for the fullest deliberation on the part of the executive. Under these circumstances an execution will never or but very rarely occur in Massachusetts. The labor of myself of my son and of many others from 1829 to 1852, may, in a good degree be considered as crowned with success.

The states of Rhode Island & Michigan and the territory of Minnesota have abolished the punishment of death and the state of Maine has some ten or twelve years ago placed it on the same footing as it now is in Massachusetts. Thus, I have been spared to witness the blessed success of one of my reformatory measures. I have been engaged in it for twenty-three years let this long period of time during which this measure has been pursued, encourage my grandchildren to perseverance in every good object however discouraging the prospect of success may appear.

For a list of newspaper articles written by me upon this subject see page __[47].

I have, I believe, written more newspaper articles upon this subject than upon any other particular subject. I think some 70 or 80 in the whole. I delivered a lecture on the subject to large audiences in Beverly, Salem, North Danvers and Manchester. How much if any my labors have contributed towards the end of it is not possible to determine. It is a well-known proverb that "every little bit helps".

[402½] Extracts from the Journal of the House of Representatives:

"March 18th, 1831

"An order was passed appointing a committee of five members of the House to sit during the term of this legislature and report at the next session on the punishment of death.

"Messrs . Sullivan of Boston

"Rantoul of Beverly

"Kendall of Boston

"Molson of Charlestown

"Davis of Boston

"Were the Committee.

"June 10th, 1831: Mr. Rantoul of Beverly presented a report of the Committee which was read, laid on the table, and printed.

"On the 18th of June 1831, on motion of Mr. Oliver of Lynn this report was taken up in Committee to Messrs Rantoul of Beverly, Kendall of Boston, Molson of Ch. Oliver of L. & Bassett.

[402½.1] "June 21st, 1831, Mr. Rantoul from the Committee referred a reference to the next Legislative & that Hon. William Hilliard be authorized to insert a bill or bills in accordance with the report, which was accepted.

"(Journal 1832. 39, 56, 120, 200, 306, 389, 416, 418, 430, 505, 532)

"January 9th, 1832: The report presented to the House at the last session was ordered to be printed for the use of the members.

"The next day, the Speaker laid before the House a communication from the Hon. William Sullivan inclosing these bills proposed by him- laid on the table & printed."

"These bills were referred to Mr. Molson of Charlestown Brooks of Bernardston, Rantoul of Beverly, Oliver of Lynn, Little of Marshfield, who reported Feb. 1 that the

---

[47] Rantoul left this page reference blank, but he is certainly referring to page 403 of his manuscript.

bill marked A should pass with certain amendments. It was read and ordered to a second reading.

"Feb 18th: The amendments were rejected.

[403] A list of some of the articles published on the subject of capital punishment by me:

10 Articles in the Salem Gazette from March 22 to May 31, 1831.

12 in the Experiment, a Lowell paper published by Horatio Hastings Weld, from April 26 to July 12, 1832.

15 in the Worcester Palladium from July to Nov 14, 1838

5 in the Christian Register in 1838 from August to October

17 in the Gloucester Democrat in 1835, 1836

3 in the Salem Advertiser in April 1846

5 in the Prisoner's Friend

67 others not now recollected

On Friday May 28th, 1854 James Clough, aged about 21 years, was executed at Taunton Gaol for murder committed some time ago and for which he has been under sentence for more than a year and is the first who had been executed under the law suspending the issuing of a warrant for execution for a year after sentence. From newspaper accounts this execution was with as much privacy as practicable. There were about 50 persons admitted within the prison yard and spectators without the yard could not see the tragical operation within.

Doct. Webster was the last before Clough who was executed in Massachusetts.

[404] In the session of the Legislature of 1855 a bill was passed through the House of Representatives abolishing capital punishment by a majority of about 30 but it was negative by the Senate by a considerable majority.

From the Inquirer London July 12th, 1856 on the abolition of capital punishment, it is said, "probably no moment was ever more auspicious than the present for actively agitating the question. The co-operation of the public represented by the newspapers which by a large majority support the abolition is willingly accorded to the cause. It is a most encouraging fact that the London daily papers advocating the abolition exceed in number those which are opposed to such a step, and of the provincials the same may be recorded. No greater proof of an advanced public opinion upon any question can be required than this."

Notice of Robert Stephen Rintoul, Editor of the London Examiner [404.1]

The London Daily News has an editorial in eulogy to Robert Stephen Rintoul, founder and editor of the "Spectator" newspaper, who has lately deceased. He is described as an able, industrious, and honest journalist.

Boston Daily Advertiser,

May 6th, 1858.

"RS Rintoul was born in the North of Scotland. He set up a newspaper at Dundee first, then at Edinburgh and then moved to London and founded the "Spectator", and maintained it for thirty years, until near his death, which occurred on April 22nd, 1858, when he was in the seventy-first year of his age."

There is a somewhat lengthy notice in the June number of "The Living Age" 1858 taken from an English publication. This article describes him as a conscientious, industrious, indefatigable, of great independence of thought, and firm and determinate in action."

Robert Rantoul – Representative [405]

Tuesday November 3rd, 1857 my grandson Robert S. Rantoul was this day chosen a Representative to the General Court from the Beverly District by the votes of the Republican Party. On the same day Nathaniel P. Banks of Waltham was chosen Governor. He studied law in the office my son Robert and was patronized by him.

My grandson Charles W. Rantoul was on the same day appointed second mate of the ship *R.B. Forbes*, __ [48] Master. The day is noticeable for the number of agreeable circumstances in connection with my life. This ship soon afterwards sailed for Singapore. My grandson Robert S. Rantoul was appointed a Justice of the Peace March 1858.

May 13th, 1858: In the evening I attended at the home of David S. Neal in Salem the wedding of my grandson Robert S. Rantoul and Harriett Charlotte Neal daughter of David S. Neal. They were married by James W. Thompson of Salem.

Andrew Peabody, my nephew prayed the services were simple and appropriate as is used by Unitarians. A new thing to me was the passing of a ring as in the Episcopal service. There was great seriousness pervading the whole of the service. There was a very plain collation in an adjoining room. The party consisted of about fifty and were elegantly dressed. There was no singing, no music, dancing or merriment. The order was good within & without the house though there were many people, male and female gathered around the doors and windows of the house. The order was perfect <u>without</u> as well as within. The party broke up at half past nine o'clock and the newly married couple took a coach for Boston from thence to New York.

[406] January 28th (Wednesday): Wm. Endicott, Joanna Endicott, Mary E. Endicott, Robert R. Endicott, Hannah L. Rantoul & myself attended the annual examination of the Salem Classical High School at the Lyceum Hall in Salem. The occasion was interesting to me and my family because that my grandson Henry Endicott, aged about 17 years after attending this school about three years was graduated with the highest honors of the day, and as the first scholar, delivered the valedictory address which was entirely his own composition & commended the applause of the school and the approbation of everyone from whom I heard an opinion. The exemplary deportment in every respect is more grateful to

---

[48] Rantoul left this blank.

me than every other consideration. In the character of my children and grandchildren I have much comfort in old age from which god be praised. Henry's address is copied on the two next pages. In the afternoon, the past members of the Salem High School held a meeting in the Tabernacle church and were addressed by Henry K Oliver the first teacher of the School and by others ad in the evening they held a Levee and had a supper. Wm R Preston of Portsmouth attended the celebration. On Monday February 16, 1859, my grandson Henry Endicott commenced his apprenticeship in C. F. Hovey's store in N. 33 Summer street Boston. His brother William being one of the firm and his brother Charles is there as a clerk. He boards with them at the house of the widow of John Treadwell's house in Indiana Place.

[407] Address delivered at the close of the examination of the High School in Salem by Henry Endicott of Beverly of the graduating class, January 28th, 1857, at the Lyceum Hall in Salem:

"We thank you who have come hither on this occasion to show by your presence the interest you feel in the school of which you are members. It is to you we are indebted for the privileges which we have enjoyed. You have allowed us to attend school for a longer period than is usually allotted to that, and we trust that you have not been wholly disappointed at the progress we have made in our various studies. My class mates, you are now about to bid farewell to those halls in which we have studied together during the three last years. Your various duties and occupations will dispense you over different parts of the earth, some on the land and others on the lanes, but wherever you may be, may you always regard with pleasure the many hours we have spent together in study. Very many of these hours we have doubtless allowed to glide by without improving them as we ought, but we may expect in future to make amends for our negligence by increased diligence in the pursuit of knowledge. For though about to leave school we should not renounce study. We have merely laid the foundation upon which we have yet to erect the edifice. Surrounded as we are by advantage of every kind, we are in danger of forgetting the full extent of them, where everyone has a share in the government, where each [408] might depend upon his own exertions for a maintenance, but where no limit is set to the progress of any, when the humblest may become the greatest, his advancement depending not on his birth, but on merit and energy, and one of the greatest benefits we receive is from the system of free schools, and to Salem belongs the honor of having established the first free school in this country. We should be grateful to our ancestors for handing down to us such a blessing and endeavor to transmit unimpaired to future generations. The world is now before you and solely upon your class will depend whether or not you will become honored members of the community in which you live and leave behind you footprints on the sands of time.

"Footprints that perhaps another

"Sailing o'er life's solemn main,

"A forlorn and shipwrecked brother,

"Seeing shall take heart again."

"I cannot close before thanking our instructors, for so faithfully and kindly leading us forward on the path of knowledge, correcting us when in error, removing obstacles when they impeded our progress. You have told us of the bright rewards of knowledge and virtue and of the fearful recompense of ignorance and vice and may we testify to the value we place on your instructions, by our future lives, and at this time we should not forget those instructors who were with us during the earlier parts of our course but have since left for other fields of labor. May we ever think on them with gratitude for their unceasing efforts on our behalf. And now we must bid farewell to our school, our instructors, and to each other as scholars for whom the bright sun which now rolls over our heads shall set in the west we shall no longer be members of the Salem Classical and High school.

"Henry Endicott."

Institution for the Blind [405.1]

On the 4th of February 1829, I received an invitation through the hands of John Pierpont of the following form:

"Boston February 4, 1829 – Sir in consideration of the great numbers of persons incurably blind in this state and in New England, who are proper subjects of education according to the plan now passed in Europe it is proposed to lay before a number of charitable individuals a statement of the degree of education of which blind persons are capable that an association may be formed to establish an Asylum for the Blind, if any persons can be found who deem it expedient to engage in the charitable work for the purpose above mentioned you are requested to attend a meeting on Tuesday evening next, at 7 o'clock at the Exchange coffee house ,when a variety of valuable information will be communicated -

"John Pierpont

"John D. Fisher

"Edward Brooks"

On Tuesday the 10th of February, I attended the proposed meeting and was chosen Chairman. Doct. John D. Fisher explained the method of teaching. He said that reading was taught by having letters raised on the surface of stiff paper, by types made for the purpose but without any ink or coloring, so that the letters can be distinctly felt with the fingers. He described several other methods of teaching reading. A method of writing and of learning other branches of common education. These descriptions were highly interesting and at that time perfectly new to most who were present, though now very familiar to great numbers. This meeting was adjourned to the Representatives [406.1] Hall in the State House on an evening in the next week.

I attended and was chairman of the meeting. My wife and daughter Charlotte also attended. There was a large assemblage and the methods of teaching were again explained. Theodore Sedgwick of Stockbridge made an eloquent speech. Other gentlemen made speeches more or less interesting and impressive. The meeting resulted in the formation of an association for the purpose of promoting the education of the blind. "An act to incorporate the New England Asylum for the Blind was obtained by this association on the 2nd day of March 1829. The whole number of corporators was 39. William Thorndike and myself were the only members from Beverly. About one third of the whole number are dead. Four of the Trustees were to be chosen annually by the visitors, who are the Governor, Lieut. Gov., President of the Senate, Speaker of the House and Chaplains of the legislature. I was appointed a Trustee on the part of the State and have been continued from 1829 to 1849. The school was first opened in Pleasant Street, by Doct. Samuel G. Howe. Margaret Teague, daughter of Richard Teague of this town was among the first pupils, the number of whom was six and the number was small for some considerable time. Thomas H. Perkins gave a valuable dwelling house in Pearl Street to the institution, to which house it was removed and the name of the Institution has been twice changed and now is "The Perkins Institution and Massachusetts Asylum for the Blind." The school was first opened by Sam'l G. Howe in Pleasant Street. [407.1] August 29th, 1832; it was the removed to Perkins's House in Pearl Street, which was exchanged for the Mount Washington estate at South Boston, where the accommodations are ample for the largest number that will probably resort to it. The number is now about 100.

I have made a point of visiting this institution occasionally on account of my connection with it as a trustee, but I have not had it in my power to do much in promotion of its interests. A few opportunities have occurred which I have endeavored to improve but little was expected from me. I was instrumental in procuring the admission of Margaret Teague in 1833 but of no other pupil as I now recollect. I wrote the petition for her father to sign, the certificate for the Selectmen, etc. & caused it to be presented. April 23, 1840: The pupils of this institution held a concert in the Baptist Meeting house in this town. It was well attended and continued till 9 1/4th the evening.

W. Nelson superintended the exhibition and the price of admission was 25 cents. Doct. Howe visited this town with a view of examining the hair factories here. I conducted him to Phillip English's factory and Mr. English explained to him cheerfully and satisfactorily the various operations connected with the preparation of hair for use in upholstery, notwithstanding Doct Howe's design was to establish the business in the Asylum for the Blind. I believe that after a trial Doct. Howe became satisfied that the employment was not well adopted to the situation of the blind at the Asylum. I assisted Doct. Howe with advice in getting up the [408] exhibition here in 1840. I feel satisfied that this institution has proved and that it will continue to be useful and beneficial in ameliorating the physical condition and improving and enlarging the mental and moral state of those who are so unfortunate as to be deprived of sight. There always will be a considerable number of this class and so far, though but little, as I may have contributed to its establishment and progress it is a source of gratification in old age. I commend it to my grandchildren to embrace all opportunities of aiding in any degree, however small, the establishment, the growth, and usefulness of every institution which they think will be beneficial in improving the condition of the human race. Having done this, they will find their reward in their subsequent reflections and recollections. Never refrain from doing any good thing because you can do but little. Do that little heartily and cordially and when you have done it, it may open a door which you thought not of for more extended action.

Richard Teague's petition to the Governor and Council praying that his daughter Margaret might be placed at the Asylum for the Blind was (approved) in 1833. She was not born blind but soon became so from a disease of her eyes which began a few days after her birth.

Essex Bridge [409]

The Essex Bridge between Salem and Beverly, 1907.

In September 1833, I was chosen a Director of the Essex Bridge and in 1838, December, after the decease of William Leech, I was chosen President and have continued to be re-elected to that office till this time (Feb 1849). The 51 original subscribers for this Bridge in 1787 are all dead. Their names and many other particulars relating to this bridge may be found in my lecture of December 1830, on the history of Beverly, beginning at the 12th page. My connection with this corporation has nothing particularly interesting to be here recorded. Anyone who is desirous of learning the history of this bridge will find many facts in the above-mentioned lecture, from which source E.M. Stone obtained most of the facts for his history of the bridge. This bridge has very much diminished in value since the establishment of the Eastern Rail Road.

I have upon two different occasions attended the Legislature to represent the interests of this corporation, for which I received pay.

At the annual meeting of the stockholders, on the 24th of September 1856 I declined a re-election as a director, having served twenty-three years and Benjamin F. Newhall was chosen in my place. He is the largest stockholder, owning 16 shares. Nancy Bridge is the next largest owning 12 shares the whole number of shares is 200. W. Newhall was by the directors chosen President. Cotton Bennett declined a re-election as a director and John T. Baker was chose in his stead.

Salem Turnpike & Chelsea Bridge [410]

In 1822 or before that time (not having any minute of the year at hand) I was chosen a director of the Salem Turnpike and Chelsea Bridge Corporation and have continued to be re-elected to this time a period of about twenty-seven years. From 1825 to 1830 I was in conjunction with Nathan Dane and E. Hersey Derby, one of the standing committee for attending specially to the concerns of the road & bridge. For this service, I received twelve dollars per year. This office occasionally called me to go over the road with N. Dane & E.H. Derby and added to my knowledge of its situation and of the surrounding localities. I have at different times since I have been a director, represented the corporation before the legislature petitions have been pending, from any quarter that affected its interests. My attendance at the director's meetings, though numerous, has not been constant. I believe I have contributed about a fair proportion to the labors required of directors, but I cannot claim anything more and perhaps my associates, who have been numerous may not concede so much. This road has diminished in value very much since the establishment of the Eastern Rail Road.

Since writing the above I have ascertained that I was first chosen a director in October 1821. My associates at that time were Nathan Dane, Jacob Ashton, Ichabod Nichols,

Benjamin Pickman, William Mansfield, John D. Treadwill, John Derby and Ezekiel Hersey Derby. They are all dead (April 1849) but E. Hersey Derby and he is not now a director. Mr. Derby died October 28, 1852 aged 80.

[411] In September 1849, I addressed the following letter to John G. King Clerk of the corporation.

"Hon John G. King   Beverly September 14th, 1849

"Dear Sir: I beg leave to request that at the next annual meeting of the Salem Turnpike and Chelsea Bridge corporation you will give notice that I respectfully decline being a candidate for re-election to the office of a director of said corporation. The length of my service, being about twenty-eight years and my advance age, admonished me that it is time to withdraw. I am very respectfully, dear Sir,

"Your friend and Obedt Servant

"Rob Rantoul."

I named to Mr. King William Endicott as a suitable person to supply my place if it was thought expedient to have one of the directors from Beverly. September 24th, 1849, I received the following communication.

"Salem Sept. 22, 1849

"Hon. Robert Rantoul

"Dear Sir, I am directed by the Proprietors of the Salem Turnpike and Chelsea Bridge Corporation to transmit to you the following copy of a vote passed at their meeting held this day and am, Dear Sir, with very great respect and regard,

"Your friend and Obed Servant

"J.G. King.

"At the annual meeting of the proprietors of the Salem Turnpike and Chelsea Bridge Corporation on the 22nd day of September 1849. It was unanimously voted, that the thanks of the proprietors be presented to the Honorable Robert Rantoul of Beverly, who has declined a re-election to the [412] Board of Directors for his assiduous, faithful and valuable service as a director of this corporation for a long series of years. A copy from the record.

"Attest J.G.. King – clerk"

Thus ends my connection with the management of the affairs of the corporation.

Benjamin Newhall of Saugus was chosen to fill my place. He is one of the County Commissioners for Essex County. When I was first chosen it was with particular reference to the accommodation of Nathan Dane, who was President and took upon himself much of the business of the corporation and being advanced in years it was thought desirable that he should have one of the directors near him, on whom he might easily call for aid when he desired it. Probably on no other grounds would the proprietors have chosen two directors on this side of Bass River. In this situation, I remained until Mr. Dane withdrew from the direction, aiding and assisting him when he called on me, as was in my power to do.

Beverly Bank [415]

October 5th, 1846: I was elected a director of the Beverly Bank and accepted the appointment. I was chosen to this office before, about 1828 or 1829, but then from a consideration of certain circumstances, I declined its acceptance. I have been a stockholder in the Bank from its first establishment in 1802 to this time. My coming into the direction at so late a period of my life was rather from a sense of duty than from a desire of the office. The time when I should have esteemed it a ground of distinction in society had passed away. The directors with whom I associated are Albert Thorndike, President, Josiah Lovett, Henry Larcom, Ezra Ellingwood, Jonathan Batchelder & Samuel Endicott. Lovett and Larcom are older than myself. Coming into the direction so late in life I cannot be of much use. I doubted whether I ought to accept. There was a period when I should have been gratified by an election to this office and could have made myself useful in it. I will not state the circumstances which excluded me at that time- they are known to but a few, if to any, now living. The principal actors are dead. Its presidents have been Israel Thorndike, Moses Brown, Joshua Fisher & William Leech, who are all dead, Pyam Lovett who is now living but has been confined to his house for some years with sickness and Albert Thorndike the present President. Its cashiers have been Josiah Gould, Albert Thorndike and now Robert G. Bennett. It's first board of directors are all dead. In October 1849 Cotton Bennett was chosen a director in the room of Jonathan Batchelder who is gone to California.

[416] Previous to and also at the stockholders meeting on the 3rd of October 1853, I gave notice that I did not wish to be a candidate for re-election and Albert Thorndike gave the like notice. Votes of thanks were passed to him and to me for his faithful services as president, a piece of plate of the value of fifty dollars was voted to be presented. Thanks was also voted to Rob G. Bennett for his faithful services as cashier. Andrew T. Leech and William Endicott were chosen directors in the places of A. Thorndike and myself. Samuel Endicott was subsequently chosen president by the directors. Henry Larcom retired from the direction in 1852 and Josiah Lovett was omitted in 1851 and in the room of these two Abraham Edwards and John Pickett were chosen. Edwards in 1851 and Pickett in 1852.

This finishes my connections with the management of the Beverly Bank. Coming into it so late in life I did not take a very active part in its concerns. In March 1854, a new bank was incorporated with the name of the Bass River Bank. I regret that an attempt is to be made to put another Bank in operation. One Bank is more than sufficient for the business of the town at this time and the competition of the two will make both of them undesirable as a place of investment. The new one, if put in operation, will have to struggle hard for continued existence and if it should stop or fail it will be attended with much loss by its stockholders, many of whom will be drawn into the concern by reckless speculators.

Joanna Quiner – Bust [417]

Bust of Robert Rantoul by Joanna Quiner.

January 12th, 1842: I began to sit at Joanna Quiner's house for her to model a bust for me. It claimed about 1 ¾ hours. She measured my head, nose and mouth with calipers and at the same time took various views of my countenance and continued working with her fingers upon a mas of clay provided for the purpose. While she worked she entertained me with conversation. She informed me that the mouth is generally of the same length of the nose. I attended on eleven or twelve different days, averaging about two hours each day till Feb 5th and on the 8th February the model was carried to Boston, from which a mold was formed and six casts in plaster of Paris were made which were ready for delivery on the 8th of March and I disposed of them as follows viz: One to Christopher T. Thayer, my minister – one to my nephew Andrew P. Peabody – one to my son Robert – one to my daughter Joanna, one to Joanna Quiner and one I reserved which I intend to give to my daughter Hannah after my decease. I paid Joanna Quiner fifty dollars and about the same sum to Chickey & Garey of Boston for making the mold and casting. I afterwards gave Joanna Quiner the mold from which she has made one or more casts herself. As long as the mold remains perfect casts can be made from it at pleasure. Many persons who have seen the bust speak of it as a very striking likeness. Andrew P. Peabody in his letter of the 18th March 1842 considers it a good likeness and writes in very commendatory terms of the skill of Miss Quiner, the self-taught artist.

[418] Joanna Quiner's father was born in Marblehead, about the year of 1772. He, with his father's family, removed to Manchester about 1780, and lived there until about 1794. He married a Miss ---[49] Campbell of Gloucester and removed to Beverly, where he lived until his death April 30th, 1844 at about the age of 73. He never learned to drink spirituous liquors. In his younger days, he followed the Cod fishing and used to carry a quart of rum with him for medical purposes and very frequently he brought it back again, untouched. After he left fishing he labored hard and usually accomplished more work in a given time than other laborers, he working without spirits, while they drank as usual. There was always some eccentricity of character about him, he had the reputation of strict honesty and of great industry. Joanna his daughter is remarkable for her industry and for her very extraordinary faculty in many branches of industry as well as for her genius and acquirements without the advantage of instruction, in the art of sculpture. As an evidence of the inherent persevering industry of her ancestors, she showed me a stick, made of hard wood, with which her grandmother had turned her spinning wheel for so great a length of

---

[49] Rantoul left her first name intentionally blank. Joanna's father Abraham married Susannah Cammell in Manchester-by-the-Sea on March 4, 1792 (Manchester VRs, p47).

time and with such unwearied constancy, that part of the stick embraced by the thumb and finger when used, near the foreword part, and at the hinder part of the stick where it bore upon the little finger was worn by the action of the thumb and finger about half off. This stick she keeps as a remembrance of the industry of her grandmother which trait of character has prevailed in two succeeding generations.

[419] Joanna Quiner has made busts of George Abbot, of some persons in Joshua Safford's family in Salem and of a child of John E. Thayer of Boston and of some others whose names are not now recollected. She has also made some additional Casts of mine from the mold which I gave her. One of these she has exhibited in the Athenaeum Gallery in Boston[50].

August 1851; Joanna Quiner is now making a bust of Capt. Henry Larcom.

May 1853: I had a large sized Daguerreotype by Southworth & Hawes[51] taken and from this William Endicott Jun. had a plate engraved but of a somewhat smaller size, from which he had some hundred copies printed. These he, daughter Hannah and others of my family have distributed among friends very extensively so that there will be of me no lack of pictures about in this part of the country. The Daguerreotype is said to be, by the best judges, one of the best performances of the named artists.

William Endicott has procured a second set of impressions from the plate from which he owns, of two hundred in number, so that there are now 400 copies.

The large Daguerreotype above mentioned I have given to my daughter Hannah. It costs ten dollars.

Beverly Charitable Society – Fisher Charitable Society [421]

The Beverly Charitable Society was incorporated March 1st, 1809, and its name changed to that of the Fisher Charitable Society March 28, 1836. Joshua Fisher was the founder of this society. He gave $200 at the time of its organization and $1,000 by his will. One hundred dollars, of the first donations, he directed to be kept at compound interest for one hundred years, and after that time to be at the disposal of the Society. He was the first President and died March 15th, 1833, aged 84. Thomas Davis was chosen President in September 1833 and died July 17, 1840 aged 85. I was chosen President September 1840. I was a trustee of the society from 1810 to 1840. For nearly thirty years, I aided in the annual distributions of the society. In 1812 & 1813, the sum distributed was $30, and from September 1847 to September 1848 it had increased to $145 and is still increasing. In 1850 & 1851 it was $190.

My connection with this society as trustee and as President has continued about 38 years. As an agent in distributing its funds I spent considerable time, but the office of President requires much less time and attention. The establishment of this society was a favorite object with Doctor Fisher and its funds are now so well established that a reasonable ground of expectation exists for its continuance for a great length of time or so long

---

[50] A copy of Rantoul's bust is on display in the gallery of the Boston Athenaeum.

[51] Southworth & Hawes is a photographic studio that operated in, Boston from 1843-1863

at honest, honorable and intelligent men, are willing to administer its affairs. Those in office should take very precaution to prevent its falling into other hands. [422] I would also mention as the second largest donation the sum of one thousand dollars given by George Lee, son of Joseph Lee formerly of this town. There were several sums of $100 given by different persons, among whom was Pyam Lovett. A subscription was gotten up in December 1810 but there was not much obtained.

The donation of $1,000 by George Lee was through the agency of his nephew John C. Lee of Salem and was represented to be in advance of a bequest to that amount which he had provided for in his will.

This society was organized in November 1810. The first meeting was held on the 10th and adjourned to the 19th, when the by-laws were adopted and the first officers were elected viz Joshua Fisher – President, Josiah Gould – Secretary, Thomas Davis – Treasurer, Thomas Stephens, Moses Dow & Robert Rantoul – Trustees. September 3rd, 1849 its permanent funds are $5,610.50 including the Hay-scales valued at $250.

Moses Brown gave the old Hay-scales to the society which were used until they were worn out or had become antiquated amidst the numerous improvements and they were replaced by a modern construction which cost the society $250, but is not a profitable investment as the income is only about 6 pct. over the annual repairs without looking to the expense of reconstruction at a future day, 1856. George Lee, the second in the amount of his donation, died at West Cambridge, July 22nd, 1856, aged 80 years. He was never married.

General Lafayette: His Reception [423]

August 31st, 1824: General Lafayette visited this town. A committee of arrangements was constituted to prepare for his reception. This committee invited me to make an address to him. He was so situated in regard to his stopping places at Salem and at Ipswich that he could not alight here, it was therefore arranged that he should stop with the escort and cavalcade in front of the Bank House on Cabot Street and receive the address in his coach. When he arrived at the proposed place there was a <u>very</u> heavy shower of rain, his coach stopped abreast of the front door of the house, the side door of his carriage was thrown open and I proceeded in the midst of the heavy rain from the door of the hose to the side of the coach, having first secured Nathaniel Lamson to hold an umbrella over me, I stood in the water with my hat under my arm, and read the address which I had prepared, to which he made a reply, but his foreign

"Journey of Lafayette",
a poem by Daniel S. Whitney, 1825.

accent, the excitement of the occasion and my perturbation, prevented me from fully understanding it. This being accomplished the cavalcade moved on for Ipswich amidst the cheers of the persons assembled around the Bank and the pelting of the drenching rain. A copy of my address and an account of the other proceedings on this occasion may be found in Stone's History of Beverly, to which I refer. Peter Jowder lost [424] an arm by firing of cannon on Ellingwood's Point while La Fayette was entering the town by Essex Bridge. In June 17, 1825 I, then being a member of the House of Representatives, was introduced to him in the Representative's chambers and afterwards joined the procession to Bunker's Hill where Daniel Webster delivered an oration and Lafayette assisted at the laying of the cornerstone of the monument on that hill. Joseph Thanter of Edgartown, who had been a Chaplain in the revolutionary army, offered prayers. The heat of the sun was so great as to produce a bilious attack, which obliged me to leave my seat soon after the commencement of the services and to return to my lodgings at Elizabeth Reed's in Brattle Street, Boston. The ceremonies prolonged that session of the General Court, somewhat. The circumstances attending the visit of La Fayette to this town, required that my address should be short. George Brown was the principal instrument in fixing the service upon me and I believe he was well satisfied with its performance. Nathaniel Lamson has been dead many years, but his widow Lucy and two sons Charles and Israel are now living. George Brown has died at a later period leaving a widow and several children.

John Everett, a brother of President Edward Everett was in the coach with Lafayette when he stopped here. He died soon afterwards. [425] After writing the foregoing account of the visit of La Fayette I have concluded to add a copy of my address which is as follows viz:

"General: The inhabitants of Beverly bid you welcome. We welcome you to our country – that country which owes so much to your aid in the acquisition of her independence. We receive you not merely as the friend of our beloved country, but as the friend of Man. Your labors, our sacrifices, your sufferings in the cause of liberty demand our gratitude. Tyrants receive the commanded adulation of their slaves, but to the benefactors of our race belong the spontaneous effusions of our hearts. Accept our sincere congratulations that you live to witness the order, the prosperity, the happiness that results from our free institutions and may the evening of your days be solaced with the reflection that those principles of government, to the support of which your life has been devoted, and which alone can secure the enjoyment of rational liberty are fast spreading their influence through the whole family of man. Wishing you long life and uninterrupted happiness, we bid you farewell. "

At the ensuing session of the General court I was instrumental in procuring a pension of $50 per year from the Treasury of the Commonwealth during his life, for Peter Jowder. He has lived in Hamilton principally, since he lost his arm.

[426] March 1854: I commenced writing a Biographical Sketch in 1851 of Lafayette for the Beverly Citizen, but after publishing two or three numbers, I was informed that their arrangements with their printers forbade their publishing lengthy articles, but that they would be pleased to publish matters of local interest. Thus checked, I wrote no further on the subject.

State Reform School [429]

May 15th, 1846: I was appointed a commissioner in conjunction with Alfred Dwight Foster and Samuel H. Walley Jun., to select an eligible site for a manual labor school for the employment, instruction and reformation of juvenile offenders by virtue of a resolve of the Legislature of the 16th of April 1846. In pursuance of this appointment the commissioners caused advertisements of the date of 17th of June 1846 to be inserted in twelve different newspapers inviting proposals for the sale of suitable sites, such as described in the resolve. Many proposals were received, and the Commissioners visited such places as they thought might answer the intended purposes. They thought it expedient to visit the house of reformation for juvenile offenders and the Farm School in Boston. On the 11th of September 1846, S H. Walley and myself left Boston for New York by the way of Norwich and through Long Island Sound by the superb Steamer *Atlantic,* which was soon afterwards lost with many lives by a gale of wind in the sound. At the Astor House in New York we met A.D. Foster according to a previous arrangement on Saturday morning the 12th and visited the House of Refuge for Juvenile Offenders and on Monday proceeded to Philadelphia and there visited a similar establishment after which I left my colleagues and proceeded to Cincinnati and returned home by the way of Lake Erie. A story of this journey may be found among my manuscripts. I arrived at home October 1846 and the next day was attacked with the Influenza, but it did not confine me to the house.

[430] The Commissioners after they had viewed all the places offered where they thought such a view necessary, made choice of the farm of Lovett Peters on the northerly side of Chauncey Pond in Westborough. This farm contains about 180 acres of land and comprises about one half of the margin of the pond as a boundary. The pond has surface of 178 acres and is in some parts thirty feet deep. Its water is clear and pure. The price was 9,000 dollars. Pending these proceedings, a gentleman who concealed his name from all except the Chairman of the commissioners, A.D. Foster offered the gift of ten thousand dollars from which gift the farm was paid for. It is conjectured that the gentlemen who thus concealed his name from the public is Theodor Lyman. After purchasing this farm, the commissioners procured an architect who with the advice Daniel Chandler, the very efficient superintendent of the Boston House of Reformation, since deceased, furnished the plan of the building which has since been erected. The architect who made the plan was ----[52] Melvin. He estimated the cost of the buildings at $45,000 but when proposals were issued for contractors for the building, although he had previously said that he would take the contract at that sum, yet he put in an offer to do it for some thousand dollars more, say 62,500 instead of 45,000 so that the contract was given to Daniel Davies of Boston, who contracted to do it for 52,000 dollars.

After the purchase of the farm A.D Foster received a letter from the same unknown offering another sum of from five to ten thousand dollars upon certain conditions for the aid of boys leaving the institution.

[431] I wrote the following letter in answer to one received from A.D. Foster and from S. H. Walley Jun. before the report of the commissioners was adopted.

---

[52] Rantoul intentionally left his first name blank.

"Hon Sam'l Walley Jun   Beverly November 27, 1846

"My dear Sir: I return you W. Foster's draft of a report and the other papers sent with it. I am pleased with the tenor of the report. We are, I believe, very well agreed in opinion in regard to the object of the proposed institution and in the means to be used for the allotment of the most desirable object, the reform of the vices of the young, although there may be some slight discrepancy of opinion in regard to details. I have, with great freedom, examined the draft of the report and of such parts of it as i have marked with a pencil. I respectfully invite a reconsideration. I think that if W Foster had had your draft of a bill before him he would have omitted some things as repetitions and have made others to conform more exactly to its provisions. With respect to an application to the keepers of Houses of Correction for a return of the number of commitments under the age of sixteen, I think that the value of the information would not compensate for the trouble. I am glad to find that Mr. Peters is reconciled to our having the whole of his farm, and I hope that no suggestion will be admitted into the report that there is any too much land. I have read Mr. Packarel's pamphlet and agree with you that some extracts might be useful as tending to enlighten the public mind in regard to the necessity of the proposed institution and the principles upon which it [432] should be established and conducted. Could not that part of Professor Greenleaf's letter beginning with "In regard" and ending with "Surveying etc." be appended to the report as a note? I hope Mr. Foster will be successful in procuring the plans and estimates from the source he proposed. The plan should be upon an economical scale of arrangement, to commend it to the acceptance of the Legislature, and the estimates should be just and faithful for obvious reasons, besides a regard to our own reputation in avoiding the imputation of a desire to promote the adoption of a public measure by the practice of deceptive arts. With respect to a tenant for the farm for the first year, although we might have made it a part of the bargain for the purchase, that Mr. Peter should continue his occupation for a definite period, it is doubtful whether we have authority to make an agreement with anyone else for its use., therefore our enquires upon that head should be only for the sake of information and not with any view to a contract. The proposition for establishing a fund for the benefit of boys after their discharge deserves serious consideration not only as it respects the future character and destiny of the boys themselves, but as to its effect upon society at large. Boys who leave this institution are either to be bound out to service or to be restored to their parents. In either case they will be as well off as other boys, whose honesty, fidelity and general good conduct, have never been impeached and will have the same opportunity of rising in the world except the remembrance of their juvenile delinquency and this cannot be removed by pecuniary aid. It is understood that boys who have been subjects of institution will, when they are discharged, be better off [433] than those who have always maintained a good character will it not have an injurious influence upon some minds so as to impair their efforts to sustain a virtuous character? In all charitable undertakings, it is of the first importance that nothing should be done that will operate as a <u>bounty</u> upon pauperism or upon crime or that will diminish virtuous effort. Self-control, self-dependence and self-effort are to be acquired or learned in youth, they cannot be bought with money. I hope it will not be thought that I in the least degree undervalue the noble charity of the unknown individual, who has so generously furnished the means of commencing our institution, nor impugn his motives in his suggestions in regard to the application of his future bounty, for I am sure that I most heartily concur with Mr. foster in the sentiment, that "both these offers of donations are exceedingly generous and noble hearted." I remain very truly,

"Your friend and obedient servant,

"Robert Rantoul"

The report of the commissioners was made to the governor on the 12th of January 1847, and by him sent to the House of Representative on the 15th. On the 9th of April 1847, a resolve was passed authorizing the Gov. to appoint commissioners to erect the buildings in conformity with the report. Thus far acting in concert with A.D. Foster & S.H. Walley Jun, I attended to this business visiting many places and spending some 30 or 40 days' time and saw its successful termination in the procurement of the most desirable site that has been seen before or since, and the adoption of the plan and in the <u>main</u> of the principles and regulations which we recommended.

[434] On the 21st of April 1847 I received official information that I was appointed a commissioner, in conjunction with Alfred D. Foster & Samuel Pomeroy, for erecting the buildings on the site in Westborough, purchased by the previous commission. Having some doubts about the propriety of accepting an appointment which would probably extend so far ahead, I wrote the following letter:

"Beverly April 24th, 1847.

"Hon. Alfred D. Foster,

"Dear Sir: I have received official information of an appointment as a commissioner for erecting the State Reform School buildings, and I am in doubt whether I ought to accept of this office. Before a decision, I am desirous of hearing from you, and if I should take the place under any circumstances, it will be that I have great confidence in your superior qualifications for transacting the business, and that your and Mr. Pomeroy will be content with an associate from whom you can expect only a limited participation in the more active duties. My age, distance from the location and my want of knowledge and experience in transactions of the kind are among the more prominent reasons that had me to doubt the propriety of my engaging in this, <u>to me</u>, new kind of business. If you will be kind enough to favor me with your view, I shall greatly esteem it and it will aid me to decide what is my duty in the case. I am very respectfully

"Your obed't Sev't

"Rob Rantoul"

[435] To this letter I received an answer from Mr. Foster wherein he informs me of his acceptance of the appointment and his willingness to undertake the duties of it in conjunction with Mr. Pomeroy and myself which determination of his led me to accept and I wrote him the following letter.

"Beverly May 3rd, 1847

"Hon. A.D. Foster

"Dear Sir: Your letter of the 26th ult. by a mistake of the Boston Post Office, was sent to my son's office in Boston and in consequence it was not received by me until Saturday evening and there being no mail from here until this day (Monday) I regret that the delay may prevent your proposed arrangement with Mr. Carter. Being assured of your acceptance of the office of Commissioner and of the peculiar qualifications of Mr. Pomeroy, Judge Washburn's opinion of whom is confirmed by my son, who has served with him as a director of the Western Rail Road, I have concluded to serve with you and Mr. Pomeroy and shall endeavor to afford whatever aid will be in my power to render in the execution of the important trust confided to us. I shall expect to meet you and Mr. Pomeroy in Boston, tomorrow at 10 o'clock, when we can confer upon the subject of the employment of Mr. Carter and therefore I forbear replying to your remarks respecting him. I remain, Dear Sir

"Very respectfully your Obed Serv't

"Rob Rantoul"

The commissioners proceeded to make arrangements for the erection of the buildings. They appointed Elias Carter of Springfield and James S. Savage of Southborough joint superintendent of the work. [436] Through their agency many proposals were obtained for executing the work and a contract was made with Daniel Davies for 52,000 dollars, he agreeing to build and complete it on or before the first day of December 1848. It was inserted in the written contract that no spirituous liquor should be drank by any one while at work on the building. The superintendents and contractor abstain from the use of intoxicating liquors as a drink at all places. While the buildings were progressing, I made sixteen visits to Westborough, sometimes with one or more of the commissioners and sometimes alone. We were favored with a very good temperance hotel, kept by Dexter Brigham, opposite the Rail Road Depot, where we boarded when at Westborough. I also met with the commissioners four or five times in Boston. My first journey was May 4th, 1847 and my last one February 16th, 1849. So that my journeys averaged about one in a month. The contractors informed us in the Autumn of 1848 that the buildings would be ready for use on the first day of November, being a month earlier than he had agreed to have them finished, whereupon we gave notice to the Governor who issued his proclamation authorizing courts & justices of the peace to commit boys to the State Reform School according to law on and after the 1st day of November 1848. Boys soon came and now (Feb. 8th, 1849) there are about sixty boys there on the 7th of December 1848. The buildings were dedicated under the direction of the Justices who were appointed the Governor and Council sometime before and whose names are, x Nathan Fisher of Westborough, x Doct John W. Graves of Lowell, Samuel Wilson of East Hampton, Thomas Greene of New Bedford, Otis Adams of Grafton, George Denny of Westborough and William J. Andrew of Boston.

[437] On the 7th of December 1848, I left home at seven o'clock in the morning to proceed to Westborough to attend the dedication of the Reform School and arrived at the Depot in Westborough at about 11 ½. There were many carriages in waiting to take the company about 2 ½ miles to the buildings, but not enough to take them all at one time so that some of the carriages went twice. Gov. Briggs with some members of the council and many of the most distinguished men from various parts of the state were present. A.D. Foster and Samuel Pomeroy were there, but Mr. Pomeroy, debilitated by sickness and

having lost the distinctness and animation of his voice which characterized him when we commenced our joint labors somethings more than a year and a half ago. He walks feebly. The buildings were shown to the visitors by the trustees after which the company assembled in the works shop which was fitted up temporary with a desk, settees, chairs, bench and etc. so that the whole might be comfortably seated and there listened to an able address from Amory Washburn of Lowell. The services commenced with prayer by John Peirce of Brookline. There was singing by the boys, who numbered about 26 in the whole and the conclusion by a benediction by John Pierce. The company then proceeded to the Eastern dormitory hall, where tables were spread, and an excellent dinner served up, of cold meats, pies, nuts, raisins, grapes, apples etc. The ware used on the table was what had been procured for the use of the inmates of the institution. The new white coverlids were used for table cloths. Barnabas Sears the newly appointed Secretary of the Board of Education asked a blessing. Water was the only drink. After the dinner, some toasts were read by George Denny, which in the first place led Gov. Briggs to rise and address the company which he did in a very feeling manner, and told a very pathetic story of a child that had been rescued from a gaol by a lady and restored to virtue and usefulness by her assiduous labors. He was followed by Levi Lincoln and a Mr. Foster of Boston after whom Henry Colman formerly a Minister in [438] Salem lately returned from Europe rose to speak but I was obliged to leave and did not hear him. There were only two Ladies at the table, one of whom was the wife of S Williston, a trustee. Returning I arrived at Boston at about 6 ½ pm. Lodged at the Adams House where I again met S Williston & wife & J. W. Graves. One of the boys having escaped through a 7 by 9 iron window sash it became necessary to guard the windows more effectively and on Friday I went with J.S. Savage to Daniel Safford & Co.'s shop to examine some Iron netting which it was proposed to put on the windows to increase the security against escape and I wrote to A.D. Foster approving of the netting and leaving it to his option whether it should be procured. On the 7th of February 1849 A.D. Foster & myself at the Adams House settled with Daniel Davies for his work, allowing him 52,000 on his contract and about 2,756 dollars for extra work and materials. We allowed the two superintendents five percent on the expenditure amounting to about 3,500 $ to be divided between them as they may agree. We also signed our report to the Gov. and Council and asked for another appropriation of 6,000 dollars to pay all remaining demands.

The gentleman who gave the sum of ten thousand dollars before mentioned afterwards gave another like sum, which, together with as much, say 10,000 dollars, appropriated by the State is to constitute a fund to be appropriated for the benefit of the Intuition. The same gentleman also gave the case of another farm, being about 2500 dollars, which farm, of about 70 acres, was in part bounded on Chauncey Pond and lying partly southerly and easterly and adjoining Peter's farm, which was bought at first and comprised some land lying on the easterly side of the road and some other land lying at a distance and a small dwelling house and out buildings on the land connected with the Peters farm. The land immediately connected with the institution is more than 200 acres and comprises more than half of the margin of the pond. [439] There are two commodious dwelling houses on the land in addition to the buildings erected for the school. These houses will furnish accommodations for a farmer, a teacher or other officers who cannot well be lodged in the main building.

October 8th, 1846: In connection with the first commission, Sam'l H. Walley Jun. and myself visited the farm school on Thompson's Island in Boston harbor. We left Liverpool wharf in Boston, in the Hingham Steam Boat, *Mayflower* at 11 o'clock am. This boat is small but very commodious for a considerable number of passengers. There were in the boat Deacon Grant, who was the conductor of the visitors, Minot Thayer of Braintree, an old acquaintance of mine, W. Poales of Hingham, Mr. Whitney of Braintree, who had just been appointed a teacher in the school, some other gentlemen and about fifty women and children going to see their relatives and to witness the examination of the school. We had a pleasant passage down but were delayed some time near the island by the state of the tide not being high enough to allow the boat to come to the wharf and we landed at about 12 o'clock. We found the boys in the school room. hey soon came to order after they had greeted their relations and friends who visited them, the first class read, they were examined in Geography, History and Spelling and Declaimed. Deacon Grant led in the examination. He spoke very encouragingly to the boys and read an interesting letter from one who was sent to the school when four years of age and is now a minister of the Gospel. I made a short address as did Mr. Walley. The school was dismissed, and the boys were allowed free intercourse with their friends and visitors. When the company were about leaving one little boy clung to his mother and going with her to the wharf, cried most loudly. He was separated from her not without some force and led back by Deacon Grant to the house. It was remarked that this boy had been there but a short time and that his mother visited him too soon.

[440] The boys formed in procession and with a drum marched down to the wharf followed by the visitors and opening right and left the company passed through their ranks and went on board the boat to return to Boston. The boys gave three cheers at the departure of their friends though some of them shed tears of some. The minister whose letters Deacon Grant read was John H Wilson, of Huron, Wayne county New York. He remained three years in the school and at 7 years of age went to live with Thomas Gold of Pittsfield, father of the first wife of Nathan Appleton. At 19 years of age he became religious. Went to Lowell as a clerk – fitted for college – entered Williams college 1832 – graduated 1836 – taught school four years, became a minister and settled as above. He expressed his gratitude to Joseph Austin, Thomas Gold, Nathan Appleton, the managers of the Farm school and to others. I was favorable impressed with the general appearances of this school intended for boys who cannot be well governed at home.

General Theodore Lyman that President and the most munificent benefactors in the institution died at Brookline July 18, 1849, aged 57. He was much distinguished for his philanthropy. He gave not only his money but his time to do works.

In May 1849 William Livingston of Lowell and Burnill A. Giggs of Lanesborough, are appointed trustees in the place of Nahum Fisher and John W. Graves whose time expires of the state reform school at Westborough. Rev. Stone, chaplain and principal teacher, O.H. Hutchinson, assistant teacher Deacon James Leech steward and farmer Wm R. Lincoln superintendent. 143 boys there. Rev Mr. Stone resigned in January 1850.

[441] Lemuel Pomeroy of Pittsfield who was one of the commissioners for building is about my own age. Alfred D. Foster was born in 1800 and being so much younger than either of the other two and being chairman also, he has taken the principal charge of the business. Mr. Pomeroy and myself have given him what aid we could and certainly we have not interposed any obstructions to his progress. My intercourse with both has been only pleasant and agreeable, as also it was with Samuel Walley Jun. on the first commission. Mr. Foster has risen in my opinion from this occasional intercourse for the two or three past years. I knew him several years ago as a member of the House of Representatives and I renewed this acquaintance at Amherst in August 1845. He has a deservedly high reputation for is excellent moral and religious character his kindly feelings and his benevolence and liberality. I saw Mr. Pomeroy and was introduced to him at Pittsfield in April 1819 when I was there to examine the Agricultural bank. When I met him at Westborough in 1847 I had no recollection of his person. He has a fine, stately, noble figure, florid countenance and very pleasant and agreeable in conversation. His affability makes him friends at sight. In the summer of 1848 he had a paralyzed attack from the effects of which he did not entire recover. I saw him probably for the last time in this world at Westborough, on the 7th of December 1848, I have this day (Feb 13, 1849) received information of his being again prostrated on a bed of sickness and that he is not expected [442] to recover. With S.H. Walley Jun., who I suppose is about six years younger than A D Foster, I had no previous acquaintance but my connection with him on the first commission in 1846 and into January 1847 left upon my mind a most favorable impression of the goodness of his heart and of the correctness of his character. His mother was a daughter of Lieut. Gov. William Phillips of whose hospitality I frequently partook when I was in the House of Reps and when I had often seen his father and his mother at the dinner table. Mr. Walley is now (March 1849) afflicted with disease which has disqualified him for business for some months past.

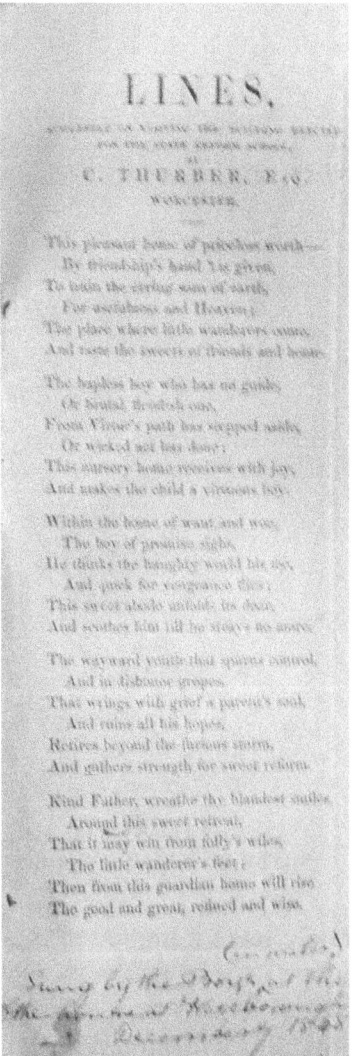

"Lines", sung by children at the State Reform School, Westborough, 1848.

Although when I entered on the second commission I had some misgivings, yet I now have no reason to regret my engagement inasmuch my life, health and strength have been spared to its completion and I have thus another opportunity of serving the commonwealth and of giving my aid in the establishment of an Institution which I trust will be fraught with great benefits to society in rescuing from crime, misery and wretchedness, many of the young.

July 9th, 1849: I called at S.H Walley Jun. office in Boston and was there informed that he had not been able to resume his business and was still an invalid.

August 25, 1849 Saturday at 8 o'clock in the evening Lemuel Pomeroy died aged 71. He was an enterprising and successful manufacturer and highly esteemed.

Rev. Mr. Todd preached a sermon at his funeral in Pittsfield

[443] On the 4th of August 1849, I met with A.D. Foster at Westborough (Mr. Pomeroy being still sick) for the purpose of settling some bills which closes our concern as commissioners saving that we have a report to make of our doings. We visited the Reform School now in full operation with 209 boys. About a third of them are employed in sewing and knitting under the charge of two women. The principal teacher is Miss Porter of Salem. About the same number of boys are employed in shoe making. The residual are employed in the cultivation of the farm and in household labor, such as cooking, washing, ironing, cleaning etc. We visited the school but at the time we were present only singing was attended to. Mr. Foster and myself made some remarks to the school. The Trustees have made several improvements and alterations in regard to the out buildings. They have removed one of the barns to the rear of the principal buildings for a piggery and stable for the horse used for a carriage and for a place for emptying and filling the beds with straw, for all of which purpose it is conveniently situated. As the pigs will be fed mostly from the waste of the house, it is good economy to have them near at hand. They have a new barn for stock on the farm at the cost of more than $4,000. There are now 15 cows, but it is thought that an improved cultivation will sustain double that number so that will make a large part of the [444] diet of the boys as well as furnishing butter and cheese for the family. Considerable has been done in gardening and eventually they will have a beautifully located garden, extending from the front of the main building towards the pond. The supply of water is inadequate, and the trustees have it in contemplation to bring water from the pond, by a wind mill, to the main building to an elevated reservoir so that it may run to every part of the house. Mr. Foster informed me that the decease of Gen'l Theodore Lyman had relieved him from the injunction of secrecy and that he was now at liberty to say that the 20,000 dollars which passed through his hands was given by Theodore Lyman under a strict charge of secrecy during Mr. Lyman's life.

We have settled all the demands for the building without any difference excepting that of Mr. Melvin for making the working plan. We thought his demand so extravagant that we rejected it but offered him $75 which he refused to take so that it remains unsettled. He proposed a reference which we declined. We should have been gratified to have completed the whole concern without this difference. Mr. Carter & Mr. Savage the

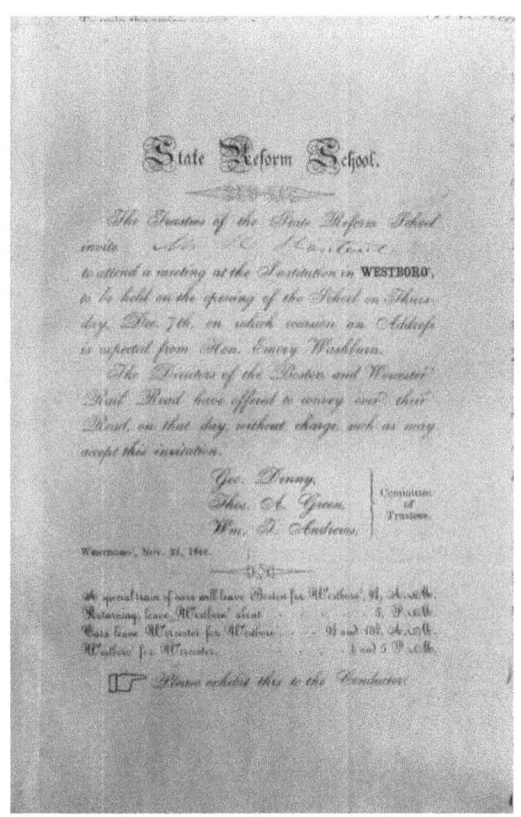

Rantoul's invitation to meeting at the State Reform School November 23rd, 1848.

superintendents employed by us, were judicious, faithful and good tempered so that we were saved from those collisions with workmen which frequently occur in such large undertakings. Mr. Pomeroy has been confined to his bed for most of the time since February last and he was not advised of our meeting in August as his son wrote to Mr. Foster that it would be useless and perhaps injurious to inform him of it.

[445] Copy of the final report of the commissioners for erecting the State Reform School buildings

"To his Excellency George Briggs, Governor and to the Honorable Executive Council of the commonwealth of Massachusetts.

"The commissioner for erecting the State Reform School buildings at Westborough, having as they suppose discharged their commission in full, herewith present, for settlement, their final account. All bills incurred by them have been paid with one exception. In regard to that one, they state the following facts, because they have reason to believe it will be brought to the notice of the Legislature, by petition from Mr. Isaac Melvin.

"The commissioners for selecting a site and procuring plans of buildings for this school upon the recommendation of Capt. Daniel Chandler, the superintendent of the house of Refuge for Juvenile Offenders at south Boston, employed Mr. Isaac Melvin, architect, to draw the plans, which they were to procure and present to the consideration of the Legislature. He performed that service and furnished written explanations of the plans, for which he charged, and was paid the sum of two hundred dollars. Those plans came into the hands of the present commissioners as stated in former reports, the commissioners employed Elias Carter & James Savage Esquire, both [446] reliable and competent men to superintend the erection of the buildings. Working plans and specifications were necessary and might have been prepared by them, but they thought professional courtesy required that Mr. Melvin should have opportunity to prepare all the plans as he had furnished the design. They were authorized to employ Mr. Melvin to draw the working plans and to write out the specifications. What he did will appear from the papers herewith presented. His claim for the service was three hundred and fifty-eight dollars ($358). Mr. Carter has for years been extensively employed as an architect and builder, and Mr. Savage is well known as the builder of the Bunker Hill monument, and other extensive works in Boston and its vicinity. Both these gentlemen considered fifty dollars to be an ample compensation for the service rendered by Mr. Melvin, and more than it was worth. Not to rely on their judgment alone two other competent architects were asked for what they would do the like work. One said for thirty dollars, the other for fifty dollars. The Commissioners wished to have no difficulty with Mr. Melvin and to have nothing pertaining to their duties undischarged. They therefore directed to Mr. Savage to tender to Mr. Melvin the sum of seventy-five dollars. It was done, and the tender declined. Subsequently the subscribers had an interview with Mr. Melvin discussed the whole matter, and the tender of seventy-five dollars was by them renewed. Mr. Melvin declined it again [447] saying that he told Mr. Savage he would rather have nothing than so inadequate a compensation and he adhered to that decision. The subscribers could not justify themselves in paying more than they tendered and thus the claim now remains unsatisfied.

"They forbear making any comments however great the temptation to make them. They are satisfied that they have done their duty by the lamented sickness and death of Mr. Pomeroy the subscribers have been deprived of his counsel and assistance in closing their commission.

"He was able however, to advise with them in regard to everything except the very last item of work done.

"Alfred Dwight Foster

"Rob Rantoul

"October 15, 1849

"The charges of the commissioner for their time and expense are as follows viz:

"A D Foster   276.28
"Lemuel Pomeroy   284.75
"Rob Rantoul   290.92
                   $851.95"

Mr. Foster did the greater part of the business but he, living within 12 miles of Westborough, incurred much less expense for travelling than Mr. Pomeroy wo is 120 miles and myself 50 miles from that place. I attempted many more times than Mr. Pomeroy.

[448] On the 26th of November 1849, there was a notice in the Salem Register that the whole number of 300 were admitted to the school and that no more could be received without first consulting the superintendent to know if there were vacancies. Thus, in about three weeks more than a year from the house being opened the whole number for which it was prepared had been committed to it. In the course of another year there will be many discharged or bound out as apprentices.

On the 12th of May 1854 on the complaint of his mother Sarah Field widow of Russell Field, I committed Joseph Henry Millward to this institution, he being a stubborn child, a little more than eleven years of age, being a truant and disobeying the commands of his mother. This is the only commitment which I have made thus far.

1856 September – Since writing the above I have committed two other boys. One of them a son of Jesse Dame has been discharged and has been a fishing this summer past.

[449] Hon Theodore Lyman, a mayor of Boston, President of the Boston Farm School, Prison Discipline Society and holding other and important offices in society died at his residence in Brookline, of consumption on the eighteenth day of July 1849. He returned from France on the 4th of July in feeble health. His death is a public loss as his charity to the poor and interest in many benevolent avocations will testify. Mr. Lyman was formerly republican in his politics and as such was elected Mayor of Boston. Latterly he was denominated a Whig. He was attaché' at Paris at the time Crawford was minister to France. He was born in 1792 and graduated at Harvard in 1810. (from the Traveler[53])

---

[53] Boston Traveler newspaper.

He is understood to be the munificent donor of 22,500 for the establishment and support of the State Reform School at Westborough. He was a member of the Legislature while I belonged to it and I there formed some acquaintance with him. He was kind and affable in his demeanor and always subsequent to this slight acquaintance, he recognized me when passing him in the street. I believe that Mr. Foster kept the secret of his gifts to the Reform School inviolable during Mr. Lyman's life, though public opinion had settled upon him as the donor for a considerable time before his decease. By his will he has given 50,000 dollars to the Reform School, 10,000 dollars to the Farm School and 10,000 dollars to the Horticultural Society. [450] Thus has he given evidence in the last act of his life, of the noble feelings and principles which guided the whole of it, he has left behind him the memory of a character elevated refined disinterested and consistent. It is one which should not be suffered to die, and it will not be for "the memory of the first is blessed"

Gov. Briggs in his inaugural address January 1850 suggests to the Legislature the propriety of giving the name of Lyman to the institution, in consideration of his gifts, amounting in the whole to 72,500 dollars and his personal interest in getting the institution up. The particular friends of Mr. Lyman being opposed to this measure, it was not carried into effect[54].

[451] August 28th, 1849: I this day at 3 ½ pm Tuesday, received the following letters-

"Pittsfield 27 Aug '49

"Hon A.D. Foster, D Sir: Our respected father died on Sat 7 Aug at 8 o'clock. The funeral is to be on Tuesday at 3 pm. The funeral is to be on Tuesday at 3 p. Your kind sympathy in his long sickness he often expressed leads me in behalf of his afflicted family to invite you and his colleague, Mr. Rantoul to be present if consistent with your many duties. Will you do us the favor to communicate this to Mr. Rantoul

"Rev. Doherty and friend

"Thos. Pomeroy"

"Hon. Mr. Rantoul

"I received this too late for the mail this day and of course too late for you to accept the invitation to attend the funeral of our associate tomorrow. I shall write you soon

"Yrs Truly Dr. A.D. Foster

"August 27th /49

"6 PM."

I could not of course attend the funeral to which I was invited as the invitation came to hand too late. My respect and regard for the deceased grow out of my acquaintance

---

[54] Rantoul added a footnote, "The letters and other papers relating to this subject are in a bundle by themselves".

with him since April 1847. At our first meeting, he appeared more hale and hearty than most men of his years.

The following notice is from the Boston Daily Advertiser of September 1, 1849.

"Pittsfield August 28th Lemuel Pomeroy Esq., one of the most intelligent public spirited and energetic citizens of Pittsfield and a large woolen manufacturer in this place [452] was buried this afternoon. His funeral was attended by a large concourse of sympathizing citizens, who deeply deplore his loss. Rev. John Todd delivered the funeral sermon over his remains in the Congregational Church. It was a powerful and eloquent delineation of the character of the deceased as a citizen a business man and a Christian. Mr. Pomeroy was 71 years of age. His ancestors were connected with a long line of English nobility, two of whom emigrated to Boston in 1633. They settled some years after in South Hampton Mass. Where an original estate of nearly 1000 acres is still in the Pomeroy family. In 1809 Mr. Pomeroy began the manufacture of muskets for the national government, and his contracts were faithfully performed for 37 years. In 1812, he began the manufacture of woolens in Pittsfield which business he continued up to the time of his death, having accumulated a large fortune by industry and integrity. He left 50 children and grandchildren, most of whom were present at the funeral ceremonies. Among my pamphlets is the sermon of Rev John Todd delivered at the funeral which contains some interesting historical facts. "

On Tuesday, August 10th, 1852 Alfred Dwight Foster died at Worcester, very suddenly, aged about 52. He was attacked with the Gout to which he was subject by hereditary descent. It struck in to his stomach on Monday and on Tuesday afternoon he died. He was very exemplary in the performance of every duty. He was a religious man. A public-spirited man. An amiable man and highly esteemed wherever he was known.

[453] January 14th, 1857: Being Wednesday, my daughter Hannah and myself left home at about 11 am for Westborough to attend the installation of the Superintendent of the State Reform School at Westborough, on Thursday the 15th, by invitation of Simon Brown, J. A. Thayerweather & John Fitch, committee of the trustees. We arrived at Boston about 12 o'clock noon, called on Capt. Charles Pearson's wife at the United States Hotel was there introduced to Col __ [55] Thayer of Braintree who has been employed in engineering. Exchanged a few words with him and but very few because the time of departure of the train for Westborough was near at hand. At 1 ½ o'clock left Boston and arrived at the Westborough Hotel at about 3 o'clock. At about 6 ½ o'clock we went to Doctor Bingham's house to see his family and at 7 o'clock went to the Town Hall to hear a Lyceum Lecture by Edward Everett Hale on the British government's Barque *Resolute*, abandoned in the Northern Ocean by her British officers and ever after they had remained by her, frozen in for two winters. Afterwards she floated out of the ice and was fallen in with by an American Whaling ship and carried in to New London in Connecticut state, was there purchased by the United States government and sent to England as present to Queen Victoria. His lecture was interesting, and our attendance gave an opportunity to speak with him and with the Rev. Mr. Gage, the minister of the Unitarian Society in Westborough, the Rev. Doct. Allen of Northborough, & Mr. Peters of Westborough, 88

---

[55] Rantoul left the first name blank.

years of age and who was the owner of the farm were the Reform School stands. The next morning, we were carried to the Reform School at about ten o'clock and after introduction to several of the Trustees and others, the boys to the number of 576, being assembled in the Chapel, the visitors to the number of about 200 were conducted in. The account of the proceedings will be found in print on the next page but one. We left Westborough for home at about 4 ¾ o'clock and arrived at Boston at about 6 ½ o'clock but too late for the last Eastern train for Beverly, so we went to the Adams House and we then met several friend and acquaintance. On Friday in the forenoon we called on Mrs. Nourse & Mrs. Kingman, the daughter of Rufus Anderson, and visited the State House, going into the library room the Senate chamber and the western gallery of the house. We left Boston at 2 ½ pm for home and arrived at about 3 ½ o'clock well pleased with our journey which was unattended with any of the unpleasant circumstances which frequently attend on journeying in the middle of winter. The printed account of the proceedings is tolerably correct but not absolutely so. At the Adams House on Friday morning I met Mr. David Wells Atwood of Greenfield and Abel Cushing of Dorchester and his wife and other friends. On Friday morning, the temperature was below zero, but soon became warmer so as not to be uncomfortable while moving. February 27, 1857: I received, by mail, several copies of the address of Mr. Boutwell and of the whole proceeding in a pamphlet form, giving a more correct and full report of the speeches and services therein contained on the next page but one. This pamphlet may be found in a volume No. __[56] of my collection.

---

[56] Rantoul left this number blank.

[Reported for the Journal.]

Inauguration of a New Superintendent of the Reform School for Boys at Westboro'.

JAMES M. TALCOTT having resigned the Superintendency of the above institution, the inauguration of WM. E. STARR, Esq., as his successor, took place at the institution yesterday, and was attended by many of the ladies and gentlemen of Westboro', as well as from other parts of the State. Among the officials present besides the Trustees of the Institution, were Lieut. Gov. Benchley and several members of the Executive Council; members of the Board of Agriculture, who now have charge of the farm; the venerable Robert Rantoul, who was one of the commissioners for the erection of the building; Mr. Lincoln, Superintendent of the Maine State Reform School, and first Superintendent of this institution; Rev. B. K. Pierce, Superintendent of the Industrial School for Girls at Taunton; and others.

The services were held in the Chapel, at 11 o'clock. Previous to that time the boys, under the superintendence of their teachers, were marched in and seated in regular order. There were 576 of them, and among them some as smart-looking boys as can be found anywhere. They occupied the body of the chapel. The seats on the sides and near the desks were occupied by the spectators.

The devotional exercises were conducted by Rev. Mr. SEAVER, the excellent Chaplain of the institution, and commenced with the singing of the hymn commencing—

"O Lord, I would depend on thee."

Prayer was then offered by Rev. HORACE JAMES of Worcester.

REMARKS BY HON. SIMON BROWN.

Hon. SIMON BROWN, one of the Trustees and the Chairman of the Committee of Arrangements, then introduced to the Trustees, to the friends gathered there, and to the boys, Mr. WILLIAM E. STARR, the Superintendent elect. To the boys he would say that Mr. Starr did not seek this place, but the Trustees sought him for it, because they thought him to be a man eminently qualified for the station. He comes to you, boys, he said, with a loving heart, to do you good. You have been cut off from your natural parents, and have been deprived of your liberties. But here you may be greatly benefited by your Superintendent. He comes to you with a father's love, and to benefit you. And now you must resolve that in all his requirements you will obey him with cheerfulness and alacrity. Then, when you go out into the world, it will be bright and cheerful to you, and you will be good citizens.

REMARKS BY THE SUPERINTENDENT.

Mr. STARR then made a brief and appropriate address in response, thanking the trustees for the confidence reposed in him, and the chairman of the committee for his kind introduction. He then addressed his fellow officers, asking and expressing his conviction that he should receive their hearty co-operation in instructing the ignorant, restraining the wayward, and guiding the erring who might come under their care. The motive of this work should be love—love of those committed to our charge—love of the right, of God and of man. The means to be used are numerous and various. He besought them by united efforts to endeavor to make the institution sustain the high reputation which it now enjoys. To the boys he said: "I have come here to do you good; I am desirous to do you all the good I can, and to do it in the kindest manner possible. Though now I am a stranger to the most of you, I trust I shall not be long. God grant that when you may leave the institution, you may leave it wiser and happier than when you entered it, and then may you live long, useful and happy lives, and finally enter into the rest prepared for those who love God and keep his commandments."

A select choir of the boys then sang, in a very fine manner, the sentence commencing—

"Wait on the Lord."

ADDRESS BY HON. GEO. S. BOUTWELL.

Hon. George S. Boutwell, the Secretary of the Board of Education, was then introduced to make a brief address. He spoke but fifteen or twenty minutes—and in a manner which interested his audience. In commencing he said he had chosen rather to address himself to the friends of the school than to the boys, hoping at some future time to be able to address them under more favorable circumstances. As the mariner (he said) on the ocean, though wafted by favoring breezes, tests and marks his course by repeated observations, so we have come to note the progress of this humanity freighted vessel over an uncertain sea, yet destined to reach a peaceful and desired haven. All are voyagers upon this sea. The course of some lays in light and some in darkness—according as they choose the way of good or evil. The wisdom of a wise choice is manifested in the history of this institution. It has now had eight full years experience, and enough is seen of its results to justify the course of its patrons, and to realize their early cherished hopes. The name of Lyman will ever command the admiration of the citizens of this Commonwealth, and stimulate our youth to acquire and practice the virtues of their patron. Since its establishment some 3000 boys have been admitted. The chaplain in his report of 1854, says that

under its fostering care will be saved to a life of virtue and respectability. This the speaker said suggested some important reflections. Massachusetts is relieved by this result from the presence of one thousand criminals; or, on the other hand, she receives one thousand full grown, active, industrious, useful men to add to her productions; one thousand enemies of the public peace are transferred into good citizens. And again the criminal class are not a producing class. And he estimated that the result of saving this number of boys from the ways of crime, and making them virtuous and industrious, would in twenty years add two millions of dollars to the productive power of the State. This however was a low consideration compared with the other considerations of intellect, morals, and the public virtue.

He then alluded to the remark of Mr. Lyman, the liberal pastor of the Institution, that "it should not be regarded as an experiment to be abandoned, even if it failed at the outset." Mr. Lyman saw obstacles in its way. It has encountered those obstacles, and yet its progress has been more rapid than his ardor even anticipated.

The speaker then alluded, happily, to the generous patrons of the institution, alluding particularly to those who have passed away—Lyman, Lamb, Denny, Woodward, Shaw and Greenleaf—and then passed to some excellent and judicious remarks upon the position and duties of the new Superintendent. We have not space to sketch this portion of the address. He said he must unite here the influences of the home and the school; he must secure equality, uniformity and certainty in the administration of law; he must not rely upon the visible weapons of authority, but must appeal to the sentiment of veneration and love; first, he must secure good government—not a reign of terror—but a government whose power, uniformity, equality and certainty, must be experienced by all alike, and by all respected, reverenced and obeyed—and next, the genial influences of home and school must be added. In conclusion, he would have it remembered that this institution is not an end but a means—a means to fit the boys to enter upon a course of life which will make them wise and good citizens.

The address was listened to with much interest, not only by the adults to whom it was addressed, but by the boys also.

OTHER ADDRESSES.

Mr. BROWN then spoke to the boys of the little word LOVE. It is the power of that little word, he said, which has brought these friends of various ages to see you here to-day. To prove this, he introduced to the boys the Hon. ROBERT RANTOUL, to say a few words.

Mr. Rantoul said it was suitable that the old and young should meet together on an occasion like this. He spoke as the representative of the old persons present, and expressed his gratification at the order manifested here. He reminded the boys of the advantages which they enjoyed—in some particulars superior to boys who are at large in the world, and he was glad to be grateful for them. He was pleased to meet with children—as it recalled his boyhood days, and excited feelings of gratitude to God for the improvements which had been made for protecting and benefiting the youth of this day. He counseled them to reverence their teachers; and commended, in closing, this useful institution to the blessing of God.

Lieut. Gov. BENCHLEY was next introduced, and expressed regret that the Governor was unable to be present. He was, he said, formerly associated with Mr. Starr in Worcester, and believed him to be fully qualified for the discharge of the duties devolving upon him here. He congratulated the Trustees upon the wisdom of their choice, and then addressed a few words to the Superintendent appropriate to his entering upon his new duties. He said a few words to the boys—relating one or two incidents imparting useful lessons to his youthful hearers in regard to the power of extraneous influences—and cautioning them against evil temptations. He counseled them to be obedient to their teachers, and then they would become useful members of society.

Rev. BRADFORD K. PIERCE, Superintendent of the Industrial School for Girls, was then introduced, and made a beautiful and appropriate address to the boys, full of instructive and interesting anecdotes, which we cannot sketch, but which enchained the attention of his young audience. The speech was both beautiful and appropriate.

Rev. Mr. VAISEY of Seekonk was next introduced, who made a good address to the boys.

Mr. LINCOLN, the former Superintendent of the Institution, was next introduced, and alluded to the changes which had taken place in the Institution since he left. He added a few words of excellent advice to the boys, impressing upon them the importance of their co-operation in order to secure to themselves the greatest benefits of the Institution.

The doxology—

"Praise God, from whom all blessings flow,"

was then sung, and the services were closed with a benediction by Rev. Mr. RICHARDSON of Westboro'.

Article on Inauguration of William E. Starr, Superintendent of the Reform School in Westboro, 1857.

Essex Agricultural Society [457]

In 1818, I became a member of the Essex Agricultural Society principally with the intention of promoting its establishment by adding my name to the list of its members and paying the fee for membership. I have attended several of the annual meetings and have given such other aid as has been convenient, which has been but little. The whole number of members belonging to Beverly from 1818 to 1849 is 26 – two of these have removed from this county – <u>sixteen</u> are dead and <u>eight</u> are now living, of whom four or five only are of the original members. Thus, in looking back I find everywhere that clearly has thinned the ranks of my associates in middle life as well as of my youth. I attended the annual meeting in Salem in September 1849.

Business in Probate Court – Guardian – Trustee [457]

The first business which I did in the Probate court was in reference to the estate of my brother in law, John Lovett, in 1805, his mother being administratrix and I her attorney. I have been Executer to nine or more persons and have besides administered upon fifteen or more estates and have as an attorney to Administrators and Executors settled, in fact, many more estates. I have many times been an appraiser a divider and a commissioner of insolvent estates. I have been guardian of a spendthrift and of fourteen or more minors. I have been a trustee under wills and otherwise in many cases. I have transacted other business in the Probate court, to some extant under Judges Samuel Holten and Daniel S. White and the Registers Daniel Noyes and Nathaniel Cord and have rarely met with any difficulty either in court or out.

[454] As a Justice of the Peace I have joined only two couples in marriage. I have thought that this duty had better by performed by a Clergyman and I have therefore discouraged its being done otherwise. Other justices of the Peace in town have been called on for this business more than I have. My attention to Probate business has brought me in connection with many widows and other females, as attorney, advisor and otherwise. From many of these I have received warm expressions of gratitude and they have continued their kindly feelings to my old age. This is one of the solaces which I have earned, and which is now enjoyed. With some it has been merely a business transaction. I have done what business they wanted to be done, and they have paid me for the doing of it, and no particular kindly feelings have been expressed or apparently entertained. To the first class I feel under great obligations for their gratitude and kindness to the latter class which I am happy to say is the smaller in number, I can only say that they owe me nothing and I owe them nothing except to advise them to cultivate feelings of respect, gratitude and kindness towards those who serve them and not content themselves with merely discharging their pecuniary obligations towards them. This advice is for their own advantage morally as well as pecuniary. If they follow this advice they may have a willing servant, but if they neglect it they will have a hireling only. The exchange of kindly feelings has a greater value in what makes up the enjoyment of life than is always appreciated.

[455] I have avoided guardianships as much as I well could because it involved a responsibility in regard to the conduct of the ward, which is very frequently, from the want of moral power, but very poorly executed and from the want of efficient control over the ward he suffers in his morals and the guardian is subjected to infinite vexations which he

knows not how to prevent nor how to control. I have therefore sometimes undertaken guardianships simply with reference to the care of the property of the ward under an agreement with the friends that they would take the whole care of his person. It is altogether inadmissible in a guardian to employ the property to be kept distinct and separate and not exposed to any risk beyond what necessarily results from its investment in securities which will give the usual rate of income. Honesty, fidelity and a disinterested regard for the interest of those administrator, trustee or guardian, without all these, talent, shrewdness, knowledge and learning are to be thought little of. If any of my grandsons desire these offices, let them above all things cultivate the virtues which will secure a fast confidence in them, and to these add the knowledge which will be useful to them in performing the duties of these offices with satisfaction to themselves and with the approbation of those immediately interested.

[456.1] My intercourse with society has had its peculiar characteristics and has probably had its full influence in the shaping of my own character. I see in my own failings and know from my own experience that which could the young have a realizing sense of without the same failings and without the experience which comes with age, could be immensely beneficial to them in the conduct of life.

But in whatever situation in life they may be led virtue be the first object of desire and pursuit; business the acquisition of property, office, fame ambition, the love of distinction must all be kept in subjection not to be disregarded and neglected, but to be duly regulated or pursued with reference to the highest principles of religion and morality. The sum of the whole matter is to "fear God and keep his commandments, for this is the whole duty of man".

I will further add as a caution to my grandsons "not to be in haste to get rich". The disregard of this maxim has been the cause of very much suffering, calamity and misery. Some have engaged in speculations far beyond their ability to carry through and thus have involved themselves in much sorrow loss of their property, bankruptcy and ruin. In regard to the acquisition of property, be content with small gains and you will be sure of accumulating a competency with peace, a quiet conscience and the enjoyment of what you have accumulated by honest means and by persevering industry.

Silas Stickney, Andrew Peabody & Others [457.1]

My most intimate early associates in Beverly were Silas Stickney and Andrew Peabody. They boarded with me at Martha Burke's. Stickney was the Grammar School Master and married for his first wife Betsey Thorndike, a half-sister of Mrs. Burke's. He as a graduate of 1791 of Dartmouth College and a native of Byfield. Although he went through college regularly, yet he had very little taste or inclination for reading of for intellectual cultivation. He kept on in a beaten track in his school, without change or progress until the public became tired of him. He was a regular daily visitor at my shop for many years and we harmonized well until the acrimonious feelings engendered by the party politics of the times gradually produced coldness and alienation in part, though we still kept up a degree of intercourse until he removed from this town to Charlestown, where he died. In politics he was always a Democrat, while at the time he lived in this town I adhered strongly to the Federalists. In my opposition to him, my ardent zeal frequently outran my prudence and discretion and thus gradually lessened the intimacy and confidence which was founded on my earliest associations in Beverly. I would commend it to my grandchildren to avoid <u>frequent</u> discussion with their particular friends and associates upon topics in regard to which it is well known that there is a settled and decided difference of opinion. By a different course which I pursued in the younger part of my life, I not infrequently [458] disturbed my own equanimity but made my opponents more pertinacious in their adherence to their opinions. Converts are but rarely made under such circumstances. For many years last past, I have inflexibly avoided discussions with opponents unless coolly invited. This course may be safely relied on for the preservation of the harmony of social intercourse and is consistent with that candor and frankness which will always lead to the open avowal of one's decided opinions in politics religion or any other important concern under circumstances which call for such disclosure. Under this course of conduct converts are sometimes made to one's own side of a question. Mr. Stickney lived long enough to know that notwithstanding my strong adhesion to the political party which in my youth I had joined, for the greater part of my life and which in the warmth of my feeling I had so frequently endeavored to convert him to the belief of, I had joined the same party to which he had always belonged. Though in the main, Mr. Stickney was a well-disposed man, yet he could not be called amiable. He governed his school more by the fear inspired by punishments than by any love engendered in the hearts of the scholars by kindness and affability. He was orthodox in his religious views and left the First Parish and joined the Baptist Society before he removed from this town. He was irascible, reserved, subject to jealous discontented and envious feelings with his qualifications he had many good traits of character which would discover themselves amid circumstances which were unfavorable to their development.

[459] Andrew Peabody was not a graduate of any college, he had however, made some progress in the Latin & Greek languages and was well versed in English Grammar and of a more literary taste than My Stickney, he was exact and particular in everything that he did or said. He wrote a very good hand and was well gratified to instruct in all the branches required in his school. His health was feeble and his constitution weak, but by a most exact attention to diet, exercise warmth and every other particular connected with health, he was very rarely kept from his accustomed avocations by sickness. He at first kept a secondary school in the Town Hall until Mr. Stickney left when he took the Grammar School and continued it until he left it to keep shop. His conscientiousness pervaded all his conduct. His religious opinions were of the liberal aspect which distinguished one portion of the congregational church from another portion who were more strictly Calvinistic but there was not <u>then</u> a line of separation drawn between the two portions as has since been done. His temper was mild and his morals pure and his conduct exemplary in every respect. He read as much as his regard to his health would permit in addition to his other necessary employments. In May 1808, he was married to my sister Polly and he died December 19th, 1814 in the 42nd year of his age. A constant, uninterrupted intimacy and daily intercourse for eighteen years made me to feel his loss very sensibly. [460] I have seldom felt a deprivation of a friend so much as in the loss of Mr. Peabody. A confidential, harmonious kindly feeling had grown up between us from our first acquaintance which was strengthened by his marriage with my sister and continued until I saw his eyes closed in death. He left two children who are now settled in Portsmouth, New Hampshire and who inherit his virtue.

Next to Mr. Stickney and Mr. Peabody my greatest intimacy was with Thomas Stephens and Thomas Davis. The occasion of the separation between them and me is stated under other heads. I regretted this separation in both cases, but it seems to be the lot of human nature to suffer from time to time from the alienation as well as from the death of beloved friends. I feel more and more impressed with the importance of guarding against the incipient stages of difference. Whenever any such occurs let it be healed instantly and forgotten as soon as possible. Avoid recurring to it in word and even in thought, if possible. An old, tired friend is better than many new ones, and no effort should be spared to preserve such a one. The suffering from lacerated feelings is not to be disregarded or thought lightly of by any one. There are many things connected with my social relations which I refer to with regret and sorrow. I have not always been duly regardful of the feelings of others. Otherwise I should have saved myself [461] from many unpleasant feelings and unhappy hours. I particularly commend it to my grandchildren to be kindly affectioned one towards another. To be forbearing – self-denying – sociable – courteous, but still preserving their self-respect and independence. It is those duties which occur most frequently well or ill discharged that, in the main, constitute the happiness or unhappiness of life. What are sometimes called the smaller duties which are in every body's way there should receive the most careful attention and be most diligently preformed. Great occasions occur but seldom in one life and perhaps not at all, while lesser opportunities for doing good are of constant perpetual occurrence.

Installation of Dexter Clapp at Salem [465]

December 17th, 1851: I this day attended the installation of Doctor Clapp at the East Church in Salem. He's about thirty-two years old, has been settled some four or five years in West Roxbury, is slim in person and rather tall. I have before noticed the ordination of William Bentley, September 24th, 1783 as colleague with James Diman. In September 1821, I attended the installation of James Flint who is still pastor now aged 72 years and was the successor of William Bentley who died December 29nd 1819 and was born June 22, 1759. I was a delegate from the First Church in Beverly and dined at the same place which is now the Essex House but then called by another name. The dinner then was for large company and Wine and Cigars were used by clergymen and others at the table. I now attended the dinner at the Essex House which was in good style but without any liquor save water and no smoking. This change is now noticeable in many public entertainments but not in all. There was no organized council upon the occasion of the installation of Mr. Clapp, but letters of invitation were sent to neighboring churches inviting the brethren to attend and on this invitation, I was present. The several parts were performed by Clergymen invited by the Society. This course seems to be superseding the usual practice of convening an Ecclesiastical Council of Pastors and Delegates of the Churches.

It has its greater simplicity to commend it to use while the departure from the established custom of the Congregational Churches in New England is not without its regrets.

[466] The services were as follows viz:

1 Voluntary, 2 Anthem. 3 Introductory prayers selection from the Scripture by O.B Frothingham. 4 Hymn. 5 Sermon by George Putnam from John Putnam from John ch. 10-9-6. 6 Hymns 7 Installing prayer by Rev. Francis. 8 Charge by James

Flint. 9 Right hand of Fellowship by Rev. Doct. Thompson of Salem. 10 Address to the people by F. D. Huntington. 11 Concluding prayer by Rev. Thos. F. Stone. 12 Anthem. 13 Benediction.

Nathaniel Silsbee then gave an invitation to Clergymen, members of churches invited and others to repair to the Essex House to dine at 2 ½ o'clock. There were about a hundred persons at the tables. They were mostly Salem people. I received particular attention from Issacharah Silsbee, a brother of my fellow apprentice at Wm. Stearns store. He is about sixty-eight years of age and was the last child baptized by James Dimon in the East Church.

Mr. Stone, who is the last Unitarian minister before Mr. Clapp who was settled in Salem was introduced into the pulpit by some of the lay members of the Church, not only without the assistance of a Council, but without the services of any clergyman. This was the first Church in Salem, which is the successor of the first Church in Massachusetts proper, and is in coincidence of the proceedings, in the installation of the first minister at Salem. Then it was a matter of necessity as there were no Congregational Ministers nearer than in the Plymouth Colony. Mr. Stone had been previously ordained as a minister at Machias in Maine.

[467] The greater ease and conscience and the frequent changes of the ministerial relations will induce some Churches to resort to these methods of inducting their ministers, but I wish that the ancient practice of settling ministers for life and the custom of their remaining in their first place of settlement during life, with the exception of some cases of necessity, might again be restored and then the ancient formalities of their settlement would be restored inasmuch as the frequencies of new settlements would not discourage their use. The clergy would regain a portion of their lost influence and the people would be gainers by the prominency of the connection. The East Society is the second in Salem and they have had two meeting houses. The first, which was taken down a few years since, was enlarged from what it was when first used. They have had five ministers besides Mr. Clapp viz: Robert Staunton 1719, William Jamison 1728, James Dimon 1737, William Bentley 1783, and James Flint 1821. The last three are within my recollection. The first meeting house was a little further down than the present Town school house on the southerly side of Essex Street, which is below the Common. The present house fronts on the northwesterly side of the Common. In elegance and splendor, it is in entire contrast with the former house. I have been thus particular in regard to this house society because I was born there, so to say. The house where I was born was directly opposite to the old East Meeting House.

Celebration at Danvers, of the Incorporation of the Town [468]

Wednesday June 16, 1852. By invitation of the committee of arrangements I attended the centenary celebration of the incorporation of the Town of Danvers. It was a very hot day. Thermometers indicated from 93 degrees to 98 degrees. I was invited to ride in the procession in an open Barouche so that I felt the full power of the sun. The procession was large, containing some 1,500 children. The address in the church was by John W. Proctor. Rev. Mr. Promes presided at the dinner.

There were about a thousand persons dined under a tent in a field. There were many speeches made and a letter from George Peabody of London, a native of Danvers, was read tendering a gift of $20,000 dollars for a Lyceum & Library for the free use of the inhabitants of Danvers.

The want of time prevented the performance of the whole that was intended. The performances began at 9 o'clock in the morning and continued till 8 o'clock in the evening. A letter from son Robert was read at the table and was published in the Essex County Freeman in Salem. C.T.Thayer made a speech in response to the toast referring to Beverly which it was expected I should have done, but I left before the proper time therefore. I left at about 7 o'clock P.M.

Death of Son Robert [469]

August 1852: My only son Robert, being at Washington attending to his duties as a Representative in Congress, on Wednesday August 4th, 1852, a Telegraphic dispatch was received that he was sick not dangerous. On Thursday in the afternoon another dispatch was received that he was sick with the Erysipelas and his wife was wanted. About the same time, she received a letter from him dated on Tuesday the 3rd wherein he stated that he had a sore on the side of his head which made him sick but did not think it necessary for his wife to come to him as he should probably get well before she got there. On Thursday evening the 5th she left home for Boston to start from there for Washington, which she did the next morning at 7 o'clock. She arrived there at about six o'clock on Saturday morning and she caused a dispatch announcing that his sickness was not without danger. He was so sick that he could not open his eyes to see here but had them opened that he might see her, and although his mind had been wandering he knew her and conversed with her and she remained with him until he died at about half past ten o'clock on Saturday night the 7th of August. His death was communicated here on Sunday evening and at the same time it was announced that Jane would leave Washington at four o'clock on Sunday afternoon with the body of the deceased and would arrive here on Monday night by the way of Springfield. Monday evening Jane arrived, and the corpse was carried to the First Parish Meeting House enclosed in a metallic coffin, made airtight with solder. [470] Followed by a long procession of the inhabitants of Beverly who had assembled for the occasion. Jane was in a state of exhaustion as well she might be, having since Friday morning travelled near nine hundred miles and witnessed the last hours of the sickness and the death of her husband. The funeral took place at the meeting house on Tuesday the 10th, at three o'clock in the afternoon with every public demonstration of mourning that could well be shown with such a short time to make preparations.

The suddenness of this afflictive bereavement filled my house with grief. He would have been forty-seven years of age had he lived until the 13th of August. He was weakly in his infancy and never robust. His independence of thought, of speech and of action always placed him in antagonism to a strong body of conservatives. Through continued and unrelenting opposition, he had raised himself without extrinsic aid, to high honors and the field was open to him for still farther advances. The ground he took in Congress in relation to the fugitive slave law will immortalize his name with the state's rights party. He was taken away in the midst of his laborious performance of high duties to the public and his loss is mourned by all with whom he had acquaintance. The last time that I heard him speak in public was at Salem in Mechanic hall, on the 5th of July 1852, when he spoke about an hour and three quarters to a very large audience and was enthusiastically applauded. [471] He left home for Washington on the 8th of July and we had several letters from him without any complaints in regard to his health. But in a short month after his leaving here he was dead.

Upon the occasion of this bereavement I and my family have the strongest reasons for gratefully acknowledging the very numerous acts of kindness and sympathy which have been realized from almost every individual in town and from very many persons from other places. This kindness and sympathy has for exceeded all my expectations. Light alienations of friendship have been overcome by individuals who have called on members of my family and many other indications of sorrow and feeling have been expressed by those who have been expressed by those who have had no particular connection with us before. These circumstances lead me to think more favorably of mankind. This bereavement should have a tendency to wean me from the world and lead e to think more of eternity. It throws new duties into m path while it leaves the infirmity of age to cope with them.

My son prepared for college at Phillips Academy in Andover, beginning September 7, 1819. He entered Harvard College as a freshman in 1822. Graduated in 1826. He commenced the study of Law with John Pickering in Salem but after a few months Mr. Pickering removing to Boston he went into Leverett Saltonstall's office and finished his course of study with him, and in 1829 being admitted to [472] practice he opened an office in a chamber in Stearn's building corner of Washington & Essex street in Salem. He removed from Salem to South Reading in 1831. He removed from South Reading to Gloucester Feb 21, 1833. He removed from Gloucester to Beverly March 27th, 1839, where he resided until his death, keeping his office in Boston.

My Cousin Sarah S. Rintoul, of London, to whom I sent a portrait, says in a letter dated Nov 26th, 1852 that "in the portrait we can perceive a family likeness, there is some resemblance to my eldest brother, specially about the forehead and upper part of the face."

John Howard of Salem and my aunt Susanna Preston have said that he resembled his grandfather, my father, with whose looks they were both well acquainted.

[473] Copy of a letter to the Citizens of Beverly

"Doct. Charles Haddock   Beverly August 11, 1852

"Dear Sir

"You having had the goodness to wait upon me with a copy of certain resolutions passed at a meeting of the citizens of Beverly, held for the purpose of taking measures in relation to the sudden death of my dear son, I beg leave to make my acknowledgements to you for your respectful attention and through you to express the grateful sense entertained by myself as well as by the widow and relative of the deceased of the numerous acts of kindness and sympathetic feeling manifested by the Citizens of Beverly and very many others upon this afflicting occasion and to express our entire satisfaction with and approbation of the prompt and very appropriate measures adopted and so very well carried out, to evidence their high respect and esteem for the departed and the most considerate regard to our feelings. The impression which the whole course of proceedings has made upon my mind and heart give me renewed evidence of the kind and friendly disposition of my fellow citizens and of which I shall always retain the most grateful remembrance

"I am very respectfully, Dear Sir, you Ob't Serv

"Rob Rantoul

"August 22, 1852."

The committee of arrangements by John Lovett waited on me to propose having a Eulogy pronounced on my son Jane having been consulted referred the matter to me and I expressed my disapproval of the measure so strongly that it put an end to any further movement.

Some friends in Salem caused a Portrait to be painted from Daguerreotype likenesses and presented to Jane Rantoul, handsomely framed and of a large size. A Lithograph of a medium size has been published by __[57] of Boston and sold at one dollar each. The publishers sent Jane several copies and one to me.

[474] A memoir and a collection of speech's reports, addresses and other publications, edited by Rev. Luther Hamilton, who was the minister at Gloucester a part of the time which Robert resided there and who died very soon after he had prepared the work and put it into the hands of the printer, was published in November 1853. It is an octavo volume of 864 pages published by John P Jewett & Co. Boston. 1400 copies are subscribed for at two ½ dollars per copy and an edition of 3000 copies are printed. The volume was first seen in Beverly on the 19th of November 1853. The day of his birth is erroneously printed in the beginning of the volume. It should be August 13th, 1805. Luther Hamilton died August 30th, 1853 aged 57 years at Roxbury after a few weeks confinement from sickness and while his book was in course of printing. The summer of 1854, his son informed me that the 3000 copies printed were about all sold.

January 17th, 1854: This day a neat and chaste monument was erected over the grave of Robert Rantoul Jun at the expense of numerous friends in Essex County mostly. The inscription was prepared by Charles Sumner, his successor in the Senate of the United States. It is in my family burial lot in the town burying ground. It rests upon a square massive foundation of finished granite, and is composed of an upright, four-sided Italian marble shaft, capped and finished at the summit in a flat pyramidal form. The expense is about five hundred dollars, which has been defrayed by one-dollar subscriptions among his friends.

The following inscription occupies the front face of the monument.

"Here lies the body of Robert Rantoul Jr. who was born at Beverly the 13th August 1805 and died at Washington 7th August 1852: An upright lawyer, a liberal statesman, a good citizen, studious of the past yet mindful of the future.

---

[57] Rantoul left the lithographic company name blank.

"Throughout an active life he strove for the improvement of his fellow men. The faithful friend of Education he upheld our Public Schools. A lover of virtue, he opposed Intemperance by word and example

[475] "For the name of Justice and Humanity he labored to abolish the punishment of death.

"Inspired by Freedom, he gave his professional services to a slave hunted down by public clamor and bore his testimony in court and congress, against the cruel enactment which sanctioned the outrage.

"He held many places of official trust and honor but the good works filling his days were above these.

"Stranger! At least in something imitate him."

This inscription was written by Charles Sumner of Boston, who was the immediate successor of my son in the Senate of the United States in the Legislature of 1857. Sumner was reelected to the Senate for six years from the fourth day of March next, by large majorities in both branches.

On the 22nd May 1856 Charles Sumner was severely beaten in the Senate Chamber with a cane by Preston Brooks, a Representative in Congress from South Carolina, on account of a speech made by Sumner in answer to Senator Butler of South Carolina. For the assault Brooks was tried in the Criminal Court at Washington and fined $300. A majority of the House voted to expel him, but it requires two thirds vote which was not obtained. He immediately resigned but was very soon re-elected and resumed his seat. Sumner was so much injured as to prevent his resuming his seat for the remainder of the session. He still (Sep 22nd, 1856) keeps himself away from his home to avoid the excitement of the Presidential election of this autumn. The excitement is unusually great for the occasion. Mr. Sumner left Boston for Washington the latter part of February 1857.

[476] The following inscription was copied from a monumental stone in the congressional burying ground in Washington by Harriet C. Neal February 1857.

"Erected to the memory of Hon. Robert Rantoul Jr., member of Congress of the United States from the State of Massachusetts   Died August 7th, 1852 Aged ___ years."

Extract from Rev. Samuel Osgood's address to the class of 1832 to which my son Samuel belonged. Delivered at Cambridge commencement week July 15, 1857.

"We changed much alike in number and in development of character during our undergraduate years. A considerable number left us, and more joined us. Of those who left us, six were removed by death and their names should be spoken of affectionately here to night—Bradford, Hodges, Peters, Rantoul, Treadwell, Welch. Each of these might fitly have a special word but I name particularly the two who were in our section. Peters, a man of considerable humor and shrewdness, and with not a little genuine fellowship under his awkward exterior and <u>Rantoul</u> a quiet, sensible, genial, loveable fellow, whose lameness seemed to quicken instead of slowing him and who made up by the playful freedom of his tongue for the want of as ready locomotion in his limbs. He was a quiet and kindly philosopher in his way, and not inaptly called

"Cool Sam". These and the whole six who died before we graduated, we remember as part of ourselves"

Massachusetts 2nd Convention 1853 [477]

On the seventh day of March 1853 a town meeting was held to choose two delegates to the state convention for amending the constitution. The voting resulted as follows:

In whole number of votes 567

Necessary for a choice	284
Robert Rantoul had	360
Joseph E. Ober	355
Frederick W. Choate	202
Levi S. Abbot	202
Scattering	15

It is now nearly thirty-three years since I was chosen a delegate to a similar convention held in Boston November 15th, 1820 and continued to January 9th, 1821. At the meeting in this town to choose four delegates to which at that time they were entitled held on the 16th of October 1820, the whole number of votes given in was 64 and the persons elected viz x Nathan Dane, Deacon John Low, Rev Nathaniel W. Williams and myself, had from 52 to 55 votes each. There were eight other persons voted for. This state of the vote shows the difference of interest in public affairs at that time and at this day. The town was then declared by a large majority now it is divided into three parties the Whig, the Democratic and Free Soil. The coalition of the two last effected the election of Joseph E. Ober of the Free-Soil Party and myself of the Democratic party. In all elections which have turned on political party politics I have been in the minority for about twenty years last past, now in my old age I am again in a position to stand fairly for elections but it's so late in life with me that it is of little value, though I feel a good degree of satisfaction in the belief that my fellow townsmen are coming nearer to my views in regard to public affairs. For the last twenty years I have in a great measure been shut out from free conversation with those who I most frequently met with by my difference with them in politics and with whom I had been in free intercourse for more than thirty years previously.

[478] In the convention of 1820 there were __[58] persons who were members of the convention of 1780 who framed the constitution. These were John Adams ex-President of the United States aged 85, chosen from Quincy. Doct. Parker Cleaveland chosen from Rowley and I think one other, but I am not certain. For the present proposed convention of those who were members of that of 1820 the following persons are chosen viz –Nathan Hale of Boston, Rufus Bullock of Royalston and James C. Doane of Cohasset, Larkam Marcy of Greenwich and Philip Eames of Washington and myself.

---

[58] Rantoul left this number blank.

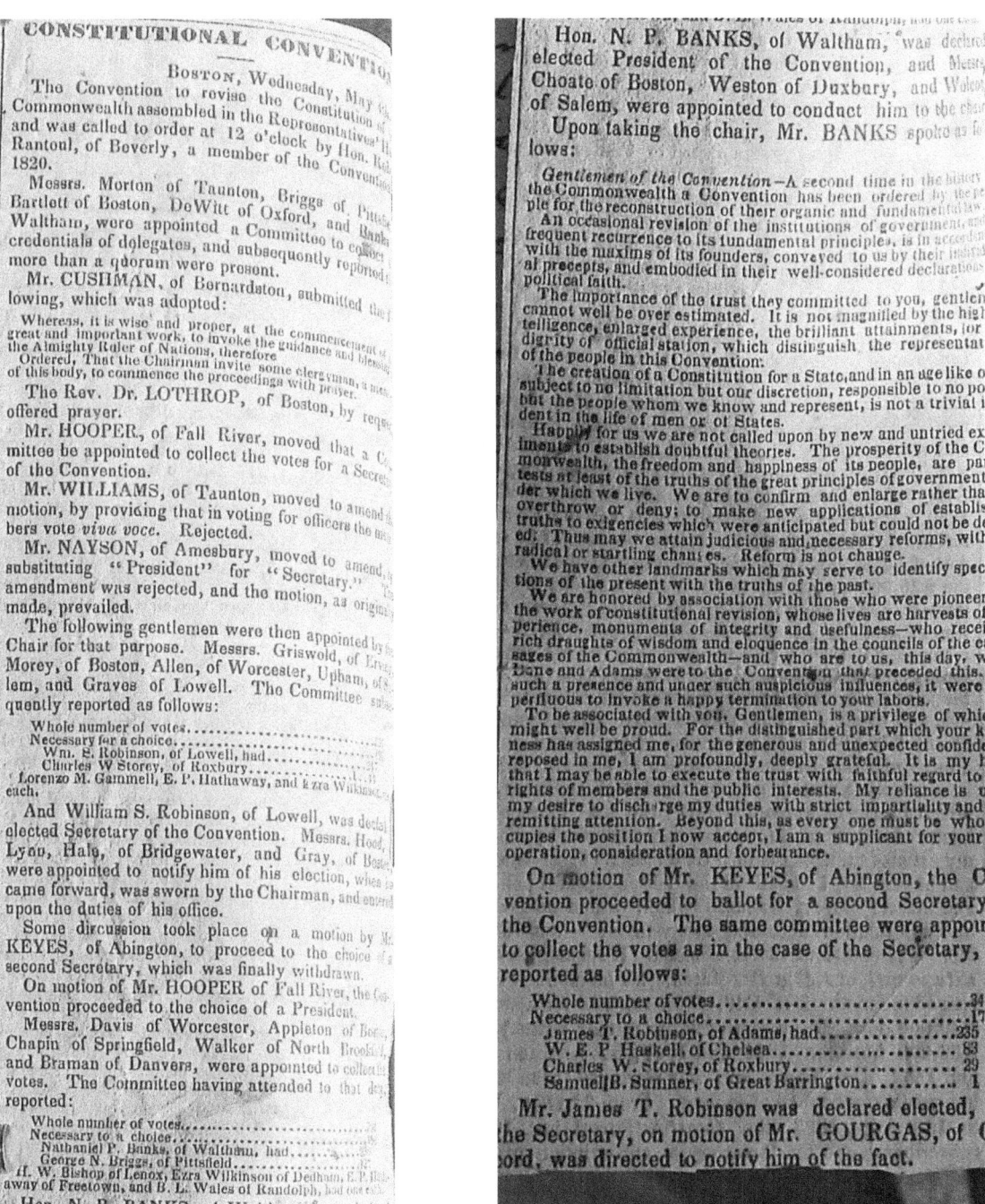

Newspaper article covering the 1853 Convention

The Convention met on Wednesday May 4, 1853 and at 12 o'clock and I being the senior in Legislative standing though not in years and being thereto requested, took the chair and called the convention to order and presided until after the choice of a president, Nathaniel Banks Jun, who on being conducted to the chair made an address to the convention and alluded to me as a colleague with Nathan Dane in the convention of 1820. Samuel French of Berkley aged about 76 years is the oldest member in years and I stand next to him. I was treated with much deference and respect by the members of the convention throughout the session and was enabled to attend in my place on a part of every sitting day. I was invited by the President at one time to preside in committee of the whole, but

I requested to be excused on account of my deafness and of course the invitation was not renewed. On Monday August 1st, 1853, there were three sessions the last of which commenced at 8 o'clock in the evening and continued until six minutes before two on Tuesday morning when the convention adjourned sine die[59] I continued in my seat until the final adjournment and then between 2 & 3 o'clock in the morning went to the Marlborough Hotel and went to bed and in the forenoon of Tuesday returned to Beverly. My health was tolerably good through the session but at sometimes suffered from debility occasioned by heat and long confinement.

[479] I did not speak much in the convention, but on the subject of the House of Representatives on the 15th June., I spoke about one hour and on the subject of the rights of juries I spoke twice, but not at much length. I also spoke at some other times but shortly. I was listened to with respectful attention however little deserving thereof. I was appointed ion the committee on the subject of representation which consisted of 21 members; ten of whom were in favor of a district system of representation and eleven in favor of town representation. I went with the minority and signed a minority report in favor of a districting system, which report was drawn up by Nathan Hale and supported by him in a speech on Tuesday June 4th. I, together with the other members of the convention of 1820 had an appropriate seat assigned to us by the messenger and received other marks of attention on account of our relation to that convention.

The new constitution was rejected by the people by a majority of about five thousand votes. I voted in favor of its acceptance generally. I was induced to do so by the putting in of an article providing for a district system in 1856 to be submitted to the people for acceptance.

Although the convention has thus failed of accomplishing its object, yet I believe that it will become the legislature to make a strenuous effort to affect the more necessary changes in the way provide for amendments in the constitution as it now is.

Transcriber's Note: Here ends the handwritten manuscript of the professional autobiography of Robert Rantoul Sr., except for an unrelated note at the very end of the journal that perhaps can be seen as a fitting reminder to us or our own mortality and the changes that time makes.

[481] "Lydia Smith widow of my friend Ebenezer Smith did on Wednesday April 23, 1856 aged 80 years of Cancer. I have been acquainted with her for about 60 years. The number of my earlier acquaintances has become very few. It is the common lot of old age to be without most of the associates of their early and middle life."

---

[59] Sine die: "without a date."

Index

Abbot, Abiel 137
Abbot, Adeline 109
Abbot, Ann Wales 137
Abbot, Dudley 86
Abbot, Emily 109, 190
Abbot, George 224
Abbot, George W. 131
Abbot, Levi S. 250
Abbot, Rev. Abiel 32, 89, 103, 104, 105, 106, 108, 132, 133, 180, 190
Abbot, Rev. Joseph 140, 141, 187
Adam, Mr. 22
Adam, William 23, 120
Adams House 190, 231
Adams, Daniel 86
Adams, Hannah 121
Adams, Moses 71
Adams, Otis 230
Adams, President John 102, 171, 176, 250
Adams, President John Quincy 70, 165
Adams, Thomas 86, 93
Africa, steamer 36
African race 51
Agricultural Bank at Pittsfield 168
Allen, G.W. 44
Allen, John 87
Allen, Mary Elizabeth Dana (Lovett) 44
Allen, Rev. Isaac 106, 238
Allen, William H. 131
American Tract Society 180
American Unitarian Association 105, 116, 117
Ancilla 51

Anderson, Elizabeth (Lovett) 40, 45
Anderson, Rev. Rufus 39, 40, 104, 117, 239
Anderson, Robert Rufus 45
Anderson, Sally (Hale) 57
Andrew, William J. 230
Andrews, Abel 99
Annable, Daniel 96, 185
Appleton, Edward 137
Appleton, Isaac 83, 86
Appleton, James 105
Appleton, John 82
Appleton, Nathan 232
Appleton, Thomas 102
Archer, Jonah 24
Archer, Jonathan 27, 29
armed police 92
Armstrong, Lieut. Gov. Samuel F. 181
Ashton, Jacob 220
Astor House 227
Astrea, ship 67
Atlantic, steamer 227
Atlantic House tavern 185, 186, 194
Atwood, David Wells 239
Austin, Joseph 232
Austin, Rev. David 106
Babbige, Miss Lydia 54, 60
Babbige, Rev. Charles 53
Babbige, Susannah 53
Baglies, William 175
Baker, Allen 90
Baker, Isaac W. 71

Baker, John Chipman	87
Baker, John E.	109
Baker, John I.	84, 93, 97, 146
Baker, John T.	131, 220
Baker, Judith	146
Baker, Samuel	86
Baker, Stephens	96, 117, 142, 147, 192
Baker's Island	64
Ball, John	182
Balles's Beach	70
Balliol, John	41
Baltimore Sermon	168
Bancroft, Thomas P.	55, 59
Bank House	225
Banks, Gov. Nathaniel P.	151, 216
Banks, Nathaniel Jun.	251
Baptist Meeting House	157, 204, 219
Baptist Society	104, 243
Barker, Stephen	152
Barlow, Rev. David H.	106
Barnett, Elihu	205
Barrett, Hannah (Hamden)	162
Barrett, Lois (Symonds)	161
Barrett, Lydia (Smith)	162
Barrett, Thomas	161
Bartlett Street	95
Bartlett, Israel	168
Bartlett, William	188
Barton Square Church	115
Barton, Samuel	34
Bass River Bank	222
Bass River District school	193
Batchelder, Caleb	39
Batchelder, Doct. Josiah	85
Batchelder, Doct. Josiah Jun.	149
Batchelder, Ezra	95, 96
Batchelder, Hannah	39
Batchelder, Jonah Jun.	86
Batchelder, Jonathan	222
Batchelder, Josiah	27, 39, 77, 78, 102, 132
Batchelder, Josiah Jun.	150
Batchelder, Nathaniel 2nd	109
Bates, Rev. Joshua	106
Bay State newspaper	162
Baylies, Francis	206
Becker, Isaac W.	131
Beckford, Benjamin	46
Beckford, David	46
Beckford, Ebenezer	46, 74
Beckford, Elizabeth	46
Beckford, Eunice	46
Beckford, Hannah	46
Beckford, John	46
Beckford, Jonathan	46
Beckford, Mary	46
Beckford, Pinson	46
Beckford, Rebecca	46
Beckford, Samuel	46
Beckford, Sarah	46
Beckford, William	86
Beckwith	205
Beckwith, George C.	93
Beecher, Doct. Lyman	160
Bell tavern	65
Bell, John	117
Bell's building	71
Bell's Hall	93, 184
Bennet, Ebenezer	88
Bennett, Cotton	220, 222
Bennett, Robert G.	222
Bentley, Rev. William	51, 55, 58, 69, 115, 149, 244, 245
Bernard, Rev. ___	115
Bernett, Robert G.	131

Beverly, ship 119
Beverly Academy 136, 138
Beverly Bank 222
Beverly Charitable Society 224
Beverly Citizen newsaper 162
Beverly Common 149
Beverly Depot 96
Beverly Light Infantry 85, 91, 93
Beverly Lyceum 157
Beverly Marine Insurance Company 68, 162
Beverly Total Abstinence Society 182
Bible Society of Salem 107, 112
Bigelow, Rev. Andrew 32, 106, 111
Bigelow, Rev. William 106
Bigelow, Sen. Lewis 172
Bigelow, Timothy 175
Bingham, Doct. 238
Bishop, Miss. 39
Blackbourne, Henry 209
Blake, Sen. George 172, 174, 175
Boston Athenaeum 224
Boston Farm School 236
Boutwell, Mr. 239
Bowditch, Nathaniel 115
Bowdoin College 102, 194
Bowers, Ishmael 101
Bowers, Sally 101
Boyden, Doct. Wyatt C. 84, 98, 108, 131, 189, 196, 198
Boyden, James Woodberry 137
Boyles, Hannah 78
Bradstreet, Edward 137
Breed, Holton J. 31
Breed, William B. 152
Breed's Tavern 90
Bridge, Nancy 109, 110, 220
Briggs, Enos 67

Briggs, Gov. George N. 190, 194, 209, 230, 231, 235, 237
Brigham, Dexter 230
Brimble Hill 134
Brimmer, Hannah 109
Briscoe Hall 85, 110, 134
Brodie, Mr. 22
Brooks, Charles 93
Brooks, Edward 184, 218
Brooks, Luke 62
Brooks, Mary 62
Brooks, Sen. Peter C. 172
Brooks, Sen. Preston S. 175, 249
Brown, Benjamin. 91
Brown, George 226
Brown, James 87
Brown, John 29
Brown, Martha 29
Brown, Moses 83, 129, 150, 162, 169, 222
Brown, Nancy 109
Brown, Nathan 87
Brown, Rev. John 106
Brown, Simon 238
Brown, Walter 88
Brown's Hill 134
Bruce, Robert 41
Bryant, James 131
Buck, Henry 87
Bullock, Rufus 250
Bunker's Hill 226
Burbank, Johnson 86
Burbank, William 86
Burke, Capt. John 75
Burke, Martha (Thorndike) 75, 76, 77, 242
Burley, Edward 131
Burley, John 151
Burley, William 135

Burnap, Rev. George W. 106
Burnham, Col. James..................................85, 88
Burton, Rev. Warren.......................................106
Bush, Doct. Benjamin.....................................180
Cabot Street 84, 95, 96
Cabot, John..84
Cabot, Sebastian 84
Cadets of Temperance 190
Camel, barque 31
capital punishment..................42, 158, 206, 213
Carnatie, ship 28
Carrico, Thomas 87
Carter, Elias 230, 234, 235
Cary, Robert 88
Casey, Robert 93
Castle Hill 65, 69
Caty, schooner 27
Cave, Mr. 79
Cave, Philis 79
Chandler, Capt. Daniel 227, 235
Channing, Rev. William Ellery 168
Chapin, Harvey..156
Chapman, Abner................... 104, 132, 163, 168
Chapman, Capt. Isaac 37, 104
Chapman, Homer..37
Chapman, Mrs. 104
Chase, Francis Esq...152
Chebacco Meeting House 95
Cheever, George B. 189
Cherry Hill Farm 94
Cherry Hill Farm School 138
Chipman, Joseph......................................94, 161
Chipman, Rev. John..................................94, 161
Choate, Frederick W............. 146, 148, 185, 250
Choate, Hon. Stephen Esq., ...156
Choir of the East Society 56
Cholera 198

Christian Register newspaper 117, 158, 159, 215
Citizens Bank 120
Clap, Rev. Elisha 106
Clapp, Doct. Dexter.......................................244
Clark, Robert 168
Clark, Stephen M...211
Clarke, Augustus N. 131
Claxton, William 75
Cleaveland, Doct. Parker.......................156, 250
Cleaves, Deacon Benjamin...24, 36, 37, 87, 105, 129
Cleaves, John...128
Clement, Rev. Jonathan 106
Clough, James 215
Coffin, Rev. W. 141
Cogswell, Hon. George 151
Cole, Benjamin 131
Cole, Hannah...109
Colman, Henry..231
Colon Street...84, 95
Columbian Sentinel 171
Columbus, Christopher..................................84
common law 101
compulsory support of worship 103
Conant Street 84
Conant, Roger...84
Congress Street...96
Cook, Charles 34
Cook, Hannah 34
Coombs, Isaac 209
Cord, Nathaniel 241
Cornelius, Rev. 149
Cornwallis, Lord...51
corporeal punishment 63
cotton factory...60
County Fife 21
County Kinross...21

county prisons	159
cow hide	63
Cox, Nathaniel	71
Cox, Sarah D.	109, 133
Crane, Col.	161
Cranmore, Malcome	41
Crawley and Elger	75
Cray, Peter	26
credit	75
Crowninsheild, Benjamin William	54
Crowninsheild, Edward	55
Crowninsheild, Francis Boardman	54
Crowninsheild, Richard	54
Crowninshield, Benjamin William	99
Crowninshield, Capt.	39
Crowninshield, George	99
Crowninshield, Jacob	149
Crowninshield, Richard Jun.	211
Cummings, Judge	79
Cushing, Abel	239
Cushing, Caleb	206
Cutler, Doct. Manasseh	149
D'Israeli, W.	41
Dame, Jesse	236
Damhead	21
Dana, Judge	99
Dana, Rev. Samuel	104
Dane Street Church	104, 105, 107, 187, 205
Dane Street Meeting house	90
Dane, Nathan	102, 129, 171, 175, 220, 221, 250
Daniel Safford & Co	231
Danvers, Town of	245
Danvers plains	65
Darling, ship	23
Daughters of Temperance	158, 182, 183, 184
David Copperfield	58
David, Thomas	102
Davies, Daniel	227, 230
Davis, Charles	111, 116, 131, 151
Davis, John B.	207, 209
Davis, Joseph W.	185
Davis, Judge	101
Davis, Thomas	83, 95, 102, 103, 105, 107, 116, 129, 142, 144, 147, 148, 163, 168, 170, 177, 179, 224, 225, 244
de Preston, Leolphus	41
Decker, William	131
Declaration of the County of Essex	169
Defense, brig	27
Dempsey, Elizabeth	109
Dennis, Charles	142, 183
Denny, George	230, 231
Derby Wharf	67
Derby, Capt.	27
Derby, Elias Hasket	67
Derby, Ezekiel Hersey	111, 220
Derby, John	221
Dexter, Franklin	131
Dickens, Charles	58
Dickinson, Rev. Pliny L.	106
Dike, Abigail	39
Dike, John	89, 102
Dike, John Jun.	87, 95
Dike, Samuel	193
Dilworth's School Master's Assistant	55
Diman, Rev. James	51, 211, 244, 245
Dinmore, James	211
Diomede, privateer	39
Doane, James C.	250
doctrine of the Trinity	104
Dodge Street	84, 94
Dodge, Aaron	146, 147
Dodge, Caleb	183
Dodge, David L.	203
Dodge, Ezra	142, 147

Dodge, Israel 183
Dodge, Maj. Levi 89
Dodge, Samuel 87
Dodge, Seth 87, 93
Dodge, William 86
Dodge's Hill 111
Dodge's Row 84
Dole, Rev. George 184, 189
Dow, Rev. Moses 31, 32, 225
Dowling, James 142, 147, 198, 202
Duke of Kingstown, ship 22, 24
Dutton, Warren 175
Dyson, Abigail 109
Dyson, John 102, 103, 142, 147
Eames, Philip 250
East Church 211, 244, 245
East Farm School 198
East Meeting House 71, 77
East Town School 55, 63, 211
Eastern Rail Road 69, 96, 220
Eastman, Sen. Samuel 172
Eaton, Joseph 86
Edward I 41
Edwards, Abraham 95, 142, 147, 222
Edwards, Col. Abraham 96
Election cake 66
Election Day 65
Elkins, Henry 51
Elkins, Mrs. 29
Elkins, widow 51
Ellingwood, Ezra 198, 202, 222
Ellingwood, John 46
Ellingwood, John Jun. 46
Ellingwood, John Wallis 87, 89
Ellingwood, Mary (Endicott) 46
Ellingwood's Point 226
Elliott Street 84

Elliott, Andrew 84
Ellis, Rev. M. 115
embargo 81, 149
Emerson, Rev. Joseph 104
Endicot, Mrs. 36
Endicott, Augusta Rantoul 34, 35, 45
Endicott, Capt. Samuel 120
Endicott, Charles 34, 45, 122, 217
Endicott, Elizabeth 45
Endicott, Hannah (Endicott) 46
Endicott, Henry 34, 45, 80, 122, 216, 217
Endicott, Joanna Lovett (Rantoul) 35, 44, 82, 216
Endicott, John 45
Endicott, Martha T. 115
Endicott, Mary 34, 45, 117
Endicott, Mary (Holt) 46, 47
Endicott, Mary Elizabeth 34
Endicott, Mary Elizabeth (Rantoul) 115, 121, 216
Endicott, Mrs. Martha 121
Endicott, Nathan Hale 46
Endicott, Nathan Holt 45
Endicott, Robert 34, 45, 46, 47, 102
Endicott, Robert Jun. 46
Endicott, Robert Rantoul 34, 44, 98, 216
Endicott, Samuel 46, 47, 109, 110, 123, 199, 202, 222
Endicott, Sarah F. (Endicott) 46
Endicott, William ... 34, 35, 44, 45, 83, 109, 116, 131, 216, 217, 221
Endicott, William Jun. 24, 25, 30, 34, 35, 36, 121, 130, 131, 224
English, Phillip 131, 219
Episcopalian College 194
Essex, frigate 66
Essex Agricultural Society 241
Essex Bridge 64, 220, 226
Essex County Convention of 1812 169

258

Essex County Temperance Society	182
Essex House	244
Esty Tavern	94
Eurofice, steamer	36
Eustis, Gov.	165
Everett, Ebenezer	107, 170
Everett, Gov. Edward	194, 209, 226
Everett, John	226
Fairfield, William	33
Farley, Michael	210
Fay, Samuel P.	175
Federal party	100, 169, 171
Felt, Nathaniel Henry	47
Field, Russell	236
Field, Sarah	236
fire department	179
First Baptist Society	184
first distillery	183
First Parish	107, 188
burying ground	150
Church	243, 244
clerks	128
division of Third Parish	102, 176
Meeting House	75, 77, 89, 122, 158, 200
organ	123
Prudential Committee	103
records	129, 197
Sexton	161
social library	130, 131
Sunday school	108, 111
Vestry	109, 110, 129
First Universalist Church in Boston	161
Fisher Charitable Society	224
Fisher, Doct Joshua	129, 169, 195, 222, 224
Fisher, Doct. John D.	218
Fisher, Nahum	232
Fisher, Nathan	230
Fisher, Rev. Mr.	210
Fisher's corner	95
Fisk, Eldridge	109, 117
Fisk, Hannah K.	109
Fitch, John	238
Flagg, Isaac	108, 116, 162
Flagg, Thomas Wilson	109
Flanders, Rev. Charles W.	110, 184
Flint, Rev. James	71, 244, 245
Ford, Edward	95, 123, 198, 202
foreigners	62
Fornis, Henry	157
Fornis, John	86
Fort Pickering	65
Foster, Abigail Dike (Lovett)	44
Foster, Alfred Dwight	227, 230, 233, 234, 236, 238
Foster, Joseph	109, 128
Foster, Josiah 3rd	142, 147
Foster, Josiah L.	96, 131
Foster, Maj. Israel	89
Foster, Mr.	231
Foster, William	44
Foster, William Lovett	44
Fourth Congregational Church	110
Francis, Col. John	85
Francis, Rev.	244
Free Masons	190
Freeman, Capt. Constance	161
French, Samuel	251
Fromentin, Sen. Eligius	68
Frost, Barzillac	187
Frothingham, Rev. O.B.	244
Fry's tavern	65
Gage, Rev. Mr.	238
Galloupe, Charles W.	131
Gambling	65

Gardner, Joseph 69
Gardner, Nancy 109
Garrison house 37
General Lafayette 225
George, ship 120
Gerrymander 172
ghost stories 52
Gibbs, Mr. 22, 23
Giddings, Charles S. 131
Giddings, John E. 47, 109
Giddings, Martha (Leech) 109, 110
Giddings, Martha Thorndike 47
Giddings, Mrs. Martha F. 117
Giddings, Nancy 109
Giggs, Burnill A. 232
Giles, Deacon 189
Gloucester Democrat newspaper ... 158, 160, 215
Glover, Lucy 109
Goganian, Sue xiii
Gold, Thomas 232
Goodwin, Enoch 85
Goodwin, Nathaniel 132, 142, 147, 168, 170
Gore, Gov. Christopher 171
Gould, Jacob 99
Gould, Josiah 85, 88, 150, 222, 225
Gould, Lieut. Josiah 88
Gould, Mr. 148
Gouldsberry, Joseph 86
Gove, Timothy Blake 86
Grand Turk, ship 67, 68
Granger, Gideon 149
Grant, Deacon Moses 187, 232
Graves, Doct. John W. 230, 231, 232
Gray, Francis C. 175
Gray, Sen. William 172
Gray, William 27, 51, 89
Gray, William Shepard 29

Great Pasture 69
Great Temperance Dinner 184
Green, John I. 131
Green, Rev. James D. 106
Greene, Thomas 230
Greenwood, W. 28
Groce, Obadiah 76
Grover's Hollow 94
Groves, John 109
guardianship 241
habits 57, 58, 60
Haddock, Charles 131
Haddock, Doct. Charles 247
Hale, Edward Everett 238
Hale, Nathan 250
Hale, Rev. John 55
Hale, Robert 128
Hale, Sally 57
Hamilton, Rev. Luther 248
Hamis, Alden 185
Hartford Convention 169
Harvard College 194
Haskel, Eunice 109
Haskel, Sally 109
Haskell, Samuel 95, 131
Hastings, Horatio 215
Hatch, Gamaliel 86
Hatch, John 86, 88
Hathorne, Benjamin Herbert 29
Haven, Franklin 131
Hawkins, John W. 187
Hazeltine, William 129
Healey, Hammond 86
health 195
Health Committee 198, 200
Henry, ship 67
Herrick, Abigail 46

Herrick, Andrew	46
Herrick, Daniel	102
Herrick, David	46
Herrick, Elizabeth	39, 47
Herrick, George	46
Herrick, Henry	76
Herrick, Jedediah	33, 43
Herrick, Jonathan	39, 46, 47
Herrick, Joseph	87
Heyde, Elizabeth Herrick (Lovett)	44
Heyde, Henry	44
Higginson, Rev. Mr.	193
high school	98
Hildreth Soap and Candle factory	183
Hildreth, Daniel	131
Hildreth, Eldridge	185
Hildreth, Paul	121
Hildreth, Rev. Hosea	182
Hill, Hannah	107, 109, 112
Hill, Hugh	169
Hill, James	153
Hills, Samuel	76
Hind, ship	48
Hoar, Sen. Samuel Jun.	172, 175, 187
Hodges family	38
Hodges, Capt. Benjamin	71
Holden, Oliver	207
Holland, Frederick W.	117
Holmes, John	175
Holmes, Rev. Doctor	32
Holt, Hannah (Holt)	47
Holt, Mary	45
Holt, Nathan	45, 47
Holt, Peter	47
Holt, Sarah	45
Holten, Judge Samuel	241
Holyoke, Doct. Edward Augustus	72, 115
Homans, Maj. William	85
Homans, Peter	24
Homans, Stephen	88, 208, 210
Hooper, Nathaniel	168
Hope, schooner	27
Hopewell, brig	27
Hopkins, Rev. Daniel	104
Hopkinsians	104
Hovey, C.F.	3, 217
Hovey, Thomas	102
Howard, John	27, 247
Howe, Doct.	78
Howe, Doct. Abner	157, 195
Howe, Doct. Samuel G.	219
Howe, Mary	121
Hubbard, Samuel	175
Hubbard, Sen. Samuel	172
Hudson, Sen. Charles	208
Hunewell, Sen. Jonathan	172
Huntington, Asahel	187
Huntington, F.D.	245
Huntoon, Rev. Benjamin	106
Hutchinson, O.H.	232
impeachment	173
India Rubber factory	95
Ingersol, S.	79
Ingersol, Samuel	142, 147
inoculation	69
intemperance	145
intoxicating drink	76
Iris, ship	27, 37, 47, 48
Jackson, Ebenezer	83, 86
Jackson, President Andrew	167
Jackson, W.	83
Jamison, Rev. William	245
Jefferson, President Thomas	171
Jeffries	101

Jowder, Peter 226
Juniper Fort... 65
Junis, Rev. William H.................................. 106
Jupiter Bunn... 79
Juryman 99
Kelly Bridge 21
Kendal, Deacon Thomas....................... 206, 213
Kendal, Thomas... 207
Kilham, Austin D... 131
King James 42
King, Daniel P. 205
King, James 175
King, John Glen 168, 175
King, John Glen. 221
Kingman, -- (Anderson) 239
Kinross-Shire 21
Kitteridge, Doct. Ingalls 131
Knapp, John Francis 211
Knapp, Joseph Jenkins Jun. 211
Kneeland, Abner 102
Knocker's Hole boys 55
Knowlton, John S.C....................................... 108
Knowlton, Mark 123
Knowlton, Nancy 109
Knowlton, Nehemiah 174
Kuhn, Jace C.. 173
Laborin, George... 24
Laborin, Sarah (Rintoul)............................ 25, 26
Laborin, W... 26
Ladd, William.. 204
Lambert, Elizabeth... 33
Lambert, Joseph................................... 33, 38, 51
Lambert, Margaret 33
Lambert, Mary 33, 37
Lambert, Priscilla... 33
Lambert, Sarah 33
Lamson, Benjamin................................... 86, 142

Lamson, Charles 226
Lamson, Francis 40, 77, 86, 93, 99, 102, 142, 146, 154, 185
Lamson, Francis Jun. 142, 147
Lamson, Henry 146
Lamson, Israel 226
Lamson, Judith 40
Lamson, Lucy 226
Lamson, Nathaniel................ 142, 147, 225, 226
Lamson, William 87, 93
Lamson's corner 110
Landlord Thorndike... 75
Lang, Master 59, 62, 63
Larcom, Capt. Henry 224
Larcom, Henry. 37, 142, 147, 168, 198, 202, 222
Larrabee, William 131
LaScelles, ship 28
Laurence, Abel 183
learning to write... 58
Ledder, Mayor John... 90
Lee, George 225
Lee, John C.. 225
Lee, Joseph 183, 225
Lee, Larkin F. 109
Lee, Seaward 86, 109, 129
Leech, Andrew 75
Leech, Andrew J.. 131
Leech, Asa 149
Leech, Deacon James 232
Leech, Elizabeth 109
Leech, William 47, 122, 123, 220, 222
Lefavor, Elizabeth 38
Lefavour, Amos 44, 131
Lefavour, Issachar 137
Lefavour, J... 134
Lefavour, Nancy Lovett................................... 44
Lefavour, Raney (Lovett) 44

Leland, Sherman 175
Liberal party... 107
Lincoln, Gov. Levi 166, 175, 200, 231
Lincoln, William R. 232
Lindsey, Eleazer.. 29
Lion, man of war 48
Little, Hannah 109
Littlehale, Joseph 86
Livingston, Edward... 207
Livingston, William 232
Loch Leven 21
Long Wharf... 27
Longfellow, Stephen 170
Longley, Sen. Thomas 156, 172
Lord Dingwall 41
Lord, William... 211
Loring, Charles G. 131
Lothrop Street 84, 95
Lothrop, Capt. Thomas 84
Lothrop, Rev. Samuel 106
Louis XVI 70
Louverture, Toussaint 158, 162
Lovett Street 96
Lovett, Abigail (Dike) 44
Lovett, Ann (Gage) 44
Lovett, Augustus 39, 45, 82
Lovett, Augustus Sidney 45
Lovett, Benjamin Jun. 129
Lovett, Bethia () 44
Lovett, Capt. Benjamin 74
Lovett, Capt. Jonathan H. 85, 88
Lovett, Capt. Josiah 2nd 164
Lovett, Caroline (Cressy) 44
Lovett, Charles Thorndike 44
Lovett, Charlotte 40, 44, 45
Lovett, Charlotte (Wallis) 44
Lovett, Col. 150

Lovett, Col. Jonathan H. 89, 90, 149, 150
Lovett, Deacon Joshua 107
Lovett, Edmonds.......................................40, 45
Lovett, Elizabeth 31, 39, 75, 77, 109
Lovett, Elizabeth (Herrick) 40, 44, 47
Lovett, Elizabeth Augusta........................40, 44
Lovett, Emily Francis......................................44
Lovett, Ezra..81, 83
Lovett, Frederick William....................39, 44, 45
Lovett, George Augustus 44
Lovett, Hannah................................44, 79, 109
Lovett, Hannah (Batchelder)................40, 44, 45
Lovett, Hannah Batchelder 40, 44
Lovett, Henry Francis 44
Lovett, Henry Hall 45
Lovett, Hezekiah...45
Lovett, Horace Ray 44
Lovett, J.P. 43
Lovett, James 43, 128
Lovett, James Albert 44
Lovett, Jeremiah......................................81, 83
Lovett, Joanna...........................31, 39, 40, 77
Lovett, Joanna B. 78, 80
Lovett, John 31, 39, 40, 43, 47, 77, 78, 80, 81, 198, 241, 248
Lovett, John 4th 129
Lovett, John C..44
Lovett, John Francis.......................................45
Lovett, John Prince 44, 81
Lovett, Jonathan Herrick.....................39, 44, 89
Lovett, Joseph 39, 43, 82, 83
Lovett, Joshua 109
Lovett, Josiah 39, 45, 168, 222
Lovett, Josiah 2nd 117, 123, 168, 183
Lovett, Judith (Lamson)..................................45
Lovett, Judith (Lovett) 45
Lovett, Lucy Ann (Fornis) 45

Lovett, Lydia (Ray) 44	Lyman, Mary (Rantoul) 35
Lovett, Maj. Jonathan H. 89	Lyman, Mary Rantoul 35
Lovett, Mary 44	Lyman, Theodore 27, 227, 236
Lovett, Mary (Pride) 44	Mackey, Elizabeth (Smith) 71, 72
Lovett, Mary (Shaw) 44, 81	Mackey, Mr. 73
Lovett, Mary Ann (Bishop) 45	Mackey, Samuel G. 71, 75, 197
Lovett, Mary Sprague 44	Madison, President James 171
Lovett, Mrs. Susan 109, 111	Magee, James 67
Lovett, Nancy 39	Maj. Swasey tavern 156
Lovett, Nancy (Lovett) 44	Manchester Lyceum 157
Lovett, Nancy Foster 44	Mann, Ezra 86
Lovett, Pyam 74, 168, 222, 225	Mann, Horace 194
Lovett, Raney (Foster) 44	Manning, Jacob 38
Lovett, Rebecca 39	Manning, Richard Esq. 38
Lovett, Rebecca (Woodberry) 44	Manning's Livery Stable 69
Lovett, Samuel 178	Mannings, Sarah 32
Lovett, Samuel Ingersol 39, 45	Mansfield, William 221
Lovett, Samuel P. 71, 109, 116, 142, 147	Marcy, Larkam 250
Lovett, Sarah 45	Marlborough Chapel 184
Lovett, Sarah Ellen Everett 45	Marlborough Hotel 252
Lovett, Susan (MacDonald) 45	Mary Lambert 33
Lovett, Swan J. 45	Massachusetts Colonization Society 76
Lovett, William Edmonds 45	Massachusetts Peace Society 203, 204
Lovett, William Herrick 39, 44, 85, 86, 88, 89, 131	Massachusetts Society for the Suppression of Intemperance 180
Low, Deacon John 250	Massachusetts Sunday School Society 110
Low, John 102, 175	Master Lang's school 55
Lowell Experiment newspaper 158, 215	Master Watson's school 54
Lunt, Hon. George 152	Masury, George 194
Lunt, Jacob 184, 194	Matthew, Father Theobald 189, 192
Lutton, Rebecca 74	*Mayflower*, steamboat 232
Lyceum Hall 216	McCleary, Samuel F. 173
Lyman, Dora 35	McDonald, Donald 145
Lyman, Gen. Theodore 232, 234	McDonald, Susan 39
Lyman, Isaac 31	McKean, Rev. Joseph 77, 102, 104, 106, 129, 159, 188
Lyman, John P. 31, 79, 117	McLovett, Joseph 117
Lyman, John Pickering 35	Meacam, Edward 131

Meacom, Abby Stevens (Foster) 44
Meacom, Capt. Edward 44
Mead, Rev. Samuel 106
Mechanic Hall 100
Melvin, Isaac 227, 234, 235
Melzesend, Thomas 47
Mercantile Bank 89
Messervy, John 86
Metcalf, Mrs. Eunice 121
Middleton, Cleish Parish, County Kinross, Fifeshire 21
military connections 85
military training for children 91
Militia 90, 92
Militia Drills, abolition of 206
Miller, C. 25
Mills, John 156
Millward, Joseph Henry 236
Milton Hill 97
Milton Street 96, 97
Mingoes Beach 37, 91
Minot, Judge 99
Miss Barbauld's Hymns in Prose 112
Monroe, President James 171
Montier, Elizabeth Augusta (Lovett) 45
Montier, Francis 45
Morgan, Charlotte 44
Morgan, Charlotte (Lovett) 44
Morgan, Henry 44
Morgan, Luke 132
Moseley, Ebenezer 168
Murray, Elizabeth 83
Murray, John 117
Murray, Rev Mr. 161
Mussey, Doct. Reuben 74, 194
Mynick, Sen. George 172
Napoleon I 39

Nash, Lonson 169
Nash, Nancy 78
National Bank 165
National Republican party 171
Neal, Caroline Frothingham 39
Neal, David Augustus 39
Neal, David S. 115, 216
Neal, Elizabeth Mattingini Whitteridge 39
Neal, Harriet Charlotte 39
Neal, Jonathan 38, 39
Neal, Margaret Maria 39
Neal, Theodore Augustus 39
Neal, Theodore Frederick 39
Negro fiddler 65
Nelson, Joseph S. 85
Nelson, Oliver F. 194
Nelson, W. 219
New England Asylum for the Blind 218
New England Christian Academy 138
New England Primer 54
New Light Christians 104
Newcomb, Horatio G. 175
Newhall, Benjamin 221
Newhall, Benjamin F. 220
Newhall, James R. .... xii, 159
Nichols, Ichabod 220
Noble, Daniel 168
Noble, Richard 47
North Church in Salem 115
North Parish 94
Northey, William 59
Nourse, John 137
Nourse, John Freedom 35
Nourse, Mrs. 36, 239
Nourse, Mrs. Bonnie Thorndike 35
Nourse, Stephen 109
Nourse's Corner 95

Noyes, Daniel 241
O'Meara, Barry 39
Obear, Oliver 168
Ober, Andrew 103, 142, 146, 147
Ober, Andrew Jun. 142, 147
Ober, Augusta 131
Ober, John 128
Ober, Joseph E. 250
Ober, Oliver 142, 147
Ober, Peter 75
Ober, Richard 2nd 102
Ober, Sally 109
Ober, Samuel S. 204
Ober, William 128
Ober, Zebulon 75
Odd Fellows 190
Oliphant, Rev. David 105, 133
Oliver, Doct. 115
Open doors 103
Orne, Doct. 210
Orne, William 27
Osborne, Doct. George 153, 155
Osborne, Rachel 78
Osgood, Benjamin 168
Osgood, Joseph 69, 72, 73, 74, 197, 211
Osgood, Lucretia (Ward) 72
Osgood, Polly (Beckford) 74
Osgood, Rev. Samuel 249
Osgood's Tavern 65
Overseers of the Poor 97, 146, 148, 153
Owens, Jenny 75
Packarel, Mr. 228
Page, John 89
Page, Woodberry 95
Palmer, W. 28
Park, Rev..Harrison G. 184
Parkman, Doct. George 212

Parrot, William W. 168
Parsons, David 86
Parsons, Hon. Isaac 40
party spirit 171
Patch, John 117
pauperism 144
Peabody, Andrew 76, 216, 242, 243
Peabody, Andrew Preston 30, 31, 34, 79, 121, 159, 182, 184, 208, 223
Peabody, Augustus 175
Peabody, Caroline Eustis 35
Peabody, Catherine Langdon 34
Peabody, Charles G. 137
Peabody, Ellen Langdon 35
Peabody, George 246
Peabody, Helen 35
Peabody, Maria Ladd 35
Peabody, Mary R. 137
Peabody, Mary Rantoul 31, 35
Peabody, Polly (Rantoul) 31, 243
Peabody, Robert Rantoul 35
Peace Society 122
Pearson, Daniel 185
Pearson, Daniel H. 211
Peele, Rebecca 37, 47
Peele, Willard 99
Peirce, Rev. John 186, 231
Peirpont, John 99, 218
Peirpont, Rev. John jun. 186
Penidges, Alice 134
Percy, Ralph 41
Perkins, Rev. George W. 106
Perkins, Thomas H. 219
Perth Shire 21
Peters, Lovett 227
Peters, Mr. 238
Phillips Academy 247

Phillips, ---	33
Phillips, Elizabeth	52
Phillips, Lt. Gov. William	233
Phillips, Sen. John	172
Phillips, Stephen	111
Phillips, Stephen C.	187
Phillips, Stephen H.	151
Phillips, William E.	134, 135
Phoenix, brig	27
Pickard, Thomas	87, 93
Pickering, Col. Timothy	55
Pickering, John	55, 247
Pickering, Timothy	115, 169
Picket	144
Pickett, John	131, 222
Pickett, Thomas	132
Pickman, Benjamin	221
Pickman, Dudley L.	168
Pierce, Benjamin	86
Pierce, Osgood	131
Poales, W.	232
Polland, Benjamin	175
Pomeroy, Lemuel	233, 234, 238
Pomeroy, Samuel	229, 230
Pomp	211
Poor, Rev. Ebenezer	105
Porter, Billy	169
Porter, Miss	234
Porter, Samuel	131
Porter, William	131, 198
Pousland, Edward	198
Precinct of Salem and Beverly	111, 129, 161
Prescott, Judge James	172, 175
Prescott, Maj. William	88
Prescott, William	175, 176
Presson	*See* Preston
Preston family arms	42
Preston, Alfred	40
Preston, Andrew	29, 30, 36, 37, 38
Preston, Benjamin	37
Preston, Captain	42
Preston, Daniel	42
Preston, David	38
Preston, Edward	42
Preston, Eliza Ann	47
Preston, Elizabeth	37, 43
Preston, Hannah	38
Preston, Henry	41
Preston, Increase	33
Preston, John	37, 38, 42, 43, 47, 48
Preston, Jonathan	38
Preston, Joseph	37, 43, 47
Preston, Lucy	37
Preston, Lydia	43
Preston, Marcie (Seales)	41
Preston, Margaret	47
Preston, Mary	30, 37, 43
Preston, Mary (Blodgett)	43
Preston, Mary Lambert	47
Preston, May	79
Preston, Polly	38
Preston, Priscilla	36, 43
Preston, Randall	36, 37
Preston, Rebecca	79
Preston, Roger	42
Preston, Ruth	43
Preston, Samuel	40, 43
Preston, Samuel Lambert	37
Preston, Sarah (Bridges)	41
Preston, Sir Amicus	42
Preston, Sir Jacob Henry	42
Preston, Sir John	42
Preston, Sir Robert	41
Preston, Sir Thomas	42

Preston, Sir William 41
Preston, Susan..37
Preston, Susanna 36, 37, 38, 247
Preston, Susanna (Gutterson)............................43
Preston, Susannah..43
Preston, Thomas 42
Preston, William 36, 37, 38, 43, 52
Preston, William Rantoul 47
Price, ---...41
Price, Harriet Charlotte......................................39
Price, James 39
Price, Mary 39
Prince, Joanna (Batchelder)............. 78, 107, 112
Prince, John 37, 88, 101
Prince, Josiah B. 121
Prince, Rev. ___ 115
Prince, Rev. John 210
Prince, Warren 129
Prisoner's Friend newspaper........... 158, 159, 215
Probate court..241
Proctor, John W. 245
Promes, Rev. Mr. 245
prosperity...81
public worship 77
Puffer, W. 36
Pulcifer, Israel..101
punctuality 60
Putman, Rufus 133
Putnam, David 89
Putnam, John 244
Putnam, Rev. George..............................212, 244
Putnam, Rufus 131, 140
Putnam's tavern 65
Quaker 59
Quincy, Edmund 29
Quincy, Josiah 47, 203
Quiner, Abraham 223

Quiner, Joanna.. 223, 224
Quiner, Susannah (Cammell) 223
R.B. Forbes, ship 216
Rae, Isaac... 147
Rail Road Avenue 96
Rail Road Station..96
Rambler coach 111
Rammohun Roy...................................... 118, 120
Ramsdell, Polly 34
Ramsdell, William 34
Rand, Abel..36
Rand, Asa 36
Rand, Edward S. 168
Rand, Rev. Samuel 38
Rand, Sophia 38
Randall, Rev.. Mr. 35
Ranoul, William 48
Rantoul Street 95, 96
Rantoul, Harriett Charlotte (Neal) 36
Rantoul, Augusta 197
Rantoul, Charles W. 216
Rantoul, Charles William 34, 45
Rantoul, Charlotte 32, 218
Rantoul, Elizabeth Augusta Lovett..................32
Rantoul, Hannah...... 24, 25, 26, 79, 93, 97, 115,
    117, 121, 131, 198, 216, 223, 224
Rantoul, Hannah Lovett............................. 32, 45
Rantoul, Harriett Charlotte (Neal) 216, 249
Rantoul, Jane 79, 248
Rantoul, Jane Elizabeth (Woodberry)........ 36, 45
Rantoul, Joanna 34, 198, 223
Rantoul, Joanna (Lovett) .... xii, 44, 47, 79
Rantoul, Joanna Lovett 31
Rantoul, Mary (Preston) 31
Rantoul, Mary Elizabeth...................................32
Rantoul, Polly.............................. 29, 30, 31, 54
Rantoul, Robert 23, 28, 30, 31, 44, 45

American Tract Society 180
American Unitarian Association 116
application for Post Master 149
Beverly Academy 136
Beverly Bank 222
Beverly Common 150
Beverly Light Infantry 85, 88, 91
Beverly Marine Insurance Company 162
Beverly Total Abstinence Society 182
Bible Society 109
bust 223
candidate for Elector of President 156
capital punishment 207
Commissioner of Highways 151, 183
Constitutional Convention of 1820 175
Daguerreotype 224
Deacon 105, 107
Essex Bridge Corporation 220
Essex County Convention of 1812 169
Essex County Temperance Society 182
family bible 24
Fisher Charitable Society 224
Health Committee 199, 202
influence of father's character 61
Institution for the Blind 218
Justice of the Peace 150, 151
land 83
Mass. Const. Conv. 1820 250
Mass. Const. Conv. 1853 250
Overseer of the Poor 142, 147, 148
Parish Clerk 102, 103, 123, 129
Reform School Commission 227
Representative to the General Court. 163, 170
run over by horses 68
School Committee 132
social library 129, 132
State Reform School 236

Sunday School Superintendent 108
Town library 131
Town Treasurer 175
Union Fire Society 179
Union Temperance Society 181
Washington Street 83
Rantoul, Robert P 45
Rantoul, Robert Samuel 34, 36, 98, 193, 198, 216
Rantoul, Samuel 31, 32, 45, 54, 249
Rantoul, Sen. Robert 32, 34, 45, 79, 108, 109, 110, 184, 185, 190, 193, 194, 208, 223, 246, 248
Rantoul, William 28, 31
Raymond, Josiah 87
Rea, Isaac 142, 163, 168
Rea, Joseph 129
Read, Doct. Nathan 75
recreation 66
Reed, Doct. 28
Reed, Elizabeth 226
Rentoul, Robert 27
Representatives Hall 204
Republican party 100
Resolute, barque 238
Rial Side school 71, 134
Rial Side Road 94
Rich, Mr. 140
Rich, Rev. Thomas 106
Rickett, Richard 131
Rintoul 21
Rintoul, Anna (Browe) 26
Rintoul, Betty 22, 23
Rintoul, Charles 22, 23
Rintoul, Christian 28
Rintoul, Christian (Miller) 26
Rintoul, David 22, 23, 24, 26, 30
Rintoul, Elizabeth 25

Rintoul, George	28
Rintoul, Helen	26
Rintoul, Janet	23
Rintoul, Jean	22, 23
Rintoul, Jeanie	23
Rintoul, Jenny	22, 23
Rintoul, John	26
Rintoul, Margaret	25
Rintoul, Margaret (Miller)	26
Rintoul, Mary	24, 30
Rintoul, Mrs.	22, 28
Rintoul, Nelly	22, 23
Rintoul, Rev. Mr.	22, 24
Rintoul, Robert	21, 22, 23, 24, 25, 26, 30
Rintoul, Robert Stephen	215
Rintoul, Robert William	24, 28
Rintoul, Sarah	24, 30
Rintoul, Sarah (Laborin)	24
Rintoul, Sarah Sinclair	21, 28, 30, 247
Rintoul, Thomas	26
Rintoul, W. Robert	22
Rintoul, William	21, 22, 23, 24, 26, 28, 121
Roberts, Catherine W.	31
Roberts, Edmund	31
Robinson, Rev. Ebenezer	117
Rogers, John	54
Roman Catholics	62
Ropes, Daniel	33
Roundy, Benjamin	185
Roundy, Deacon Robert	105
Roundy, Nehemiah	199, 202
Rowe, Seth	86
Rowsland, Edward	132
Roy, Ebenezer	147
Rubly Hill	95
Russel, Maj. Benjamin	171
Sabourn, George	30
Safford, John	142, 147, 168
Safford, Joshua	224
Safford, Nathaniel	147
Salem Advertiser newspaper	158, 159, 161, 184, 215
Salem Artillery	92
Salem Cadets	92
Salem Classical and High school	216, 218
Salem Female Charitable Society	72
Salem Gazette newspaper	158, 159, 208, 215
Salem Latin School	63
Salem Neck	69
Salem Regiment	92
Salem Turnpike and Chelsea Bridge Corporation	220
Salem Work House	146
Salter, Marie	47
Saltonstall, Leverett	115, 156, 247
Sandemanian	161
Saunderson, Deacon Jacob	99, 115
Savage, James S.	230, 231, 234, 235
Sawyer, Amos	83
Seales, James	41
Seales, Sarah	41
Sears, Barnabas	231
Sedgwick, Judge Theodore	100, 206, 218
Seger, James	208
Sewall, Rev. Edmond L.	106
Sharp, Doct.	213
Shehan, Bryan	211
Shelden, Amos	147, 168
Shelden, Jesse	168, 198, 202
Sheldon, Amos	142
Siewers, Joseph Henry	138
Sikes, Rev. Oren	76
Silsbee, Issacharah	245
Silsbee, Mayor Nathaniel	115, 192, 245
Silsbee, William	56, 57, 70, 71

Slack, Charles W. 193
small pox 33, 69, 157
Small, W. 38
Smith, Capt. Elias 71
Smith, Ebenezer 71, 252
Smith, Francis 129
Smith, Jonathan 84, 95
Smith, Lydia 252
Smith, Mrs. 79
Smith, Nehemiah, Jun. 86
Smith, Samuel 27, 79
Smith, Sidney 131
Smith, William 168
Snelling, Jonathan 55
Snelling, Master 62
social library 129, 132
Sons of Temperance 182, 184, 189, 190, 192, 194, 195
South School District 139
Southwick, John 55, 56, 59, 62, 64, 73
Sparhawk, Nathaniel 27
Sparks, Rev. Jared 168
Spaulding, Rev. Joshua 104
Spaulding, Shaniliah 86
Spear, Charles 209
Spear, John M. 209
Spectator newspaper 215
Sprague, Joseph 70
Sprague, Joseph E. 56, 70
Sprague, Maj. Joseph 70
Sprague, William B. 159
St. James's boys 55
Stack, Charles W. 189
Stage Point 67
Standley, Andrew W. 185
Standley, Samuel Downing Gently 146, 147
State Reform School 227, 230

Staunton, Rev. Robert 245
Stearns, Doct. William 56, 60, 70, 71, 73, 74
Stearns, Joseph Sprague 70
Stearns, Rev. Samuel H. 106
Stearns, William 245
Stebbins, Doct. 122
Stephens, Charles 93, 116, 123, 162, 168, 199, 202
Stephens, Joseph 95
Stephens, Thomas . 103, 116, 129, 142, 147, 149, 162, 163, 168, 191, 225, 244
Stephens, Thomas Jun. 166, 168
Stephens's Hill 97
Sterns, Nathaniel 76
Stetson, Rev. Caleb 189
Stickney, Amos 87
Stickney, Betsey (Thorndike) 77, 242
Stickney, Ebenezer 87
Stickney, Eliza 109
Stickney, Ensign Samuel 93
Stickney, Joseph 174
Stickney, Matthew 27
Stickney, Samuel 39, 88, 93
Stickney, Samuel, Jun. 86
Stickney, Silas 76, 77, 242
Stone, Deacon John 189
Stone, Edward 86, 93
Stone, Hannah 34
Stone, Israel O. 87
Stone, Mr. 245
Stone, Rev. Edwin M. ...... xii, 109, 111, 116, 117, 139, 159, 220, 232
Stone, Rev. Thomas. F. 245
Stone, Robert 56
Stone, Thomas 193
Stone, Thomas B. 193
Story, Judge 101
Stow Lyceum 203

Stowe, Rev. Calvin E. 106
Strickland, George W. 117
Strict Calvinists 104
Stuart, Gilbert 172
Styles, Simon 86
Suchmore Bridge 21
Sullivan, Gov. James 90, 150
Sullivan, Sen. William 172
Sullivan, William 207, 209
Sumner, Charles Pinkney 175
Sumner, Sen. Charles 175, 248, 249
Sunday school 107, 110
Swasey, Maj.tavern 169
Swett, Maj. Samuel 89
Symmonds, John 87
Symonds, Daniel Jun. 87
Tabernacle Society in Salem 156
Tam, Rev. Jonathan 106
Tavern House 95
Taylor, President Zachary 200
Teague, Margaret 219
Teague, Richard 219
temperance reform 180, 182, 184
Tessenden, Rev. John 106
Thanter, Joseph 226
Thayer, John E. 224
Thayer, Minot 232
Thayer, Rev. Christopher Toppan.34, 35, 79, 98, 106, 107, 108, 109, 110, 111, 116, 117, 120, 131, 132, 133, 135, 139, 140, 141, 159, 184, 187, 198, 200, 204, 210, 223, 246
Thayerweather, J. A. 238
The Perkins Institution and Massachusetts Asylum for the Blind 219
Third Congregational Society 103, 104
Thissel, Samuel Morse 87, 93
Thompson, Rev. James W. 106, 216, 245
Thompson, W 189

Thompson's Island 232
Thorndike, Albert 35, 36, 44, 107, 108, 109, 116, 117, 162, 222
Thorndike, Charles 44
Thorndike, Clara 36
Thorndike, Clarissa 36
Thorndike, Col. Larkin 75, 77, 129, 188
Thorndike, Doct. Larkin 77
Thorndike, Helen M. (Stephens) 116
Thorndike, Israel 81, 171, 176, 222
Thorndike, Joanna Batchelder (Lovett) 44
Thorndike, John 75
Thorndike, Nicholas 36, 91, 168, 170
Thorndike, Samuel, K, Lothrop 44
Thorndike, Thomas Stevens 44
Thorndike, William 44, 108, 116, 142, 160, 168, 208, 218
Thorndyke, John 82
Titch, Eunice 29
Titch, Timothy 29
Tittle, Oliphert 109
Todd, Rev. John 234, 238
Torrey, Doct Augustus 80
Town affairs 94
Town hall 124
Town library 130, 132
Town School 59
Townsend, Hannah 33
Townsend, Moses 33
Townsend, Shipley 161
Training-field 149
Trask, Doct. James Dowling 199
Trask, Ebenezer 87, 93
Trask, Israel 142, 147
Trask, Israel 5th 146, 148
Trask, Menasseh .... xiii, 95
Trask, Oliver 96
Trask, William 96

Treadwell, John 217
Treadwell, Nathaniel 86
Treadwill, John D 221
Tremont Temple 187
True, Henry 76
True, Rev. Henry 76
Trumbull, Mr. 120
trust deeds 159
Tuck, George 92
Tuck, Robert 87, 91, 92
Tucker, Ichabod 156
Tuckerman, Joseph 115
Underwood, --- 33
Underwood, Sarah 52
Union Fire Society 177, 179
Union Temperance Society 158, 181, 183
Union Wharf 27
Unitarian convention
    Boston 1852 117
    Boston 1857 122
    Montreal 1854 121
    Portland 1849 .... 38, 117
    Portsmouth 1851 117
    Providence 1855 121
    Salem 1847 117
    Springfield 1850 117
    Worcester 1853 120
Unitarian Sunday School Association of Massachusetts 115
Unitarianism 117
Universalist Meeting House 190
Upper Parish 105, 111
Usher, Capt. Daniel 88
van Buren, President Martin 156
Veitch, Mary 26
Very, Samuel 31
Very, William Rantoul 31

Vezia, Rev. Samuel 106
Wales, Andrew F. 162
Walley, Samuel H. Jun 227, 232, 233
Wallis, Andrew 75, 109
Wallis, Bartholomew 93
Wallis, Bartholomew, Jun. 86
Wallis, Benjamin Jun. 131
Wallis, Caleb 86, 128
Wallis, Ebenezer 86
Wallis, Ebenezer 2nd 86
Wallis, Eleazer 142
Wallis, Israel W. 93, 129
Wallis, John 2nd 86
Wallis, Nancy 109
Wapping boys 55
Ward, Joshua 72
Warren, Doct. John C. 190
Warren, Rev..Mr. 189
Washburn, Amory 231
Washburn, Mrs. 210
Washburn, Rev. Ira 162, 184, 193, 210
Washington Hall 70, 158
Washington Street 83, 95
Washington Street Church 204
Washington, Gen. George 55, 59, 60
Washingtonian Lyceum 157, 158
Watch House Hill 89
Water Street 95
Waters, Richard Palmer 130, 131
Watson, Master 68
Webber, Israel 87
Webber, John 93
Webber, John Porter 87, 131
Webber, John Porter Jun. 131
Webber, Josiah 87
Webber, William Jun. 85, 89
Webster, Daniel 174, 175, 176, 226

Webster, Doct John	211
Webster, Mrs.	212
Webster, Redford	212, 213
Webster, Sen. Daniel	172
Weld, Horatio Hastings	158
Weld, Mary	121
Weld, Mary F.	134
Weld, Mary Thorndike	137
Weld, Mrs. Mary	133
Wells, Sen. John	172
Wenham Lake	111, 134
West Farm	98
West Point Military Academy	194
West, Benjamin	27
West, Thomas Barnard	137
Western Rail Road	230
Westfield Normal School	134
Weston, Gersham B.	187
Wetmore, William	88
Whetmore, Judge	99
White, Daniel A.	115
White, Henry	94
White, Joseph	211
White, Judge Daniel S.	88, 241
White, Margaret	52
White, William	33
Whitman, Bernard	105, 108
Whitmarsh, Ann	109
Whitney, Capt. Israel	118, 119
Whitney, Clarissa (Lovett)	74
Whitney, Doct.	83
Whitney, Doct. Elisha	74, 75
Whitney, Dorothy	109
Whitney, Elisha	74, 83
Whitney, Michael	95
Whitney, Mr.	232
Whitney, Swan	89
Whitteridge, Elizabeth Boardman	39
Whitteridge, Susan Lovett Mead	39
Whittridge, Hannah	109
Whittridge, Livermore	129, 132
Whittridge, Thomas	86, 93
Wilde, Judge	102
Wilde, Samuel S.	170
Wildes, Asa W.	152
Wildes, Rev. George D.	152
Wilison, Samuel	230
Willard, Charles W.	193
Willard, Rev. Joseph	188
William the Lyon	41
Williams, Antriss	32
Williams, George	33
Williams, Henry	33
Williams, John	32
Williams, Mary	33
Williams, Mary E.	137
Williams, Rev Nathaniel W.	250
Williams, Rev. Nathaniel W.	110, 175
Williams, Roger	121
Williams, Ruth	33
Williams, Samuel	28
Williams, Sarah	32
Williams, Sen. John M.	172
Williston, Mrs. S.	231
Wilson, John	131
Wilson, Joseph	131
Wilson, Miss	135
Wilson, Rev. John H.	232
Winn, Benjamin	85, 88
Winn, Capt. Joseph	88
Winn, Joseph	152, 196
Witteridge, Thomas Cook	39
Wood, Israel	128

Wood, Joseph .. 95, 102, 103, 128, 142, 143, 147, 151

Wood, Robert G. 87

Woodberry, Asa 142, 147

Woodberry, Augustus 193

Woodberry, Curtis 37

Woodberry, Debby 34

Woodberry, Elizabeth 109

Woodberry, F.B. 131

Woodberry, Hon. Levi 152

Woodberry, Isaac 95

Woodberry, Israel 86

Woodberry, Jacob 123

Woodberry, Jacob T. 131

Woodberry, Jane Elizabeth 34

Woodberry, John 86

Woodberry, Joseph 5th 87

Woodberry, Judge Levi 30

Woodberry, Peter 34, 86

Woodberry, Robert 128, 129

Woodberry, Thomas 82

Woodberry, William 37

Worcester Palladium newspaper 158, 159, 215

Worcester, Doct. Noah 203

Worcester, Rev. Samuel 104

Work House 97, 142

Worsley, Mary 109

Worsley, Mary Elizabeth 141

Wright, Sir Robert 102

Wyer, Timothy 86, 88, 89, 91, 92

www.ingramcontent.com/pod-product-compliance
Lightning Source LLC
Chambersburg PA
CBHW080546230426
43663CB00015B/2728